Lecture Notes in Economics and Mathematical Systems 515

Springer
Berlin
Heidelberg
New York
Barcelona
Hong Kong
London
Mailand
Paris
Tokyo

Gerald Heisig

Planning Stability in Material Requirements Planning Systems

Springer

Author

Dr. Gerald Heisig
Faculty of Economics and Management
Otto-von-Guericke-University Magdeburg
P.O. Box 4120
39016 Magdeburg
Germany

Cataloging-in-Publication data applied for

Die Deutsche Bibliothek - CIP-Einheitsaufnahme

Heisig, Gerald:
Planning stability in material requirements planning systems / Gerald Heisig. - Berlin ; Heidelberg ; New York ; Barcelona ; Hong Kong ; London ; Mailand ; Paris ; Tokyo : Springer, 2002
(Lecture notes in economics and mathematical systems ; Vol. 515)
ISBN 3-540-43015-6

ISSN 0075-8450
ISBN 3-540-43015-6 Springer-Verlag Berlin Heidelberg New York

Springer-Verlag Berlin Heidelberg New York
a member of BertelsmannSpringer Science+Business Media GmbH

http://www.springer.de

Typesetting: Camera ready by author
Cover design: *design & production*, Heidelberg

Printed on acid-free paper SPIN: 10860410 55/3142/du 5 4 3 2 1 0

Preface

In logistics systems, the issue of planning stability has obtained more and more importance. This is mainly due to an increasing integration of planning systems both within and across companies. Hereby even small changes within a plan at a specific stage of materials flow may cause replanning of many other actions in an entire supply chain. This propagation of adjustments in planning systems first acquired wide attention when MRP systems were employed as standard planning tools for material coordination in companies. Managers became aware that MRP application within a rolling horizon framework produced considerable planning instability which was perceived as some kind of nervousness and created a plethora of problems in implementing plans. In assessing this nervousness syndrome it seems clear that planning instability origins from uncertainties in the planner's exogenous environment which make it impossible to develop precise forecasts and thus necessitate planning adjustments as time goes by. But it also is true that size and frequency of adjustments may have endogenous sources, since they can be affected by planning systems and decision rules. In order to understand how planning stability is influenced by endogenous and exogenous factors, one has to gain insight into how these factors interact.

For bringing more light into these complex interdependencies in the field of material requirements planning systems, a lot of simulation studies have been made. However, due to the simulation methodology, all these studies lack being able to create a precise and systematic knowledge of functional dependencies. For that reason, analytical techniques have to be applied to describe and analyse how precisely planning rules and parameters affect the level of planning stability under given uncertainties in the planning environment. This book presents a high-level analytical investigation that gives deep insight into the effects that different kind of inventory control rules have on the stability of material planning systems under stochastic demand. To this end, the author extends the theory of stochastic inventory control to a new dimension. In traditional inventory theory decision rules are investigated with respect to their cost and service level performance. In this book, however, the stability of decisions in subsequent planning cycles resulting from the choice of alternative control rules and control parameters is considered. The in-depth analysis given by the author provides us with very interesting and novel findings. We learn how different control rules can affect the degree of planning stability in a very different way. We find how the level of stability precisely depends on the level of control parameters, which enables us to determine which policy parameter constellation leads to highest stability, and avoid settings resulting in highest nervousness. We also gain a systematic insight into the stability effects of exogenous parameters like the degree of demand uncertainty and the length of the planning horizon.

Summarising, this book presents an excellent scientific work which considerably contributes to the field of analytical studies of the nervousness phenomenon. The results of this investigation are such that they will not only be interesting and impressive for people from academia, but also will provide materials managers with useful insights that may help them to handle their systems in a manner in which planning stability can be improved.

Magdeburg, October 2001 Karl Inderfurth

Acknowledgements

While researching and writing my thesis at the Faculty of Economics and Management at the Otto-von-Guericke-University of Magdeburg I was fortunate to receive a great deal of support from those around me. First of all, I wish to convey my sincere thanks to Prof. Dr. Karl Inderfurth, who was open to discussion and to give advice at all times throughout my work. I wish also to express my special thanks to my two assessors Prof. Dr. Alfred Luhmer and Prof. Dr. Ton de Kok: It was Prof. Dr. Alfred Luhmer who awakened my sustained interest in Operations Research during my business studies degree at the University of Bielefeld, an interest that Prof. Dr. Engelbert Dockner further intensified. I would like to thank Prof. Dr. Ton de Kok for his great interest in the subject matter and for the discussion and advice he provided, both at the outset of this work and during the final stages.

I wish also to convey my appreciation to my former colleagues Dr. Thomas Jensen, Dr. Dirk Meier-Barthold, Dr. Stefan Minner, Rainer Kleber and Gerd Lindner for their contributions to discussion on this subject, and also for the pleasant working atmosphere in the faculty. My special thanks go to Dr. Thomas Jensen and Dr. Stefan Minner for their invaluable advice throughout this thesis. I would also like to thank Dr. Moritz Fleischmann for his contributions on the analysis of planning stability in product recovery systems. Furthermore, my sincere thanks go to Rainer Kleber for his technical support in putting together the final version of this work, and to Jill Trace for improving my English.

This study has only been possible with the continued support of my parents, to whom I owe my greatest heartfelt thanks, and to whom this thesis is dedicated.

Heidelberg, October 2001 Gerald Heisig

Contents

1. Introduction

1.1 Research Motivations

In recent years, supply chain management has attracted increased attention and interest in the field of business logistics. For researchers, the optimization of the supply chain is a major task. In practice, different approaches have been developed to establish an efficient supply chain between companies, such as, e.g., Efficient Consumer Response (ECR). Moreover, recent standard Enterprise Resource Planning (ERP) packages consider the entire supply chain starting with the suppliers' suppliers and ending with the customers' customers. It is crucial that material and information flows are coordinated in order to achieve the overall efficiency of a supply chain.

In particular, "one of the most important enablers for efficient supply chain operations" is ***schedule stability***[1]. Suppliers of parts to vehicle manufacturers cited "schedule stability" as the fifth most important source of potential cost reductions. Additionally, "stable schedules" has been listed as the seventh most important task recommended by the U.S. automotive industry to increase the U.S. competitiveness (see Arthur Andersen [2]). Schedule instability in a Just-in-Time (JIT) environment causes significant problems for suppliers. Suppliers are forced to react to unexpected changing requirements resulting in increased costs due to increased overtime, inventory, or material handling, for example [2]. Moreover, instability is usually amplified from one supplier to the succeeding supplier[3] (see Inman and Gonsalvez [66]).

[1] Inman and Gonsalvez [66] define a schedule as stable "if the production requirement forecasts for a given period do not change and equal the actual production requirement for that planning period". In fact, stability implies that a given production plan will be followed, whereas instability means not following the plan.

[2] For instance, Van Donselaar et al. [133] point out that stability reduces the need for expensive emergency orders.

[3] See also the early work of Forrester [40] on the cyclical variations of stocks in supply chains. The same holds for the different levels in the product structure in multi-stage production systems controlled by a Material Requirements Planning (MRP) system (see Section 2 and Section 3, respectively).

As a consequence of increasing dynamics and uncertainties in the environment of enterprises, planning systems must be able to react to unexpected developments. The ability of a system to do so is referred to as "flexibility"[4]. Thus, flexibility is certainly an important deciding factor for a company's competitiveness. Because the speed of the information flow is ever-increasing, there is more time to react to disturbances and to implement the necessary adjustments. However, on the other hand, the time between plan revisions is reduced, and due to the networking between planning systems, disturbances are amplified in integrated systems.

In the field of production and material requirements planning, the problems resulting from frequent plan revisions have been discussed in literature since the middle of the seventies, using the term "nervousness" (see, e.g., Steele [124], and Mather [86].). In Material Requirements Planning (MRP) systems, there are various negative aspects of frequent plan revisions. First, frequent replanning leads to a general loss of confidence in planning. In particular, production decisions that are continually altered generate confusion at an operational level and on the shopfloor. Furthermore, in multi-level production systems, nervousness on the top level, i.e. Master Production Schedule (MPS) level, propagates throughout the entire system, and disturbances may be amplified, just as in supply chains. Consequently, throughput times and inventories may increase, and service-levels as well as capacity utilization may decrease as a result of inappropriate priorities set by the planning system (see, e.g., Penlesky et al. [99], and Ho [53]). Notice that, as already mentioned above, also the application of a JIT concept requires a "stable" master production schedule (see, e.g., Chapman [24], and Spencer and Cox [118]). Since in JIT lot sizes are reduced as much as possible[5], the equipment utilization level is increased. Moreover, inventories are decreased systematically, and there are no buffers, such as safety stocks, times, or capacities[6]. Therefore, unexpected disturbances in the system lead directly to disruptions on the shopfloor[7]. However, because of the abandonment of buffers, plan revisions significantly impair the planning and production system.

To cope with uncertainties, the planning system is usually embedded in a framework which permits the incorporation of new information into decision

[4] The terms "planning stability", "flexibility" as well as "robustness" are clearly defined in Section 3.2.

[5] A necessary requirement for small lot sizes are small setup times.

[6] For a discussion of these buffers against uncertainties in the production environment see Section 2.3.2.

[7] Although the philosophy of JIT seeks to eliminate waste and uncertainties (see, e.g., Silver et al. [116], pp.632), disturbances cannot be avoided completely. In Arthur Andersen [2], one supplier points out:"... JIT is great until schedule changes occur, and you as a supplier damn well better not cause a line shutdown".

making from one planning period to the next one[8]. The decisions made by the top planning level provide input data for subsequent lower planning levels. Therefore, the adjustment of plans for a specific planning level may lead to additional uncertainties at adjoining planning levels[9]. Conventionally, buffers are used to protect against disturbances. If these buffers are not coordinated between the different planning levels, then an unnecessarily large amount of buffers may be built up (see, e.g., Jensen [68], p.4, and Van Donselaar [131], pp.51).
Additionally, amplifications or temporal shifts of changes may occur if decision rules are applied which amplify uncertainties in a rolling horizon schedule[10], or, if decisions are triggered by only a minor violation of tolerance intervals for the relevant states of the system (see Jensen [68], p.4). Then, adjustments are generated, the extent of which exceeds the amount of data changes which have triggered them.

The property of planning concepts and decision rules to generate reliable and "stable" plans, even in the case of changes of input data, has an origin value (see, e.g., Jensen [68], p.4, or Van Donselaar [131], p.17). However, the performance of these procedures with regard to stability must be compared with other performance criteria such as costs or service levels. Nevertheless, to make this comparison it is necessary to analyze the stability performance of underlying decision rules. Furthermore, the term "planning stability" has to be strictly defined and a measurable formalization, independent of the decision rule, must be given[11].

1.2 Planning Stability in Material Coordination Systems

Within the entire production decision making framework, master production scheduling and material planning are central components of the system (see, e.g., Silver et al. [116], p.540). The major task of material planning is to determine detailed production/procurement schedules (timing and quantities) of all components and raw materials which are necessary to produce the finished goods established in master production scheduling (see, e.g., Silver et al. [116], p.543.). On the one hand, short-range MPS scheduling and material planning are closely connected to preceding medium-range aggregate

[8] In practice, a rolling horizon schedule is usually applied, see also Section 2.3.1 and Section 3.1, respectively.

[9] See also Section 2.2 for the distinction between primary and secondary disturbances, and Section 3.1.2 for a classification of plan revisions.

[10] Notice that also the opposite effect may occur, i.e. uncertainties may be compensated one another.

[11] In this work the same definition of planning stability as introduced by Jensen [68] is used, and a very similar measure of stability is applied. Nevertheless, the main difference in this investigation compared with Jensen's examination is the underlying analytical approach (see also Section 1.3).

production planning, and, on the other hand, they provide input data for the shorter run operations, such as short range scheduling. Furthermore, in capacity planning, the feasibility of the MPS and material planning is checked. Thus, planning at different levels in the product structure is not only connected vertically because of technological relations, but also horizontally due to capacity utilization. Therefore, material planning (including master production planning) is the core element of production planning and scheduling. Besides the its close connections with other planning stages within production planning, material planning is also an important interface between marketing, procurement, and production[12]. Therefore, different sources of disturbance occur in the material planning system, namely, uncertainties in demand and supply, and stochastic influences in the production process itself, such as machine breakdowns or scrap[13]. Thus, these uncertainties and the close relationship between different planning modules require frequent adjustments of decisions with respect to actual developments in the environment. Since these decisions directly affect operational planning, the relevance of "stable" material requirements planning is greater still.

A major problem in material coordination is the determination of lot sizes (see also Section 2). In inventory theory, much work has been done to develop models and solution procedures for stochastic problems[14]. Models for determining lot sizes in multi-level production systems within a stochastic environment taking into account the above-mentioned dependencies are, in general, too complex to solve (see, e.g., Schneeweiß [112]). Thus the decision problem is often decomposed into a deterministic multi-level lot-sizing and a stochastic buffering problem. The determination of lot sizes is then based on a quasi-deterministic modeling of the stochastic environment. Here, forecasts are used instead of stochastic data, and deterministic lot-sizing rules are applied. Conventionally, safety stocks[15] are used to cope with uncertainties. However, due to the separation of the decision problem, dependencies between lot sizes and the amount of safety stock are not taken into account[16]. The operating flexibility of the system (see, e.g., Inderfurth and Minner [65])is another means of protection against demand uncertainties. In such a scenario, emergency actions are implemented, such as accelerating internal processing, or ordering express deliveries from an external source. This flexibility at an operational level is also related to the fact that, in MRP-like material coor-

[12] Silver et al. point out that the MPS "serves as the primary interface between marketing and production" (see Silver et al. [116], p.540).

[13] A detailed description of the types of uncertainties in a material planning framework is given in Section 2.2.

[14] See, e.g., Graves et al. [42], Nahmias [95], and Sherbrooke [115].

[15] See also Section 2.3.2 for alternative buffering methods.

[16] For instance, in Inderfurth [60] a lot-for-lot policy is assumed for determining safety stocks in a multi-level system. Moreover, Van Donselaar [131] uses single-stage lot-sizing rules.

dination systems, fixed planned processing lead times are used which are, in reality, fairly variable (see, e.g., Vollmann et al. [135]). Nevertheless, this operating flexibility is not explicitly taken into account in stochastic inventory control models.

Finally, the impact of inventory control rules on the stability of planned decisions in a rolling horizon schedule are also not taken into account. The application of a specific inventory policy may increase relatively small variations in input data by the aggregation of demand of several periods. Moreover, because of the dependencies of inventory control rules in multi-level production systems, plan revisions may be amplified from one stage to the other. Consequently, plan revisions in future periods on top levels in the product structure may enforce immediate replanning activities on lower levels, and, in particular, at the operational level.

1.3 Objectives and Structure of Analysis

The aim of this examination is to provide an analytical approach giving insights into the dependencies of different stochastic inventory control rules on planning stability in a rolling horizon planning framework. This study considers a single-stage production system as well as a product recovery system. Both systems usually apply basic, simple inventory policies. The performance of these decision rules with respect to costs and customer service has been examined extensively in literature, but, up to now, a comprehensive analytical investigation of their impact on planning stability has not been carried out[17]. Therefore, the consideration of planning stability may serve as an additional reason for integrating these lot-sizing rules into production planning and material coordination systems. However, Jensen [68] has examined the stability performance of inventory control rules in a single-stage production system within a simulation study. Since simulation studies do not give a systematic insight into the inter-dependencies between critical parameters, for example, order quantities, or length of the planning horizon, and planning stability, an analytical approach is provided in this work. For analytical tractability, some specific assumptions have to be made, in particular concerning the type of stability, the forecasting process of demand, and the characteristics of the demand distribution. Nevertheless, the kind of nervousness which is mainly disruptive in the execution of the planning process is dealt with in this study.

[17] Note that only in Inderfurth [61] and De Kok and Inderfurth [32] analytical examinations of stochastic inventory control rules with respect to planning instability are presented. Nevertheless, there is a comparable broad range of literature concerning the impact of deterministic lot-sizing rules on nervousness (for details see Section 3.6).

Moreover the underlying demand distributions for the single-stage production system are fairly general, and do not limit the results. Besides the influence of lot-sizing parameters on stability, the impact of other factors of the operating environment is shown. A central aspect of the investigation is to analyze if one of the examined inventory control rules is favorable with respect to stability aspects. Furthermore, the differences between a "traditional" inventory system and a recovery system regarding stability are of particular interest. This work is organized as follows.

Chapter 2 addresses different concepts for material planning. The types of uncertainty that occur in a production environment are presented, as are the methods that exist to cope with these uncertainties. Since, in practice, the Material Requirements Planning (MRP) concept is conventionally used in connection with a rolling horizon schedule, the main focus is on the presentation of the MRP approach and its additional features in an uncertain environment. Furthermore, the relationship between Stochastic Inventory Control (SIC) and MRP are presented. Finally, alternative material planning concepts are briefly explained.

In Chapter 3 the term "planning stability" is first defined. This is followed by a detailed explanation of material planning in a rolling horizon planning framework. Different causes for plan revisions in such a framework are presented, and plan changes are classified according to specific criteria. After a clarification of the stability-related terms "robustness" and "flexibility", the application of a technical stability measure is justified. The nervousness measure used in the analysis of different inventory control rules is then introduced. Finally, different strategies for coping with nervousness are presented, and their performances to increase planning stability are compared to each other.

Chapter 4 contains a steady-state analysis for examining the impact of reorder point policies on planning stability in a single-stage production system. There is a analysis of the dependency of stability on the length of a so-called stability horizon, which is closely connected to the planning horizon, the weighting of periods within this horizon, the forecast accuracy, and the demand variability.

Chapter 5 analyzes the two basic inventory control rules in slightly different recovery systems. First, the necessary adjustments of the MRP concept in product recovery systems are explained, and the basic recovery model is introduced. Then, the underlying inventory control rules applied in the two different recovery systems are explained and analyzed with respect to nervousness.

Chapter 6 concludes the examination with a summary of the main findings and some suggestions for further research topics.

2. Material Requirements Planning and Inventory Control

This chapter gives an overview of different approaches for material planning in manufacturing systems. The main focus is on the comparison of necessary information for each concept, and the explanation of the coordination between different stages of production. A description of how uncertainty is taken into account in these different concepts is given, and in Section 2.3.1 different planning methods for dealing with uncertainties are explained. Contrary to the decision making concepts introduced in the other subsections[1], these planning concepts may also be applied in other decision problems in companies, such as investment decisions, for example.

The aim of material requirements planning in a multi-stage manufacturing system is to determine the amount of all products[2] which are necessary to produce a forecasted quantity of end-items within a given planning horizon and to determine the timing of the matching production and procurement decisions. To develop a detailed production and procurement schedule, certain information is essential (for details see, e.g., Silver et al. [116], pp.597, or Van Donselaar [131], pp.13). First, the Bill of Material (BOM) must be provided[3]. It shows all of the components and component numbers required to manufacture one unit of the parent item. Second, the planned lead times for manufacturing/purchasing components or raw materials, respectively, are required. Third, information about lot-sizing rules and buffering policies used on the different manufacturing levels must be given. This is the static input data of most of the planning models for material coordination. In addition, some dynamic data must be provided. This refers to the (time-phased) requirements, the scheduled receipts which contain those orders that are already released but not yet received, and the inventory on hand. The output data of a planning model is current and planned order releases (with respect to timing and quantity) for production and procurement within a given time period. Some of these releases lead to immediate manufacturing/purchasing of components, others are only forecasts for planning in future periods. The planning model

[1] See Sections 2.1, 2.3.2 and 2.3.3).

[2] These are components and raw materials.

[3] Notice that there are different forms of BOMs; for instance, in the so-called modular form, only the immediate components are shown.

also provides exception messages which give information about late or early scheduled receipts. To cope with uncertainty and the dynamic environment, planning of materials is generally embedded in a rolling horizon schedule (for details see Section 2.3.1).
Material planning is a core element of a company's entire production planning system (see, e.g., Silver et al. [116], pp.535). It belongs to the short range[4], operational production decisions. Material planning is directly related to customer demand (in-house production of manufacturing orders) and suppliers (purchasing of components and raw materials). Thus, uncertainties in demand and supply frequently lead to plan revisions in material planning. Moreover, stochastic influences in the manufacturing process itself, such as breakdowns of machines or scrap, may lead to plan changes. Since the results of material planning are input data for several other operational decisions, such as short-term scheduling, plan revisions may cause replanning activities directly on the shopfloor. If there are a lot of plan changes, then a general loss in planning confidence will occur. Because of this loss of goodwill towards the planning system, people who are engaged in the execution of production plans get frustrated; and, maybe as a final consequence, the shop foremen do not accept any plan at all and develop their own schedules. Furthermore, material planning also relays information to capacity planning. Therefore in the case of joint utilization of capacities, plan changes may not only lead to replanning activities on lower stages in the manufacturing system, but may also cause plan revisions at the same level in the product structure. Ultimately, the decision rules used in material planning may differ from one level to the other. Therefore, plan revisions at an upstream stage may be increased due to the decision rule at its successor[5].

The next section describes different methods for material planning. They differ mainly with regard to the information used. Other differences concern lot-sizing rules, material coordination between different production stages, and procedures to cope with stochastic disturbances.

2.1 Concepts for Material Planning

2.1.1 Stochastic Inventory Control (SIC)

Using stochastic inventory control, the orders at each production stage are driven by the use/assumption of specific demand distributions and the application of forecasting methods. The input data required concerns the components/raw materials used in the past. Therefore, the application of a (stochastic) inventory control rule on the basis of expected/forecasted demand at

[4] According to Silver et al. [116], p.538, the time horizon for short range is lower than 6 months.

[5] The arguments in this paragraph are taken from Jensen [68], pp.15.

each production stage (or stocking point, respectively) leads to released and planned manufacturing orders at this stage. The manufacturing orders are determined independently of the requirements of downstream stages, i.e. information about future demand at succeeding stages is not used for calculating the size of the replenishment order at upstream stages. Thus, this concept can be identified as a "pull" control system, because independent downstream stages pull stock from their supplying predecessors (see, e.g., Pyke and Cohen [102]).

The major advantage of SIC is the use of relatively simple, local inventory control rules at each stocking point. The parameters of these policies can be determined on the basis of local information at the corresponding production stage. The rule itself is also applied only taking into account local information about the inventory position (i.e. inventory on hand plus on order minus backorders) at this stage as well as its lead time, and the requirements which result from the manufacturing orders of its downstream stages.

In SIC, usually two-parametric inventory control rules are applied. These inventory policies can be distinguished between decision making with respect to the quantity and the timing of an order. They are summarized in Table 2.1[6].

Table 2.1. Stochastic inventory control rules

	fixed order cycles	variable order cycles
fixed order quantities	–	(s, Q) policy
variable order quantities	(R, S) policy	(s, S) policy

In the case of an (R, S) policy, orders can only be placed after a fixed number of (R) time periods. Then, the inventory position is raised to a predefined order-up-to-level S. In the case of so-called reorder point policies, orders are placed if at any review time the inventory position reaches or drops below a predefined reorder point s. This leads, in general, to variable order cycles. Then, with respect to the reorder quantity, a further differentiation is possible. Applying an (s, S) policy means that the inventory position will be brought up to a specified reorder level (order-up-to-level) S by placing an order. The use of an (s, Q) policy differs from the (s, S) rule in that an order consisting of a fixed quantity Q is released to raise the inventory level above the reorder point[7]. Notice that an (R, S) policy with $R = 1$, and an (s, S)

[6] See, e.g., Zahn and Schmid [147], p.383.

[7] To ensure that stock is really raised above s, frequently an (s, nQ) policies is applied. Then, as many lots (n) of Q are ordered, so that inventory position after replenishment exceeds the reorder point.

policy with $s = S$ lead to a simple order-up-to-level (S) policy.
Furthermore, inventory control models can be classified into periodic or continuous review models (see, e.g., Nahmias [95], p.215 and p.267). Periodic means that replenishment decisions are only made at discrete points in time whereas in continuous models, orders can be released at all times. Therefore, the application of an (R, S) policy is only useful in periodic review models where R coincides with the review times. The reorder point policies can be used efficiently in both periodic and continuous review models.

Nevertheless, the application of such an inventory control rule in multi-stage systems causes some serious problems related to the fact that each stocking point is controlled locally. This results in a lack of material coordination between successive stages (see Van Donselaar [131], pp.48): information about the actual inventory position at downstream stages is not used, and future requirements of downstream stages are also not taken into account at upstream stages. In particular, if the lot size of a downstream stage is large, then this new information is given to the upstream stage with long delays. These delays result from the fact that upstream stages only receive information if the downstream stage releases an order. Moreover, because of the lack of information on upstream stages, variations are amplified; for example, a change in the requirements of a downstream stage may lead to a change in the parameters of the underlying inventory control rule on the upstream stage (see Van Donselaar [131], p.24 and p.50). Therefore, SIC should only be applied in multi-stage production systems which are characterized by stable, continuous requirements and small lot sizes at each stage. This leads to Just-in-Time (JIT) systems which are controlled by Kanbans[8]. Finally, because of its simplicity, SIC can also be used for cheap products (see, e.g., Van Donselaar [131], p.51).
A variation on the SIC concept introduced above is a base stock control system. Here, information about demand for the end-product are available for decision making at all production stages, i.e. global information is used (see, e.g., Silver et al. [116], pp.489). Different from the aforementioned locally controlled system, the replenishment decisions at each stocking point are based on customer demand instead of replenishment orders from the next downstream stage. The order decisions at each stocking point are then based on the echelon inventory position[9].
Comparing the performance of local control and base stock control in multi-stage systems, the latter leads to less variability, lower safety stocks, and, consequently, to a reduction of inventory carrying costs (see, e.g., Tempelmeier [126], pp.415, and Silver et al. [116], pp.491).

[8] A detailed description of the JIT concept is given in Silver et al. [116], pp.631.
[9] For details see, e.g., Silver et al. [116], pp.491.

2.1.2 Material Requirements Planning (MRP)

MRP logic has been explained in depth in numerous textbooks (see, e.g., Orlicky [97], Baker [7], and Silver et al. [116], Chapter 13 and 15). Material planning in MRP is coordinated centrally. The starting point is the (independent) demand for the end product. The Master Production Schedule (MPS) contains information about what quantities of each end product will be produced at what time (order release dates) within the planning horizon. The time basis is discrete, and conventionally a one week period or time bucket is used[10]. The MPS is a time-phased plan for the completion of products, i.e. a schedule for final assemblies. Besides the MPS, the other types of input in MRP systems, such as Bill of Materials (BOM), production and procurement lead times, or the current inventory status, have already been mentioned above. To meet the requirements of the MPS, a sequence of steps called explosion, netting, offsetting, and lot-sizing at each production level is conducted (see, e.g., Baker [7], pp.573).

Explosion refers to the computation of gross requirements for the components along the information in the BOM, at the next upstream stage in the product structure. This procedure is applied for each level in the product structure, resulting in a new sequence of (gross) requirements by time period. In the next step, the existing inventory position and safety stock is set against the gross requirements, leading to a modified series of net requirements of each item by time period. The timing of order releases is then calculated by working backward from the dates at which net requirements take place. Therefore, planned lead times are used either for purchased parts (vendor response time) or manufacturing orders (setup time, processing time, transportation time, queueing time). Finally, the batch quantities, which will be purchased or produced to satisfy the net requirements, are determined using lot-sizing procedures. In literature, different lot-sizing heuristics, such as Silver-Meal, or part-period-balancing method are discussed[11]. Nevertheless, a simple type of solution known as lot-for-lot strategy is quite often appropriate (see, e.g., Silver et al. [116], p.603). Lot-for-lot means that each net requirement is covered with a separate replenishment quantity. This method performs well if the requirements pattern is very erratic, or, if the setup costs are very low.

Two other very familiar ways to calculate the order quantity in an MRP system are the fixed order quantity (FOQ) and the period order quantity (POQ) (see, e.g., Wemmerlöv [138], or, Van Donselaar [131], pp.20). Using FOQ means that the order quantity is a (multiple of a) fixed lot-size, whereas the quantity is variable for a POQ policy. These lot-sizing rules frequently used in MRP systems can be interpreted as simple stochastic inventory control rules (see Anderson and Lagodimos [4], [78]): the use of an (s, S) control rule can be interpreted as applying POQ, and the implementation of an (s, Q) policy coincides with FOQ planning.

[10] See, e.g., Wemmerlöv [138], or, Silver et al. [116], p.602.

[11] For an overview on lot-sizing heuristics see, e.g., Nahmias [95], pp.345.

To sum up, the gross requirements, net requirements, planned order receipts, and planned order releases for each item are determined in MRP. Finally, the amount and timing of planned replenishment orders for manufacturing and purchasing are obtained. Notice that MRP can be identified as a "push" control system, because stock is pushed to the locations that need it most in order to satisfy the requirements of the MPS (see, e.g., Pyke and Cohen [102]).

Contrary to stochastic inventory control, the MRP logic takes a deterministic view. Therefore, for instance, buffers are incorporated into the MRP concept to cope with uncertainty (a detailed discussion can be found in Section 2.3.2). Moreover, MRP must be able to handle updates[12]. In periodic review, the procedure mentioned above is carried out once per basic time period. However, changes in input data may occur not only once per period, for example, changes in the MPS due to direct external demand, discrepancies in inventory records, machine breakdowns, and so on, can occur (see, e.g., Silver et al. [116], p.611). Replanning activities are then necessary, which lead to nervousness in the MRP system[13]. A disadvantage of the MRP logic is that buffers such as safety stocks are often not used to avoid or reduce plan revisions[14]. Then, planned orders only serve to raise safety stocks to their desired level.

As in SIC, if lot-sizing rules are applied which only use local information at the corresponding level in the product structure, information about customer demand is also lost in MRP systems. Because of the direct connection between requirements of subsequent stages, the MRP system is very prone to diffuse and amplify disturbances. This effect is increased by the fact that capacity constraints are not taken into account appropriately in MRP logic. Furthermore, no adjustment is made to buffers, since only information on the local inventory position is given at each stage. Therefore, stocks possibly still at downstream stages are not used to dampen disturbances on upstream levels. This leads to unnecessarily high stock levels at the individual stages[15].

---

[12] Notice that MRP systems are used in connection with a rolling horizon schedule to incorporate new available information, see also Section 2.3.1.

[13] This topic will be discussed in detail in Chapter 3. Furthermore, the use of a rolling horizon schedule itself leads to plan revisions.

[14] See, e.g., Wemmerlöv [140], Sridharan and LaForge [123], or Carlson and Yano [23].

[15] For a detailed discussion of the ineffective use of inventories in an MRP system see, e.g., Van Donselaar [131], pp.51.

2.2 Types of Uncertainty in a Production Environment

This section addresses different kinds of uncertainty taking place in production planning systems. Uncertainty generally refers to the probability that the realization will differ from the expectations or estimates respectively (see, e.g., Van Donselaar [131], p.5).
First, one may distinguish primary from secondary disturbances (see, e.g., Schneeweiß [113], p.132). The former are carried into the planning system from an external source, and lead to a change in the available information. Secondary disturbances occur as a consequence of primary uncertainties. They can further be divided into vertical and horizontal disturbances.
A second distinction concerns uncertainty in timing and in quantity (see, e.g., Whybark and Williams [141]). Timing uncertainty means that the realization takes place later or earlier than expected, whereas quantity uncertainty describes the extent to which the realization differs from its expectation. Notice that deviations in time usually cause major problems in the execution of the planning process (see, e.g., Jensen [68], p.23).
A further classification refers directly to the uncertainties in a production environment (see, e.g., Van Donselaar [131], pp.6). A production environment consists of suppliers, customers, the production system and the matching planning and control system. In such a system, different kinds of uncertainties may occur. First, customer demand may be uncertain. This directly affects material requirements planning. Then there may be process uncertainty, unexpected scrap or breakdowns of machines for example. Material availability, capacity requirements and availability are directly influenced by process uncertainties. Supply uncertainty concerns the supply of raw materials or purchased components, e.g. materials are not delivered in time, or in the right quantity/quality[16]. This kind of uncertainty again affects material availability. Finally, there are uncertainties in the planning and control system, for example, errors in the BOM, the current inventory status, or in the norms of capacities. If this is the case, material requirements and availability (inventory counting errors) as well as capacity requirements and availability (errors in the norm of capacities) may be affected. In each planning period, the planning and control system derives new plans and decisions. This planning is based on historical data from former plans, and the current data from suppliers, customers, and the planning system itself. This data is analyzed, and a new plan is established and communicated to the suppliers, the production system, and customers. Any error made in this process contributes to uncertainties in the planning and control system. Moreover, not only the

[16] Notice that this coincides with the classification of Whybark and Williams [141]: supply uncertainty can be distinguished into uncertainty in timing (materials are not delivered in time), or uncertainty in quantity (materials are not delivered in the right amount). The same holds for demand timing and demand quantity uncertainty, respectively. Furthermore, according to the classification of Schneeweiß [113], supply as well as customer uncertainties are primary disturbances.

lack of information or the uncertainties in data lead to errors in the planning system, but also the lack of communication between production planning and other departments of a firm (e.g. marketing) can lead to disturbances in the production production planning process (see, e.g., Van Donselaar [131], pp.7, or Schneeweiß [113], pp.122). Notice that uncertainties in the planning and control system may also occur because of the modification in the parameters of an underlying decision rule, for example, a change of a reorder point, or lot size.

2.3 Methods for Coping with Uncertainty

This section focuses on different methods to cope with uncertainty. In Section 2.3.1 two general planning methods, which may also be applied in other decision problems are explained. How uncertainty is taken into account in wide-spread MRP applications is then examined. Finally, two other material planning concepts designed for a stochastic environment are introduced.

2.3.1 Planning Concepts in a Stochastic Environment

A general planning concept to cope with uncertainties is to set up a plan for a given number of time periods, i.e. a predefined planning horizon. This study presents two basic planning concepts for determining a plan for a finite number of periods.

2.3.1.1 Stochastic Dynamic Programming

Dynamic Programming is a systematic procedure for calculating the optimal combination of inter-related decisions (see, e.g., Hillier and Lieberman [52], Chapter 11, pp.393). The solution procedure of Dynamic Programming is designed for determining an optimal policy for the underlying overall planning problem. This overall problem is divided into stages. Each stage has a number of states, and a policy decision is required at each stage for each of the possible states. In the case of deterministic Dynamic Programming, the state at the next stage is determined completely by the state and the policy decision of its predecessor. This is not true for stochastic Dynamic Programming, where only a probability distribution describes what the next state will be. This means that the structure of the stochastic processes for all relevant states is assumed to be known completely. The possible states and decisions at all stages are frequently summarized in a decision tree (see, e.g., Hillier and Lieberman [52], p.420). Thus, the procedure of stochastic Dynamic Programming determines (inter-related) decisions for all possible future states already at the beginning of the planning process, i.e. in the planning period. The major deficiency of this approach is the fact that all possible states as well as all available decision alternatives in these states must be known at the beginning of the planning process. Moreover, if there is a greater number of future states then the planning effort is intractable. Further to this, the procedure does not take into account the possible gaining of new information in the future. This procedure is therefore not feasible for many real planning problems.

2.3.1.2 Rolling Horizons

Contrary to stochastic dynamic programming, the rolling horizon method does not provide a decision scheme for all possible future situations. Instead of stochastic data, forecasts about future developments are used, leading to a quasi-deterministic planning concept. Applying a rolling horizon procedure means that, in general, only the first period decision of a P-period planning problem is implemented[17]. After the first period has passed, the full P-period problem is rerun to determine a new first period's decision. For each time period, planned decisions are based on the actual state of the system. After each period, the decision maker has new information concerning the realization of the decisions from the previous plan as well as stochastic data. Notice that the decisions in future periods are not directly implemented, but in multistage production systems planned orders on the MPS level in periods at the end of the planning horizon may lead to order decisions in the actual period at lower levels in the product structure. Therefore, due to MRP time phasing, plan revisions in future periods may lead to plan changes in the imminent period.

Besides the length of the planning horizon (P)[18] and the rolling interval length[19], the number of periods and their decisions which are implemented directly are the third design parameter of the rolling horizon planning procedure. This is is what is called "freezing" a part of the plan, or "frozen zone", respectively[20]. The freeze length interval, called ΔP, is the proportion of the overall planning horizon that is frozen[21]. The freeze length interval has

[17] In some applications not only the first period's decision is implemented, but also the decisions for some of the first periods. This will be discussed in detail below.

[18] Notice that in a rolling horizon planning framework the planning horizon is also called "forecast window".

[19] For instance, in an MRP system, the length of the replanning interval, i.e. the rolling interval length, describes how often the MPS is replanned.

[20] In MRP systems the approach of freezing the MPS, especially over the cumulative lead time of a product, is frequently used in practice. A detailed description of this procedure can be found in Vollmann et al. [135].

[21] Notice that a further distinction may concern the freezing method. For instance, in an MRP system one may differentiate between period and order based freezing method. These procedures are describe in Section 3.6.1 in more detail.

a certain impact on the frequency of replanning activities[22]. A variant of this procedure is the freezing of all decisions within the planning horizon, i.e. $P = \Delta P$ (see, e.g., Blackburn et al. [14]). Then, there are no plan revisions.

2.3.2 MRP Logic in a Stochastic Environment

This section examines how the uncertain environment is taken into account in MRP logic. The main method of reducing uncertainty is the use of buffers (see, e.g., Wijngaard and Wortmann [142], Chu and Hayya [25], Murthy and Ma [94], and Van Donselaar [131], pp.31).

2.3.2.1 Safety Stocks, Safety Times, and Safety Capacities

A widespread approach for coping with uncertainty in MRP systems is the use of safety stocks. In general, safety stock is defined as the average net inventory at the end of an arbitrary period, just before a replenishment arrives (see, e.g., Silver et al. [116], p.234). Safety stocks protect against "larger-than-average" demand during the effective replenishment lead time. In contrast, safety time means that orders are scheduled for completion (slightly) ahead of the required time for manufacturing (see, e.g., Silver et al. [116], p.613). The main difference between both approaches is that safety times lead to buffers only in the case of a scheduled order, whereas explicitly planned safety stocks are always kept. Both methods lead to an increase in inventory levels. The surplus of capacity available (with respect to employees and/or machines) is called safety capacity (see, e.g., Van Donselaar [131], p.32). Safety capacities should ensure that the capacity requirements for manufacturing the scheduled orders can always be satisfied. Since safety capacity is fairly costly, it is rarely used intentionally in a typical industrial practice (see Milwaukee Chapter Inc. [?]). Moreover, unused capacity is considered as a "waste" in current operating environments[23].

Conventionally, safety stock and safety lead time are used to protect the production system against uncertainty. Though it is not entirely clear which method should be used under specific conditions, safety stock is usually the preferred method in the case of quantity uncertainty, while the use of safety lead time is conventionally favorable in cases of timing uncertainty[24]. However, Grasso and Taylor [41] suggest to use safety stocks instead of safety lead

[22] See, e.g., Sridharan et al. [119]. A discussion of the impact of design parameters of a rolling horizon procedure on nervousness can be found in Section 3.6.1.

[23] An examination of the effectiveness of the three different methods to deal with production uncertainty can be found in Schmitt [111].

[24] See, e.g., Whybark and Williams [141], and Van Donselaar [131], pp.31.

times for buffering against supply/timing uncertainty. Buzacott and Shanthikumar [18] have found that safety time only performs better than safety stocks when the forecasts of future required shipments over the lead time are accurate.
An additional problem in multi-stage systems is the determination of the optimal location of buffers, i.e. at which level in the product structure safety stock or safety time should be kept. Moreover, the optimal amount of safety stock and safety time respectively, has to be calculated[25]. Lagodimos and Anderson [78] have found that for serial systems, safety stocks should be kept at the end-item level, whereas for divergent systems, the result depends on different factors, such as variability of demand, total amount of safety stock available, structure of lead time. A recent study on the amount and location of safety stocks in production networks is presented by Minner [92].
However, in MRP systems, the most common method is to keep safety stocks primarily for end-items, since they are directly available to satisfy customer demand. Nevertheless, safety stocks at lower levels can be used in a more flexible way, and, in general, lead to a lower capital commitment. Moreover, safety stocks at upstream stages may be used to protect against the negative consequences of frequent plan revisions (see, e.g., Lagodimos and Anderson [78]). A practical guideline for the possible use of safety stocks and safety times is given by Silver et al. [116], p.613.

2.3.2.2 Hedging and Overplanning

Besides safety stocks, quantity buffers can be set up by hedging[26], option overplanning[27], and order overplanning[28], respectively. All methods "overplan" the requirements. This leads to excess inventories at all levels of the product structure, but the management of the system is different as for safety stocks.

Hedging means that requirements are increased by using time-phased extra requirements which are called hedges. Option overplanning overestimates the requirements by raising the explosion factor in the planning BOM (see also Van Donselaar [131], p.175). Order overplanning anticipates future requirements by utilizing information about each customer. This information is gathered during the customer's purchasing process prior to actual order placing. The major difference between order overplanning and hedging or option overplanning is that order overplanning uses two different units in the MPS

[25] See, e.g., Lagodimos and Anderson [78] for the discussion of the optimal positioning of safety stocks in MRP systems.
[26] See, e.g., Miller [88].
[27] See, e.g., Van Donselaar [131], pp.175.
[28] See, e.g., Bartezzaghi and Verganti [8].

and forecasting process. The MPS unit is an end item, while the forecast unit is a single customer order.
Portioli [101] compares the performance of option overplanning and safety stocks to cope with uncertainty in multi-level production systems. Within his simulation test, Portioli has found that the best alternative depends on demand uncertainty, product cost structure and desired service level. His results indicate that the service level is most important, and that at low service levels (e.g. 85 %), safety stocks are better than overplanning. For high service levels, overplanning outperforms safety stocks, for example, for service levels larger than 95 % overplanning has been the best choice in most cases. Bartezzaghi and Verganti [8] deal with order overplanning to manage demand uncertainty in environments characterized by heterogeneous, undispersed, and erratic demand. They point out that order overplanning is appropriate when demand is sporadic, and when information about single sources of uncertainty leads to an increase in the quantity and quality of information about future requirements.
However, Van Donselaar [131] argues that the combination of MRP and hedging or overplanning is not a good alternative (see Van Donselaar [131], pp.180). He shows that planned orders are not realistic, and, consequently, each plan that uses these planned orders as input data, is distorted. This holds, for example, for capacity requirements planning. Moreover, the buffer policies mentioned above do not use individual, component-dependent safety stocks. The buffers on upstream product levels are directly deduced from the buffers used at downstream stages. Therefore, component specific uncertainties resulting from different suppliers, different production processes, or different planning procedures, for example, cannot be taken into account. He concludes that MRP and hedging or overplanning, only fit together when capacity requirements planning is not essential and the product structures are not convergent, or no component dependent stocks are needed.

2.3.3 Alternative Concepts in a Stochastic Environment

Since the MRP concept is not very efficient in a stochastic environment, the aforementioned buffers are integrated to cope with uncertainty. Nevertheless, the MRP concept still has a number of disadvantages[29], for example, any flexibility in the requirements is ignored due to the loss of information, i.e. MRP only explodes the planned orders of the parent product. Thus, alternative concepts for materials coordination have been developed.

[29] See, e.g., Van Donselaar [131], pp. 51, and Van Donselaar [132] for a detailed analysis of MRP weakness in a stochastic environment.

2.3.3.1 Line Requirements Planning (LRP)

The LRP concept is based on the base stock and echelon concept already mentioned above[30] (for details see Van Donselaar [131], pp.55). The echelon stock at a stage in the product structure is defined as the stock at this stage plus the stock at all its (direct or indirect) successor stages plus stock in transit minus backorders at the end-item level. Planned orders are then released by applying a dynamic reorder point inventory control rule based on the cumulative lead time of the echelon.
Comparing MRP and LRP, the main advantage of the latter concept is the fact that it explodes information on inventories and requirements separately and in their basic form to upstream stages. This leads to a higher transparency and fewer plan revisions[31] than in an MRP system. The main disadvantage of LRP is that it does not take into account lot-sizing inflexibility[32]. Moreover, firm planned orders[33] of downstream stages cannot be taken into account in LRP, whereas in MRP, the MPS should consist of firm planned orders.

2.3.3.2 Flexible integral Requirements planning STrategy (FiRST)

An extension of LRP is the FiRST concept which tries to avoid the disadvantages of MRP and LRP (for details see Van Donselaar [131], pp.82). According to Van Donselaar, FiRST combines the strong features of MRP and LRP, and leads to stabilized production, reduced inventories, and a flexible and transparent planning instrument. FiRST is based on LRP, and planned orders for a parent product and its components are determined according to the LRP planning concept. Therefore these planned orders are denoted by "planned orders LRP". Contrary to LRP, FiRST also takes into account lot-sizing of the planned orders for the components.
To incorporate lot-sizing in FiRST, Van Donselaar introduces a design parameter called Lot size Inflexibility Factor (LIF): the quantity of any order should be at least equal to a given predefined percentage of the standard lot size (which might also be the firm planned order). This percentage is denoted by LIF, and it has to be determined for each product separately. Contrary to

[30] Notice that the echelon concept, which has been introduced by Clark and Scarf [27], is an extension of the base stock concept developed by Magee [85].

[31] In Section 3 considers the impact of LRP on nervousness, see also Van Donselaar et al. [133].

[32] On upstream stages, LRP always assumes that the inventory can be used, regardless of lot-size restriction on downstream stages.

[33] Firm planned orders have their quantities, due dates, and start dates set manually by the planner. The quantity, start and due date of a "normal planned order" is automatically calculated by the MRP program using planned order quantities and lead times. Note that firm planned orders cannot be changed automatically by the computer.

MRP, where the planned orders are checked with respect to "normal" lot size restrictions imposed by the parent product, FiRST checks the planned orders LRP for violations of "minimal" lot size restrictions. Therefore, minimal planned orders for the parent products, which will constitute the minimal requirements for the component, must be known in FiRST. Using these minimal requirements, FiRST checks whether the planned orders LRP for the component are released or should be replanned. Notice that setting LIF=100 %, FiRST generates the same requirements as the standard MRP concept, whereas LIF=0 % leads to LRP requirements (see Van Donselaar [131], p.100).
Besides the treatment of flexible lot-sizing, the main advantage of this approach is that inventories are reduced. In MRP, existing inventory at upstream stages which is not sufficient to produce a standard lot size of the parent product, leads to "remnant stock", i.e. stock which is not used. In FiRST, because of the Lot size Inflexibility Factor, existing inventory at upstream stages may be used to produce minimal planned orders of the parent product. Furthermore, because of the introduction of the Lot size Inflexibility Factor, FiRST tends to be less nervous than MRP (see Van Donselaar [131], p.115, and Jensen [68], p.35).

2.4 Summary

The previous sections indicate a number of uncertainties which disturb the execution of planned decisions in multi-stage production systems. They result either from a stochastic environment or from deficiencies in the planning process which may be caused by a lack of information and/or coordination between different levels in the product structure. However, the uncertainty of the environment leads to frequent plan revisions, because new information about stochastic data, or consequences of previous decisions must be taken into account. Therefore, each of the aforementioned procedures for material planning tends to be more or less nervous. Besides the rolling horizon schedule environment in which these concepts usually are embedded, the respective underlying planning procedure itself causes plan revisions; for instance, in multi-stage production systems the use of lot-sizing rules may even increase nervousness. Further to this, the approaches for coping with uncertainty, such as safety stocks or safety times, can also amplify disturbances. Consequently, in multi-stage production environment, nervousness at the top level is propagated throughout the entire system.

3. Nervousness in Material Requirements Planning Systems

In practice, material planning is usually conducted using MRP systems. Up to now, the use of alternative concepts such as LRP or FiRST is not widespread. Consequently, the analysis of nervousness in MRP systems is the main focus in literature and in the subsequent analysis.
In literature, MRP nervousness is defined in several ways. In an early work, Steele [124] defines a "nervous MRP" system as one that causes excessive changes to low-level requirements when the master schedule is not changed significantly. He identifies the following reasons for nervousness in MRP systems.

- Master schedule changes/Unplanned demand:
  Rescheduling the MPS, in general, leads to replanning activities on low-level items. Because of lot-sizing, even minor time-phasing changes on the MPS level may lead to major rescheduling actions on lower stages. In particular, changes in lot sizes on the MPS level may cause rescheduling of released orders at lower levels (see also Mather [86]).
- Allocation not issued in expected quantity: (or contrary to the plan, Type I)
  The difference between the actual demand and expected (planned) demand of a component may lead to changes in the due date of the replenishment requirement. An allocation gives the planned issue for a shop requirement, and if it is not available in the expected quantity, then the forecasted run-out date will shift. Similar problems occur if a machine breaks down, or a supplier cannot deliver the material for a component in time[1]. Then, assemblies on which these components are used must be delayed (see, e.g., Mather [86]).
- Order released in unplanned quantity: (or contrary to the plan, Type II)
  The impact of this is the same as for type I, i.e. subordinate requirements will again jump forward, but in this case, all components are influenced. The same holds for unexpected scrap which causes planned orders to be needed earlier (see, e.g., Mather [86]).

[1] Notice that these problems can often be kept to a minimum by using preventive maintenance programs and choosing reliable suppliers.

- Order released prematurely: (or contrary to the plan, Type III)
  Here, all lower-level requirements jump from a future period to the actual period.
- Parameter changes:
  Finally, a change in a system parameter at downstream levels in the product structure, for example lot size, safety stock, or lead time, also generates revisions at lower stages.

Mather [86] defines nervousness as "changing the required due date on a related replenishment order for either a purchased or manufactured material". He identifies some additional causes for nervousness in MRP systems. These are ***engineering changes*** which lead to changes in the BOM and consequently to changes in the requirements within the MRP program. However, if these changes can be made "well in the future", then they can be implemented without significant rescheduling. Another reason for nervousness may be *record errors* in any of the used data, e.g. on-hand inventory, or BOM. Finally, Mather points out that ***unplanned transactions*** which change the inventory level for an item will alter the plan to replenish this item, and, consequently, rescheduling activities are necessary. Since, according to Mather, many of these actions are not necessarily urgent, they could be delayed if they cause significant problems. A control of these transactions can also help to reduce/eliminate record errors.
Blackburn et al. [13] consider MRP system nervousness as "instability in planned orders" caused by uncertainty in demand (and supply of components) and variations in lot-sizing decisions.
Minifie and Davis [90] point out that nervousness in an MRP system is normally indicated by the generation of exception reports, which show that the previous schedule has changed. According to Minifie and Davis, the three basic types of exception situation are (1) the need for expediting, (2) rescheduling (delaying or cancelling) open orders, and (3) releasing planned orders. Expedite messages occur when actual requirements cannot be covered by current inventory and scheduled receipts. Then, it may be necessary to pull forward a scheduled order to meet the requirements. Reschedule messages take place whenever excessive immediate coverage of requirements occur. In such circumstances, an order can be pushed back or it must be delayed. The release message is generated when actual scheduled receipts provide insufficient coverage to meet present requirements. These exception reports, in general, are caused by schedule quantity and/or timing imbalances. The reasons for these imbalances are, for example, imperfect end-item forecasts, MPS changes, or lot-sizing effects[2].

The aim of our analysis is to determine and compare the stability performance of different lot-sizing rules in subsequent planning cycles of a rolling horizon schedule. Therefore, planning stability is defined as follows (see Jensen [68],

[2] As an example, one may think of using only multiples of a lot size.

p.37).

Definition: *Planning stability*

The planning stability of a decision rule or planning method is represented by the extent to which decisions for a certain time period and planning cycle remain unchanged for the same time period in the subsequent planning cycle.

The following sections present a measurable formalization of nervousness, or lack of planning stability. Since material planning systems are used in connection with a rolling horizon schedule, at first, a detailed description of a rolling horizon planning procedure is given, followed by a more detailed and structured overview on the reasons for plan revisions. Section 3.2 provides a specification of the underlying term of nervousness in this analysis. Therefore, the term "planning stability" is defined more precisely, and it is delimited from "robustness" and "flexibility", respectively. This section concludes with a explanation as to why technical instead of cost-oriented stability measures should be used. Concepts for measuring stability are introduced, and the application of the measure used in our analysis is motivated. Finally, different strategies for coping with nervousness are introduced, and their performance to reduce nervousness is compared.

3.1 Rolling Horizon Planning Framework

3.1.1 General Approach

Usually, material planning concepts are embedded in a rolling horizon planning framework. Because of the permanent processing of new information and the realization of stochastic data, a rolling schedule procedure is almost always used to adjust former replenishment decisions to current conditions in applications of material planning systems. In particular, though order quantities are calculated over the entire planning horizon, only the imminent decision is realized (see, e.g., Silver et al. [116], p.199). In the next period, i.e. at the time of the next decision, new information is used to determine the updated production schedule.
Assume that a planning cycle of P periods is started at the horizon. That means that replenishment decisions are planned for the current plus the next $P-1$ periods[3]. Orders for the current period are released immediately, whereas future decisions are only preliminary and may be updated in later periods. Consequently, in each period, orders for the current plus the next $P-2$ periods are updates of previous plans. The replenishment order size in

[3] Note that it is assumed that there is no frozen zone, which means that the complete schedule is replanned after each planning period.

period t as planned in period i is denoted by $\hat{q}_t^i$. Analogously, $\hat{Z}_t^i$ describes the inventory position at the beginning of period t before replenishment, as planned in period i. Finally, $\hat{D}_t^i$ denotes the demand per period t as projected in period i. To sum up, at the beginning of each period t, a sequence of planned production orders $(q_t, \hat{q}_{t+1}^t, \hat{q}_{t+2}^t, ..., \hat{q}_{t+P-1}^t)$ is generated[4]. This procedure can be seen in Figure 3.1 for three subsequent planning periods, or planning cycles (see, e.g., Inderfurth [61]). Here, D_t denotes the realized demand in period t.

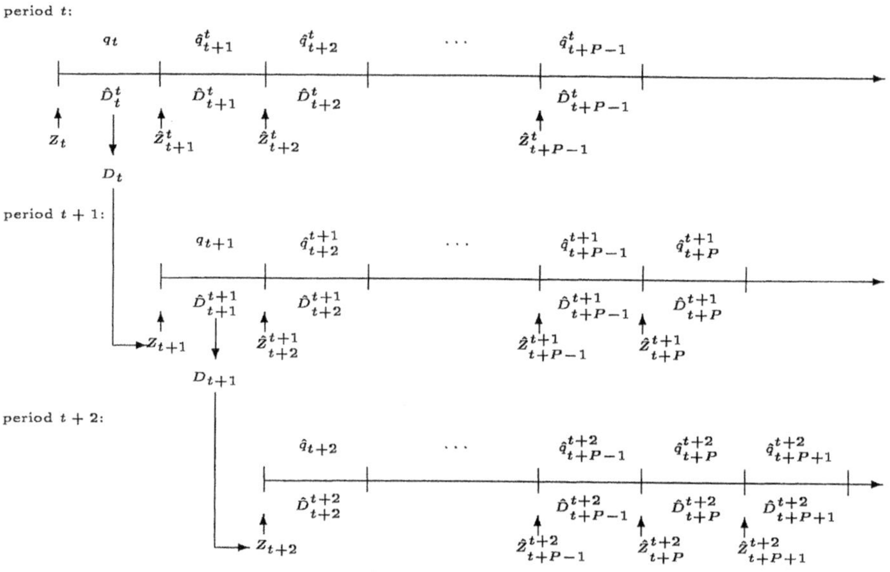

Figure 3.1. Planning cycles and order decisions in a rolling horizon framework

The state of the planning system at the beginning of each planning cycle t is described by the inventory position before replenishment (Z_t). This inventory position, in general, is defined as stock on hand minus backorders plus outstanding orders of the previous periods which have not yet been added to the stock on hand due to a positive, deterministic lead time. Throughout this study, for the purpose of simplifying documentation, it is assumed that all orders are delivered instantaneously[5]. Consequently, there is no lead time

[4] Notice the definition $\hat{q}_t^t = q_t$, and analogously for Z_t.

[5] Note that a deterministic lead time can easily be incorporated in the standard way by appropriately redefining the inventory position. Assuming a lead time of Λ periods, the inventory position of period t is given by stock on hand in t minus back orders in t plus outstanding orders of periods $t - \Lambda, ..., t - 1$.

and there are no outstanding orders. This analysis assumes that unsatisfied demand is back-ordered. In the case of lost demand, the inventory position must be adjusted by leaving out the back orders.
Now, the replenishment decision for period t (q_t) is planned on the basis of inventory position Z_t and the underlying lot-sizing rule. If, for example in the case of a reorder point policy, Z_t is smaller than the reorder point s, then an order will be made, i.e. $q_t > 0$[6]. Since this lot size is released immediately, the inventory position after replenishment is given as $Y_t = Z_t + q_t$. Consequently, the planned inventory position of the subsequent period is given as $\hat{Z}^t_{t+1} = Y_t - \hat{D}^t_t$.

Analogously, the replenishment decisions for subsequent periods are planned by taking into account planned inventory positions $\hat{Z}^t_{t+i}$, planned lot sizes $\hat{q}^t_{t+i}$ and projected demand $\hat{D}^t_{t+i}$ (for all $i = 1, ..., P-1$).
After period t has passed, the realization D_t of the stochastic demand is known, and the inventory position of period $t+1$ can be updated accordingly. An updated sequence of realized/planned order decisions for periods $t+1$ to $t+P$ is obtained using the adjusted inventory position Z_{t+1}. This action is repeated after each period.

Typically, in multi-stage production systems ruled by an MRP system, the above mentioned procedure is done at the end-item level in master production scheduling (MPS level), and at all upstream stages (see also Section 2.1.2). Therefore, plan changes on the top level are propagated throughout the entire planning system. Due to MRP time-phasing, even replanning activities in future periods near the end of the planning horizon enforce order revisions at lower levels in the first planning periods, or even the current period. Consequently, nervousness in future periods on the MPS level may influence planning stability at the beginning of the planning process at upstream stages.

3.1.2 Characterization of Plan Revisions

This subsection highlights some characteristics of plan changes[7]. Frequent plan revisions lead to nervousness in the planning system, and consequently, the production system may be unable to react appropriately to plan changes.

Definition: *Plan revisions*

plan revisions = deviation of a planned replenishment decision for a certain period and planning cycle from its planned value for the same period in a later cycle

[6] Note that the exact amount of the order depends on the lot-sizing rule, see Section 2.1.1, p.9.

[7] In this study, the expressions "plan changes" and "plan revisions" are used synonymously.

Thus, in general, nervousness arises when a formerly fixed order decision for a certain period is replanned in a later planning cycle. Using the notation introduced above, instability occurs, if for any j and v:

$$q_j^t \neq q_j^{t+v} \quad \text{for} \quad j \geq t \geq v > 0. \tag{3.1}$$

Note that this kind of nervousness can be characterized as planned orders nervousness.

On the one hand, replanning activities may be caused by realizations of stochastics of the system as well as new available planning information in each planning cycle. This kind of ***factors for plan changes***, e.g. from cycle t to $t+1$, are (see Jensen [68], pp.42):

- Realization of demand D_t, which is different from the projected demand $\hat{D}_t^t$, i.e. forecast error
- Deviation of actual forecasts ($\hat{D}_{t+i}^{t+1}$) from their projected values ($\hat{D}_{t+i}^t$) in the previous planning period (for all $i = 1, ..., P-1$)
- Influence of forecasted demand $\hat{D}_{t+P}^{t+1}$ for new planning period $t+P$

On the other hand, additionally, the underlying decision rule has a significant impact on the frequency of plan revisions. For instance, assume that the planned lot sizes are generated by different inventory control rules. It is obvious that the more these inventory policies are restricted, the fewer replanning actions take place. However, strong restrictions of the decision space lead to certain disadvantages with respect to other performance criteria, for instance, costs[8].

Plan revisions, in general, lead to some undesirable consequences in the planning process. First, plan changes generate a considerable amount of short-run and medium-term adjustment efforts. Furthermore, frequent replanning actions lead to a general loss of confidence in planning[9]. Since in many situations these negative aspects cannot be valued in terms of costs, they cannot be integrated into the underlying objective of the decision maker[10]. Therefore, plan revisions are described as changes in decision variables due to the application of a specific decision rule, for example, changes in lot sizes due to the use of a certain inventory control rule.

[8] Notice that a simple order-up-to-level policy generates production setups in all planning periods with positive (projected) demand. Therefore, instability with respect to setup changes is very low. Nevertheless, considering the average cost performance under a fixed plus convex cost structure this policy is worse than the optimal (s, S) policy (see, e.g., Lee and Nahmias [80], pp.25).

[9] Campbell [20] shows that the inappropriate handling of rescheduling problems may lead to higher rescheduling costs, fluctuation in capacity utilization, and confusion on the shopfloor (see also Chapter 1.1).

[10] See also Section 3.3 for the motivation of using technical stability measures.

In a first classification, plan changes may be distinguished according to the *cause* of their occurrence (see Jensen [68], pp.45):

- Plan revisions taking place because of rolling forward the planning horizon in a rolling horizon planning framework
- Plan revisions occurring as a reaction to disturbances

The first cause results from the use of a specific planning concept, i.e. the application of a rolling horizon schedule. Because of the inclusion of new information at the end of the planning horizon in each subsequent planning cycle, nervousness is influenced directly by the use of a rolling horizon planning framework. Even if all data in previous periods remains unchanged, then new information in the last period of the planning cycle may lead to a change in the planned decisions of the previous periods[11]. The reason for such kinds of plan revisions is the decomposition of the planning problem in successive, partially overlapping periods. Because of the dynamic environment, this decomposition does not have to lead to the overall optimal solution of the problem. Consequently, plan revisions frequently occur.

Plan changes taking place as reactions to disturbances can further be differentiated as follows[12]. Firstly, revisions may occur because of deviations between realizations of stochastic data from its projected values. Secondly, plan changes may take place due to plan revisions at preceding planning stages in a multi-level production system. Then, for the succeeding planning stage, these plan changes are "stochastic". Notice that the same applies to the adjustment of forecasts in successive planning cycles caused by the actual realization of the projected data (see Jensen [68], p.47).

A further categorization of plan revisions concerns their *distance from the planning period* (see Jensen [68], pp.47). One may distinguish between *short-term* and *long-term* plan revisions. Short-term nervousness only describes changes in the current period's decision that refers to the planned decision for this period in the previous planning cycles. For instance, in Figure 3.1, assume that the current period is $t+1$. Short-term nervousness with respect to only the preceding planning cycle is represented by the deviation of $\hat{q}^t_{t+1}$ from q_{t+1}. Notice that because of lack of information or communication between planning stages, this planned current decision may not necessarily be implemented, for instance, if in a multi-stage production system the planned lot size cannot be produced because of a shortage at an upstream stage. Contrary to this short-term consideration, long-term instability considers all planned decisions of overlapping periods within the entire planning horizon.

[11] See also the remarks on the meaning of a so-called decision horizon for the stability of lot-sizing rules (refer to Section 3.6.1).

[12] See also the distinction between primary and secondary disturbances in Section 2.2, p.13.

In Figure 3.1 this means that for cycle t and $t+1$ the planned decisions from period $t+1$ to $t+P-1$ have to be compared with regard to long-term nervousness.

One may further distinguish between plan revisions which affect the *timing* or the *amount* of a decision variable (see Jensen [68], pp.48). The latter kind of instability means that the original date of an action is not altered, but that the quantity of the decision variable is changed. Shifting a decision from one period to another leads to a change in the timing of a decision variable, where its size remains unchanged. This kind of plan revision, in general, leads to more problems in the execution of the planning process, because a completely new planned action has to be integrated into the plan, whereas in the case of pure quantity changes, the timing of a previous planned decision is confirmed.
In the field of material requirements planning and inventory control, a change in the timing of an order occurs if, in a new planning cycle a previously planned lot size is cancelled, or if, vice versa, a new order is planned. Since these plan revisions influence production setups, this kind of nervousness has been denoted as *setup-oriented* instability. Analogously, *quantity-oriented* instability measures deviations in the lot size quantities of successive planning cycles (see, e.g., Jensen [67], or Inderfurth [61]). Note that equation (3.1) represents quantity-oriented instability, whereas pure changes in order setups can be measured as $\delta(q_j^t) - \delta(q_j^{t+v})$ with $\delta(q) = 0$, for $q = 0$, and $\delta(q) = 1$, else[13]. In many practical situations, companies focus on changes in timing of planned orders. For instance, Van Donselaar et al. [133] report that DAF[14] and its suppliers want to minimize disruption in the production sequence, because this would imply additional setup time. The special relevance of setup-oriented stability results from the consequences of setup changes at all succeeding stages of the production planning process. In particular, capacity planning and short-range scheduling are considerably influenced by changed setups. Compared with pure changes in quantities, setup changes more often lead to a delay in capacity requirements. Since, in general, capacities should be used at their maximum availability, a delay in requirements frequently leads to considerable, and more complex additional plan changes. Setup changes create more serious problems on the shopfloor than quantity changes, because a completely new action has to be executed. In the case of revisions in the order quantity, the timing of the lot size is already known, and only the previously planned level of the action has to be adjusted (see Jensen [68], p.49).

[13] In Sections 3.4.1 and 3.4.2, respectively, concrete measures for setup-oriented and quantity-oriented instability are presented.

[14] DAF is a truck manufacturer in The Netherlands.

Plan revisions can be further be divided according to their ***direction*** into *loosening* or *increasing* plan changes (see Jensen [68], p.49). The first kind describes those plan revisions which lead to a (partial) withdrawal of a previously planned action whereas the latter need an additional or increased action. Thus, in general, the planning effort for increasing plan revisions is larger.

Finally, notice that plan revisions may also occur because of variations in the parameters of a decision rule, for example, resulting from a change in the cost parameters or service level constraints[15].This examination does not consider plan revisions and plan changes as a result of changed objectives of the decision maker.

3.2 Clarification of Terms: Robustness, Planning Stability, and Flexibility

Besides nervousness, there are other concepts to evaluate the sensitivity of planning methods on changes in stochastic and/or dynamic input data. "Robustness" characterizes the insensitivity of decision and planning methods as well as parameters on changes in input data. In statistics, the robustness of tests and estimations for analyzing random samples is of particular interest. For instance, in statistical time series analysis, an estimator is called robust if its performance is acceptable for the case that the "true" distribution of input data deviates from the distribution used for the determination of the estimator (see, e.g., Stockinger and Dutter [125]). In engineering, the term "robust" describes how, in dynamic systems, variations in parts of the system are tolerated without exceeding predefined tolerance boundaries in the vicinity of some nominal dynamic behaviour (see Weinmann [137]).

Robustness, flexibility, and planning stability of solution methods are of special interest in business administration for solving decision problems in an uncertain and dynamic environment. Robustness is often considered in connection with flexibility.

Robustness is defined as the invariability of initial decisions[16], or the persistence of complete decision sequences[17]. Schneeweiß defines robustness as insensitivity of a strategy to stochastic disturbances (see Schneeweiß [113],

[15] See, e.g., Richter and Vörös [105], [106] for a sensitivity analysis of the solutions of multi-level, deterministic, dynamic lot-sizing problems with respect to a change in the cost parameters.

[16] See, e.g., Rosenhead et al. [109].

[17] See Kühn [77].

p.157). Here, a strategy means a sequence of conditional decisions of a problem which has been solved by stochastic Dynamic Programming (see also Section 2.3.1). Robustness may also be interpreted as a service level or a specific measure of flexibility, (see Kühn [77], pp.77, and Schneeweiß [113], pp.157)[18]. In Gupta and Rosenhead [46] both terms, flexibility and robustness, are used synonymously. Within hierarchical production planning, Lasserre and Mercè [79], and Zäpfel [146] argue that each feasible decision sequence is "robust" because the restrictions of the decision space of the problem are not violated by a feasible decision sequence. Daniels and Kouvelis [29] have dealt with the problem of robust schedules. Schedule robustness is described as the "determination of a schedule whose performance, relative to the corresponding optimal performance, is relatively insensitive to the potential realizations of the task parameters". Furthermore, Kouvelis et al. [74] as well as Rosenblatt and Lee [108] have applied the robust decision-making formulations introduced by Gupta and Rosenhead [46] and Rosenhead et al. [109] to operational decision problems[19]. However, a consistent definition of the term robustness has not been established in literature.
Flexibility is defined as the capability of companies to adjust to different environmental constellations in the future[20], or, to decrease "optimal" the deviations of a realized state from its planned state, respectively[21]. According to Schneeweiß [113] the responsiveness of a system is determined by the number of available measures (volume of actions), the speed at which deviations are reduced, and the probability with that an action can be executed as it has been planned beforehand. Additionally, flexibility is influenced by the uncertain environment, i.e. the stochastic development of all relevant environmental constellations (see Schneeweiß [113], p.143). Meier-Barthold [87] introduced a standardized measure of flexibility by means of the cardinality of all feasible strategies (see Meier-Barthold [87], pp.51).

In general, the flexibility of a planning or decision system can be defined as its capability to adjust to the development of all relevant environmental states. Note that this incorporates a responsiveness with respect to the dynamics of the environmental conditions as well as the ability to cope with the uncertainties in the environment. Then, robustness describes the extent to which this adjustment can be achieved without a change in the behavior of the system. Nevertheless, contrary to flexibility, robustness only refers to the insensitivity of a system towards stochastic disturbances, the dynamic nature of the environment is not considered (see Jensen [68], pp.53).

[18] Kühn [77] and Schneeweiß [113] define the robustness of a decision sequence in a stochastic and dynamic environment by means of the probability that an economic aspiration level is satisfied.

[19] The concept of Rosenhead et al. [109] is briefly described on p.31.

[20] See Hanssmann [48], p.227.

[21] See Schneeweiß [113], p.145.

This definition of robustness is similar to the definition of planning stability (see p.23), since both terms deal with the insensitivity of a system to uncertain impact factors. But robustness only describes plan revisions as a result of stochastic influences, whereas planning stability also considers plan changes caused by the dynamic environment. This understanding of robustness supposes implicitly that each time a decision is made, the development of all relevant environmental constellations is known and used to find the solution.

Since a rolling horizon schedule is, in practice, commonly used to cope with uncertainty, a brief description of measures for robustness in such a planning framework is given in this study[22].

Rosenhead et al. [109] define an initial decision as robust, if the number of ex ante available "good" strategies is not reduced by the execution of the initial decision[23]. Then, robustness of an initial decision is measured as the fraction of the number of ex post available good strategies to the amount of ex ante available good strategies. This measure is not suitable for measuring planning stability, because on the one hand it is not clear how "good" strategies can be evaluated[24], and on the other hand, the definition only considers the impact of initial decisions on the available scope for action. Thus, only a part of the possible actions for plan revisions in a rolling horizon schedule is considered. The main contribution of this measure for developing a measure for planning stability is the standardization of robustness by the number of available strategies. Analogously, nervousness could be measured by relating the number of real plan changes in successive planning cycles to the number of available plan revisions (see Jensen [68], p.57).
Robustness is also defined as the insensitivity of a strategy towards stochastic disturbances in the case of a given technology[25] (see Kühn [77], p.69). Then, robustness R of a specific strategy a is given by the probability $\mathbb{P}$ that for a given technology Ω and predefined aspiration level $\hat{c}$ the realization of an objective $C(a)$ is reached by the application of this strategy, i.e. $R(a) := \mathbb{P}\{C(A) \leq \hat{c}|\Omega\}$. Note that the determination of the aspiration level restricts the set of all possible decisions. Since Kühn's concept for measuring flexibility[26] should not be affected by a restriction of feasible strategies, Kühn interprets the robustness measure mentioned above as a risk measure

[22] As mentioned before, the definition of robustness is closely connected to flexibility. A detailed description of concepts for measuring flexibility can be found in Meier-Barthold [87], pp.25.

[23] Note that ex ante means the number of available good strategy decisions before the determination of the initial decision, whereas ex post means the number of available good strategies after the implementation of the initial decision.

[24] See also Section 3.3 for the motivation of using technical stability measures.

[25] The technology of a system is described by the available scope for action and the possible speed in which actions can be executed.

[26] See Kühn [77], pp.77.

for the underlying strategy. Besides flexibility, he suggests using robustness as an additional criterion for the evaluation of a strategy[27]. However, this measure of robustness is also not appropriate for computing planning stability of decision rules (see Jensen [68], p.59). It considers the deviations between the actual objective $C(a)$ and the predefined aspiration level $\hat{c}$. At first, only "negative" plan changes with respect to the desired objective value are considered. Moreover, robustness does not only depend on the decision rule, but also on the objective function. One main shortcoming of this approach is that the interpretation and measurement of deviations depends both on the underlying objective and the decision rules applied. Finally, the aspiration level must be determined consistently with the expected consequences of plan revisions. This seems to be impossible because of the complex interrelations between the impact factors on plan changes, their treatment by the underlying decision rules, and their effects on the objective function.

To sum up, the definitions of robustness found in literature cannot be used to determine planning stability according to its definition at the beginning of this chapter (see p.23). Nevertheless, robustness is closely connected to flexibility, i.e. the ability of a system to cope with the dynamic environment and stochastic influences.

A flexible planning concept or decision rule is generally characterized by a large amount of available alternative courses of action (see, e.g., Meier-Barthold [87], pp.51). It is important therefore to analyze if the application of flexible decision rules must coincide with decreasing planning stability. For instance, Wild [143] has found that high stability is connected with low flexibility[28] whereas De Leeuw and Volberda [33] have shown that an increase in stability may also lead to rising flexibility[29].
Meier-Barthold [87] analyzes the flexibility of inventory control rules of (R,S)-, (s,nQ)- and (s,S)-type. He has found that, in general, an (s,nQ) is more flexible than an (s,S) policy, which is superior to an (R,S) policy. Regarding stability, in general, an (R,S) policy performs best, whereas there is no clear superiority between the reorder point policies (see, e.g., De Kok and Inderfurth [32] for an analytical investigation of short-term nervousness, and Jensen [68]). The high stability of an (R,S) policy results from a reduction of the scope for action in comparison to the reorder point policies where the time of placing an order is not fixed. Therefore, one may conclude that planning stability is just the opposite of flexibility. But Jensen has also shown that an increase in the stability performance of inventory control rules

[27] Note that Kühn's robustness measure is also considered as a specific measure for flexibility, see Schneeweiß [113], pp.157.
[28] Note that Wild [143] considers the flexibility of plant agreements for labor time.
[29] De Leeuw and Volberda [33] deal with the flexibility in the organization of companies.

may also coincide with an increase in flexibility (see Jensen [68], pp.200). By introducing a stabilization parameter, reorder point policies are applied in a more flexible manner, and, additionally, planning stability is increased (see also Section 4.5, pp.125).
Moreover, Van Donselaar [131] shows that a more flexible planning system like FiRST may lead to lower levels of nervousness (see Van Donselaar [131], pp.82). Note that Van Donselaar et al. [133] have also found that, on average, an MRP system is 4 to 5 times more nervous (with respect to setup-oriented instability) than a material planning system controlled by LRP (for details see also Section 3.6.6).

3.3 Explanation of Technical Stability Measures

This section explains why a technical stability measure is used in further analysis. Alternatively, costs for plan revisions may be introduced to evaluate nervousness of a planning system (see also Section 3.6.2).
In Stochastic Inventory Control (SIC), shortage costs are frequently used to ensure a desired service level. Analogously, one may also think of using schedule change costs to ensure a certain level of planning stability; for instance, the extent of plan revisions can be influenced by using modified setup costs (see the explanations regarding the work of Carlson et al. [22] in Section 3.6.2, p.55). However, as in the case of the determination of appropriate shortage costs[30], the settling of schedule change costs causes some serious problems.

On the one hand, the (cash-outlay) costs[31] caused directly by plan changes can generally be determined reasonably easily, but, on the other hand, the costs of the indirect consequences of plan revisions cannot be calculated sufficiently precisely (see also Jensen [68], pp.49). The setup costs for an additional setup, or the additional inventory carrying costs resulting from a change in timing or size of an order quantity can surely be quantified. Because of the execution of plan changes on time, expediting measures and shortfalls can generally be avoided. The question then arises if, in a cost-oriented evaluation of plan revisions, these consequences should also be considered, e.g., how to treat the additional revenues caused by evaded shortages.
Moreover, in multi-level production systems the allocation of schedule change costs is doubtful. They can be assigned either to the production level where the adjustment costs occur, or to the stage where the adjustment is triggered as a result of a previous plan change.

[30] See, e.g., Silver et al. [116], pp.244, for different types of shortage costs. For a discussion about the dependencies between shortage costs and service levels, see, e.g., Alscher and Schneider [1].
[31] For instance personnel costs and cost of materials for computing a new plan.

As mentioned, frequent plan changes lead to a general loss in planning confidence. In particular, production decisions that are continually being altered generate confusion on the shopfloor (see, e.g., Campbell [20]), and mainly capacity planning decisions become rather difficult. Furthermore, in multi-level production systems, plan revisions at downstream stages become stochastic inputs for preceding stages. Consequently, throughput times and inventories may increase, and service levels as well as capacity utilization may decrease because of incorrect priorities set by the planning system. Similar to the loss of goodwill in the case of shortages, these consequences cannot be expressed in monetary terms[32].

Because of these problems, it is useful to deal with planning stability as an independent criterion for assessing an inventory control system. This procedure is comparable with the application of different service levels[33] which, in general, cannot be replaced by revenues or cost values in most practical situations. For this reason, planning stability is treated as a specific attribute of an inventory control system. Then, similar to service level constraints in inventory control, the additional factor of planning stability can be included by using analogous stability constraints[34].
This study presents the underlying technical stability measure developed by Jensen[35] for the analysis of basic inventory control rules used in traditional production and inventory systems as well as product recovery systems[36]. A brief literature review of other technical stability measures is provided.

3.4 Concepts for Measuring Planning Stability

In literature, there are several suggestions for measuring stability, but, unfortunately, most of the examinations use (slightly) different definitions of plan changes. Therefore, most of the results are hardly comparable. However, all examinations consider deviations from planned decisions of successive planning cycles for a certain period, i.e. the level of nervousness of planned decisions is measured.
Carlson et al. [22], and Kropp and Carlson [76] consider the shift of scheduled setups. They define system nervousness as a change of the first period's setup decision, or a shift in the period with the first planned setup, respectively.

[32] See, e.g., Alscher and Schneider [1] for the difficulty of quantifying and allocating shortage costs.
[33] See, e.g., Lagodimos and Anderson [78] for the definition of different types of service levels.
[34] See also Kimms [73] for the addition of stability constraints into mathematical programming models.
[35] See Jensen [67] [68].
[36] See Chapter 4 and Chapter 5, respectively.

Here, setup changes in the first period of the planning horizon are weighted equally to changes in later periods, although in many practical situations, changes at the beginning of the planning horizon are more crucial, because there is less time to react on them. Additionally, pure changes in order quantities are not taken into account.

Blackburn et al. [14] define instability as the number of times an unplanned order is made in the first period when the schedule is rolled forward[37]. They count the number of times that changes take place in the imminent period of the planning horizon.

Minifie and Davis [90], [91] as well as Ho [53], and Ho and Ireland [56], [57] define nervousness by means of the exception reports and expediting measures generated by an MRP system. Here, the measurement of nervousness is reduced to the registration of plan revisions which have to be implemented immediately. Furthermore, the MRP system only indicates the need for a plan revision, the exact amount of replanning activities is not known. Finally, the measurement depends on the logic of the underlying MRP system. Notice that Ho [53] measures nervousness as the equally weighted sum of the number of reschedule-in notices and the number of reschedule-out notices. Ho and Ireland [56], [57] define nervousness as a weighted value of the number of rescheduling messages generated by the MRP system, i.e.

$$WR_{i,t} = q_{i,t} \cdot |NDD_{i,t} - ODD_{i,t}|,$$

where

$WR_{i,t}$	=	weighted rescheduling measure (for item i in period t)
$q_{i,t}$	=	order quantity of the open order of item i in the tth period to be rescheduled,
$NDD_{i,t}$	=	new due date of item i in the tth period,
$ODD_{i,t}$	=	original due date of item i in the tth period.

Then, the total weighted rescheduling measure (WR) is given as the sum over all items i and periods t. Minifie and Davis [90] define MRP nervousness as "the degree to which upper level plan revisions are directly reflected in lower level exception conditions". They are therefore not taking into account plan changes on the same production stage in later periods.

In other (simulation) studies, only ad-hoc measures of nervousness are used to describe the influence of different planning parameters on system nervousness in MRP systems[38]. A further deficiency of these measures is that they are not

[37] This type of nervousness has been characterized as short-term setup-oriented nervousness.

[38] See also Section 3.6, and, for instance, Blackburn et al. [15], or Yano and Carlson [144].

normalized. Different decision rules and planning concepts as well as scenarios with different impacting factors can therefore not be compared appropriately. Only Sridharan et al. [120], Kadipasaoglu and Sridharan [71], Kimms [73], and in a more general sense, Inderfurth [61] and Jensen [67], [68] provide a systematic discussion and development of stability measures. Notice that the measure proposed in Jensen [68] has been used (in a slightly modified manner) by De Kok and Inderfurth [32], as well as Heisig [49] and Heisig and Fleischmann [50]. Nervousness is measured by relating the expected (setup or quantity) deviations of orders to the expectation of maximum deviations that can occur under worst case inventory control.

This study first describes the measure proposed by Sridharan et al. [120]. Some general requirements for a nervousness measure are then presented (see Jensen [68]), and Jensen's measure for (setup- as well as quantity-oriented) instability is explained.

Sridharan et al. [120] measure nervousness as the weighted average of changes in planned replenishment quantities over subsequent planning cycles, i.e.

$$\nu_{SBU} = \frac{1}{M} \sum_{j=1}^{N-1} \sum_{i=j}^{P+j-2} |q_{t+i}^{t+j-1} - q_{t+i}^{t+j}|(1-a)a^{i-j}, \tag{3.2}$$

where

q_t^i	=	replenishment order size in period t as planned in cycle i
N	=	number of planning cycles
M	=	total number of orders over all planning cycles
a	=	weight parameter to represent the criticality of plan revisions $(0 < a < 1)$.

Since plan changes in periods near the end of the stability horizon may not have the same urgency as replanning activities in the imminent periods of the planning horizon, the weight parameter a is used to assign decreasing weights to subsequent periods within the planning horizon. On the one hand, the assumption that changes in the first periods are more important than those in future periods is reasonable, because there is less time to react to them. But, on the other hand, in a multi-stage production system, nervousness in future periods at the end-item level may influence planning stability in the first periods at upstream stages. Notice that a can take on values in the interval (0,1). With a close to 0, the weighting of plan revisions in later periods decreases rapidly, while values of a close to 1 imply that all periods within the horizon are (almost) equal in weight which may be relevant in multi-stage production systems. Therefore by choosing the weight parameter appropriately, both aspects, the reaction time as well as the fact that nervousness propagates throughout the whole MRP system, may be integrated in the measure.

Furthermore, Sridharan et al. [120] suggest relating the measure in (3.2) to the average lot size. As approximation for this average lot size they use the well-known Economic Order Quantity- (EOQ-) formula (see, e.g., Silver et al. [116], pp.151). The modified nervousness measure is then given as

$$\nu_{SBU}^{mod} = \frac{\nu_{SBU}}{EOQ}. \tag{3.3}$$

This standardized measure is based on the assumption that the average order cycle, or time between orders (TBO), is equal to the ratio of the EOQ and average or expected demand ($\bar{D}$), respectively, i.e. $TBO = \frac{EOQ}{\bar{D}}$.

These measures are not free of shortcomings either (see also Jensen [68], pp.66). First, there is no distinction between pure changes in setup decisions and changes in quantities. However, setup nervousness can easily be measured by modifying (3.2) (see also equation (3.4) in Section 3.4.1). This measure nevertheless remains non-standardized.
Furthermore, in (3.3), the standardization by the EOQ is questionable because ν_{SBU}^{mod} is still not normalized between a minimum and maximum value of nervousness. Also, since the measure in (3.3) is standardized by the EOQ, the simplifying assumptions of the EOQ are implicitly used to evaluate plan revisions. For instance, in the case of capacity restrictions, the EOQ is not a good approximation of the real average lot size. Additionally, the value of the EOQ depends on the inventory carrying and setup costs, and, consequently, the same holds for ν_{SBU}^{mod}. A nervousness comparison of different scenarios may therefore be considerably distorted. Finally, in the numerator of (3.3), period-specific weights are used, whereas the denominator consists of a simple average lot size.

Because of the shortcomings of the nervousness measures mentioned above, Jensen defines some general requirements on an instability measure (see Jensen [68], pp.67):

- A distinction between pure changes in timing of replenishment decisions, i.e. setup-oriented instability, and plan revisions with respect to order quantities, i.e. quantity-oriented nervousness, is possible
- Differences between planned decisions of all overlapping periods of subsequent planning cycles are considered
- The nervousness measure is normalized between values of 0 and 1, i.e. maximum stability and maximum nervousness, respectively
- The measure is, as far as possible, independent of the chosen parameters of the planning framework
- A (decreasing) weighting of periods depending on the distance of the planning period to the planning horizon is possible
- The measure can easily be modified to consider some specific aspects of nervousness, for instance, measuring short-term instability

- Plan changes occur because new information is gained in successive planning cycles. Since the extent of schedule adjustments depends significantly on changes in the information, nervousness is defined relatively with respect to the stability of this information

The derivation of nervousness measures according to these requests will now be briefly summarized (for details see Jensen [68], pp.71). Since this examination deals with long-term, setup-oriented stability, the main focus is on presenting this measure. The analysis must be restricted to setup stability, because long-term quantity-oriented stability cannot be examined analytically. Furthermore, from a practical point of view, setup stability is more interesting than quantity stability (see also Section 3.1.2).

3.4.1 Setup-Oriented Stability

The measure of setup-oriented nervousness ν can be defined as (see, e.g., Heisig [49])

$$\nu_S = \frac{\sum_{j=1}^{N-1} \sum_{i=j}^{P+j-2} |\delta(q_{t+i}^{t+j-1}) - \delta(q_{t+i}^{t+j})|(1-a)a^{i-j}}{(N-1)\sum_{t=1}^{P-1}(1-a)a^{t-1}}. \tag{3.4}$$

Despite of the fact that this measure takes into account setup changes, it is rather similar to the measure proposed by Sridharan et al. (see equation (3.2), p.36). Nevertheless, contrary to (3.2), the measure in (3.4) is normalized between the value space $[0, 1]$. It is determined by relating the weighted number of periods with changed setups to the weighted total number of periods that can be compared. If ν_S is equal to zero, then maximum stability can be found. For $\nu_S = 1$ there is maximum nervousness, i.e. the planned setup decisions from one planning cycle to the subsequent one are different in each planning period.

Consequently, the measure of setup planning stability is given as

$$\pi_S = 1 - \nu_S. \tag{3.5}$$

According to the requirements mentioned above, this stability measure can be modified to consider specific aspects of plan revisions.
As limiting value of (3.4) with $a \to 1$ we obtain the special case that all periods are weighted equally (see, e.g., Jensen [67], and Inderfurth and Jensen [62])[39]

[39] In this study, symbol "$-$" indicates the case that all periods within the stability horizon are equal in weight.

$$\bar{\pi}_S = \lim_{a\to 1} \pi_S = 1 - \frac{1}{(N-1)(P-1)} \sum_{j=1}^{N-1} \sum_{i=j}^{P+j-2} |\delta(q_{t+i}^{t+j-1}) - \delta(q_{t+i}^{t+j})|. \quad (3.6)$$

The short-term planning stability which measures stability with respect only to the first period's replenishment decision, i.e. $P = 2$, is given if i in the second summation of expression (3.4) is fixed to j (see Inderfurth [61])[40], i.e.

$$\pi_{IS} = 1 - \frac{\sum_{j=1}^{N-1} |\delta(q_{t+j}^{t+j-1}) - \delta(q_{t+j}^{t+j})|}{(N-1)}. \quad (3.7)$$

The relevance of this measure results from the fact that the planned setup in the first period of a planning cycle is realized immediately in the next (actual) planning cycle. Thus, plan changes directly influence the shopfloor.

Furthermore, if one considers a stationary inventory policy (i.e. the control parameters will neither change from period to period nor from planning cycle to planning cycle) for an infinite number of planning cycles, then the stability in (3.5) can be interpreted as the probability that the setup decisions will not change from one planning cycle to the subsequent one[41]. Since setup decisions in each planning cycle depend on the stochastic initial inventory position and demand, π_S is a random variable[42]. The measure of setup stability is now given by

$$\pi_S = \mathbb{E}[1 - \nu_S]. \quad (3.8)$$

Finally, one gets[43] (for cycle t to cycle $t+1$)

$$\pi_S = \frac{1-a}{1-a^{P-1}} \Big[\mathbb{P}\{\delta(\hat{q}_{t+1}^t) = \delta(q_{t+1})\} + a\mathbb{P}\{\delta(\hat{q}_{t+2}^t) = \delta(\hat{q}_{t+2}^{t+1})\} + \ldots + a^{P-1}\mathbb{P}\{\delta(\hat{q}_{t+P-1}^t) = \delta(\hat{q}_{t+P-1}^{t+1})\}\Big]. \quad (3.9)$$

Notice that planned setups also depend on the (possible) changes in the projected demand, i.e. $\hat{D}_t^{t+i} \neq \hat{D}_{t+1}^{t+i}$ $(i = 1, ..., P-1)$. If demand is forecasted on the basis of past demand values, then the distributions of the demand forecasts $\hat{D}_{t+1}^{t+i}$ depend on the distributions of the demand in former periods. Therefore, the calculation of expected stability as indicated in (3.9) requires the determination of rather complicated conditional probabilities. Chapters

40 Note that $\lim_{a\to 0} \pi_S$ is equivalent to this short-term consideration.

41 In this steady-state situation it is sufficient to determine stability for two arbitrary successive planning cycles.

42 It is evident that the setups also depend on the underlying inventory control rule, but the inventory policy has no "stochastic" impact. Moreover, the demand forecasting process also influences setup decisions.

43 See, e.g., Heisig [49].

4 and 5 demonstrate that for specific inventory control rules, general demand distributions, and a relatively "simple" forecasting process the probability in (3.9) can be determined analytically.

Jensen also introduces two (unweighted) measures of setup stability which distinguish between the stability of setup and non-setup decisions.[44] (see Jensen [68], pp.74).

$$\bar{\pi}_S^+ = 1 - \frac{\sum_{j=1}^{N-1} \sum_{i=j}^{P+j-2} [\delta(q_{t+i}^{t+j-1}) - \delta(q_{t+i}^{t+j})]^+}{\sum_{j=1}^{N-1} \sum_{i=j}^{P+j-2} \delta(q_{t+i}^{t+j-1})}, \tag{3.10}$$

where $[x]^+$ defines an indicator function with $[x]^+ = x$, if $x > 0$, and $[x]^+ = 0$, else.

Here, $\bar{\pi}_S^+$ describes the average fraction of setups that are neither cancelled nor shifted to another period in the subsequent planning cycle. Consequently, $1 - \bar{\pi}_S^+$ represents the average fraction of periods in which a setup previously planned is cancelled.

Analogously, $\bar{\pi}_S^-$ represents the extent to which non-setups decisions are maintained from one planning cycle to the other. It is determined by

$$\bar{\pi}_S^- = 1 - \frac{\sum_{j=1}^{N-1} \sum_{i=j}^{P+j-2} [\delta(q_{t+i}^{t+j}) - \delta(q_{t+i}^{t+j-1})]^+}{\sum_{j=1}^{N-1} \sum_{i=j}^{P+j-2} (1 - \delta(q_{t+i}^{t+j-1}))}. \tag{3.11}$$

The latter is mainly disruptive to the execution of the planning process, because $1 - \bar{\pi}_S^-$ describes the average fraction of periods of a planning cycle in which new setups are planned. These replanning activities are rather critical, because, in general, they directly influence upstream stages and capacity planning.

Finally, Jensen also defines a measure to distinguish between plan revisions that occur due to additional new planned setups and plan changes which are generated by temporal shifts of setups (see Jensen [68], pp.76). Because of analytical tractability, this measure is not considered in this analysis, nor are the special cases in (3.10) and (3.11) dealt with.

---

[44] The weighting of periods can easily be integrated in these measures. But for ease of notation, the weights have been omitted. Moreover, short-term stability can also be included.

3.4.2 Quantity-Oriented Stability

Analogously to setup-oriented stability (see equations 3.4 and (3.5)) the quantity-oriented stability can be defined as

$$\pi_Q = 1 - \nu_Q \tag{3.12}$$

with

$$\nu_Q = \frac{\sum\limits_{j=1}^{N-1} \sum\limits_{i=j}^{P+j-2} |q_{t+i}^{t+j-1} - q_{t+i}^{t+j}| a^{i-j}}{\Delta q_{max}}. \tag{3.13}$$

Here, the calculation of the maximum quantity Δq_{max} that can be changed between two successive planning cycles is a more complicated task, since it depends on the characteristics of the demand distribution. In order to determine this value, some additional assumptions are necessary (see Jensen [67] [68], pp.78). It is assumed that an upper limit for the maximum reasonable demand per period can be given. This is denoted by D_{max}. Then, the maximum quantity changed per planning cycles is given when the maximum demand per cycle is aggregated to one lot size, and when it is scheduled in an other period in the subsequent cycle: $\Delta q_{max} = (2 \sum\limits_{t=1}^{P-1} a^{t-1} + 1) D_{max}$, i.e. $\Delta q_{max} = (2 \frac{a^{P-1}-1}{a-1} + 1) D_{max}$. The addition of one unit of maximum demand is related to the fact that a backorder in the first period of the second planning cycle may occur. Only backorders in this period have to be considered, because a new planning cycle is started after each period, and planned backorders are not allowed [45].

The measure in (3.13) can be interpreted as the weighted average percentage of quantity per cycle, which is not changed in a new planning period related to the weighted maximum possible amount of changes per planning cycle.

With the same arguments as for setup-oriented stability, the unweighted quantity stability can be measured as (see, e.g., Jensen [68], p.79)

$$\bar{\pi}_Q = 1 - \frac{1}{\Delta q_{max}} \sum_{j=1}^{N-1} \sum_{i=j}^{P+j-2} |q_{t+i}^{t+j-1} - q_{t+i}^{t+j}|, \tag{3.14}$$

where $\Delta q_{max} = 2\, P\, D_{max}$. Here, Jensen implicitly assumes that planned backorders are feasible, i.e. a backlog may occur in each period. According to the aforementioned assumption, where planned backorders are forbidden, Δq_{max} would be given by $(2\,(P-1)+1)\, D_{max}$, i.e. $\Delta q_{max} = (2P-1)\, D_{max}$.

[45] Notice that this measure leads to a slightly different value of q_{max} as Jensen's measure for the unweighted consideration in (3.14).

Moreover, short-term planning stability is given by

$$\pi_{IQ} = 1 - \frac{\sum_{j=1}^{N-1} |q_{t+j}^{t+j-1} - q_{t+j}^{t+j}|}{\Delta q_{max}}, \tag{3.15}$$

with $\Delta q_{max} = 3\ D_{max}$, or $\Delta q_{max} = 4\ D_{max}$, depending on the treatment of backorders.

In a steady-state situation, in the case of a sufficiently large planning horizon, the expected maximum demand per planning cycle can be approximated by the expected value of the demand per period ($\bar{D}$) multiplied by the length of the planning horizon, i.e. it holds in (3.14) that $\Delta q_{max} = 2\ P\ \bar{D}$. For the short-term consideration, Δq_{max} is given by $\hat{D} + \bar{D}$, where $\hat{D}$ represents the constant forecasted value of the demand per period (see also De Kok and Inderfurth [32]).
Analogously to setup stability in (3.10) and (3.11), quantity-oriented stability can also be divided into plan changes which occur because of a reduction of order quantities, and revisions that take place due to an increase of orders, respectively (see Jensen [68], pp.83).

Kimms [73] provides an alternative approach to measure quantity-oriented stability. Contrary to the previous analysis in Jensen [68], Kimms considers a multi-item situation on the MPS level and integrates a frozen zone in the rolling horizon schedule. He assumes that a P-period problem is solved N times, i.e. $N \geq 2$ represents the number of planning cycles. Then, nervousness for two subsequent planning cycles ι and $\iota - 1$ is compared. This leads to a production plan for the periods $(N-1)\Delta P + P$ where ΔP indicates the length of the frozen zone. In each run $\iota = 1, ..., N-1$, the plan for the periods $(\iota - 1)\Delta P + 1, ..., \iota\Delta P$ is implemented whereas the plan for $\iota\Delta P + 1, ..., (\iota - 1)\Delta P + P$ is only preliminary.
For this situation, Kimms defines an item-specific instability measure with respect to the production plan of item h $(h = 1, ..., H)$ as

$$\nu_{KI}^{h}(\iota) = \frac{|\ \ddot{q}_h^{\iota} - \dot{q}_h^{\iota-1}\ |}{max\{\ddot{q}_h^{\iota}, 1\}}, \tag{3.16}$$

where

ι = number of run, $\iota \geq 2$,

$\dot{q}_h^{\iota}$ = $\sum_{t=1}^{P-\Delta P} \Upsilon_{h,t}\ q_{h,t+\iota\Delta P}^{\iota}$ for $\iota = 1, ..., N-1$
(weighted production quantities for item h, temporarily scheduled),

$\ddot{q}_h^\iota \quad = \quad \sum_{t=1}^{P-\Delta P} \Upsilon_{h,t} \, q_{h,t+(\iota-1)\Delta P}^\iota \quad$ for $\iota = 2, ..., N$
(weighted production quantities for item h, after rescheduling in overlapping periods),

$q_{h,t} \quad = \quad$ production quantity for item h in period t $(h = 1, ..., H; \, t = 1, ..., P - \Delta P)$,

$\Upsilon_{h,t} \quad = \quad$ item-specific weights for item h in period t $(h = 1, ..., H; \, t = 1, ..., P - \Delta P)$.

Note that the item-specific weights are positive, and non-increasing over time. As an example, Kimms proposes the use of item-independent weights. For instance, $\Upsilon_{h,t} = \frac{1}{t}$ (for $h = 1, ..., H$ and $t = 1, ..., P - \Delta P$) means that there is no preference for keeping the schedule more stable for some items than for some others. If this is not valid, an item-specific definition should be chosen. Since the weights are non-increasing over time they have the same interpretation as the weight parameter a.
Thus the instability measure in (3.16) for an item h gives the relation of production plan changes of this item to the total quantity that is scheduled, taking into account what run ι can affect. Values of (3.16) close to zero describe a high stability. However, the measure in (3.16) is not normalized, because values larger than 1 may occur. Note that for $\Delta P = P$ there is no nervousness at all.
Now, Kimms considers several alternatives to measure the instability of the overall plan. Then, the aggregated nervousness measure under consideration is given by

$$\nu_{KI}(\iota) \in \{\nu_{KI}^{max}(\iota), \nu_{KI}^{mean}(\iota)\}$$

where

$$\nu_{KI}^{max}(\iota) = max\{\nu_{KI}^h(\iota) | h = 1, ..., H\} \tag{3.17}$$

represents maximum instability, and

$$\nu_{KI}^{mean}(\iota) = \frac{1}{H} \sum_{h=1}^{H} \nu_{KI}^h(\iota) \tag{3.18}$$

describes mean instability.

For the special case $\Delta P = 1$ and two subsequent planning cycles 1 and 2, in (3.16) one sees that

$$\nu_{KI;\Delta P=1}^h(2) = \frac{| \ddot{q}_h^2 - \dot{q}_h^1 |}{max\{\ddot{q}_h^2, 1\}}, \tag{3.19}$$

where $\dot{q}_h^1 = \sum_{t=1}^{P-1} \Upsilon_{h,t} \, q_{h,t+1}^1$, and $\ddot{q}_h^2 = \sum_{t=1}^{P-1} \Upsilon_{h,t} \, q_{h,t+1}^2$.

Thus, Kimms' instability measure for a specific item h is very similar to the quantity-oriented nervousness measure introduced by Jensen (see (3.13)). From (3.13) with $t = 1$, i.e. planning cycle 1 and 2, one gets

$$\nu_q = \frac{\sum_{i=1}^{P-1} |q_{i+1}^1 - q_{i+1}^2|(1-a)a^{i-1}}{\Delta q_{max}},$$

whereas from (3.19) we obtain

$$\nu_{KI;\Delta P=1}(2) = \frac{\sum_{t=1}^{P-1} |q_{t+1}^1 - q_{t+1}^2| \Upsilon_t}{max\{\sum_{t=1}^{P-1} \Upsilon_t \, q_{t+1}^2, 1\}}.$$

By choosing adequate weights, i.e. $\Upsilon_t = (1-a)a^{t-1}$, both measures almost coincide. They only differ in the standardization in the denominator. As previously mentioned, Kimms' measure can take on values larger than 1.

3.4.3 Extensions

The measures introduced by Jensen can be modified to include throughput times, or to calculate stability in multi-stage systems, (see Jensen [68], pp.84).

3.4.3.1 Throughput Times

If throughput times are taken into account, then, in the case of the application of a reorder point policy, the value of s must be adjusted appropriately. The size of the reorder point is then determined by the sum of the expected demand during lead time (plus review period) plus a safety stock depending on the predefined service level. In MRP logic, taking into account a throughput time Λ means that the requirements in a period t must be ordered at the latest $t - \Lambda$ (or $t - \Lambda - 1$, respectively) periods before (see also Figure 3.1). Therefore each planning cycle t should only consider the requirements of periods $t+\Lambda$ to $t+P-1$, because the requirements of periods t to $t+\Lambda-1$ cannot be fulfilled by planning activities which are effective after the processing time Λ[46]. Consequently, considering planning stability, the planning horizon P must be reduced by the throughput time. This means, for instance, that in the case of setup stability with equally weighted periods the term $P-1$ in the denominator of (3.6) must be substituted by $P - 1 - \Lambda$. The other

[46] In the case of allowing for backorders, this argumentation is only true if there is no need for a subsequent delivery of unsatisfied demand in periods earlier than t.

stability measures must be modified accordingly.
Jensen also discusses the inclusion of stochastic throughput times in the stability measures mentioned above (see Jensen [68], pp.85). Then, the common distribution of the stochastic demand and the stochastic lead time must be known to determine, for instance, the upper limit D_{max}. Moreover, an analytical examination of setup stability does not seem possible, because rather complicated convolutions of the expected stability occur (see Section 4)[47].
Although this study deals with setup stability in single-stage production systems, it will briefly describe how stability can be measured in multi-stage systems to give a complete overview of measuring planning stability in material planning systems.

3.4.3.2 Stability Measures in Multi-Stage Systems

Again, it is important to distinguish between setup-oriented and quantity-oriented stability. The measure of setup planning stability can be used in the same manner as introduced in Section 3.4.1 for a single-stage system. One only has to take into account the throughput times on the different levels in the product structure. Then, the (level-dependent) setup stability measure has to be modified according to the procedure mentioned in Section 3.4.3.

Jensen suggests aggregating the setup stability measures ($\pi_{S,k}$) of each level k for all stages $k \in K$ to a setup-oriented stability of the entire production system[48] (see Jensen [68], p.95):

$$\pi_S^K = \frac{1}{|K|} \sum_{k \in K} \pi_{S,k}, \tag{3.20}$$

where $|K|$ represents the cardinal number of the set of production stages.
Here $\pi_{S,k}$ describes the expected number of setup changes which, on average, occur at each level in the product structure. This measure is also normalized in the value space $[0, 1]$.
Moreover, considering the ratio between the setup stability π_S^A of a specific part A of the product structure with $A \subset S$, and the aggregated stability measures π_S^K, values of $\frac{\pi_S^A}{\pi_S^K} > 1$ indicate that this part A, on average, possesses a higher setup stability than the complete production system. In particular, the corresponding analysis of the final stages $f \in F$ of a multi-stage system are useful[49], i.e. considering $\frac{\pi_S^F}{\pi_S^K}$. Then, the effects of plan changes on the

47 Notice that Jensen also shows how time-variant demand can be taken into account. However, with the same arguments as for stochastic lead times, an integration of time-variant demand prevents an analytical calculation of setup as well as quantity-oriented planning stability.

48 K represents the index set of all stages in the product structure. The stages of this multi-stage system are represented by a stage index $k \in K$.

49 F represents the index set of final stages.

end-item level on upstream stages can be observed (see Jensen [68], p.96).

For quantity-oriented stability, a specific problem is the calculation of maximum demand of a period on upstream stages (see Jensen [68], pp.92). The demand on upstream stages depends on the forecasted demand of final products and the matching production coefficients. Moreover, in general, because of the application of specific lot-sizing or inventory control rules, the information about end-item demand is lost on upstream stages[50]. Consequently, there are two possibilities to determine the maximum demand of a period on upstream stages. It can either be based on end-item demand or on the available information about lot-sizing policies on the direct successors in the product structure. Jensen prefers the first approach, because the measure of quantity stability for each level in the product structure should be defined independently on the decisions of downstream stages. Moreover, this dependence can be analyzed by other measures (see Jensen [68], p.94). Thus, the maximum demand of a preceding stage $i \in U$ is given by[51]

$$D_{i,max} = \sum_{f \in N(i) \cap F} p_{i,f}^F D_{f,max} \tag{3.21}$$

where $N(i)$ describes all (direct or indirect) successors of stage i, and the production coefficient $p_{i,f}^F$ referring to the end-item level represents the requirements for stage i which are necessary to produce one unit of the end product at the final stage f (see Jensen [68], p.93). Then, according to the definition in (3.14) for a single-stage system, the maximal quantity changed per planning cycle at an upstream stage i is given by $\Delta q_{i,max} = 2\,P\,D_{i,max}$. Using these values, quantity-oriented stability of each level in the product structure can be determined, and, analogously to (3.20) for setup stability, an aggregated quantity-oriented stability measure can be defined.

Finally, an alternative approach for measuring quantity-oriented stability is discussed[52]. Kadipasaoglu and Sridharan [71] have modified the measure ν_{SBU} (see (3.2)) by incorporating a weight parameter b to assign decreasing weights to the changes in subsequent levels of the product structure.

$$\nu_{KS} = \sum_{j=1}^{N-1} \sum_{k=0}^{m} \left[\sum_{h=1}^{n_k} \sum_{i=j}^{P+j-2} |q_{h,k,t+i}^{t+j-1} - q_{h,k,t+i}^{t+j}|(1-a)a^{i-j} \right] (1-b)b^k, \tag{3.22}$$

where

k = item level, $k = 0, ..., m$ (based on low level coding),

[50] See also Section 2.1. Only in the case of a base stock control system global information about customer demand is used at each stocking point.

[51] U denotes the index set of preceding stages.

[52] Notice that this measure can easily be modified to determine setup stability.

h = item h at level k, $h = 1, ..., n_k$,
$q^i_{h,k,t}$ = replenishment order size for item h at level k in period t as planned in cycle i,
b = weight parameter for levels $(0 < b < 1)$,

using N, and a as introduced in Section 3.4, p.36. As a, the parameter b can take on values in $(0, 1)$ where large values of b assign slowly decreasing weights. Contrary to ν_{SBU}, the nervousness measure is not divided by the total number of orders over all planning periods (M).
Kadipasaoglu and Sridharan [71] argue that this measure is superior to the metric of Blackburn et al [14] (refer to p.35) and the (multiple) use of ν_{SBU} in (3.2) for measuring stability in a multi-stage system. According to Kadipasaoglu and Sridharan, the main advantages of their measure is that (1) changes in open orders are explicitly included, (2) different weights to items at different stages in the product structure can be assigned, and (3) (3.22) is not biased by TBO and the corresponding item cost structure (see equation (3.3), p.37). However, the major deficiency of this measure is that it is still not standardized between a minimum and maximum value of nervousness. Different scenarios can therefore not be compared (see also the discussion above for non-standardized measures in single-level production systems).

3.5 Strategies for Reducing Nervousness

In an early work, Steele [124] gives the following instructions for stabilizing an MRP system. First, minimize causes for nervousness, i.e. reduce master schedule changes and unplanned demand, follow the plan with respect to allocations, order quantities and timing, and control parameter changes. Second, use pegging. Pegging, in general, means that the gross requirements on an upstream level resulting from the explosion of the production schedule of its successor are "pegged" with an identification of the item generating them. Thus, if a shortage of this item occurs, it is evident which (sub-)assemblies, finished products, and customer orders are influenced (see, e.g., Silver et al [116], p.611). Third, stabilize lot-sizing[53], and finally, use firm planned order.

Table 3.1 provides a more detailed overview of procedures for reducing nervousness as identified in literature (see, e.g., Ho et al. [59], p.33). As in Table 3.1 indicates, system nervousness is dealt with in different ways. Here, the strategies will be briefly described. A detailed literature review is provided in Section 3.6, because most of the examinations do not only consider one

[53] To stabilize lot-sizing Steele suggests the use of fixed order quantity on the top level, fixed order quantity or lot-for-lot ordering on intermediate levels, and period order quantity on the bottom level. However, a systematic development of these proposals is not given.

aspect.
A first method for coping with nervousness is to choose "stable" lot-sizing rules. To include the "cost of nervousness" in lot-sizing rules, Carlson et al. [22] introduce the change cost procedure (see also Section 3.6). The setup costs for a period are modified by considering some additional costs that depend on the previous schedule. These new costs are called change costs. For periods in which no setup was previously planned, the "effective" setup cost is the sum of the old setup cost plus the change cost, while for those periods for which setups were scheduled, the "effective" setup cost equals the old setup cost. These "effective" setup costs are then used to solve the new lot-sizing problem. As a result, the schedule only changes when the joint consideration of setup, inventory carrying, and changing costs indicates that it is economically useful to do so. To stabilize lot-sizing, Blackburn et al [13], [14], and [15] suggest using the lot-for-lot policy on upstream stages ("lot-for-lot policy after the final product stage"), i.e orders are placed in the same period at all stages. Thus, only the size of the order at each level may be altered, and there are no new, previously unplanned orders.

Table 3.1. Overview of methods for reducing nervousness

orientation	methods
lot-sizing	"stable" lot-sizing rules
inventory-oriented buffering	safety stock safety lead time safety capacity overplanning
eliminating causes of nervousness	rolling horizon schedule parameters (e.g. freeze MPS) forecasting beyond planning horizon control engineering changes eliminate transaction errors minimize supply uncertainty
local-oriented	demand management time fencing lead-time compression pegged requirements firm planned orders
dampening procedures	static dampening procedure automatic rescheduling procedure cost-based dampening procedure

A second approach deals with system nervousness applying different buffering techniques (refer to Section 2.3.2 for a description of these buffering methods). For instance, safety stocks at the end-item level are carried to reduce nervousness. A sufficiently large safety stock will eliminate order changes at lower production stages, but inventory holding costs are likely to increase. Mather [86] suggests overplanning the MPS to offset the system's nervousness resulting from changes in the MPS. The major deficiency of this concept is that it is not clear to which extent the end-item orders have to be increased to reduce nervousness, and how the inventory carrying costs are raised.

A third stream tries to eliminate the reasons for system nervousness. As mentioned at the beginning of this chapter, there are several causes for instability, e.g. MPS changes, lot size and safety stock changes, supply/demand uncertainty and engineering changes [54]. Some of these reasons (such as engineering changes, or record errors) can be controlled to a certain degree[55]. For instance, by freezing the MPS schedule within the planning horizon there are no plan revisions (see, e.g., Blackburn et al. [13], [14], [15]). Then, all decisions within the entire planning horizon are implemented. In Figure 3.1 this means that the order releases for periods t through $t + P - 1$ are implemented, and then orders for periods $t + P$ to $t + 2P - 1$ are generated and implemented, and so on. However, freezing the complete MPS schedule is not a realistic approach for coping with uncertainty. Therefore, a variation on this strategy is to freeze only some of the periods within the planning horizon (see Section 2.3.1). Another method for reducing plan revisions is to forecast demand beyond the planning horizon (see, e.g., Blackburn et al. [13], [14], [15]). This is done to protect against an order being placed near the end of the planning horizon, because this order will be most likely changed in the subsequent planning cycle.

Additionally, dampening rules[56] may be implemented in MRP software packages as constraints on certain variables (see, e.g., Minifie and Davis [90]). They are used to limit the number of exception reports (or, in other words, rescheduling messages) generated (see, e.g., Orlicky [98], and Steele [124]). One may differentiate between local and global dampening procedures (see, e.g., Ho et al. [58]). The global methods can be applied to any type of rescheduling problem, whereas the local dampening procedures are developed to deal with a specific kind of rescheduling problem.
Local dampening procedures can be classified by the level in the product structure (upper or lower level) and the nature (timing or quantity) of the

[54] For details see p.21.

[55] Notice that in the long run also supply uncertainty can be minimized by choosing reliable suppliers, but in the short run it is uncontrollable.

[56] A dampening procedure is a filtering process to screen out "insignificant" rescheduling activities generated by the MRP system. Insignificant are those messages which are expected to have only a slight negative influence on the ability of the system to meet the desired due date (see, e.g., Ho [53]).

rescheduling problem. A first method is demand (or MPS) management. The aim is to maintain a stable MPS when only slight changes (in terms of timing, quantity, or both) in customer orders occur. Therefore, a realistic and attainable MPS is necessary (see, e.g., Ho et al. [58]). Another kind of constraint is a time fence which can be selected so that only certain types of changes taking place in a specific time interval, i.e. "emergency" types of exceptions, are reported. It is possible to distinguish between planning time fences and demand time fences (see, e.g., Ho et al. [59]). Planning time fences give the number of periods from the beginning of the planning horizon in which the MPS cannot be changed by the MRP system. These fences suppress messages in the short term (for example a two week period) as well as in the long term (beyond e.g. ten weeks)[57]. This means that the vendor cannot change a delivery that is less than two weeks away, and that he is not interested in a change of a long term delivery date (see also Mather [86]). A demand time fence defines "the plan's final commitment to the schedule within which almost no rescheduling will be accepted without meeting stringent rules", e.g., engineering changes must be carefully considered within demand time fences. Lead time compression is suggested for coping with timing uncertainty (see, e.g., Mather [86]). It is defined as the systematic reduction of normal planned lead time to a shorter desired lead time in response to an unplanned event. Contrary to "traditional expediting", which is a kind of informal rescheduling initiated by the subjective judgement of shopfloor foremen, it can be seen as "formal expediting" initiated by rescheduling messages generated by the MRP system itself. Finally, pegged requirements have been suggested as a means of dealing with rescheduling problems at the component level by splitting the lot size of the parent item (see, e.g., Steele [124], Orlicky [98], and Mather [86]). This technique is usually applied to deal with quantity uncertainty, in particular when lot-sizing leads to coverage problems (a detailed description of the pegged-requirement technique can be found, e.g., in Ho et al. [59]). Moreover, the firm planned order technique can be combined with the procedures mentioned above. Steele [124] and Mather [86] propose the use of pegged requirements/firm planned orders to solve rescheduling problems at the component level. Time fencing/firm planned order as well as lead time compression/firm planned order can also be combined (refer to Ho et al. [58] for a detailed explanation of these combinations).

From an information-oriented point of view, global dampening methods can be divided into static, automatic, and cost-based dampening procedures[58]. In a static dampening procedure, the parameters will rarely be changed in time (see, e.g., Mather [86]). Using an automatic dampening procedure means that all released open orders are automatically rescheduled when the MRP system recommends doing so (see, e.g., Steele [124]), only the rescheduling within a

[57] Notice that planning time fences can also be interpreted as frozen zones.

[58] Notice that from an inventory-oriented point of view, applying global dampening methods means the use of "slack", e.g., safety stock, or safety lead time.

"minimum lead time" is not allowed[59]. Cost-based procedures take into account cost trade-offs of rescheduling[60]. An additional information system is therefore necessary to calculate the costs of rescheduling and not rescheduling for each exception report. A rescheduling message will then be suppressed, if the cost of rescheduling is greater than the cost of maintaining the previous schedule (see, e.g., Ho [53]).

To sum up, many strategies have been developed to cope with nervousness in MRP systems. The next section presents a literature review on the performance of these methods to establish "stable" material requirements planning systems.

3.6 Influence of Operating Environment on Planning Stability

3.6.1 Rolling Horizon Schedule Parameters

3.6.1.1 Length of Planning Horizon

The first important decision is the determination of the length of the planning horizon for each planning cycle in a rolling horizon planning framework. The length of the planning horizon may influence the quality of the resulting plan for a certain decision problem. Furthermore, solution procedures with finite planning horizon which are embedded in a rolling horizon planning framework are used frequently for decision making in an uncertain environment and an infinite planning horizon. However, applying a rolling horizon schedule and solving a decision problem with the optimal procedure for a finite planning horizon does not have to lead to the optimal solution for the infinite horizon. This even applies in a deterministic environment, e.g., for the Wagner-Whitin algorithm to solve deterministic, dynamic lot-sizing problems.
Within the environment of dynamic lot-sizing[61] a great deal of work has been done to investigate when an extension of the planning horizon does not affect the plan in previous periods. Then, in some cases, a so-called decision horizon[62] can be calculated (see, e.g., Bean et al. [9], Blackburn and Kunreuther

[59] The minimum lead time is defined as the necessary lead time for the completion of an order under highest priority (see, e.g., Orlicky [98]).

[60] Notice that this procedure is derived from the concept of "cost of nervousness" introduced by Carlson et al. [22].

[61] See also Section 3.6.2.

[62] This means that the optimal solution of the subproblem consisting of the initial period up to the decision horizon is a part of the overall optimum solution, i.e. it will remain the same, even if the input data in periods which exceed the matching planning horizon are changed.

[16], and Federgruen and Tzur [34], [35]). Thus, the schedule is stable for all periods within this decision horizon. However, these results, in general, can only be applied for deterministic lot-sizing problems. Moreover, the input data within the corresponding planning horizon cannot be changed.
In an early study, Baker [5] has shown that rolling schedules for production planning are very efficient for coping with uncertainty. Baker compares the optimal solution for dynamic lot-sizing problems with 48 periods to the solutions found by applying the Wagner-Whitin algorithm in a rolling horizon schedule with varying length of the planning horizon. The average cost deviation from the optimum has been within 10 %. One important result is that in many cases "less information is better than more". That means that the longest possible planning horizon is not always the best. Baker suggests setting the length of the forecast window equal to the length of the "natural cycle", i.e. the TBO in an EOQ model (see also Section 3.4, p.37). Nevertheless, Baker's studies underline that the planning horizon should not be smaller than the natural cycle. In general, costs are minimized when the forecast window is an integral multiple of the TBO of an end-item. Lundin and Morton [83] have found that planning horizons with a length of at least 5 TBO lead to cost deviations less than 1 %. Furthermore, Zhao and Lee [151] have found that, under deterministic demand, a planning horizon of eight TBO leads to a better stability and cost performance than a horizon of four TBO. The general result that the planning horizon should be chosen as an integral multiple of the TBO has also been confirmed by the examinations of Carlson et al. [21], and Baker and Peterson [6].

Chung and Krajewski [26] have analyzed the interaction between MPS and aggregate production planning within a deterministic hierarchical planning system. They define a linear programming model to minimize the deviations between MPS and foregoing aggregate production planning. It turns out that the length of the planning horizons for both problems do not necessarily have to coincide.
Furthermore, in Lin and Krajewski [82], the cost performance of a rolling horizon schedule with respect to the choice of the forecast window (as well as the choice of the freeze length) is examined analytically. Costs consist of forecast error costs, MPS change costs, setup and inventory carrying costs. Lin and Krajewski's model can be used to estimate the expected costs depending on the forecast error, the length of the planning horizon, and freeze interval, respectively.

In Jensen [68], the influence of the planning horizon length on the quantity and setup-oriented stability[63] of reorder point policies in a single-stage production system is analyzed (see Jensen [68], pp.192). He finds that for an (s, S) as well as an (s, nQ) control rule for lot sizes which are larger than the expected demand per period with increasing planning horizon, both stabil-

[63] As stability measures (3.14) and (3.6), respectively, are used.

ity measures generally decrease. The same applies to the weighting of periods, i.e. with increasing weight parameter[64], stability decreases for $Q-$values which are larger than $\hat{D}$. In particular, for small planning horizons, an increase in the planning horizon leads to a comparably high reduction in stability, but for large horizons the decrease of stability is hardly remarkable. For both policies with rising horizon, stability converges from above to a lower bound.

3.6.1.2 Freeze Interval Length

The influence of different lengths of freeze interval on the costs of production and inventory carrying is analyzed in a simulation study by Sridharan et al. [119][65]. As a result it appears that freezing up to 50 % of the horizon slightly influences production and inventory costs. Furthermore, an order-based freezing method is better than a period-based procedure[66]. Using the stability measure as indicated in equation (3.2)[67], Sridharan et al [120] find that freezing a small proportion of the MPS (up to 50 % of the planning horizon) has only a relatively small influence on stability. If the frozen portion exceeds 50 percent, then the impact on stability can be significant. Thus, combining both findings, they conclude that the proportion of the horizon that is frozen should be larger than 50 % to increase stability substantially, but this is achieved at the expense of higher costs. Moreover, a comparison of the cost as well as stability performance[68] of different MPS freezing methods can be found in a subsequent simulation study by Sridharan and Berry [121]. The replanning frequency, i.e. the rolling interval length, and the MPS freeze interval length have a greater impact on MPS instability and costs than the length of the planning horizon or the type of the freezing method (i.e. an order or period-based freezing method).

Zhao and Lee [150], [151] examine the influence of the aforementioned MPS freezing parameters on total cost, schedule instability and service levels in

---

64 Notice that Jensen uses a slightly different weighting scheme as presented in Section 3.4.1 and Section 3.4.2 (see Jensen [68], pp.195).

65 Notice that they also examine the impact of the freezing method and the planning horizon length on cost.

66 Period-based freezing means that some periods of the MPS are frozen. An order-based freezing approach means that some future orders cannot be changed. Both "frozen periods" and "frozen orders" can be varied to balance between schedule stability and production and inventory costs.

67 See Section 3.4, p.36. Because of the incorporation of a freeze interval, the measure has to be modified slightly (for details, see Sridharan et al. [120], p.150). Moreover, all periods are weighted equally.

68 Here again the metric in (3.2) with equally weighted periods is used.

multi-level MRP systems under deterministic and uncertain demand[69]. These studies extend the investigations of Sridharan et al. [119] [120] for multi-level MRP systems[70]. Increasing the planning horizon improves the MRP performance under deterministic demand, whereas under uncertain demand the MRP performance worsens. In the case of deterministic demand, nervousness and costs decrease for a higher freezing proportion [71], and service levels are not influenced. Consequently, the best performance is achieved by freezing the entire planning horizon. For uncertain demand, total costs often increase while service level and instability are reduced[72]. Regarding the freezing method in terms of costs, order based freezing is favorable in most cases. Concerning customer service with a freezing proportion of 100% the period-based approach is worst. Concerning stability, with a freezing proportion of 100% the period-based approach is best. Freezing only a proportion of 25 % high service levels are achieved by using the period-based method. Moreover, under both demand conditions, the higher the replanning frequency is, the lower total costs as well as nervousness and the higher service level will be. Therefore, less frequent replanning result in better system performance.

Jensen [68] has examined the impact of the length of the freeze interval on the stability of (s, S) and (s, nQ) policies in a single-stage system (Jensen [68], pp.212). He has found that by rising the length of the frozen zone, setup and quantity-oriented stability increase. However, with respect to service levels and costs, the performance of freezing a part of the planning horizon is worse than when lot-sizing policies are stabilized by introducing a modified reorder

[69] Zhao and Lee [150] have also investigated the impact of forecasting errors on the selection of MPS freezing parameters and system performance. The major outcomes are that forecasting errors reduce service level and schedule stability, and increase costs.

[70] As a measure for instability they use the metric of Sridharan et al. [120] (see equation (3.2), p.36). They apply this measure sequentially to calculate stability in a multi-stage system.

[71] Note that this finding contradicts the outcome by Sridharan et al. [119] [120] in single-level systems. Sridharan et al. [119] [120] have shown that in single-level systems, increasing the freezing proportion leads to lower nervousness but higher costs. Therefore, Zhao and Lee [151] conclude that freezing the MPS is more beneficial in multi-level systems than in single-level systems.

[72] Notice that these findings coincide with the results of Kadipasaoglu [69] who has examined the impact of the freeze length in multi-level MRP systems on costs and service level. Under uncertain demand, total costs decrease substantially as the freeze length is increased to cover the cumulative lead time, a further increase beyond the cumulative lead time leads only to a small cost reduction. Furthermore, increasing the freeze length decreases the customer service level. Thus, lower costs are achieved at the expense of poorer customer service. With known demand, total costs only change insignificantly if the freeze length is increased to cover the cumulative lead time. A further increase leads to significantly higher costs.

point[73] (for a description of these modified reorder point policies see Section 4.5, pp. 125).

Venkataraman [134] addresses the problem of replanning frequency for a rolling MPS in a process industry environment. He demonstrates how an appropriate replanning frequency can be determined under several constraints, such as minimum batch-size restrictions, multiple products and production lines, capacity constraints, or minimum inventory requirements. Venkataraman defines a weighted integer goal programming model for the MPS to analyze the replanning frequency. In a case study, actual data from a paint company is used to illustrate the solution procedure. It indicates that the replanning interval should be set equal to the length of the planning horizon to achieve significant cost savings. This means that changes within the planning horizon are avoided.

3.6.2 Lot-sizing

3.6.2.1 Schedule-Change-Cost based Approaches

In two early papers, Carlson et al. [22] as well as Kropp and Carlson [76] consider the shifting of scheduled setups. They deal with nervousness stemming from lot-sizing rules. As previously mentioned, nervousness is defined as a change in the first period's setup decision, or a shift in the period with the first planned setup. Carlson et al. [22] introduce a schedule change cost function where they use the "effective" setup costs as introduced in Section 3.5. Furthermore, Kropp and Carlson [76] differentiate between costs for adding a new setup, i.e. a change from no setup to a setup in the schedule for a certain planning period, and costs for cancelling a setup. In both approaches, the Wagner Whitin algorithm (see Wagner and Whitin [136]) is used, together with the assumption that a schedule already exists[74]. The cost of schedule changes are then included with setup costs and inventory holding costs in evaluating and comparing schedules. The production schedule will only be changed if the sum of these costs indicates that a change is economically beneficial[75]. Their approach strikes a balance between the cost of nervousness and the savings that schedule changes can effect.

---

[73] See also Jensen [67].

[74] Wagner and Whitin do not assume that a schedule exists at the beginning of a planning period, and therefore they do not need any costs of rescheduling

[75] Notice that although Carlson et al, as well as Kropp and Carlson use the Wagner Whitin algorithm to solve the problem, their procedure is not optimal in the dynamic rolling schedule environment.

3.6.2.2 Comparison of Lot-Sizing Procedures

In simulation experiments, Wemmerlöv and Whybark [139] and Wemmerlöv [140] have analyzed the cost performance of different single-stage lot-sizing procedures. They have found that the ranking of lot-sizing rules operating under demand uncertainty differs significantly from that with certain demand. However, in the case of uncertain demand, the cost differences occurring in a deterministic environment between different lot-sizing rules decrease with rising demand uncertainty. For instance, Wemmerlöv and Whybark [139] found that in the case of uncertain demand, for some situations the application of an EOQ rule shows almost the same performance as the use of the Wagner-Whitin algorithm.

Blackburn and Millen [10], [11] analyze the influence of a rolling schedule implementation on the performance of the part-period-balancing, Silver-Meal[76], and Wagner-Whitin algorithm. Note that the decisions generated by the Wagner-Whitin algorithm are relatively sensitive to the length of the selected planning horizon. The extension of the horizon by one period may lead to a change of some (or perhaps all) decisions (see, e.g., Blackburn and Millen [10]). Heuristic approaches, such as part-period balancing, do not have the same degree of nervousness since they do not take into account all future information for planning the actual order decision. Thus, in a rolling schedule environment, the myopic procedure of the heuristics may reduce the amount of schedule instability in comparison to the Wagner-Whitin algorithm. Furthermore, it turns out that - under certain circumstances - the Silver-Meal heuristic provides the best cost performance[77], it is even superior to the Wagner-Whitin procedure. Thus, schedule stability does not necessarily have to be achieved at the expense of poorer cost performance.

In Kropp et al. [75] the effectiveness of modified Silver-Meal and part-period balancing procedures[78] in comparison with the modified Wagner-Whitin algorithm is tested. They have found that the modified Silver-Meal approach leads to only slightly more costs than the modified Wagner-Whitin algorithm[79],

[76] They have also dealt with cost-modified versions of the heuristics, e.g. McLaren's setup cost adjustment, to improve the performance of the procedures in a multi-stage environment (see, e.g., Blackburn and Millen [12]). For an overview on lot-sizing heuristics see, e.g., Nahmias [95], pp.345.

[77] The costs are determined by the sum of inventory and setup costs over the planning horizon.

[78] The modifications are included to reduce MRP system nervousness. Then, nervousness is described by the costs of schedule changes (see also Section 3.6.2). This paper considers only changes to a period where no setup was planned, but where a change has been made resulting in a setup.

[79] Although the Wagner-Whitin algorithm has not been designed for a rolling schedule framework, its modified version with the change-cost adjustment performs best.

whereas the modified part-period-balancing method performs poorly. In a later simulation study, Sridharan and Berry [121][80] found that the (non-modified) Silver-Meal heuristic leads to a more stable MPS in comparison with the (non-modified) Wagner-Whitin algorithm, but this is connected with higher costs.

Zhao and Lee [150], [151][81] have found that, in terms of total costs, schedule stability and service levels, the cost-modified Silver-Meal heuristic (see, e.g., Blackburn and Millen [11]) performs better than the non-modified rule, and it also outperforms the cost-modified part-period balancing rule in most conditions. In subsequent simulation studies, Zhao et al. [148], and Zhao and Lam [149][82] analyze the influence of 14 different lot-sizing rules and freezing parameters in a multi-level production system under probabilistic and deterministic demand, respectively. Among these 14 rules for both deterministic as well as uncertain demand, under most conditions the cost-modified Silver Meal/lot-for-lot[83], the cost-modified Silver-Meal[84], the Silver-Meal/lot-for-lot, and the cost-modified part-period balancing/lot-for-lot show the best performance with respect to total costs and schedule stability. In the case of uncertain demand, the period order quantity/lot-for-lot rule also performs very well, whereas the non-modified Silver-Meal rule is also rather good for deterministic demand. Finally, they found that the interaction effects between the lot-sizing rule and MPS freezing parameters are fairly significant. Therefore, the MPS freezing parameters should be chosen under (additional) consideration of the operating parameters of the MRP system.

3.6.2.3 Analysis of Stochastic Inventory Control Rules

In simulation studies Jensen [67], [68] analyzes the long-term stability performance with respect to pure setup as well as quantity changes of reorder point policies, i.e. (s, nQ) and (s, S) inventory control rules [85]. The major finding is that there is no general superiority with respect to long-term setup

[80] As mentioned in Section 3.6.1, the underlying nervousness measure is given by the equation (3.2).

[81] See also Section 3.6.1.

[82] In both studies, stability is again calculated according the measure of Sridharan et al. [120] as indicated in equation (3.2), p.36.

[83] This notation, in general, means that the former is used for the end-item level, and the latter for the dependent components.

[84] This means that the same lot-sizing rule is used for both independent and dependent items.

[85] Chapter provides 4 an analytical examination of long-term setup stability of (s, nQ) and (s, S) inventory control rules in single-stage production systems. Therefore only a brief description of Jensen's results concerning this aspect is covered here. Additional explanations for the specific development of stability are given in Chapter 4.

as well as quantity stability of one control rule in comparison to another. In single-stage production systems, the reorder point s has no impact on stability, whereas the lot size Q, and $S - s$, respectively, have a considerable impact. The influence of the lot sizes for both policies is, on the one hand, quite similar because, as a general tendency, high (setup as well as quantity) stability is achieved for either relatively small values of Q or $S - s$, respectively, or for sufficiently large values. On the other hand, for the (s, S) policy, there are cyclic patterns in the development of π_S and π_Q depending on the minimum lot size $S - s$. For values of $S - s$, which are multiples of the projected demand per period, stability decreases significantly. Moreover, the stability performance of an (s, S) policy with (approximately) optimal parameters s^* and S^* depending on setup and inventory carrying costs is analyzed[86]. The outcome is that the development of both stability measures is almost the same as for non-optimal parameter values, in particular the oscillating patterns remain[87].
For both policies, the development of quantity stability is quite different from the development of setup stability. In the case of large lot sizes, setup stability converges to 100 %, whereas quantity stability only converges to an upper bound which is considerably lower than 1. Jensen analyzes the influence of different forecasting methods[88] and the impact of demand variability on stability, too. As demand uncertainty increases, stability decreases.
Jensen has also introduced a stabilization parameter to improve stability performance of reorder point policies (see Jensen [67]). A detailed description of this procedure can be found in Section 4.5, pp.125.
As multi-level systems, Jensen [68] has considered two-stage serial as well as divergent systems. The result is that the stability performance of the entire system is mainly affected by the control rule applied at the end-item level (see Jensen [68], pp.219).

Both Inderfurth [61], De Kok and Inderfurth [32] and Heisig [49] present analytical examinations of the stability performance of reorder point policies. In Chapter 4 the analysis in Heisig [49] is presented in detail, including some enhancements and more detailed explanations. Inderfurth [61] analyzes the short-term setup stability of (s, S) and (s, nQ) policies for exponentially and uniformly distributed demand. De Kok and Inderfurth [32] examine short-term setup as well as quantity-oriented stability of (R, S), (s, S) and (s, nQ) policies for more general demand distributions. Since the results in Inderfurth [61] and De Kok and Inderfurth [32] with respect to setup stability of reorder point policies are special cases of the analysis in Chapter 4, they are

[86] To calculate these values, Jensen has used an approximation method developed by Schneider and Ringuest [114].
[87] For ratios of setup and inventory costs which lead to an optimal minimum lot size Q^* that represents a multiple of the expected demand per period, stability diminishes considerably.
[88] See Jensen [68], pp.186, and Section 4.5.

mentioned there. Concerning the results with respect to short-term quantity-oriented stability, De Kok and Inderfurth [32] found that this kind of stability is independent of the lot size Q for an (s, nQ) policy. Moreover, the application of an (s, nQ) inventory control rule always leads to a higher stability than the use of an (s, S) policy with $S - s = Q$. Finally, because of its constant replenishment cycles, the (R, S) policy shows the best quantity as well as setup-oriented stability performance, but for high setup costs its cost effectiveness is fairly poor.

3.6.3 Buffering Methods

In simulation studies, Sridharan and LaForge [122], [123] analyze the effectiveness of holding safety stock at the MPS level to reduce schedule instability. Besides the stability measure of Sridharan et al. [120][89], they also use a cost error measure and customer service level as performance criteria. The cost error measure is given as the percentage deviation from the optimal total setup and inventory carrying costs, which are calculated by the Wagner-Whitin algorithm. This proves that an increase in safety stock does not necessarily lead to more stability or to a higher cost error, whereas customer service is improved by higher safety stocks. In fact, providing safety stock may even produce more schedule instability. Sridharan and LaForge [122] conclude that the effectiveness of using safety stocks to reduce nervousness is limited. They suggest improving forecasting accuracy and reducing setup costs as useful alternatives for increasing stability. Furthermore, Sridharan and LaForge [123] show that the use of safety stocks in connection with a frozen zone can considerably increase planning stability. Nevertheless, freezing the schedule seems to be the better alternative for reducing nervousness[90].

Campbell [19] discusses three different methods used to determine safety stock levels. He finds that the length of the frozen zone, the length of the planning horizon, and the characteristics of the demand distribution all have a significant impact on the performance of the proposed safety stock strategies.

Bartezzaghi and Verganti [8] have found that order overplanning[91] tends to increase MRP system nervousness. They argue that most plan revisions are due to rescheduling-out messages which are automatically managed by the MRP system, and that rescheduling-in messages seldom occur. Moreover, they point out that scheduling instability at the MPS level may also be neutralized by classical operating factors, such as lot-sizing rules.

---

[89] See equation (3.2), p.36.

[90] This result coincides with the findings of Blackburn et al. [14], [15], see also Section 3.6.5, p.60.

[91] Refer to Section 2.3.2.

3.6.4 Forecast Accuracy

The influence of forecast errors on MRP nervousness is examined in a simulation study by Ho and Ireland [56], [57][92]. The results indicate that increasing forecast errors reduce the cost performance of the MRP system, but do not necessarily lead to higher MRP system nervousness. This effect occurs because other operating factors, such as the use of a lot-sizing rule, may neutralize the influence of forecast errors. The lot-sizing rule should therefore be chosen carefully when demand is uncertain and forecast errors exist[93]. Thus, instability may be reduced by applying an appropriate lot-sizing rule, such as lot-for-lot, or Silver-Meal heuristic.

3.6.5 Comparison of Different Strategies

Minifie and Davis [91] analyze the interaction effects of different dampening mechanisms in a simulation study. These dampening mechanisms are lot-sizing rules, levels of quantity and time triggers, firm planned orders, and master schedule policy fences (refer to Section 3.5). The major finding of their examination is that the MRP system nervousness is very sensitive with respect to lot-sizing. They conclude that "there appears to be a dominating effect of lot-sizing over the other treatments...".

Blackburn et al. [14], [15] have compared five strategies for reducing nervousness[94] in MRP systems, i.e. freezing the schedule over the planning horizon, lot-for-lot ordering after the final product (stage), safety stocks, forecasting beyond the planning horizon, and the change cost procedure (for details see Section 3.5). The performance of these strategies is examined by a series of simulation studies where the lot-sizing procedures, the length of the planning horizon, the cost parameters, the forecast error, and the product assembly structure are varied. They have found that in most circumstances the change cost method or freezing the schedule play the most important role in reducing nervousness.

Kadipasaoglu and Sridharan [70] compare the performance of freezing, end-item safety stock, and lot-for-lot scheduling below the final product stage for reducing nervousness in a multi-level MRP system under uncertain demand. They found that, under the condition that the freeze length covers the cumulative demand, freezing the master production schedule performs best in terms of nervousness and cost[95]. This outcome coincides with the findings of

[92] For a description of the underlying nervousness measure see Section 3.4, p.35.

[93] See also the studies of Wemmerlöv and Whybark [139] and Wemmerlöv [140] mentioned in Section 3.6.2.

[94] Notice that they only deal with short-term stability.

[95] As measure for instability they use the technical formula as introduced by Sridharan et al. [120]. Since Kadipasaoglu and Sridharan examine a multi-stage system,

previous research (see, e.g., Blackburn et al. [14], and Sridharan and LaForge [122]).

3.6.6 Comparison of MRP and LRP with respect to Nervousness

In Van Donselaar et al. [133] the influence of demand information, i.e. either to use an MRP or LRP concept, on planning stability in supply chains is analyzed in a simulation study. Besides demand information, Van Donselaar et al. also show which other operating factors (such as demand uncertainty, lot sizes, and product structure) have an impact on nervousness. They deal with setup stability as defined by Heisig [49]. They use data from DAF, a truck manufacturer in The Netherlands, which currently uses LRP logic to calculate material requirements. Applying LRP means that information about end-item demand is not lost[96]. In their simulation experiment, Van Donselaar et al. consider linear as well as divergent product structures. As performance criteria, they determine service level (as the average probability of stock-out during a replenishment cycle), inventory levels (as the average total amount of component(s) and raw material), and nervousness (as setup changes). Demand is uniformly distributed, its variability is defined as the deviation between maximum and average demand in terms of a percentage of the average demand. The lot sizes for component(s) as well as raw material depend on the number of periods of net requirements[97]. In the simulation experiment, on average, service levels are slightly higher with MRP than with LRP, but inventory on hand is also significantly larger with MRP. However, it turns out that the planning of the component(s) is less nervous with MRP, whereas with LRP, planning of the raw material is much more stable. Because of the additional inventory in raw materials resulting from the MRP logic, MRP is able to meet the planned orders of the component(s), and stability on this (these) stage(s) is larger. If the inventory level in the LRP simulation is raised to the inventory level obtained in the MRP simulations, then service levels and stability at the components' levels are almost equal for both planning systems. However, Van Donselaar et al. argue that instability at the component level for LRP does not play a role at all, because the old planned orders at this level are not used. Thus, a deviation of the actual orders from planned orders is meaningless for strictly linear and divergent product structures. Van Donselaar et al. found that, on average, MRP was 4 to 5 times more nervous than LRP (with both systems having the same inventories and service levels). In the worst case (i.e. small lot sizes, low demand variability,

this measure has to be adjusted accordingly by incorporating the order decisions on lower levels. Costs include inventory carrying costs and setup costs.

[96] Note that this transparency of the supply chain was one of the main reasons for DAF to use LRP logic.

[97] For instance a lot size is given by "4 weeks of net requirements".

and a divergent product structure) the MRP logic was 17 times more nervous than LRP planning. Moreover, with increasing demand uncertainty[98], or decreasing lot sizes, stability is reduced.

3.6.7 Filtering Processes

Contrary to the examinations mentioned above, filtering processes are implemented to screen out rescheduling messages (see also Section 3.5).

Penlesky et al. examine how the number of plan changes generated by an MRP system can be reduced by the application of filtering methods. In a first simulation study Penlesky et al. [99] compare two different techniques for dealing with due date changes in a job shop scheduling system, i.e. the fixed and the dynamic due date approach, by using customer service level and total inventory level as performance criteria. Applying dynamic due date maintenance means that each rescheduling message is implemented, whereas in the case of a fixed due date approach, the initial order due dates established at the time the orders were released to the shop are never changed. The advantage of dynamic due date maintenance is that, under the assumption that most critical orders are processed first, high customer service can be achieved even with low inventory levels. The major disadvantage is that job priorities can be changed so quickly that scheduling decisions become inconsistent, and, consequently, mean flow time of shop orders as well as work-in-process inventory is increased, leading to reduced service levels. Since a fixed due date approach ignores all rescheduling messages, these problems will not occur (see Penlesky et al. [99]). The result is that, from an operational point of view, the dynamic approach is superior to the fixed due date procedure, because across a wide range of operating conditions in terms of customer service and total inventory, it is as good as, or better than the fixed due date approach[99]. Nevertheless, operating conditions, such as MPS nervousness, capacity utilization, length of planned lead time, and lot sizes, have a specific impact on the relative performance of the two approaches. Therefore, as the primary implication for practitioners, Penlesky et al conclude that "care should be exercised in using the dynamic due date maintenance approach". There are many strategies between the two extremes of changing or maintaining all due dates, where some but not all of the rescheduling messages generated by an MRP system are implemented. For this reason, in a subsequent study Penlesky et al. [100] examine different filtering procedures which make it possible

[98] The same holds for single-stage inventory systems, see, e.g., Heisig [49], and Chapter 4.

[99] Notice that the dynamic approach, in general, reduces total inventory by decreasing component and work-in-process inventory, but finished goods inventory increases. Thus, the level of inventory investment may increase, since finished goods usually have the highest value.

to distinguish between "important" and "unimportant" due date changes[100].

Simulation studies by Ho [53], Ho et al. [59], Ho [54], and Ho and Carter [55] examine the influence of operating environments on MRP system nervousness. Besides the impact of dampening procedures[101] on nervousness, they also analyze the influence of demand variability, capacity utilization, cost structure[102], lot-sizing rules[103], component commonality[104], length of lead time and planning horizon on instability. The performance measures are total related costs (as sum of setup, inventory carrying, shortage, and back-order costs), finished-goods delay (as the total amount of delay of end-item orders released for production and finished by the assigned due date), and nervousness[105]. The result is that the static dampening procedure leads to the lowest nervousness in the MRP system, whereas the automatic procedure performs worst. Additionally, the performance of the favorable static and cost-based procedures depends on the lot-sizing rule. Furthermore, the lot-for-lot rule shows a better performance than the EOQ rule. Finally, high-capacity utilization leads to more nervous systems, because it is very sensitive to uncertain events when the facility is working at full capacity.

3.7 Summary

The previous sections dealt with different concepts for measuring nervousness in a rolling horizon planning framework, and different dampening strategies as well as their influence on nervousness. Since the application of cost-based nervousness measures has several shortcomings, the use of a technical nervousness measure is explained. A systematic development of technical instability measures is only given in Sridharan et al. [120], Kadipasaoglu and Sridharan [71], Kimms [73], and Jensen [67], [68]. Since the first of the aforementioned measures is not free of certain deficiencies, the subsequent analysis of long-term setup stability of reorder point policies uses the measure of Jensen [67], [68]. Here, nervousness is measured by relating the expected setup (or quantity) deviations of orders to the expectation of maximum deviations that can

[100] In Penlesky et al. [100] an overview on filtering methods is given.

[101] Ho et al. consider static, automatic, and cost-based dampening procedures (for details, refer to Section 3.5).

[102] This means the ratio between the cost of earliness and that of lateness.

[103] Ho et al only compare the dynamic lot-sizing rule "lot-for-lot" with the static EOQ-formulae.

[104] The same component is used by various products.

[105] Note that in Ho [53], a "technical" nervousness measure is applied (see also Section 3.4, p.35), whereas in Ho [54], Ho et al. [59], and Ho and Carter [55] a cost-based nervousness measure analogously to the concept introduced by Carlson et al. [22] is used.

occur under worst case inventory control.

Section 3.5 addressed several strategies for reducing nervousness (refer to Table 3.1, p.48). Both local and global dampening procedures can be applied to reduce the number of rescheduling messages generated by an MRP system. One problem is the evaluation of which rescheduling messages can be screened out by a filtering process, i.e. it may be difficult to determine ex-ante which rescheduling activities are "insignificant". Moreover, the causes of nervousness are not analyzed systematically. Another focus in literature is the elimination of reasons for nervousness. Some of the causes can be controlled to a certain degree, others are hard to influence.
Section 3.6 presents several examinations of the impact of MRP design factors on nervousness[106]. Besides the application of unsophisticated stability measures, the additional major shortcoming in most of the examinations mentioned above is the underlying simulation approach. Therefore, they do not give a precise and systematic insight into the dependence of the respective dampening method on stability. Only Inderfurth [61], De Kok and Inderfurth [32], and Heisig [49] present an analytical approach for examining the stability performance of reorder point policies in a rolling horizon planning framework[107].

Since an MRP system is used in connection with a rolling horizon schedule, a detailed analysis of the parameters of such a framework on nervousness is desirable. In MRP systems, specific lot-sizing techniques are applied. Frequently, simple rules such as POQ or FOQ are used. These rules can be interpreted as applying an (s, S) policy, or an (s, nQ) rule, respectively. By determining the reorder point s, the size of the safety stock is predefined.
Due to these facts, the impact of (s, S) and (s, nQ) inventory control rules[108] on the stability measure introduced by Jensen [67] for a single-stage production system is analyzed in detail in the next chapter. In a subsequent chapter nervousness in product recovery systems is dealt with, where slightly different inventory control rules are applied.

---

[106] Moreover, the MRP planning concept is compared with LRP logic in terms of nervousness. There is proof that MRP tends to be less stable than LRP. But since in practice material planning is usually based on MRP logic, MRP logic will be considered later in this study.

[107] Notice that Grubbström and Tang [44] dealt with modeling rescheduling activities in a single-level production and inventory system in which the schedule may be modified at only one point in the future. They examine analytically when a schedule should be changed at this point in time and when not. The difference between the "stay" and "rescheduling" alternatives can be computed from their model, and this gap can be compared with rescheduling costs which are given exogenously by the management.

[108] Moreover, due to the relevance of stochastic disturbances for triggering replanning activities and because of the trade-off between service level and planning stability, it is useful to deal with stochastic inventory policies (see also Jensen [68], p.140).

4. Single-Stage Production Systems

This chapter analyzes the setup stability of inventory control rules of the (s, S) and (s, nQ) type in a single-stage production and inventory system with stochastic demand. These policies are applied within a rolling horizon schedule framework, and Jensen's concept (as introduced in Section 3.4.1) is used to measure setup stability. Besides examining the influence of external parameters such as the length of the so-called stability horizon[1], the weighting of periods within this horizon, the demand uncertainty, or the accuracy of demand forecasts, the main goal of the analysis is to show the impact of lot-sizing parameters on setup stability. Moreover, the comparison of both inventory control rules with respect to setup stability is central to this investigation.

4.1 Motivation of Underlying Inventory Control Rules

As discussed in Chapter 2, the planning of lot sizes in an MRP framework is done within a rolling horizon schedule. Due to external as well as internal disturbances, plan revisions frequently occur. Furthermore, the parameters of the lot-sizing policies themselves generate continuous replanning activities in different planning cycles (see Section 3.1.1).
This analysis is restricted to two basic inventory control rules of the types (s, S) and (s, nQ). There are several reasons for considering these policies (see Section 2.1).

As mentioned, in an MRP context these policies can be interpreted as applying period order quantity planning (POQ) planning, or fixed order quantity (FOQ) planning (see, e.g., Lagodimos and Anderson [78]). Moreover, policies of an (s, S) type have proven to be optimal for a wide range of problems under pure cost considerations. Additionally, the (s, S) policy is very flexible, i.e. order timing and replenishment quantity are variable. Finally, it is fairly simple and can be applied in practice relatively easily.
The last fact also applies for an (s, nQ) policy. Though the (s, S) policy is

[1] The meaning of the stability horizon is specified in Section 4.2.1.

rather simple, and from an average cost perspective superior to an (s, nQ) policy, there may be, e.g., technical or organizational restrictions and interdependencies which prevent its application in practice. One may think of a supply chain where in the case of an (s, S) policy, the production quantity for the supplier is not predictable. Using a fixed reorder quantity suppresses this shortcoming. A final remark: the total costs of the best (s, S) system can certainly not be greater than those of the best (s, nQ) system, but the computational effort to find the optimal values of s and S is much higher (see, e.g., Silver et al. [116], pp.238).

To conclude, both policies are applied frequently in practice. Furthermore they are examined in inventory theory with respect to the optimal determination of their parameters according to their performance in costs and service. Thus it is very useful to analyze their performance with respect to (setup) planning stability.
The next sections provide first a detailed presentation of the production and inventory system being considered. Some general stability results for both policies are then derived. Finally, the impact of the critical parameters will be indicated.

4.2 Steady-State Analysis

4.2.1 Assumptions and Notation

The stability performance of a stationary (s, S) and (s, nQ) inventory control rule with periodic review within a rolling horizon planning framework is analyzed. The stationarity of both policies implies that the control parameters will neither change from period to period nor from one planning cycle to another.
It is assumed that the stochastic demand per period $(D_t)_{t \in \mathbb{N}}$ performs a stationary and independent sequence of random variables D with continuous distribution function Φ_D, density ϕ_D, and an expected value of $\mathbb{E}[D] = \bar{D} > 0$. For each planning cycle, the demand of all future periods is forecasted by using (quasi-deterministic) constant forecasting values, i.e. $\hat{D}_t = \hat{D}$ for all periods t within the planning horizon (with $\hat{D} > 0$). Backordering of unsatisfied demand is permitted and, for notational convenience, the lead time is assumed to be zero. However, the analysis can easily be extended to include positive deterministic lead times by shifting the replenishment decisions with the corresponding number of periods[2].
Moreover, a planning horizon of P periods is considered (see Section 3.1.1). Since some periods (at the end of this planning horizon) may not be relevant

[2] Note that the introduction of stochastic lead times is not trivial and leads to some additional analytical problems (see also the discussion in Section 3.4.3).

with respect to stability aspects, a so-called ***stability horizon*** is introduced which contains exactly those periods where deviations in setups are perceived to be disadvantageous. The length of the stability horizon is a management decision, similar to the determination of the length of the planning horizon. However, the planning horizon length is mainly determined by the longest cumulative lead time for the company products, and in many cases an extra margin is added (see, e.g., Wemmerlöv [138]). This lead time certainly influences the length of the stability horizon, but the stability horizon may also be set lower than , equal to, or even larger than this lead time[3]. It is given by a number of $T+1$ periods[4]. This implies that plan revisions in periods which exceed the stability horizon are not taken into account. Nevertheless, note that the stability horizon can also be equal to the planning horizon, i.e. $1 \le T \le P-1$ applies (see also Figure 4.1). Since the planning horizon parameter P is meaningless for this further analysis, only the stability horizon parameter T will be referred to. Finally, as mentioned, the parameter a is used to assign decreasing weights to subsequent periods within the stability horizon.

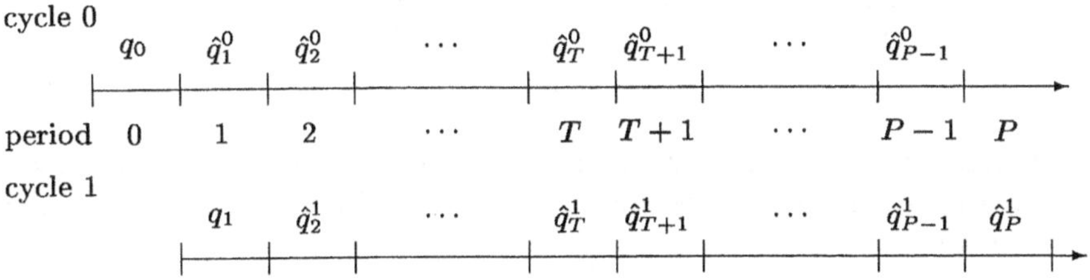

Figure 4.1. Connection between planning horizon P and stability horizon $T+1$ for two subsequent planning cycles 0 and 1

Then, for this steady-state situation with an infinite number of planning cycles, the expected long-term setup stability of the system is described by (3.9) (see Section 3.4.1) where for notational convenience the first planning cycle is denoted by 0 and the second by 1. Then, π is given by[5] (see also Fig. 3.1)

[3] Nevertheless, the stability horizon cannot exceed the planning horizon.

[4] As a special case, setup stability for an infinite stability horizon is also determined.

[5] Later in this study, setup stability π_S is denoted simply by π, because in the subsequent sections only setup stability is dealt with.

$$\pi = \frac{1-a}{1-a^T}\Bigg[\mathbb{P}\{\delta(\hat{q}_1^0) = \delta(q_1)\} + a\mathbb{P}\{\delta(\hat{q}_2^0) = \delta(\hat{q}_2^1)\} + ... +$$
$$a^{T-1}\mathbb{P}\{\delta(\hat{q}_T^0) = \delta(\hat{q}_T^1)\}\Bigg]. \tag{4.1}$$

Since a constant forecasting process is used, stability only depends on the initial inventory Z_0 at the beginning of cycle 0, the planned replenishment decisions $\hat{q}_t^0 (t = 1, ..., T)$, and (with an additional stochastic influence by D_0) the setup decisions q_1, $\hat{q}_t^1$ $(t = 2, ..., T + 1)$ are random variables.
Maximum stability, i.e. $\pi = 1$, is reached if $\hat{q}_1^0 = q_1$ and $\hat{q}_t^0 = \hat{q}_t^1$ for all $t = 2, ..., T$. Maximum nervousness, i.e. $\pi = 0$, occurs if the (planned) orders for the matching periods deviate from planning cycle 0 to 1.

Later in this study, some general results for both policies are derived.

4.2.2 General Results

The distribution function of the initial inventory position Z_0 and the inventory position after replenishment Y_0 (with $Y_0 = Z_0 + q_0$) do not only depend only on the demand distribution but also on the underlying control rule. For an (s, nQ) rule, the inventory level Y_0 is strictly limited by

$$s < Y_0 \le s + Q. \tag{4.2}$$

The same applies to an (s, S) policy if Q is defined as the distance between order-up-to-level and reorder point, i.e. it can be interpreted as the minimum lot size with

$$Q := S - s. \tag{4.3}$$

If the cdf of the stock level after replenishment, further denoted by $F_Y(.)$ (which has to be determined), and the cdf of the demand (i.e. $\Phi_D(.)$ which has to be given) are known, the probability π in (4.1) can be determined. In order to compute stability the order releases in both planning cycles must be determined. Therefore, the following relations are used.
The forecasted stock level before replenishment at the beginning of period t in cycle j is given by the forecasted stock before replenishment plus the planned order decision less the forecasted demand in the previous period, i.e.

$$\hat{Z}_t^j = \hat{Z}_{t-1}^j + \hat{q}_{t-1}^j - \hat{D}_{t-1}^j \quad \forall \quad t = 1, 2, ..., T + 1 \text{ and } j = 0, 1. \tag{4.4}$$

The expected stock level after replenishment is given by either equal to the order-up-to-level (if a setup has been planned) or equal to the inventory level before replenishment. Thus

$$\hat{Y}_t^j = \begin{cases} \hat{Z}_t^j & \text{if } \hat{q}_t^j = 0 \\ \hat{Z}_t^j + \hat{q}_t^j & \text{else} \end{cases} \qquad \forall \quad t = 1, 2, ..., T + 1 \text{ and } j = 0, 1.$$
$$\tag{4.5}$$

In the case of an (s,S) control rule, the planned inventory position after replenishment is equal to the order-up-to-level if a setup has been planned, i.e. $\hat{Y}_t^j = S$ if $\hat{q}_t^j > 0$. Using (4.5), equation (4.4) can be rewritten as

$$\hat{Z}_t^j = \hat{Y}_{t-1}^j - \hat{D} \quad \forall \quad t = 1,2,...,T+1 \text{ and } j = 0,1. \tag{4.6}$$

In order to determine setup planning stability for both inventory control rules, it is necessary to distinguish between two cases, $0 \leq Q \leq \hat{D}$ and $Q > \hat{D}$, respectively.

4.2.2.1 Setup Stability of (s,S) Inventory Control Rules

Here, a closed-form expression is derived to calculate the setup stability of an (s,S) policy. The analysis follows the lines in Heisig [49].

Case A[6]: $\boxed{0 < Q \leq \hat{D}}$

For an arbitrary period t in which a setup occurs, the expected stock level after replenishment is equal to the order-up-to-level, i.e. $\hat{Y}_t^j = S$. The planned inventory level at the beginning of period $t+1$ is given by $\hat{Z}_{t+1}^j = S - \hat{D}$. From (4.2) for $Q \leq \hat{D}$ it follows that $\hat{Y}_{t+1}^j \leq s$, thus an order is scheduled, i.e. $\hat{q}_{t+1}^j > 0$, and the expected inventory level after replenishment in period $t+1$ equals the order-up-to-level S. After the period in which the first setup is planned, an order setup takes place in each following period.
Now the period of both planning cycles in which the first setup is planned has to be determined. For the first planning cycle, this period is denoted by τ, while θ represents the first period with a planned setup in cycle 1.

Cycle 0:
From the limitation of the initial stock level (see (4.2)) it follows that in the case of $Q \leq \hat{D}$ the inventory level at the beginning of the first period is expected to be lower than or equal to the reorder point: $\hat{Z}_1^0 = Y_0 - \hat{D} \leq s$. In the first period, a setup is planned ($\hat{q}_1^0 > 0$), i.e. $\tau = 1$, and the inventory level after replenishment is equal to the reorder level, no matter what the exact stock level Y_0 may be. Note that τ only depends on Y_0. Thus in each period of cycle 0 an order is planned to be released: $\hat{q}_t^0 > 0 \; \forall \, t = 1,...,T$.

Cycle 1:
The sequence of planned order releases in cycle 1 depends on both the starting inventory position Y_0 and the actual demand D_0. Thus it is necessary to distinguish between two cases.
If demand is sufficiently large, i.e. $D_0 \geq Y_0 - s$, then a setup occurs in the

[6] The special case $Q = 0$, i.e. $s = S$, which corresponds to a simple order-up-to-level policy, is analyzed at the end of this paragraph.

first period ($q_1 > 0$), i.e. $\theta = 1$. Due to the aforementioned analysis, this leads to continuous setups, i.e. $q_1 > 0,\ \hat{q}_t^1 > 0\ \forall\, t = 2, ..., T+1$.
If, on the other hand, demand is sufficiently small, i.e. $D_0 < Y_0 - s$, then no setup is scheduled in the first period ($q_1 = 0$). The starting inventory of period 2 is given by $\hat{Z}_2^1 = Y_0 - D_0 - \hat{D}$ which has to be lower than the reorder point. From $Q \leq \hat{D}$ together with (4.2) it follows that $Y_0 \leq s+Q \leq s+\hat{D}$. Moreover, demand D_0 is not negative, and therefore one finds $\hat{Z}_2^1 \leq s$, which means that an order takes place ($\hat{q}_2^1 > 0$), i.e. $\theta = 2$. With the same arguments as above in each following period an order takes place: $q_1 = 0,\ \hat{q}_t^1 > 0\ \forall\, t = 2, ..., T+1$.

The sequence of order releases for $0 \leq Q \leq \hat{D}$ is illustrated in Table 4.1, where the figure "1" represents an order release and "0" denotes the opposite. In the line "weights", the weighting of the corresponding period is depicted (see (3.4)). For notational simplicity, the quotient $\frac{1-a}{1-a^T}$ is omitted[7].

Table 4.1. Setups in consecutive planning cycles for (s, S) policy in the case of $Q \leq \hat{D}$

weights	1	a	a^2	a^3	a^4	a^5	a^6	...		
period	1	2	3	4	5	6	7	...		
cycle 0	1	1	1	1	1	1	1	...	$s < Y_0 \leq s + Q$	$(\tau = 1)$
cycle 1	1	1	1	1	1	1	1	...	if $D_0 \geq Y_0 - s$	$(\theta = 1)$
	0	1	1	1	1	1	1	...	if $0 \leq D_0 < Y_0 - s$	$(\theta = 2)$

In cycle 0, a setup is scheduled in each period, while the sequence of order decisions in planning cycle 1 depends on the relation between the initial stock Y_0 and the amount of demand D_0. If demand is sufficiently large, then an order takes place in each period of cycle 1, otherwise in the first period no setup occurs, while in every following period an order is planned for release. In order to determine the stability measure π, so-called ***stability quotients*** are defined, which are determined by relating the weighted number of periods with identical setup decisions in both planning cycles to the weighted total number of periods that can be compared. In Case A with $Q \leq \hat{D}$ these stability quotients are denoted as

$$\alpha_\theta = \frac{\text{weighted number of periods with identical setups in demand case } \theta}{\text{weighted total number of periods which can be compared}},$$

with $\theta = 1$ for $D_0 \geq Y_0 - s$ and $\theta = 2$, else.

[7] Later in this study, the same representation of setups is used for the other cases.

Then, the probability for the setup-stability as indicated in (3.9) is given by (see Heisig [49])

$$\pi^A_{s,S} = \int_s^{s+Q} \{\alpha_1[1 - \Phi_D(Y_0 - s)] + \alpha_2 \Phi_D(Y_0 - s)\} dF_Y(Y_0). \tag{4.7}$$

The stability in (4.7) is defined by weighting the stability quotients with the corresponding demand probabilities for all possible values of the initial stock level ($s < Y_0 \leq S = s + Q$).

For $Q \leq \hat{D}$, the value of the stability quotients can easily be determined (see Heisig [49]).

In the case of a *finite stability horizon* with a given number of $T+1$ periods per planning cycle, $\alpha_1 = \frac{1-a}{1-a^T} \sum_{t=1}^{T} a^{t-1} = 1$ (an order takes place in each period of both planning cycles) and $\alpha_2 = \frac{1-a}{1-a^T} \sum_{t=2}^{T} a^{t-1} = \frac{a-a^T}{1-a^T}$, because of the single deviation of the order release in period 1 from cycle 0 to cycle 1. Altogether, the stability quotients are given by

$$\alpha_1 = 1 \quad \text{and} \quad \alpha_2 = \frac{a - a^T}{1 - a^T}. \tag{4.8}$$

For the special case that all periods are weighted equally,

$$\bar{\alpha}_1 = 1 \quad \text{and} \quad \bar{\alpha}_2 = \lim_{a \to 1} \alpha_2 = \frac{T-1}{T}. \tag{4.9}$$

In the case of an *infinite stability horizon* we get from (4.8) with $T \to \infty$ that

$$\alpha_1 = 1 \quad \text{and} \quad \alpha_2 = a, \tag{4.10}$$

where $a \cong 1$ if all periods are equal in weight, i.e.

$$\bar{\alpha}_1 = 1 \quad \text{and} \quad \bar{\alpha}_2 = 1. \tag{4.11}$$

Finally, the case of a simple order-up-to-level policy with $s = S$ is briefly discussed. Then, a setup is planned for release in each period of both planning cycles[8], and setup stability is equal to 100 %.

[8] Since the probability of zero demand is equal to zero, i.e. $\phi_D(0) = 0$, setups occur in every period of the second planning cycle (see Table 4.1).

Case B: $\boxed{Q > \hat{D}}$

To determine the order decisions, the region $Q > \hat{D}$ is divided into several intervals $(l-1)\hat{D} < Q \leq l\hat{D}$ with $l \in \mathcal{N} \setminus \{0,1\}$. The $Q/\hat{D}$-ratio-parameter l can be determined as follows (see also Heisig [49])

$$l = \lceil \frac{Q}{\hat{D}} \rceil, \tag{4.12}$$

where $\lceil n \rceil$ is the next integer larger than or equal to n. Note that l characterizes the rounded expected coverage of the minimum order size $S - s$, or, in other words, the expected time between ordering (TBO).

According to this definition, after a period t in which the first setup occurs (i.e. $\hat{Y}_t^j = S$), there are $(l-1)$ periods in which no orders are planned, because the planned inventory level at the beginning of periods $t+1, t+2, ..., t+l-1$ is larger than the reorder point: $\hat{Z}_{t+h}^j = S - h\hat{D} > s \quad (\forall\ h = 1, 2, ..., l-1)$ due to $Q > (l-1)\hat{D}$. Since the stock level before replenishment in period $t + l$ is less than or equal to the reorder point $(\hat{Z}_{t+l}^j = S - l\hat{D} \leq s)$, a setup is scheduled: $\hat{q}_{t+l}^j > 0$.
Using these arguments, it is generally the case that — as far as the stability horizon is not exceeded — orders take place in periods $t, t+l, t+2l, t+3l...$ Analogously to Case A, only the period in which the first setup is scheduled has to be determined.

Cycle 0:

The sequence of planned order releases depends on the amount of the initial stock level Y_0. If stock is sufficiently low, i.e. $Y_0 \leq s + \hat{D}$, a setup is planned in period 1 ($\hat{q}_1^0 > 0$) and the inventory level is brought up to the reorder level. If, on the other hand, the initial stock level is larger than the reorder point plus forecasted demand $\hat{D}$, then a first setup is planned in a specific period τ (with $\tau > 1$) meaning that the starting inventory Y_0 less the cumulative demand forecasts over the first τ periods is lower than or equal to the reorder point: $\hat{Z}_\tau^0 = Y_0 - \tau\hat{D} \leq s$. $s + (\tau - 1)\hat{D} < Y_0 \leq s + \tau\hat{D}$ applies, thus leading to $q_\tau^0 > 0$. Notice that from $Y_0 \leq s + \tau\hat{D}$ and $Q \leq l\hat{D}$ combined with (4.2) it follows that $l \geq \tau$ always applies.
Analogously to the definition of l (see (4.12)), the period in which the first order is released in planning cycle 0 is given by

$$\tau(Y_0) = \lceil \frac{Y_0 - s}{\hat{D}} \rceil. \tag{4.13}$$

To sum up, planned setups occur in periods $\tau + k * l$ for $k \in I\!N$ until the end of the stability horizon.
Notice that (4.13) can also be applied to Case A ($Q \leq \hat{D}$). Then, τ is equal to one, because $s < Y_0 \leq s + \hat{D}$.

For $5\hat{D} < Q \leq 6\hat{D}$, for instance, the development of the inventory level and the sequence of order releases depending on an initial stock level $Y_0 \in (s + 2\hat{D}, s + 3\hat{D}]$ are depicted in Figure 4.2. Here, the first order is planned for release in the third period. Since we have no lead time, the inventory level is immediately brought up to the order-up-to-level $S(= s + Q)$. In the next five periods no orders are planned, and the next setup takes place in the 9th period.

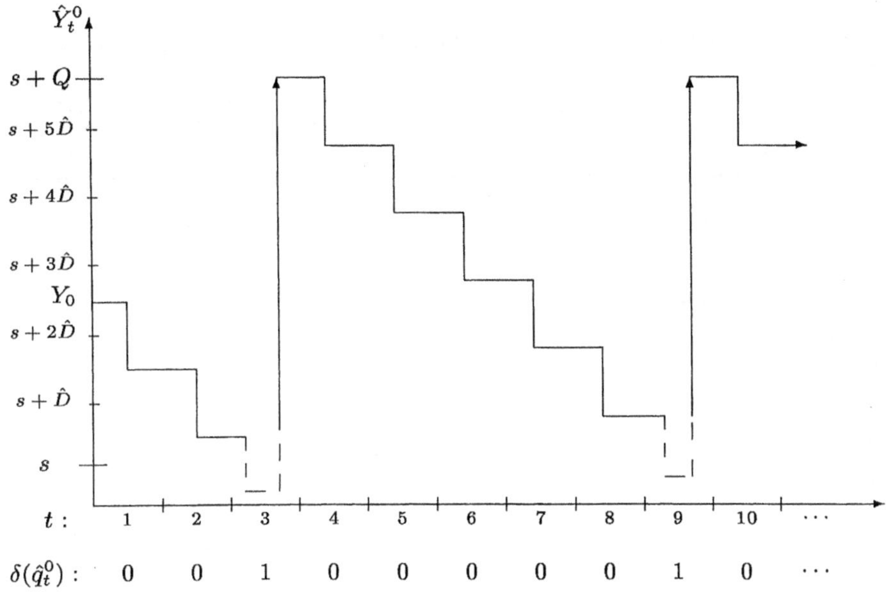

Figure 4.2. Example for development of inventory level and setups in first planning cycle for (s, S) policy

Cycle 1*:*
As for $Q \leq \hat{D}$, the period in which the first setup is planned to be released depends on both initial stock and realized demand. If, on one hand, actual demand is sufficiently high, i.e. $D_0 \geq Y_0 - s$, a setup occurs in the first period. If, on the other hand, the demand is sufficiently low ($D_0 < Y_0 - s$), a first setup takes place in a period θ ($\theta > 1$) for which the following applies: $\hat{Z}_\theta^1 = Y_0 - D_0 - (\theta - 1)\hat{D} \leq s$, i.e. $s + D_0 + (\theta - 2)\hat{D} < Y_0 \leq s + D_0 + (\theta - 1)\hat{D}$. Note that from (4.2) for $Q \leq l\hat{D}$ combined with $Y_0 \leq s + \tau\hat{D}$ and $Y_0 \leq s + D_0 + (\theta - 1)\hat{D}$ it follows that $\theta \leq \tau + 1$ for all $\tau = 1, 2, ..., l$.
Furthermore, the period in which the first setup is planned in cycle 1 is given

by

$$\theta(Y_0, D_0) = 1 + max\{0, \lceil \frac{Y_0 - D_0 - s}{\hat{D}} \rceil\}. \tag{4.14}$$

Summarizing, it is evident that planned setups take place in periods $\theta + k * l$ for $k \in \mathbb{N}$.
Note that the relation in (4.14) can also be applied to determine the value of θ in Case A.

Table 4.2. Setups in consecutive planning cycles for (s, S) policy in the case of $Q > \hat{D}$

weights	1	a ...	$a^{\tau-1}$	a^{τ} ...	a^{l-1}	a^{l}	a^{l+1} ...	$a^{l+\tau-1}$	$a^{l+\tau}$ ...	a^{2l-1} ...
periods	1	2 ...	τ	$\tau+1$ ...	l	$l+1$	$l+2$ ...	$l+\tau$	$l+\tau+1$ ...	$2l$ ...
cycle 0										
$\tau = 1, .., l$	0	0 ...	1	0 ...	0	0	0 ...	1	0 ...	0 ...
cycle 1										
$\theta = 1$	1	0 ...	0	0 ...	0	1	0 ...	0	0 ...	0 ...
$\theta = 2$	0	1 ...	0	0 ...	0	0	1 ...	0	0 ...	0 ...
	⋮	⋮		⋮			⋮		⋮	⋮
$\theta = \tau$	0	0 ...	1	0 ...	0	0	0 ...	1	0 ...	0 ...
$\theta = \tau + 1$	0	0 ...	0	1 ...	0	0	0 ...	0	1 ...	0 ...

Table 4.2 shows the sequences of lot size decisions for an initial stock level Y_0 in the intervals $(s + (\tau - 1)\hat{D}, s + \tau\hat{D}]$ with $\tau = 1, 2, .., l - 1$. In cycle 0, setups occur in $\tau, l + \tau, 2l + \tau$.....
If the demand is sufficiently high, i.e. $D_0 \geq Y_0 - s$, then an order is planned in the first period of cycle 1 ($\theta = 1$). Thus, setups will take place in $1, l+1, 2l+1$ and so on. If the demand realization lies in an arbitrary interval $Y_0 - s - (\theta - 1)\hat{D} \leq D_0 < Y_0 - s - (\theta - 2)\hat{D}$, $\theta = 2, 3, ..., \tau - 1$, then the first order is released in period θ; the next setups occur in $l + \theta, 2l + \theta$,... For the special case $\theta = \tau$ we obtain the same sequence of order decisions as for cycle 0. For the event that the demand is sufficiently low, i.e. $0 \leq D_0 < Y_0 - s - (\tau - 1)\hat{D}$, the first setup is planned in period $\tau + 1$. The following orders are scheduled in $l + \tau + 1, 2l + \tau + 1$ and so on.

The sequences of order releases for an initial stock level in $(s + (l - 1)\hat{D}, s + Q]$ have to be considered separately, because the inventory level cannot exceed the reorder level S, i.e. $Y_0 \leq s + Q$. The same results are the same as in Table 4.2, where τ must be replaced by l. Thus, in cycle 0, orders are scheduled in the periods $l, 2l, 3l$ and so on, while the moment of a setup in cycle 1 depends again on the amount of the demand realization.
Analogously to Case A, stability quotients can be defined, which are denoted

by β_θ^τ. They are given by:

$$\beta_\theta^\tau = \frac{\text{weighted no. of periods with same setups in demand case } \theta, \text{ inventory case } \tau}{\text{weighted total number of periods which can be compared}}$$

$$\forall \quad \tau = 1, 2, ..., l \text{ and } \theta = 1, 2, ... \tau + 1.$$

Then, the probability for the setup-stability in the case of $Q > \hat{D}$ is given by

$$\begin{aligned}
\pi_{s,S}^B = \Bigg\{ \sum_{\tau=1}^{l-1} \int\limits_{s+(\tau-1)\hat{D}}^{s+\tau\hat{D}} & \{\beta_1^\tau [1 - \Phi_D(Y_0 - s)] \\
& + \sum_{\theta=2}^{\tau} \beta_\theta^\tau [\Phi_D(Y_0 - s - (\theta-2)\hat{D}) - \Phi_D(Y_0 - s - (\theta-1)\hat{D})] \\
& + \beta_{\tau+1}^\tau \Phi_D(Y_0 - s - (\tau-1)\hat{D})\} \\
+ \int\limits_{s+(l-1)\hat{D}}^{s+Q} & \{\beta_1^l [1 - \Phi_D(Y_0 - s)] \qquad (4.15) \\
& + \sum_{\theta=2}^{l} \beta_\theta^l [\Phi_D(Y_0 - s - (\theta-2)\hat{D}) - \Phi_D(Y_0 - s - (\theta-1)\hat{D})] \\
& + \beta_{l+1}^l \Phi_D(Y_0 - s - (l-1)\hat{D})\} \Bigg\} dF_Y(Y_0)
\end{aligned}$$

$$\forall \quad (l-1)\hat{D} < Q \leq l\hat{D} \quad \text{with} \quad l \in \mathcal{N} \setminus \{0, 1\}.$$

As for $Q \leq \hat{D}$ stability in (4.15)[9] is defined by weighting the stability quotients with the corresponding demand probabilities for all possible values of the initial stock level ($s < Y_0 \leq S = s + Q$).

Now, the values of the different stability quotients must be determined.

[9] Notice that for $\tau < \theta$ and $l < \theta$, respectively, the sums in the second and fifth line of (4.15) are defined to be equal to zero, i.e. $\sum_{\theta=2}^{1} \beta_\theta^1 [\Phi_D(Y_0 - s - (\theta-2)\hat{D}) - \Phi_D(Y_0 - s - (\theta-1)\hat{D})] := 0$. Both cases are included in the expressions in the third and sixth line of formula (4.15). Later in this study, all sums in which the upper summation index is smaller than the lower one are predefined with zero.

If in both planning cycles the first setup occurs in the same period τ (i.e. $\theta = \tau$), then the matching stability quotient is equal to one, i.e.

$$\beta_\tau^\tau = \frac{1-a}{1-a^T} \sum_{t=1}^{T} a^{t-1} = 1 \quad \forall \quad \tau = 1, 2, ..., l. \tag{4.16}$$

In all other cases (i.e. $\theta \neq \tau$), the stability horizon parameter T influences the size of the stability quotients. In Table 4.2, there exists a certain order rhythm for a given parameter l. The order decisions of periods 1 up to l are repeated in periods $l+1$ up to $2l$, $2l+1$ up to $3l$ and so on. These recurrent setup cycles are called *order sequences.*

Due to the occurrence of one order setup in each order sequence belonging to planning cycle 0 and 1, there are exactly $(l-2)$ periods with identical lot size decisions in each order sequence. On the other hand, two periods exist in which the setup decision in cycle 0 differs from the order decision in cycle 1. In order to determine the stability quotients, the dependence between the periods τ and θ and the horizon parameter T in a specific order sequence is analyzed.

By defining an integer

$$L = \lfloor \frac{T}{l} \rfloor, \tag{4.17}$$

(where $\lfloor n \rfloor$ is the next integer lower than or equal to n) which represents the number of order sequences for a given $Q/\hat{D}$-ratio and stability horizon T — considering a comparison of two consecutive planning cycles — we can compute the value of the stability quotients (see Table 4.2). To determine the relevant stability quotients in the case of a *finite stability horizon,* it is necessary to distinguish between four cases.

(1) $\theta = \tau$

The stability quotients are then equal to one (see (4.16)).

(2) $\theta < \tau$

Then, the first setup in cycle 1 occurs at least one period before the first order is released in cycle 0. For β_θ^τ with $\theta = 1, 2, ..., \tau - 1$ and $\tau = 2, 3, ..., l$ we obtain the following results:

In each of the first $(L-1)$ order sequences there are two periods with non-identical setup decisions, i.e. in periods $\Delta l + \theta$ a setup is planned in cycle 1, but no order is planned for release in cycle 0 whereas the opposite applies to periods $\Delta l + \tau$ (with $\Delta = 0, 1, ..., L-1$). Thus, the value of β_θ^τ over $(L-1)$ order sequences is given by

$$\beta_\theta^\tau[L-1] = \sum_{\Delta=0}^{L-1} [\frac{1-a}{1-a^T}(\sum_{t=\Delta l+1}^{\Delta l+\theta-1} a^{t-1} + \sum_{t=\Delta l+\theta+1}^{\Delta l+\tau-1} a^{t-1} + \sum_{t=\Delta l+\tau+1}^{(\Delta+1)l} a^{t-1})]$$

$$= \frac{(1-a^{Ll})(a^{\theta-1} - a^{\theta} + a^{\tau-1} - a^{\tau} + a^{l} - 1)}{(1-a^{T})(a^{l}-1)}. \tag{4.18}$$

For $L = 0$ we define $\beta_\theta^\tau[L-1] := 0$.

In the Lth order sequence, the number of periods with identical setup decisions depends on the relationship between θ, τ and T. If $T < Ll + \theta$, then identical planned order releases are obtained in the remaining periods up to the end of the stability horizon. If $Ll + \theta \leq T < Ll + \tau$, then only the setup in period $Ll + \theta$ differs from planning cycle 0 to 1. For $Ll + \tau \leq T \leq (L+1)l$, there is also a different order decision in period $Ll + \tau$.
The stability quotients for β_θ^τ ($\theta = 1, 2, ..., \tau - 1; \tau = 2, 3, .., l$) are therefore given as follows (by substituting $\beta_\theta^\tau[L-1]$ from (4.18)):

(i) $T = Ll + 1, ..., Ll + \theta - 1$:

$$\beta_\theta^\tau = \beta_\theta^\tau[L-1] + \frac{1-a}{1-a^T} \sum_{t=Ll+1}^{T} a^{t-1}$$
$$= \frac{(1-a^{Ll})(a^{\theta-1} - a^{\theta} + a^{\tau-1} - a^{\tau}) + (1-a^{T})(a^{l}-1)}{(1-a^{T})(a^{l}-1)}, \tag{4.19}$$

(ii) $T = Ll + \theta$:

$$\beta_\theta^\tau = \beta_\theta^\tau[L-1] + \frac{1-a}{1-a^T} \sum_{t=Ll+1}^{T-1} a^{t-1}$$
$$= \frac{(1-a^{Ll})(a^{\theta-1} - a^{\theta} + a^{\tau-1} - a^{\tau}) + (1-a^{T-1})(a^{l}-1)}{(1-a^{T})(a^{l}-1)}, \tag{4.20}$$

(iii) $T = Ll + \theta + 1, ..., Ll + \tau - 1$:

$$\beta_\theta^\tau = \beta_\theta^\tau[L-1] + \frac{1-a}{1-a^T}\Big(\sum_{t=Ll+1}^{Ll+\theta-1} a^{t-1} + \sum_{t=Ll+\theta+1}^{T} a^{t-1}\Big) \tag{4.21}$$
$$= \frac{(1-a^{(L+1)l})(a^{\theta-1} - a^{\theta}) + (1-a^{Ll})(a^{\tau-1} - a^{\tau}) + (1-a^{T})(a^{l}-1)}{(1-a^{T})(a^{l}-1)},$$

(iv) $T = Ll + \tau$:

$$\beta_\theta^\tau = \beta_\theta^\tau[L-1] + \frac{1-a}{1-a^T}\Big(\sum_{t=Ll+1}^{Ll+\theta-1} a^{t-1} + \sum_{t=Ll+\theta+1}^{T-1} a^{t-1}\Big) \tag{4.22}$$
$$= \frac{(1-a^{(L+1)l})(a^{\theta-1} - a^{\theta}) + (1-a^{Ll})(a^{\tau-1} - a^{\tau}) + (1-a^{T-1})(a^{l}-1)}{1-a^{T})(a^{l}-1)},$$

(v) $T = Ll + \tau + 1, ..., (L+1)l$:

$$\beta_\theta^T = \beta_\theta^T[L-1] + \frac{1-a}{1-a^T}\Big(\sum_{t=Ll+1}^{Ll+\theta-1} a^{t-1} + \sum_{t=Ll+\theta+1}^{Ll+\tau-1} a^{t-1} + \sum_{Ll+\tau+1}^{T} a^{t-1}\Big)$$
$$= \frac{(1-a^{(L+1)l})(a^{\theta-1} - a^\theta + a^{\tau-1} - a^\tau) + (1-a^T)(a^l-1)}{(1-a^T)(a^l-1)}. \quad (4.23)$$

(3) $\theta = \tau + 1$ and $\tau < l$

Then, the first setup in cycle 1 is scheduled exactly one period later than the first order is planned in cycle 0, i.e. $\theta = \tau + 1$ and $\tau < l$. Analogously to the second case, for the first $(L-1)$ order sequences for $\beta_{\tau+1}^T$ with $\tau = 1, 2, ..., l-1$ the following formula applies:

$$\beta_{\tau+1}^T[L-1] = \sum_{\Delta=0}^{L-1}\Big[\frac{1-a}{1-a^T}\Big(\sum_{t=\Delta l+1}^{\Delta l+\tau-1} a^{t-1} + \sum_{t=\Delta l+\tau+2}^{(\Delta+1)l} a^{t-1}\Big)\Big]$$
$$= \frac{(1-a^{Ll})(a^{\tau-1} - a^{\tau+1} + a^l - 1)}{(1-a^T)(a^l-1)}, \quad (4.24)$$

where again $\beta_{\tau+1}^T[L-1] := 0$ is defined for $L = 0$.
By applying the same analysis as above, we obtain:

(i) $T = Ll + 1, ..., Ll + \tau - 1$:

$$\beta_{\tau+1}^T = \beta_{\tau+1}^T[L-1] + \frac{1-a}{1-a^T}\sum_{t=Ll+1}^{T} a^{t-1}$$
$$= \frac{(1-a^{Ll})(a^{\tau-1} - a^{\tau+1} + a^l - 1) + (a^{Ll} - a^T)(a^l-1)}{(1-a^T)(a^l-1)}, \quad (4.25)$$

(ii) $T = Ll + \tau$:

$$\beta_{\tau+1}^T = \beta_{\tau+1}^T[L-1] + \frac{1-a}{1-a^T}\sum_{t=Ll+1}^{T-1} a^{t-1}$$
$$= \frac{(1-a^{Ll})(a^{\tau-1} - a^{\tau+1} + a^l - 1) + (a^{Ll} - a^{T-1})(a^l-1)}{(1-a^T)(a^l-1)}, \quad (4.26)$$

(iii) $T = Ll + \tau + 1$:

$$\beta_{\tau+1}^T = \beta_{\tau+1}^T[L-1] + \frac{1-a}{1-a^T}\sum_{t=Ll+1}^{T-2} a^{t-1}$$
$$= \frac{(1-a^{Ll})(a^{\tau-1} - a^{\tau+1} + a^l - 1) + (a^{Ll} - a^{T-2})(a^l-1)}{(1-a^T)(a^l-1)}, \quad (4.27)$$

(iv) $T = Ll + \tau + 2, ..., (L+1)l$:

$$\beta^T_{\tau+1} = \beta^T_{\tau+1}[L-1] + \frac{1-a}{1-a^T}\Big(\sum_{t=Ll+1}^{Ll+\tau-1} a^{t-1} + \sum_{t=Ll+\tau+2}^{T} a^{t-1}\Big)$$
$$= \frac{(1-a^{(L+1)l})(a^{\tau-1}-a^{\tau+1}) + (1-a^T)(a^l-1)}{(1-a^T)(a^l-1)}. \tag{4.28}$$

The results for these three cases are summarized in Table 4.3.

Table 4.3. Stability quotients for $Q > \hat{D}$ with weighting of periods

	Stability quotients		
Horizon parameter T	β^T_τ $(\tau = 1,..,l)$	β^T_θ $(\theta = 1,..,\tau-1;$ $\tau = 2,..,l)$	$\beta^T_{\tau+1}$ $(\tau = 1,..,l-1)$
(i) $Ll+1,..,Ll+\theta-1$	1	$\frac{A}{D}+1$	$\frac{E}{D}+\frac{a^{Ll}-a^T}{1-a^T}$
(ii) $Ll+\theta$	1	$\frac{A}{D}+\frac{1-a^{T-1}}{1-a^T}$	$\frac{E}{D}+\frac{a^{Ll}-a^T}{1-a^T}$
(iii) $Ll+\theta+1,..,Ll+\tau-1$	1	$\frac{B}{D}+1$	$\frac{E}{D}+\frac{a^{Ll}-a^T}{1-a^T}$
(iv) $Ll+\tau$	1	$\frac{B}{D}+\frac{1-a^{T-1}}{1-a^T}$	$\frac{E}{D}+\frac{a^{Ll}-a^{T-1}}{1-a^T}$
(v) $Ll+\tau+1$	1	$\frac{C}{D}+1$	$\frac{E}{D}+\frac{a^{Ll}-a^{T-2}}{1-a^T}$
(vi) $Ll+\tau+2,..,(L+1)l$	1	$\frac{C}{D}+1$	$\frac{F}{D}+1$

where

$$A := (1-a^{Ll})(a^{\theta-1}-a^\theta+a^{\tau-1}-a^\tau),$$
$$B := (1-a^{(L+1)l})(a^{\theta-1}-a^\theta)+(1-a^{Ll})(a^{\tau-1}-a^\tau),$$
$$C := (1-a^{(L+1)l})(a^{\theta-1}-a^\theta+a^{\tau-1}-a^\tau), \qquad D := (1-a^T)(a^l-1),$$
$$E := (1-a^{Ll})(a^{\tau-1}-a^{\tau+1}+a^l-1), \qquad F := (1-a^{(L+1)l})(a^{\tau-1}-a^{\tau+1}).$$

Finally, the special case that the first setup in cycle 0 takes place in period l and the first period with a planned order release in cycle 1 is equal to $l+1$ must be dealt with, i.e.

(4) $\theta = \tau + 1$ and $\tau = l$

Here, a distinction between two basic cases is necessary, i.e. $T < l$ which means that $L = 0$, and the opposite, $T \geq l$.

(i) $T = 1, ..., l-1$:

$$\beta_{l+1}^{l} = \frac{1-a}{1-a^T} \sum_{t=1}^{T} a^{t-1} = 1. \tag{4.29}$$

(ii) $T \geq l$ (i.e. $L > 0$):
If $T = Ll$, then

$$\begin{aligned} \beta_{l+1}^{l} &= \frac{1-a}{1-a^T} \Big(\sum_{t=1}^{l-1} a^{t-1} + \sum_{\Delta=1}^{L-1} \sum_{t=\Delta l+2}^{(\Delta+1)l-1} a^{t-1} \Big) \\ &= \frac{a^{l-1} - a^{l+1} - a^{Ll+1}(a^{l-2} - 1) + a^l - 1}{(1-a^{Ll})(a^l - 1)}. \end{aligned} \tag{4.30}$$

If $T = Ll + 1, ..., (L+1)l - 1$, then

$$\begin{aligned} \beta_{l+1}^{l} &= \frac{1-a}{1-a^T} \Big(\sum_{t=1}^{l-1} a^{t-1} + \sum_{\Delta=1}^{L-1} \sum_{t=\Delta l+2}^{(\Delta+1)l-1} a^{t-1} + \sum_{t=Ll+2}^{T} a^{t-1} \Big) \\ &= \frac{(1-a^{Ll})(a^{l-1} - a^{l+1}) + (1-a^T)(a^l - 1)}{(1-a^T)(a^l - 1)}. \end{aligned} \tag{4.31}$$

For the case that all periods are weighted equally, the corresponding stability quotients are obtained by calculating the limiting values of (4.19) – (4.31) for $a \to 1$. This results in stability quotients as shown in Table 4.4.

Next, the special case of an *infinite stability horizon* will briefly be discussed. For $\theta = \tau$, it is obvious that (4.16) remains unchanged, i.e.

$$\beta_{\tau}^{\tau} = 1, \tag{4.32}$$

for all $\tau = 1, 2, ..., l$.
From (4.19) – (4.31) we get for $T \to \infty$ that

$$\beta_{\theta}^{\tau} = \frac{a^{\theta-1} - a^{\theta} + a^{\tau-1} - a^{\tau} + a^l - 1}{a^l - 1} \quad \text{for all } \theta = 1, ..., \tau - 1 \ (\tau = 2, ..., l), \tag{4.33}$$

Table 4.4. Stability quotients for $Q > \hat{D}$ without weighting of periods

	Stability quotients		
Horizon parameter T	$\bar{\beta}^\tau_\tau$ ($\tau = 1,..,l$	$\bar{\beta}^\tau_\theta$ ($\theta = 1,..,\tau-1$; $\tau = 2,..,l$)	$\bar{\beta}^\tau_{\tau+1}$ ($\tau = 1,..,l-1$)
(*i*) $Ll+1,..,Ll+\theta-1$	1	$\frac{T-2L}{T}$	$\frac{T-2L}{T}$
(*ii*) $Ll+\theta,..,Ll+\tau-1$	1	$\frac{T-2L-1}{T}$	$\frac{T-2L}{T}$
(*iii*) $Ll+\tau$	1	$\frac{T-2L-2}{T}$	$\frac{T-2L-1}{T}$
(*iv*) $Ll+\tau+1,..,(L+1)l-1$	1	$\frac{T-2L-2}{T}$	$\frac{T-2L-2}{T}$
(*v*) Ll (with $L > 0$)	1	$\frac{l-2}{l}$	$\frac{l-2}{l}$

$$\text{and} \quad \bar{\beta}^l_{l+1} = \begin{cases} \frac{T-2L}{T} & \text{if } T = Ll+1,...,(L+1)l-1 \\ \frac{l-2}{l} + \frac{1}{Ll} & \text{if } T = Ll \text{ (with } L > 0). \end{cases}$$

$$\beta^\tau_{\tau+1} = \frac{a^{\tau-1} - a^{\tau+1} + a^l - 1}{a^l - 1} \quad \text{for all } \tau = 1,2,...,l-1, \tag{4.34}$$

and

$$\beta^l_{l+1} = \frac{a^{l-1} + a^l - a^{l+1} - 1}{a^l - 1}. \tag{4.35}$$

For equally weighted periods and infinite stability horizon we get for $l \geq 2$ that[10]

$$\bar{\beta}^\tau_\tau = 1 \quad \text{for all} \quad \tau = 1,...,l, \tag{4.36}$$

$$\bar{\beta}^\tau_\theta = \frac{l-2}{l} \quad \text{for all} \quad \theta = 1,...,\tau-1 \text{ and } \tau = 2,...,l, \tag{4.37}$$

$$\bar{\beta}^\tau_{\tau+1} = \frac{l-2}{l} \quad \text{for all} \quad \tau = 1,...,l, \tag{4.38}$$

which also results from determining the limiting values of (4.32) – (4.35) for $a \to 1$.

[10] In planning cycle 0 an order is planned in $\tau, \tau+l, \tau+2l$ and so on, while in cycle 1 a setup occurs in $\theta, \theta+l, \theta+2l, ...$ In any other period we find identical non-setup decisions in both planning cycles.

4.2.2.2 Setup Stability of (s, nQ) Inventory Control Rules

Similar to the the analysis of the (s, S) policy, a closed-form expression for the setup stability of an (s, nQ) control rule is derived.

Case A: $\boxed{0 < Q \leq \hat{D}}$

Cycle 0:

From the limitation of the initial stock level (see (4.2)) it follows that in the case of $Q \leq \hat{D}$ the inventory level at the beginning of the first period is expected to be lower than or equal to the reorder point: $\hat{Z}_1^0 = Y_0 - \hat{D} \leq s$. Thus a setup is planned: $\hat{q}_1^0 = \hat{n}_1^0 Q$ with $\hat{n}_1^0 = ||\lceil \frac{s - Y_0 + \hat{D}}{Q} \rceil||$ where $||\lceil x \rceil||$ is the next integer larger than x. The inventory position after replenishment is given by $\hat{Y}_1^0 = Y_0 - \hat{D} + \hat{n}_1^0 Q > s$.

It is evident that in each following period of planning cycle 0 an order is planned for release because $s < \hat{Y}_t^0 \leq s + Q \; \forall \, t$. Since $Q \leq \hat{D}$ it follows that $\hat{Z}_{t+1}^0 = \hat{Y}_t^0 - \hat{D} \leq s \; \forall \, t$. Thus in each period of cycle 0 a setup is scheduled: $\hat{q}_t^0 > 0 \; \forall \, t = 1, ..., T$.

Cycle 1:

As for the (s, S) control rule, the sequence of planned order releases in cycle 1 depends on initial stock Y_0 and actual demand D_0. Here, two cases must be considered:

1. If demand is sufficiently high, i.e. $D_0 \geq Y_0 - s$, then a setup occurs in the first period. Since $Z_1^1 = Y_0 - D_0 \leq s$ we get $q_1 = n_1 Q$ where $n_1 = ||\lceil \frac{s - Y_0 + D_0}{Q} \rceil||$.
   As for planning cycle 0, the starting inventory level in each following period $\hat{Z}_t^1$ $(t \geq 2)$ is expected to be lower than or equal to the reorder point, thus leading to continuous setups, i.e. $q_1 > 0$, and $\hat{q}_t^1 > 0 \; \forall \, t = 2, ..., T + 1$.
2. If, on the other hand, demand is sufficiently low, i.e. $D_0 < Y_0 - s$, in the first period no order takes place $(q_1 = 0)$. The starting inventory of the second period is given by $\hat{Z}_2^1 = Y_0 - D_0 - \hat{D}$. From (4.2) with $Q \leq \hat{D}$ and non-negative demand $Y_0 \leq s + Q \leq s + \hat{D} \leq s + \hat{D} + D_0$ applies. Thus $\hat{Z}_2^1 \leq s$, which means that a setup is planned to be released $(\hat{q}_2^1 > 0)$. With the same arguments as above,an order occurs in each following period. Thus $q_1 = 0$ applies, and $\hat{q}_t^1 > 0 \; \forall \, t = 2, 3, ..., T + 1$.

To summarize, setup decisions in the case of an (s, nQ) policy for $Q \leq \hat{D}$ are exactly the same as for an (s, S) policy (see Table 4.1). In cycle 0, a setup is scheduled in each period, while the sequence of order decisions in planning cycle 1 depends on the amount of the demand D_0. If the demand is sufficiently large, then an order takes place in each period of cycle 1, otherwise in period 1 no setup occurs, while in each following period an order is released.

Thus stability can be calculated from

$$\pi^{A}_{s,nQ} = \int\limits_{s}^{s+Q} \{\alpha_1[1-\Phi_D(Y_0-s)] + \alpha_2\Phi_D(Y_0-s)\}dF_Y(Y_0), \qquad (4.39)$$

where α_θ again represents the stability quotients in demand case θ (with $\theta = 1$ for $D_0 \geq Y_0 - s$ and $\theta = 2$, else).
Since the setup decisions for an (s, nQ) and an (s, S) policy do not differ, it is evident that the value of the stability quotients are also identical. Thus the stability quotients for an (s, nQ) policy can also be calculated by (4.8) – (4.10).
Nevertheless, because of the different distribution of stock after replenishment ($F_Y(.)$) for both policies, the setup stability for an (s, nQ) inventory control rule will usually differ from the stability of an (s, S) policy.

Case B: $\boxed{Q > \hat{D}}$

In order to get analytical results for $Q > \hat{D}$, one must assume that the expected TBO $Q/\hat{D}$ is a quotient of two integers, i.e. it is a rational number. This assumption is no restriction with respect to practical applications, because in most practical situations the TBO is even an integer. Furthermore, lot sizes, in general, are integers, e.g. multiples of pallets or barrels, and the same applies to demand forecasts. Moreover, from a theoretical point of view, each number $r \in I\!R$ can be approximated arbitrarily closely by a rational number.
Definition:

$$Q = \frac{\zeta}{\eta}\hat{D} \qquad \text{with} \qquad \zeta, \eta \in I\!N \qquad \text{and} \qquad \zeta > \eta. \qquad (4.40)$$

As will be demonstrated further analysis, this assumption is required in order to derive the setup decisions for an (s, nQ) policy. Assuming $Q/\hat{D}$ to be quotient of two integers means that we can identify a "regeneration point", i.e. after a certain number of periods, which depends on the value of ζ and η, or $Q/\hat{D}$, respectively, the initial stock level will be reached again. Thus repeating order sequences occur as in the case of the (s, S) inventory control rule. If the TBO was not a quotient of two integers, then no finite sequence of setup decisions would be found, and the matching stability quotients for different inventory and demand cases could not be derived analytically.

Cycle 0:
Dividing the region $s < Y_0 \leq s + Q = s + \frac{\zeta}{\eta}\hat{D}$ into several intervals $s + \frac{\omega-1}{\eta}\hat{D} < Y_0 \leq s + \frac{\omega}{\eta}\hat{D}$ with $\omega = 1, 2, ..., \zeta$ makes it possible to determine the setup

decisions in cycle 0 by applying the following algorithm (see also the example on pp.85).

Algorithm I

For

$$s + \frac{\omega - 1}{\eta}\hat{D} < Y_0 \leq s + \frac{\omega}{\eta}\hat{D} \qquad \text{with} \qquad \omega = 1, 2, ..., \zeta, \tag{4.41}$$

we obtain:

The inventory position at the beginning of period t is given by

$$\hat{Z}_t^0 = Y_0 - \frac{c_0}{\eta}\hat{D} + \frac{c_{t-1}}{\eta}\hat{D} - \hat{D} = Y_0 + \frac{c_{t-1} - c_0 - \eta}{\eta}\hat{D} \quad \forall \quad t = 1, ..., T+1, \tag{4.42}$$

where $c_0 := \omega - 1$ and c_{t-1} can be derived from (4.45).

Then, we find that[11]

$$\begin{aligned} &\text{if} \quad c_{t-1} < \eta, \qquad \text{then} \quad \hat{q}_t^0 = \tfrac{\zeta}{\eta}\hat{D} > 0 \\ &\text{if} \quad c_{t-1} \geq \eta, \qquad \text{then} \quad \hat{q}_t^0 = 0 \end{aligned} \qquad \forall \quad t = 1, ..., T+1. \tag{4.43}$$

Thus we get

$$\hat{Y}_t^0 = Y_0 + \frac{c_t - c_0}{\eta}\hat{D} \qquad \forall \qquad t = 1, ..., T+1, \tag{4.44}$$

where

$$c_t = (c_{t-1} + \zeta - \eta) \bmod \zeta = (c_0 + t(\zeta - \eta)) \bmod \zeta. \tag{4.45}$$

Since $Y_0 > s$, $c_0 \geq 0$ and $\zeta > \eta$, it always applies that $\hat{Y}_t^0 > s$.

The numerator c_t reflects the setup decisions in periods $1, ..., t$. Due to its definition in (4.45) $0 \leq c_t < \zeta$.

The fraction $\frac{c_t}{\eta}$ gives the surplus of the stock level because of a planned setup in period t in view of the initial stock level Y_0[12]. If this surplus is larger than the forecasted demand per period $\hat{D}$, then no setup has to be released in the next period. Otherwise an order takes place, because the starting inventory position in period $t+1$ is not larger than the reorder point.

A proof of the algorithm, which is done by induction, is given in Appendix C.6, pp.224. The algorithm proceeds as illustrated by the following example.

[11] Since $s < Y_0 \leq Q$ and $Q > \hat{D}$ it is evident that $n_t^0 = 1 \quad \forall \quad t$.

[12] Note that c_0 is a kind of correction term due to the different intervals for the initial stock level Y_0 (see 4.41).

Example: $Q = \frac{7}{3}\hat{D}$.

First, the setup decisions for $s < Y_0 \le s + \frac{1}{3}\hat{D}$ will be derived in detail, i.e. $\omega = 1$.

Then, $c_0 := \omega - 1 = 0$.

$$\begin{array}{llll}
\hat{Z}_1^0 = Y_0 - \hat{D} & c_0 < 3 & \Rightarrow \hat{q}_1^0 = \frac{7}{3}\hat{D} & \hat{Y}_1^0 = Y_0 + \frac{c_1}{3}\hat{D}, \\
 & & & c_1 = (1 \cdot 4) \bmod 7 = 4. \\
\hat{Z}_2^0 = Y_0 + \frac{4-3}{3}\hat{D} & c_1 > 3 & \Rightarrow \hat{q}_2^0 = 0 & \hat{Y}_2^0 = Y_0 + \frac{c_2}{3}\hat{D}, \\
 & & & c_2 = (2 \cdot 4) \bmod 7 = 1. \\
\hat{Z}_3^0 = Y_0 + \frac{1-3}{3}\hat{D} & c_2 < 3 & \Rightarrow \hat{q}_3^0 = \frac{7}{3}\hat{D} & \hat{Y}_3^0 = Y_0 + \frac{c_3}{3}\hat{D}, \\
 & & & c_3 = (3 \cdot 4) \bmod 7 = 5. \\
\hat{Z}_4^0 = Y_0 + \frac{5-3}{3}\hat{D} & c_3 > 3 & \Rightarrow \hat{q}_4^0 = 0 & \hat{Y}_4^0 = Y_0 + \frac{c_4}{3}\hat{D}, \\
 & & & c_4 = (4 \cdot 4) \bmod 7 = 2. \\
\hat{Z}_5^0 = Y_0 + \frac{2-3}{3}\hat{D} & c_4 < 3 & \Rightarrow \hat{q}_5^0 = \frac{7}{3}\hat{D} & \hat{Y}_5^0 = Y_0 + \frac{c_5}{3}\hat{D}, \\
 & & & c_5 = (5 \cdot 4) \bmod 7 = 6. \\
\hat{Z}_6^0 = Y_0 + \frac{6-3}{3}\hat{D} & c_5 > 3 & \Rightarrow \hat{q}_6^0 = 0 & \hat{Y}_6^0 = Y_0 + \frac{c_6}{3}\hat{D}, \\
 & & & c_6 = (6 \cdot 4) \bmod 7 = 3. \\
\hat{Z}_7^0 = Y_0 + \frac{3-3}{3}\hat{D} & c_6 = 3 & \Rightarrow \hat{q}_7^0 = 0 & \hat{Y}_7^0 = Y_0 + \frac{c_7}{3}\hat{D}, \\
 & & & c_7 = (7 \cdot 4) \bmod 7 = 0.
\end{array}$$

Since $\hat{Z}_8^0 = Y_0 + \frac{0-3}{3}\hat{D} = Y_0 - \hat{D} = \hat{Z}_1^0$ the setup decisions from period 1 to 7 will be repeated in periods 8 to 14, 15 to 21, and so on. In general, it can be shown that the setup decisions from period 1 to ζ will be repeated in periods $\zeta + 1, ..., 2\zeta; 2\zeta + 1, ..., 3\zeta$, and so on (as long as the stability horizon is not exceeded). A proof of this fact is given in the remarks on Algorithm I in Appendix C.6 (see Note 2, pp.228).

The results shown in Table 4.5 are obtained in the same manner.

In Table 4.5, the setup decisions for $s < Y_0 \le s + \frac{1}{3}\hat{D}$ (i.e. $\omega = 1$) from period 1 up to the end of the stability horizon will be repeated for $\omega = 4$ beginning with period 2 and for $\omega = 7$ starting with period 3. Similarly, the same property applies to the setup decisions in the case of $\omega = 2$ and $\omega = 3$, respectively. Moreover, as the initial stock level rises Y_0 by one unit of the demand per period, the original sequence of the setup decisions will be shifted by one period, i.e. the additional demand unit may be satisfied by the initial stock level. In general, the setups from period 1 up to $T + 1$ for a certain initial stock Y_0, i.e. for a given value of ω, will be repeated in periods Θ up to $T + 1$ for an initial stock level Y_0^+, for which the parameter ω^+ is given by $(\Theta - 1)\eta + \omega$. Then, from period 1 up to $\Theta - 1$ no setups are scheduled. A

Table 4.5. Example: Order releases in planning cycle 0 for (s, nQ) policy

	weights	1	a	a^2	a^3	a^4	a^5	a^6	a^7	a^8....
ω	period	1	2	3	4	5	6	7	8	9....
1	$s < Y_0 \leq s + \frac{1}{3}\hat{D}$	1	0	1	0	1	0	0	| ...	...
2	$s + \frac{1}{3}\hat{D} < Y_0 \leq s + \frac{2}{3}\hat{D}$	1	0	1	0	0	1	0	| ...	...
3	$s + \frac{2}{3}\hat{D} < Y_0 \leq s + \hat{D}$	1	0	0	1	0	1	0	| ...	...
4	$s + \hat{D} < Y_0 \leq s + \frac{4}{3}\hat{D}$	0	| 1	0	1	0	1	0	0	| ...
5	$s + \frac{4}{3}\hat{D} < Y_0 \leq s + \frac{5}{3}\hat{D}$	0	| 1	0	1	0	0	1	0	| ...
6	$s + \frac{5}{3}\hat{D} < Y_0 \leq s + 2\hat{D}$	0	| 1	0	0	1	0	1	0	| ...
7	$s + 2\hat{D} < Y_0 \leq s + Q$	0	0	| 1	0	1	0	1	0	0 | ...

proof of this fact is given in the notes on Algorithm I in Appendix C.6 (see Note 3, pp.228).

Cycle 1:

In order to determine the setup decisions in planning cycle 1 it is necessary to differentiate between two demand cases, i.e. $D_0 \geq Y_0 - s$ and $D_0 < Y_0 - s$.

Case 1: $D_0 \geq Y_0 - s$

If the realized demand is sufficiently large, then an order takes place in the first period of planning cycle 1:

$$Z_1 = Y_0 - D_0 \leq s \qquad \Rightarrow q_1 = n_1(D_0)Q,$$

where n_1 depends on D_0 as follows: $n_1(D_0) = ||\lceil \frac{s - Y_0 + D_0}{Q} \rceil||$, i.e. for each possible demand realization D_0 and all (given) values of s, Y_0 and Q the corresponding value of $n_1(D_0)$ can be determined. Again $Q = \frac{\zeta}{\eta}\hat{D}$. For the sake notational clarity, only n_1 will be written in this study, instead of the complete expression $n_1(D_0)$.

Thus we can divide the region $Y_0 - s \leq D_0 \leq \infty$ into several intervals depending on $n_1 \in I\!N$, i.e.

$$Y_0 - s + (n_1 - 1)Q \leq D_0 < Y_0 - s + n_1 Q. \tag{4.46}$$

Then, the stock level after replenishment is given by

$$Y_1 = Y_0 - D_0 + n_1 Q > s. \tag{4.47}$$

To derive the planned setups in the following periods, the same analysis is used as for the determination of the planned order decisions in planning cycle

0. The region $Y_0 - s + (n_1 - 1)Q \leq D_0 < Y_0 - s + n_1 Q$ is divided into several intervals $Y_0 - s + (\frac{\zeta}{\eta} n_1 - \frac{\omega}{\eta})\hat{D} \leq D_0 < Y_0 - s + (\frac{\zeta}{\eta} n_1 - \frac{\omega - 1}{\eta})\hat{D}$ with $\omega = 1, ..., \zeta$.

Now, the setup decisions in planning cycle 1 from period 2 up to $T + 1$ can be determined using the following algorithm.

Algorithm II

For

$$Y_0 - s + (\frac{\zeta}{\eta} n_1 - \frac{\omega}{\eta})\hat{D} \leq D_0 < Y_0 - s + (\frac{\zeta}{\eta} n_1 - \frac{\omega - 1}{\eta})\hat{D} \quad \text{with} \quad \omega = 1, ..., \zeta, \tag{4.48}$$

we get:

The inventory position at the beginning of period t is given by

$$\hat{Z}_t^1 = Y_0 + (\frac{c_{t-1} - c_1 - \eta}{\eta} + n_1 \frac{\zeta}{\eta})\hat{D} - D_0 \qquad \forall \qquad t = 2, ..., T + 1. \tag{4.49}$$

Then, it is evident that

$$\left.\begin{array}{lll} \text{if} \quad c_{t-1} < \eta, & \text{then} & \hat{q}_t^1 = \frac{\zeta}{\eta}\hat{D} > 0 \\ \text{if} \quad c_{t-1} \geq \eta, & \text{then} & \hat{q}_t^1 = 0 \end{array}\right\} \quad \forall \quad t = 2, ..., T + 1. \tag{4.50}$$

Thus we get

$$\hat{Y}_t^1 = Y_0 + (\frac{c_t - c_1}{\eta} + n_1 \frac{\zeta}{\eta})\hat{D} - D_0 \qquad \forall \qquad t = 2, ..., T + 1, \tag{4.51}$$

where

$$c_t = (c_{t-1} + \zeta - \eta) \bmod \zeta = (c_1 + (t - 1)(\zeta - \eta)) \bmod \zeta \tag{4.52}$$

and $c_1 := \omega - 1$.

The explanation of this algorithm is similar to the comments on Algorithm I.

With $\check{s} := s + D_0 - n_1 Q$ we get from (4.48) that $\check{s} + \frac{\omega - 1}{\eta}\hat{D} < Y_0 \leq \check{s} + \frac{\omega}{\eta}\hat{D}$ with $\omega = 1, ..., \zeta$. Since $s + D_0 - n_1 Q < Y_0 \leq s + D_0 - n_1 Q$ (see 4.46) it is also true that $\check{s} < Y_0 \leq \check{s} + Q$.
The setup decisions in planning cycle 1 for $t = 2, 3, ..., T + 1$ can therefore be determined with the same algorithm as for planning cycle 0 for $t = 1, 2, ..., T + 1$. It is only necessary to substitute the formulas in (4.42)–(4.44) by (4.49)–(4.51) due to the different stock level after replenishment in the first period (see 4.47). Moreover, the determination of c_t must be adjusted.

Case 2: $D_0 < Y_0 - s$

If realized demand is sufficiently low, then no setup occurs in the first period of planning cycle 1.

$$Z_1 = Y_0 - D_0 > s \qquad \Rightarrow q_1 = 0 \qquad \text{and} \qquad Y_1 = Y_0 - D_0.$$

In order to determine the setup decisions in the following periods in demand case 2 the same algorithm is used as in demand case 1 where $n_1 := 0$ was set.

Algorithm III

For

$$Y_0 - s - \tfrac{\omega}{\eta}\hat{D} \leq D_0 < Y_0 - s - \tfrac{\omega-1}{\eta}\hat{D} \quad \text{with} \quad \omega = 1, ..., \zeta - 1,$$

and

$$0 \leq D_0 < Y_0 - s - \tfrac{\zeta-1}{\eta}\hat{D} \quad \text{with} \quad \omega = \zeta, \tag{4.53}$$

we get[13]:

The inventory position at the beginning of period t is given by

$$\hat{Z}_t^1 = Y_0 + \frac{c_{t-1} - c_1 - \eta}{\eta}\hat{D} - D_0 \qquad \forall \qquad t = 2, ..., T+1. \tag{4.54}$$

Then, it is evident that

$$\begin{array}{lll} \text{if } c_{t-1} < \eta, & \text{then } \hat{q}_t^1 = \frac{\zeta}{\eta}\hat{D} > 0 & \\ & & \forall\ t = 2, ..., T+1. \\ \text{if } c_{t-1} \geq \eta, & \text{then } \hat{q}_t^1 = 0 & \end{array} \tag{4.55}$$

Thus we get

$$\hat{Y}_t^1 = Y_0 + \frac{c_t - c_1}{\eta}\hat{D} - D_0 \qquad \forall \qquad t = 2, ..., T+1, \tag{4.56}$$

where

$$c_t = (c_{t-1} + \zeta - \eta) \bmod \zeta = (c_1 + (t-1)(\zeta - \eta)) \bmod \zeta \tag{4.57}$$

and $c_1 := \omega - 1$.

Using these algorithms for this example gives the results as shown in Table 4.6.

It is evident that the planned setups in cycle 1 for $D_0 \geq Y_0 - s$ from period 2 up to the end of the stability horizon are identical to the planned setups in

[13] Because of non-negative demand we have to adopt the left-hand side of the last interval.

planning cycle 0 from period 1 up to T. The same applies to $D_0 < Y_0 - s$ (see Algorithm I – III). In the first case in period 1 of cycle 1 an order takes place whereas in the latter one in the first period no setup is planned for release.

Table 4.6. Example: Order releases in planning cycle 1 for (s, nQ) policy

κ	weights / period	1 / 1	a / 2	a^2 / 3	a^3 / 4	a^4 / 5	a^5 / 6	a^6 / 7	a^7 / 8	a^8 / 9	... / ...
	$D_0 \geq V_0$ $(n_1 \in I\!N)$, i.e. ϑ=1										
1	$V_0 + \frac{(7n_1-1)\hat{D}}{3} \leq D_0 < V_0 + \frac{7n_1\hat{D}}{3}$	1	1	0	1	0	1	0	0	......	
2	$V_0 + \frac{(7n_1-2)\hat{D}}{3} \leq D_0 < V_0 + \frac{(7n_1-1)\hat{D}}{3}$	1	1	0	1	0	0	1	0	......	
3	$V_0 + \frac{(7n_1-3)\hat{D}}{3} \leq D_0 < V_0 + \frac{(7n_1-2)\hat{D}}{3}$	1	1	0	0	1	0	1	0	......	
4	$V_0 + \frac{(7n_1-4)\hat{D}}{3} \leq D_0 < V_0 + \frac{(7n_1-3)\hat{D}}{3}$	1	0	1	0	1	0	1	0	0	...
5	$V_0 + \frac{(7n_1-5)\hat{D}}{3} \leq D_0 < V_0 + \frac{(7n_1-4)\hat{D}}{3}$	1	0	1	0	1	0	0	1	0	...
6	$V_0 + \frac{(7n_1-6)\hat{D}}{3} \leq D_0 < V_0 + \frac{(7n_1-5)\hat{D}}{3}$	1	0	1	0	0	1	0	1	0	...
7	$V_0 + \frac{(7n_1-7)\hat{D}}{3} \leq D_0 < V_0 + \frac{(7n_1-6)\hat{D}}{3}$	1	0	0	1	0	1	0	1	0	0
	$D_0 < V_0$, i.e. ϑ=2										
1	$V_0 - \frac{1}{3}\hat{D} \leq D_0 < V_0$	0	1	0	1	0	1	0	0	......	
2	$V_0 - \frac{2}{3}\hat{D} \leq D_0 < V_0 - \frac{1}{3}\hat{D}$	0	1	0	1	0	0	1	0	......	
3	$V_0 - \hat{D} \leq D_0 < V_0 - \frac{2}{3}\hat{D}$	0	1	0	0	1	0	1	0	......	
4	$V_0 - \frac{4}{3}\hat{D} \leq D_0 < V_0 - \hat{D}$	0	0	1	0	1	0	1	0	0	...
5	$V_0 - \frac{5}{3}\hat{D} \leq D_0 < V_0 - \frac{4}{3}\hat{D}$	0	0	1	0	1	0	0	1	0	...
6	$V_0 - 2\hat{D} \leq D_0 < V_0 - \frac{5}{3}\hat{D}$	0	0	1	0	0	1	0	1	0	...
7	$0 \leq D_0 < V_0 - 2\hat{D}$	0	0	0	1	0	1	0	1	0	0

where $V_0 := Y_0 - s$

Analogous to Case A, it is possible to define stability quotients, which are denoted by $\beta^{\omega}_{\vartheta,\kappa}$. They are given by:

$$\beta^{\omega}_{\vartheta,\kappa} = \frac{\text{weighted no. of periods with same setups in demand case } \vartheta, \kappa\text{; inventory case } \omega}{\text{weighted total number of periods which can be compared}},$$

where $\omega = 1, 2, ..., \zeta$; $\vartheta = 1$ for $D_0 \geq Y_0 - s$ and $\vartheta = 2$ for $D_0 < Y_0 - s$, respectively.
For $\vartheta = 1$ we get $\kappa = 1, 2, ..., \zeta$, whereas in the case of $\vartheta = 2$, $\kappa \leq \omega$ applies.

Unfortunately, closed-form expressions cannot be derived for the stability quotients as in Case A with $Q \leq \hat{D}$, or as for an (s, S) policy.

Thus we determine these stability quotients using Algorithm I–III and comparing the matching setup decisions within the stability horizon[14]. For $Q = \frac{7}{3}\hat{D}$ and $T = 5, a \to 1$ we obtain e.g. $\bar{\beta}^5_{2,4} = \frac{1}{5}$, because for $\omega = 5$ we get from Table 4.5 the setup decisions "01010" and for $\vartheta = 2, \kappa = 4$ we find in Table 4.6 the sequence "00101".

Now, the setup-stability can be determined in the case of $Q = \frac{\varsigma}{\eta}\hat{D}$ by[15]

$$\begin{aligned}\pi^B_{s,nQ} = \sum_{\omega=1}^{\varsigma} \int_{\frac{\omega-1}{\eta}\hat{D}}^{\frac{\omega}{\eta}\hat{D}} \Bigg\{ \sum_{n_1=1}^{\infty} \Bigg[\sum_{\kappa=1}^{\varsigma} \beta^{\omega}_{1,\kappa} \Big(&\Phi_D(Y_0 - s + \frac{n_1\varsigma - (\kappa-1)}{\eta}\hat{D}) \\ &-\Phi_D(Y_0 - s + \frac{n_1\varsigma - \kappa}{\eta}\hat{D})\Big)\Bigg] \\ &+ \sum_{\kappa=1}^{\omega-1} \beta^{\omega}_{2,\kappa} \Big(\Phi_D(Y_0 - s - \frac{\kappa-1}{\eta}\hat{D}) - \Phi_D(Y_0 - s - \frac{\kappa}{\eta}\hat{D})\Big) \\ &+ \beta^{\omega}_{2,\omega} \Phi_D(Y_0 - s - \frac{\omega-1}{\eta}\hat{D})\Bigg\} dF_Y(Y_0).\end{aligned} \tag{4.58}$$

The stability in (4.58) is defined by weighting the stability quotients with the corresponding demand probabilities for all possible values of the initial stock level $(s < Y_0 \leq s + Q)$.
For $n_1 \to \infty$, the limiting values of the cdf are always considered in the further analysis.

---

[14] In order to determine the stability quotient for each value of ω, ϑ and κ the nervousness measure in (3.4) is used together with our stability measure in (3.5).

[15] As mentioned before, we define $\sum_{\kappa=1}^{0} \beta^{\omega}_{2,\kappa}[\Phi_D(Y_0 - s - \frac{\kappa-1}{\eta}\hat{D}) - \Phi_D(Y_0 - s - \frac{\kappa}{\eta}\hat{D})] :=$ 0. Furthermore, notice that n_1 in the first line of (4.58) depends on stochastic demand D_0 and stochastic initial stock Y_0, see p.86.

4.2.2.3 Summary of General Results

For further analysis, the expressions in (4.7) and (4.15) are transformed for the (s, S) policy and (4.39) and (4.58) for the (s, nQ) policy, respectively. Therefore Y is replaced by $X = s + Q - Y = S - Y$ (omitting index "0" for notational simplicity). Here, X represents the difference between maximum and actual stock at the beginning of a steady-state period (see De Kok and Inderfurth [32]). Since $s \leq Y \leq s + Q$, it is true that $0 \leq X \leq Q$.
In the case of an (s, S) control rule, (4.7) can be written as

$$\pi^A_{s,S} = \int_0^Q \{\alpha_1[1 - \Phi_D(Q - x)] + \alpha_2 \Phi_D(Q - x)\} dF_X(x). \tag{4.59}$$

Similarly, (4.15) yields to

$$\begin{aligned}
\pi^B_{s,S} = \Bigg\{ \sum_{\tau=1}^{l-1} \int_{Q-\tau\hat{D}}^{Q-(\tau-1)\hat{D}} & \{\beta_1^\tau[1 - \Phi_D(Q - x)] \\
& + \sum_{\theta=2}^{\tau} \beta_\theta^\tau [\Phi_D(Q - x - (\theta - 2)\hat{D}) - \Phi_D(Q - x - (\theta - 1)\hat{D})] \\
& + \beta_{\tau+1}^\tau \Phi_D(Q - x - (\tau - 1)\hat{D})\} \qquad\qquad (4.60) \\
+ \int_0^{Q-(l-1)\hat{D}} & \{\beta_1^l[1 - \Phi_D(Q - x)] \\
& + \sum_{\theta=2}^{l} \beta_\theta^l [\Phi_D(Q - x - (\theta - 2)\hat{D}) - \Phi_D(Q - x - (\theta - 1)\hat{D})] \\
& + \beta_{l+1}^l \Phi_D(Q - x - (l - 1)\hat{D})\} \Bigg\} dF_X(x)
\end{aligned}$$

$$\forall \quad (l-1)\hat{D} < Q \leq l\hat{D} \quad \text{with} \quad l \in I\!N \setminus \{0, 1\}.$$

For an (s, nQ) policy we get for (4.39) that

$$\pi^A_{s,nQ} = \int_0^Q \{\alpha_1[1 - \Phi_D(Q - x)] + \alpha_2 \Phi_D(Q - x)\} dF_X(x), \tag{4.61}$$

and for (4.58) we obtain that

$$\pi^B_{s,nQ} = \sum_{\omega=1}^{\zeta} \int\limits_{Q-\frac{\omega}{\eta}\hat{D}}^{Q-\frac{\omega-1}{\eta}\hat{D}} \Bigg\{ \sum_{n_1=1}^{\infty} \Bigg[\sum_{\kappa=1}^{\zeta} \beta^{\omega}_{1,\kappa} (\Phi_D(Q - x + \frac{n_1\zeta - (\kappa-1)}{\eta}\hat{D}) - \Phi_D(Q - x + \frac{n_1\zeta - \kappa}{\eta}\hat{D}))\Bigg] \quad (4.62)$$
$$+ \sum_{\kappa=1}^{\omega-1} \beta^{\omega}_{2,\kappa} (\Phi_D(Q - x - \frac{\kappa-1}{\eta}\hat{D}) - \Phi_D(Q - x - \frac{\kappa}{\eta}\hat{D}))$$
$$+ \beta^{\omega}_{2,\omega} \Phi_D(Q - x - \frac{\omega-1}{\eta}\hat{D}) \Bigg\} dF_X(x).$$

Using the results from (4.59) and (4.60) and inserting the expressions for the corresponding stability quotients, it is evident that planning stability $\pi_{s,S}$ can be written as

$$\pi_{s,S} = \begin{cases} \pi^A_{s,S} & \text{for } \; 0 < Q \leq \hat{D} \\ \pi^B_{s,S} & \text{for } \; Q > \hat{D}. \end{cases} \quad (4.63)$$

Analogously, (4.61) and (4.62) with the matching stability quotients show that

$$\pi_{s,nQ} = \begin{cases} \pi^A_{s,nQ} & \text{for } \; 0 < Q \leq \hat{D} \\ \pi^B_{s,nQ} & \text{for } \; Q > \hat{D}. \end{cases} \quad (4.64)$$

As mentioned in Section 3.4.1, De Kok and Inderfurth [32] have analyzed ***short-term stability***. It is evident that their analysis is a special case of the analysis presented in the previous sections with $T = 1$. For both policies, in Case A $\alpha_1 = 1$ and $\alpha_2 = 0$.
For the (s, S) control rule, the short-term consideration implies that in the case of $Q > \hat{D}$, the parameter l is equal to 2. Then, the matching stability quotients are given by $\beta^1_1 = \beta^2_2 = 1$, $\beta^2_1 = \beta^1_2 = 0$, and $\beta^2_3 = 1$. Thus (4.60) shows that

$$\pi_{s,S}(T=1) = \begin{cases} \int\limits_0^Q (1 - \Phi_D(Q - x)) dF_X(x) & \text{if } 0 < Q \leq \hat{D} \\ \Bigg\{ \int\limits_{Q-\hat{D}}^{Q} (1 - \Phi_D(Q - x)) + \int\limits_0^{Q-\hat{D}} \Phi_D(Q - x) \Bigg\} dF_X(x), \text{else.} \end{cases} \quad (4.65)$$

In the case of an (s, nQ) policy with $T = 1$ for $Q > \hat{D}$, it is no longer necessary to assume that $Q/\hat{D}$ is a rational number. We find a setup in cycle

0for $s < Y_0 \leq s + \hat{D}$, whereas for $s + \hat{D} < Y_0 < s + Q$ no setup is planned to be released. Analogously, we find in cycle 1 a setup if $D_0 \leq Y_0 - s$, and no setup otherwise (see also De Kok and Inderfurth [32]). Thus we have

$$\pi^B_{s,nQ}(T=1) = \int_s^{s+\hat{D}} \{[1 - \Phi_D(Y-s)] + \int_{s+\hat{D}}^{s+Q} \Phi_D(Y-s)\} dF_Y(Y).$$

With $X = s + Q - Y$ we find exactly the same result as for the (s, S) policy (see also De Kok and Inderfurth [32], pp.62.), i.e.

$$\pi_{s,nQ}(T=1) = \begin{cases} \int_0^Q (1 - \Phi_D(Q-x)) dF_X(x) & \text{if } 0 < Q \leq \hat{D} \\ \left\{ \int_{Q-\hat{D}}^{Q} (1 - \Phi_D(Q-x)) + \int_0^{Q-\hat{D}} \Phi_D(Q-x) \right\} dF_X(x), & \text{else.} \end{cases} \tag{4.66}$$

Nevertheless, because of the different cdf's of stock after replenishment ($F_X(.)$), the level of stability differs for both inventory control rules.

Since for both policies the cdf $F_X(.)$ does not depend on the reorder point s (see Hadley and Whitin [47]), it follows that the size of the reorder point has no impact on the level of the long-term setup-oriented planning stability (just like in the case of the short-term consideration, see De Kok and Inderfurth [32]). The reorder point only influences the level of the inventory process, but a change of the reorder point does not lead to a shift in planned setup sequences. This means that by adjusting the reorder point, stock-out probability and costs can be influenced, whereas nervousness of the planning system will not be affected.
The planning stability of both inventory control rules only depends on the lot size parameters $S-s$ or Q, the length of the stability horizon (T) as well as the weighting of the periods within the stability horizon (a), and the projected and expected demand ($\hat{D}, \bar{D}$), respectively. Thus $\pi_{s,S} = \pi_{s,S}(S-s, T, a, \hat{D}, \bar{D})$ and $\pi_{s,nQ} = \pi_{s,nQ}(Q, T, a, \hat{D}, \bar{D})$.

4.3 Properties of Setup Stability

This section illustrates the general forms of the stability functions in (4.63) and (4.64). Therefore three different types of demand distribution are considered, namely a special case of Mixed-Erlang distributed demand, exponentially distributed demand[16], and hyper-exponentially distributed demand. The demand distributions are characterized by their expected value

[16] Note that exponentially distributed demand is a special case of Mixed-Erlang distributed demand.

$\mathbb{E}(D) = \bar{D}$ and their coefficient of variation $c_D = \frac{\sigma(D)}{\bar{D}}$ where $\sigma(D)$ represents the standard deviation in demand. The assumption of these types of demand distributions is necessary because of the cdf of $F_X(x)$ for an (s, S) policy (for details see Section 4.3.1). For other demand distributions, the expressions in (4.63) are not tractable. However, for the (s, nQ) inventory control rule, other kinds of demand distributions are also analytically tractable. But since we want to compare setup stability of (s, S) and (s, nQ) control rules, we have to use the same assumptions and, consequently, identical demand distributions.

An Erlang-k (E_k) distributed random variable can be represented as the sum of k independent exponentially distributed random variables with the same mean value (see Tijms [128], pp.358). A generalized Erlangian distribution is formed by a random sum of exponentially distributed components. When these components have the same mean value, such a distribution can be used to approximate arbitrarily closely any distribution with its mass on the positive half-axis. Later, this study considers a special case of mixtures of Erlangian distributions, i.e. the $E_{k-1,k}$ distribution which is defined as a mixture of E_{k-1} and E_k distribution with the same scale parameters. The cdf of an $E_{k-1,k}$ distribution has the following form (see Appendix A.1):

$$\Phi_D(x) = 1 - p\sum_{i=0}^{k-2} e^{-\mu x}\frac{(\mu x)^i}{i!} - (1-p)\sum_{i=0}^{k-1} e^{-\mu x}\frac{(\mu x)^i}{i!}. \tag{4.67}$$

For $E_{k-1,k}$ distributions, only coefficients of variation between 0 and 1 can be achieved. It is true that (see Tijms [128], p.358)

$$\begin{aligned} \tfrac{1}{k} \leq c_D^2 &\leq \tfrac{1}{k-1}, \\ p = \tfrac{1}{1+c_D^2}&[kc_D^2 - \sqrt{k(1+c_D^2) - k^2 c_D^2}], \\ \mu &= \tfrac{k-p}{\bar{D}}. \end{aligned} \tag{4.68}$$

For $c_D^2 = 1$, i.e. exponentially distributed demand, in (4.68) it is true that $k = 2$, $p = 1$ and $\mu = \frac{1}{\bar{D}}$. Thus (4.67) gives

$$\Phi_D(x) = 1 - e^{-\frac{1}{\bar{D}}x}. \tag{4.69}$$

A commonly used representation for coefficients of variation greater than one is a mixture of two exponential distributions with different mean values (see Tijms [128], pp.359). The distribution of such a mixture is called hyper-exponential (H_2) distribution (of order two), and its cdf is given by (see Appendix A.2)

$$\Phi_D(x) = 1 - pe^{-\mu_1 x} - (1-p)e^{-\mu_2 x}. \tag{4.70}$$

For given $\bar{D}$ and $c_D^2 > 1$ we obtain (see [128], p.359)

$$p = \tfrac{1}{2}\left(1 + \sqrt{\tfrac{c_D^2 - 1}{c_D^2 + 1}}\right), \qquad \mu_1 = \tfrac{2p}{\bar{D}}, \quad \mu_2 = \tfrac{2(1-p)}{\bar{D}}. \tag{4.71}$$

Later in this study, closed-form expressions for setup stability of both policies are presented for the demand distributions mentioned above.

4.3.1 Stability Functions for Specific Demand Distributions

4.3.1.1 (s, S) Policy

For the (s, S) control rule the cdf of X is given by (see Tijms [128])

$$F_X(x) = \frac{M(x)}{M(Q)} \qquad 0 \leq x \leq Q, \tag{4.72}$$

where the renewal function $M(.)$ is defined as

$$M(x) = \sum_{n=0}^{\infty} \Phi_D^{n*}(x). \tag{4.73}$$

Then, (4.59) and (4.60) indicate that (see Appendices B.1.1 and B.1.2, respectively)

$$\pi_{s,S} = \begin{cases} \alpha_1 \frac{1}{M(Q)} + \alpha_2\left(1 - \frac{1}{M(Q)}\right) & \text{for } 0 < Q \leq \hat{D} \\[2ex] \left\{ \sum\limits_{\tau=1}^{l-1} \left[\int\limits_{Q-\tau\hat{D}}^{Q-(\tau-1)\hat{D}} \left(\beta_1^{\tau} + \sum\limits_{\theta=2}^{\tau+1} (\beta_\theta^{\tau} - \beta_{\theta-1}^{\tau}) \Phi_D(Q - x - (\theta-2)\hat{D}) \right) dM(x) \right] \right. \\ \left. + \int\limits_0^{Q-(l-1)\hat{D}} \left(\beta_1^{l} + \sum\limits_{\theta=2}^{l+1} (\beta_\theta^{l} - \beta_{\theta-1}^{l}) \Phi_D(Q - x - (\theta-2)\hat{D}) \right) dM(x) \right\} \frac{1}{M(Q)} \\ \qquad \text{for } \quad (l-1)\hat{D} < Q \leq l\hat{D} \quad \text{with} \quad l \in I\!N \setminus \{0, 1\}, \end{cases} \tag{4.74}$$

where the α- and β-quotients depend on T and a as derived in Section 4.2.2.

In general, both expressions for $Q \leq \hat{D}$ as well as for $Q > \hat{D}$ in (4.74) are intractable, because there are no tractable expressions for $M(.)$ except for special cases. In Appendix A an exact expression is presented for $M(x)$ for the case that the demand is distributed according to a so-called K_2-distribution. De Kok [30] shows that, in this case, the exact expression for $M(x)$ is defined by

$$M(x) = 1 + \frac{x}{I\!E(D)} + \gamma(1 - e^{-\rho x}),\ x \geq 0, \tag{4.75}$$

where γ and ρ are some constants. The rhs of (4.75) is a practically useful approximation for arbitrary renewal functions if γ and ρ are determined appropriately. In De Kok and Inderfurth [32] expressions for γ and ρ are given which are also presented in Appendix A.
Note that for the short-term stability as in [32], the expressions in (4.74) can be simplified to (see Appendix B.5)

$$\pi_{s,S}(T=1) = \begin{cases} \frac{1}{M(Q)} & \text{if } 0 < Q \leq \hat{D} \\ \left\{1 - M(Q-\hat{D}) + 2\int\limits_0^{Q-\hat{D}} \Phi_D(Q-x)dM(x)\right\}\frac{1}{M(Q)}, & \text{else.} \end{cases} \tag{4.76}$$

Obviously, the terms in (4.76) are identical to the results in De Kok and Inderfurth [32], pp.63.

4.3.1.2 (s, nQ) Policy

For an (s, nQ) control rule, the cdf of X is given by (see Hadley and Whitin [47], pp.257)

$$F_X(x) = \frac{x}{Q} \qquad 0 \leq x \leq Q. \tag{4.77}$$

With (4.61) and (4.62) this leads to (see Appendices C.1.1 and C.1.2)

$$\pi_{s,nQ} = \begin{cases} 1 - \frac{1-\alpha_2}{Q}\int\limits_0^Q \Phi_D(x)dx & \text{for } 0 < Q \leq \hat{D} \\ \frac{\eta}{\zeta\hat{D}}\Bigg\{\sum\limits_{\omega=1}^{\zeta}\int\limits_{\frac{\omega-1}{\eta}\hat{D}}^{\frac{\omega}{\eta}\hat{D}}\Bigg[\sum\limits_{n_1=1}^{\infty}\Bigg(\sum\limits_{\kappa=1}^{\zeta}\beta_{1,\kappa}^{\omega}\Big(\Phi_D(x+\frac{n_1\zeta-(\kappa-1)}{\eta}\hat{D}) \\ \qquad -\Phi_D(x+\frac{n_1\zeta-\kappa}{\eta}\hat{D})\Big)\Bigg) \\ \quad +\sum\limits_{\kappa=1}^{\omega-1}\beta_{2,\kappa}^{\omega}\Big(\Phi_D(x-\frac{\kappa-1}{\eta}\hat{D}) - \Phi_D(x-\frac{\kappa}{\eta}\hat{D})\Big) \\ \quad +\beta_{2,\omega}^{\omega}\Phi_D(x-\frac{\omega-1}{\eta}\hat{D})\Bigg]dx\Bigg\} \\ \quad \text{for } Q = \frac{\zeta}{\eta}\hat{D} \text{ with } \zeta,\eta \in \mathcal{N} \text{ and } \zeta > \eta, \end{cases} \tag{4.78}$$

where the α- and β-values depend on T and a as derived in Section 4.2.2.

In order to get the values of ζ and η for given lot size (and forecasted demand per period), the greatest common divisor (gcd) of the numerator (num) and denominator (denom) of Q is determined: $gcd(num(Q), denom(Q))$. Then, $\bar{\zeta} = \frac{num(Q)}{gcd(num(Q),denom(Q))}$ and $\bar{\eta} = \frac{denom(Q)}{gcd(num(Q),denom(Q))}\hat{D}$ are set. Now, if possible, the gcd of $\bar{\zeta}$ and $\bar{\eta}$, is determined again and the result is $\zeta = \frac{\bar{\zeta}}{gcd(\bar{\zeta},\bar{\eta})}$, $\eta = \frac{\bar{\eta}}{gcd(\bar{\zeta},\bar{\eta})}$. For instance, for $Q = \frac{40}{12}$ and $\hat{D} = 2$ we obtain $gcd(40, 12) = 4$ which leads to $\bar{\zeta} = 10$ and $\bar{\eta} = 6$. Thus we get $\zeta = \frac{10}{2} = 5$ and $\eta = \frac{6}{2} = 3$.

For the short-term consideration it follows that (see also Appendix C.5)

$$\pi_{s,nQ}(T=1) = \begin{cases} 1 - \frac{1}{Q}\int\limits_0^Q \Phi_D(x)dx & \text{for } 0 < Q \leq \hat{D} \\ \frac{1}{Q}\left\{\hat{D} - \int\limits_0^Q \Phi_D(x)dx + 2\int\limits_{\hat{D}}^Q \Phi_D(x)dx\right\} & \text{for } Q > \hat{D} \end{cases} \tag{4.79}$$

which is exactly the same as in De Kok and Inderfurth [32], pp.62.

Later in this study, some numerical examples are presented in order to gain an insight into the influence of the critical parameters on the stability measure in (4.74) and (4.78). It is assumed that $\Phi_D(.)$ is Erlangian, exponentially as well as hyper-exponentially distributed (see (4.67) – (4.70)). For this class of distributions, closed-form expressions have been derived for $\pi_{s,S}$ in (4.74) and $\pi_{s,nQ}$ in (4.78), respectively. They can be found in Appendices B.2 – B.4 for the (s, S) control rule and in Appendices C.2 – C.4 in the case of an (s, nQ) policy.

4.3.1.3 Basic Scenario for the Analysis of Stability Functions

A basic scenario is used for the subsequent numerical examples. The expected value of demand is chosen with $\bar{D} = 1$, and the forecasted demand is assumed to correspond to its expected value[17], i.e. $\hat{D} = \bar{D}$[18]. Furthermore, several (squared) coefficients of demand variation are considered, namely $c_D^2 = 0.05, 0.25$ (Erlangian distributed demand), $c_D^2 = 1.00$, and $c_D^2 = 2.00$ (exponentially and hyper-exponentially distributed demand, respectively). The shapes of the matching density functions for these distributions are

[17] Section 4.3.5 examines the influence of forecast errors on stability, including an analysis of how stability develops if the forecasted demand deviates from its expectation.

[18] For the (s, S) policy $\hat{D} = 1$ means that $l = Q$.

shown in Figure 4.3.

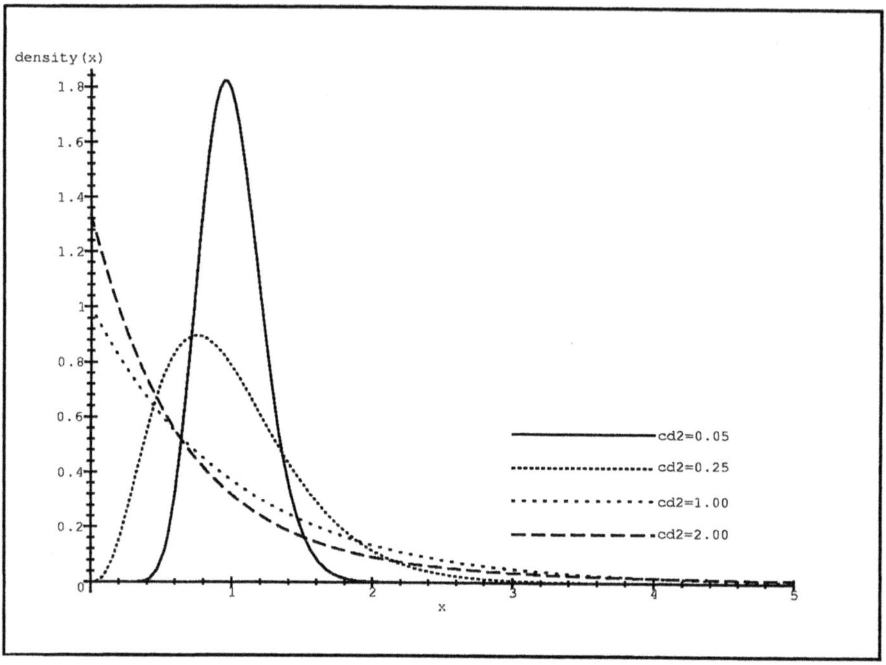

Figure 4.3. Density of underlying demand distributions

The stability horizon is supposed to consist of 6 periods, i.e. $T = 5$, and all periods are weighted equally[19], i.e. $a \to 1$. For an (s, nQ) policy in the region $Q > \hat{D}$, the analysis is restricted to lot sizes which consist of rational numbers (see Section 4.2.2). Therefore, for each stability function in the subsequent sections, 672 lot sizes Q with corresponding stability values have been determined by applying the following procedure: vary the denominator η of $Q = \frac{\zeta}{\eta}\hat{D}$ from 1 to 10 and calculate stability for 228 different values of Q with $\zeta = \eta + 1$ to $10 \cdot \eta$. For $\eta = 11, ..., 20$, $\zeta = \eta + 1, ..., 5 \cdot \eta$ is set, which leads to 384 additional lot sizes and matching stability values. In the following some of the values of the lot sizes have been noted as decimal numbers in order to ensure a better comparison of the results.

[19] In Section 4.3.3, these parameters are also varied in order to analyze the influence of T and a on stability.

4.3.2 Lot-Sizing and Demand Uncertainty Effects

First, we are interested in the development of the stability function with varying minimum lot size Q and demand variability c_D^2 for a finite stability horizon of 6 periods. The demand is forecasted by its expected value, i.e. $\hat{D} = \bar{D} = 1$.
In Figure 4.4 the shape of the stability function for the aforementioned different values of c_D^2 for an (s, nQ) policy is depicted whereas Figure 4.5 illustrates the stability function for an (s, S) policy.

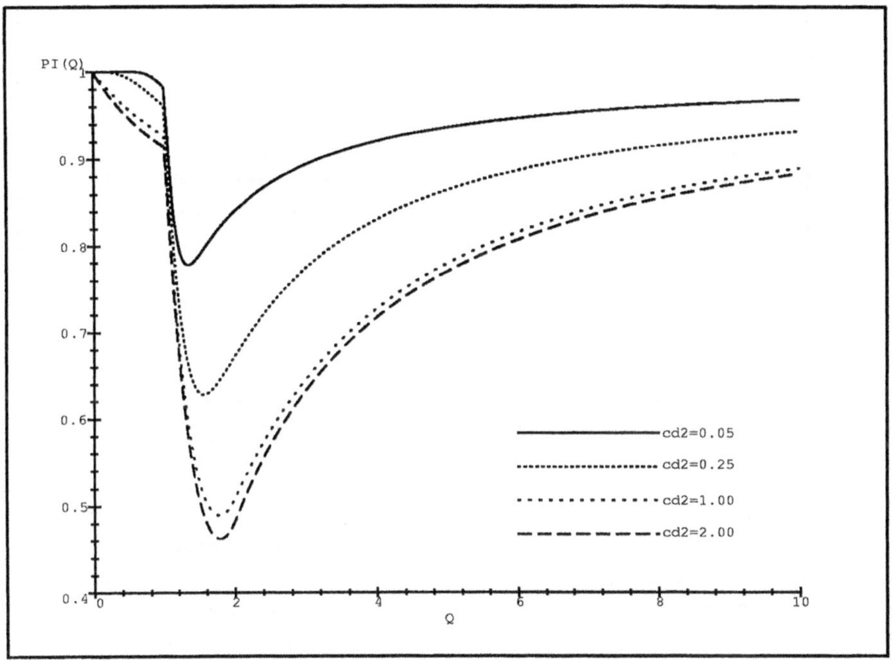

Figure 4.4. Stability function of an (s, nQ) policy for different values of c_D^2

Regarding the (minimum) lot size Q in the case of $Q \leq \hat{D}$ for both policies and for all values of c_D^2, planning stability decreases with Q approaching $\hat{D}$. For $Q > \hat{D}$, in the case of an (s, nQ) policy, stability is first reduced and reaches its minimum for values of Q which are slightly larger than the forecasted demand per period. Here, depending on demand uncertainty, minimum stability is reached for lot sizes of approximately $1.3 - 1.8$. As the minimum lot size increases, the level of stability enlarges, because periods with setups will occur more seldom, so the number of situations which may create nervousness is reduced. Thus, planning stability approaches 100 % with Q tending to infinity.

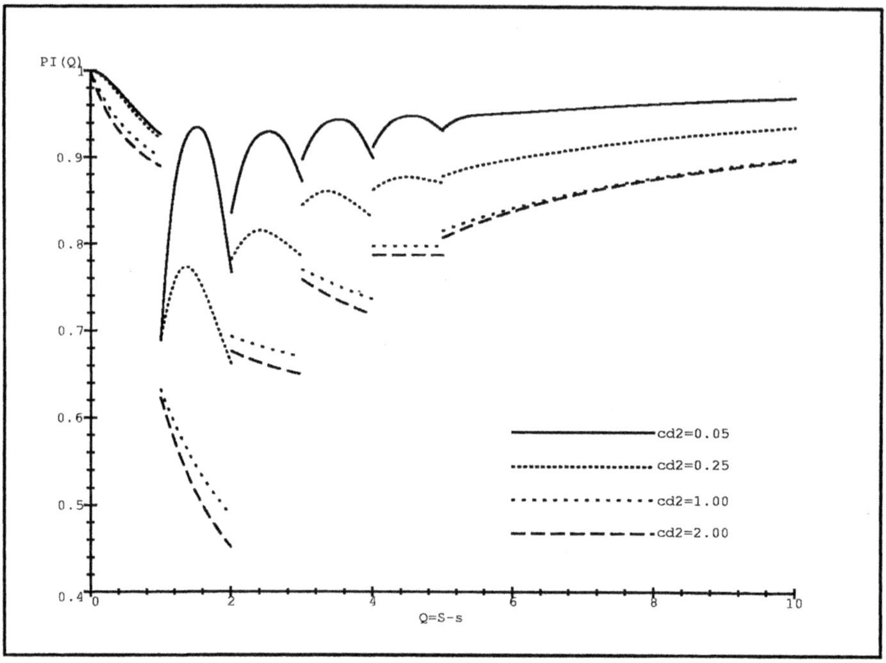

Figure 4.5. Stability function of an (s, S) policy for different values of c_D^2

This also applies to an (s, S) policy, but contrary to an (s, nQ) policy in $Q = \hat{D}$, the stability function is discontinuous. An increase of Q slightly higher than $\hat{D}$ leads to a significant reduction in the stability of approximately $30 - 40\%$ depending on depending on the demand variability. Moreover, for $Q \in ((l-1)\hat{D}, l\hat{D}]$ with $1 < l \leq T$ the stability function is discontinuous at lot size levels which correspond to multiples of the forecasted demand per period, i.e. $Q = 1, 2, 3, 4$ and 5. In these points of discontinuity, the stability function has *local minima* and increases by jumps. In the case of $l > T$, i.e. $Q > 5$, it is continuous, strictly increasing and concave. The continuous shape of the stability function in this region can be explained as follows: Since for $l > T$ the values of the stability quotients do not change with an increase in lot size Q, the stability function has to be continuous (see Table 4.2). For $l > T$ it is true that $L = 0$, and therefore the values of the corresponding stability quotients are given as $\bar{\beta}_\tau^\tau = 1$, $\bar{\beta}_\theta^\tau = \frac{T-2}{T}$ (for all $\theta = 1, ..., \tau - 1$; $\tau = 2, ..., l$), $\bar{\beta}_{\tau+1}^\tau = \frac{T-2}{T}$ (for all $\tau = 1, ..., l-1$), and $\beta_{l+1}^l = 1$ (see case (*iv*) in Table 4.4). In contrast to this for $1 < l \leq T$, an enhancement of l leads to an additional non-setup decision, and consequently to a change of the stability quotients, e.g. for $l = T$ we get $\bar{\beta}_\tau^\tau = 1$, $\bar{\beta}_\theta^\tau = \frac{l-2}{l}$ (for all $\theta = 1, ..., \tau - 1$; $\tau = 2, ..., l$), $\bar{\beta}_{\tau+1}^\tau = \frac{l-2}{l}$ (for all $\tau = 1, ..., l - 1$), and $\beta_6^5 = \frac{4}{5}$ (see case (*v*) in Table 4.4).

Similarly, for the other cases with $l < T$ the value of the stability quotients has to be adjusted according to the different cases in Table 4.4, thus leading to a discontinuous stability function.

In the case of exponentially distributed demand, the results concerning an (s, S) policy can even been shown and proved analytically. It is true that (see Appendix B.3.3)

1. The stability function is continuous, strictly decreasing and convex in Q for $Q \leq \hat{D}$ (see Section B.3.3).
2. The stability function is discontinuous in $Q = \hat{D}$ (see Section B.3.3).
3. For $Q > \hat{D}$ the development of the function $\pi^B_{s,S}(Q)$ depends on the ratio between the parameter l and the stability horizon parameter T:
   - 3.1. For $l > T$, i.e. $L = 0$, the stability function is continuous, strictly increasing and concave (see Section B.3.3, p.194).
   - 3.2. For $l \leq T$, i.e. $L > 0$, $\pi^B_{s,S}(Q)$ is discontinuous at lot size levels $l\hat{D}$ which are multiples of the expected demand per period. In the points of discontinuity the stability function increases by jumps (see Section B.3.3, pp.195). The development of the individual sections of $\pi^B_{s,S}(Q)$ limited by two consecutive points of discontinuity, further denoted by $\pi^B_l(Q)$, is characterized as follows (see Section B.3.3, pp.201):
     - A. For $\lceil \frac{T+1}{2} \rceil \leq l \leq T$, i.e. $L = 1$, we have to distinguish between four areas:
       - If $l = \frac{T+1}{2}$, then $\pi^B_l(Q)$ is a strictly increasing and concave function for $l > 6$; otherwise the individual segments of the stability function are strictly convex and decreasing.
       - If $\frac{T+1}{2} < l \leq \lfloor (2e^{-1} - e^{-2})T - 3(e^{-1} - e^{-2}) \rfloor$, then $\pi^B_l(Q)$ is strictly concave and increasing.
       - If $\lceil (2e^{-1} - e^{-2})T - 3(e^{-1} - e^{-2}) \rceil \leq l < T$, the single sections of $\pi^B_{s,S}(Q)$ are strictly convex and decreasing functions.
       - If $l = T$, then $\pi^B_l(Q)$ is strictly concave and increasing for $l > 4$. For other values of l it is a strictly convex and decreasing function in Q.
     - B. For $l < \frac{T+1}{2}$ the segments of $\pi^B_{s,S}(Q)$ are strictly decreasing and convex.
4. For $Q = 0$, and Q to infinity the planning stability approaches 100 % (see Section B.3.3, p.193, and Section B.3.3, p.194, respectively).
5. For $T > 1$, the minimum stability is reached at a critical lot size $Q = 2\hat{D}$ (see Section B.3.3, pp.203). For $T = 1$, minimum stability occurs for $Q = \hat{D}$ (see Inderfurth [61]).

Concerning the demand uncertainty for both control rules, planning stability significantly diminishes as demand variability rises. This is particularly true for $Q > \hat{D}$. Moreover, the location of minimum stability depends on the de-

mand uncertainty[20]. For both policies, the minimum of the stability function lies in the interval $Q \in (\hat{D}, 2\hat{D}]$.
In the case of an (s, nQ) policy, minimum stability is reached for lot sizes which are either equal to or a slightly larger than the forecasted demand per period. Here, for $c_D^2 = 0.05$, minimum stability is attained for $Q = 1.33 \cdot \hat{D}$[21]. With increasing c_D^2, the location of this minimum gets closer to $Q = 1.80 \cdot \hat{D}$[22] (see also Table 4.7). For an (s, S) policy, the ***global minimum*** is either reached for $Q = \hat{D}$, $Q \to \hat{D}$ (i.e. the global minimum lies in the interval $Q \in (\hat{D}, 2\hat{D}]$ and it is reached for lot sizes Q which are slightly larger than $\hat{D}$) or $Q = 2\hat{D}$ (see also Heisig [49]). Here, it is attained for $Q \to \hat{D}$ (with $\pi = 69.10$ %) if the demand uncertainty is very small ($c_D^2 = 0.05$). In all other cases it is attained for $Q = 2\hat{D}$ (see also Table 4.8). Furthermore, for $Q > \hat{D}$ the individual segments of the stability function limited by two consecutive points of discontinuity possess *local maxima* if the coefficient of variation is relatively small ($c_D^2 \leq 0.25$)[23]. Moreover, with increasing coefficient of demand variation, the location of these maxima in the matching interval gets closer to $Q \cong (l-1)\hat{D}$: for $c_D^2 = 0.05$, the local maxima are reached if the minimum lot size lies (approximately) in the middle of the corresponding interval, i.e. $Q \cong (l - \frac{1}{2})\hat{D}$, whereas in the case of $c_D^2 = 0.25$ for $Q \cong (l - \frac{2}{3})\hat{D}$ maximum stability is attained. If $c_D^2 \geq 1$, then the individual sections of the stability function are strictly decreasing, and no local maxima can be found. Comparing the shapes of the stability function for lot sizes $Q \in ((l-1)\hat{D}, l\hat{D}]$ with $1 < l \leq T$ with the development of the densities in Figure 4.3 we find that the shape of the stability function corresponds to a high degree with the shape of the matching density function.

Simulation studies show that the results here concerning the reorder quantity and the demand variability also apply to demand distributions of a beta type[24]. The basic scenario in Jensen [68] is characterized by a coefficient of demand variation of $c_D \cong 0.227$, i.e. $c_D^2 \cong 0.05$ (see Jensen [68], pp.162). Furthermore the stability horizon consists of 20 periods, and the forecasted

[20] Since the location of the (global) minimum also depends on the length of the stability horizon and the choice of the weight parameter, the topic of minimum planning stability will be investigated in Section 4.3.4 in detail.

[21] The minimum stability among the 672 calculated different lot sizes is attained for $Q = 1.33 \cdot \hat{D}$ with a stability level of 77.8 %. Nevertheless, the real minimum may deviate from this value, but as can be seen in Figure 4.4, this deviation will not be significantly large.

[22] For $c_D^2 = 0.25$, minimum stability is reached for $Q = 1.56 \cdot \hat{D}$ with $\pi = 62.8$ %, for $c_D^2 = 1.0$ it is attained for $Q = 1.78 \cdot \hat{D}$ ($\pi = 49.0$ %) and in the case of $c_D^2 = 2.0$ we find minimum stability for $Q = 1.79 \cdot \hat{D}$ with $\pi = 46.2$ %.

[23] Note that these maxima only occur as long as the parameter l does not exceed the horizon parameter T, i.e. for all $Q \in ((l-1)\hat{D}, l\hat{D}]$ with $1 < l \leq T$.

[24] The beta density is a two-parameter function which can assume quite a variety of different shapes where the specific values of the two parameters influence the skewness of the density function.

demand is equal to its expected value. In contrast to the numerical example in this study, it is found that $\hat{D} = 5$[25]. Then, for an (s, nQ) policy, the stability function is continuous and reaches its minimum for $Q \cong 6.5$ with a stability level of about 75 %. For an (s, S) policy, the stability function is discontinuous in $Q = l\hat{D}$ (for all $l \leq T$), and, additionally, in these points of discontinuity stability reaches local minima. The global minimum is attained for $Q = 5$. For $Q > 100$, i.e. $l > T$, the stability function is continuous (see Jensen ([68], pp.167).

Finally, the stability performances of both inventory control rules are to be compared directly (see Figures 4.6 and 4.7).

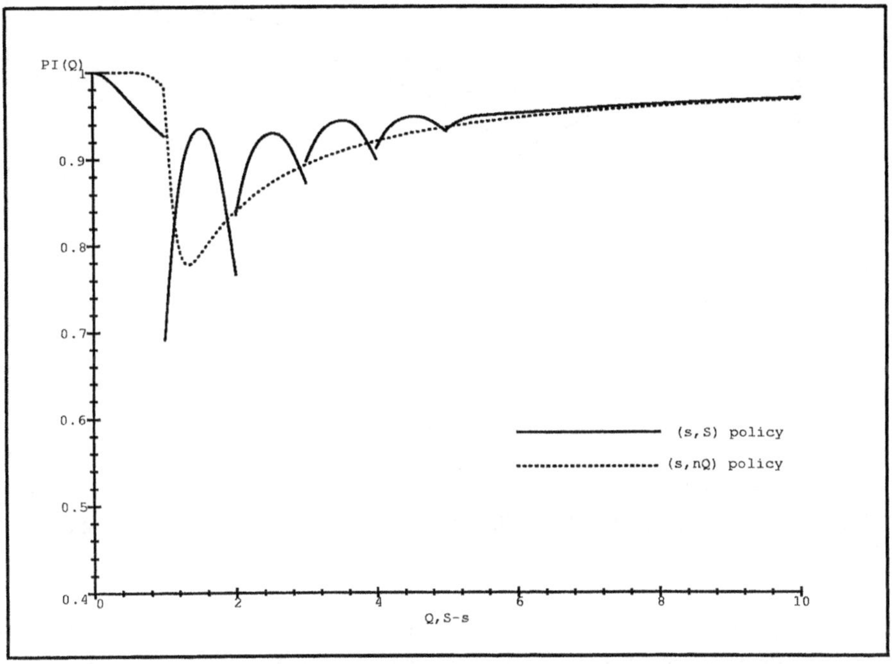

Figure 4.6. Comparison of stability functions of (s, S) and (s, nQ) policy (for $c_D^2 = 0.05$)

Considering the demand variability, it is true that stability decreases as demand uncertainty rises. Furthermore, the level of stability does not differ significantly in general. However due to the discontinuous shape of the stability function for an (s, S) policy in the region $l \leq T$, there are some lot sizes in which an (s, S) policy is superior to an (s, nQ) control rule, and vice versa. The better performance of an (s, S) policy occurs in particular for

[25] It has been decided that $\hat{D} = 1$ to keep computational effort on a minimum.

small demand variabilities if the lot size is chosen as one of the local maxima, e.g. for $c_D^2 = 0.05$ and $Q = 1.5$ we find $\pi_{s,S} = 93,5$ % and $\pi_{s,nQ} = 79,0$ %. As lot sizes increase, the superiority of the (s, S) policy for lot sizes which are set equal to the local maxima becomes less and less, and for large lot sizes with $l > T$, the shapes of the stability functions are very similar, and the differences in the levels of stability almost disappear.

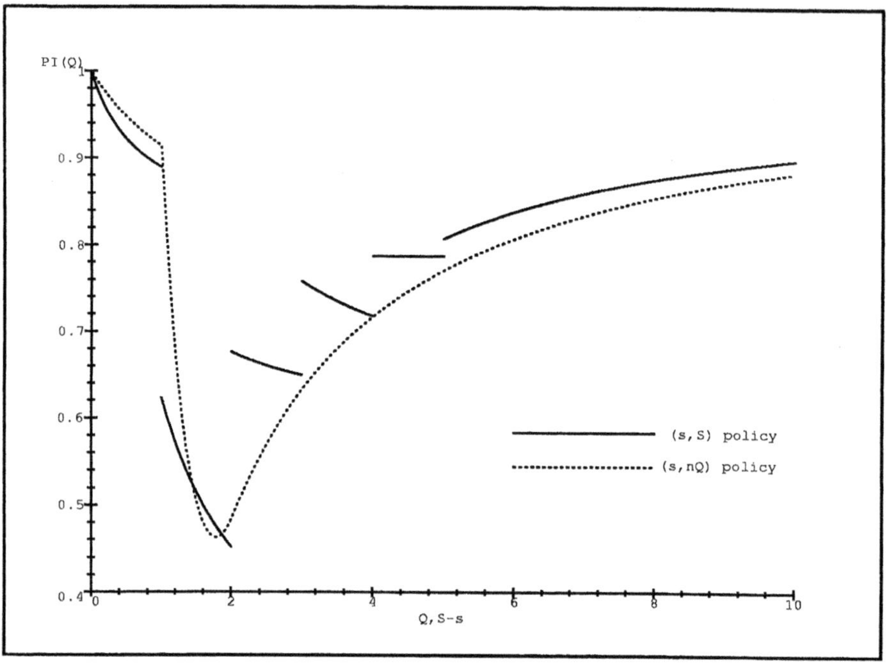

Figure 4.7. Comparison of stability functions of (s, S) and (s, nQ) policy (for $c_D^2 = 2.00$)

Comparing the the impact of the (minimum) lot size Q for both policies it can be seen that for an (s, nQ) policy, lot sizes which are equal to or slightly larger than the forecasted demand per period should not be chosen, whereas in the case of an (s, S) policy, the minimum reorder quantity should not be set to a multiple of the forecasted demand per period, in particular it should not be a slightly larger than or twice as large as forecasted demand e.g. 101 and 200 % would not be acceptable, but 180 % - though not ideal - would be acceptable. For an (s, S) policy, in any case an enhancement of Q just a bit from a multiple of the forecasted demand per period leads to a higher level of stability.

4.3.3 Influence of Stability Horizon and Weight Parameter

For $c_D^2 = 0.25$, the shape of the stability function for different stability horizons ($T = 1, 5$ and $T \to \infty$[26]) are depicted in Figure 4.8 and 4.9, respectively. The short-term consideration is also analyzed in De Kok and Inderfurth [32]. The shapes for $T = 1$ in Figures 4.8 and 4.9 correspond to the results given there.

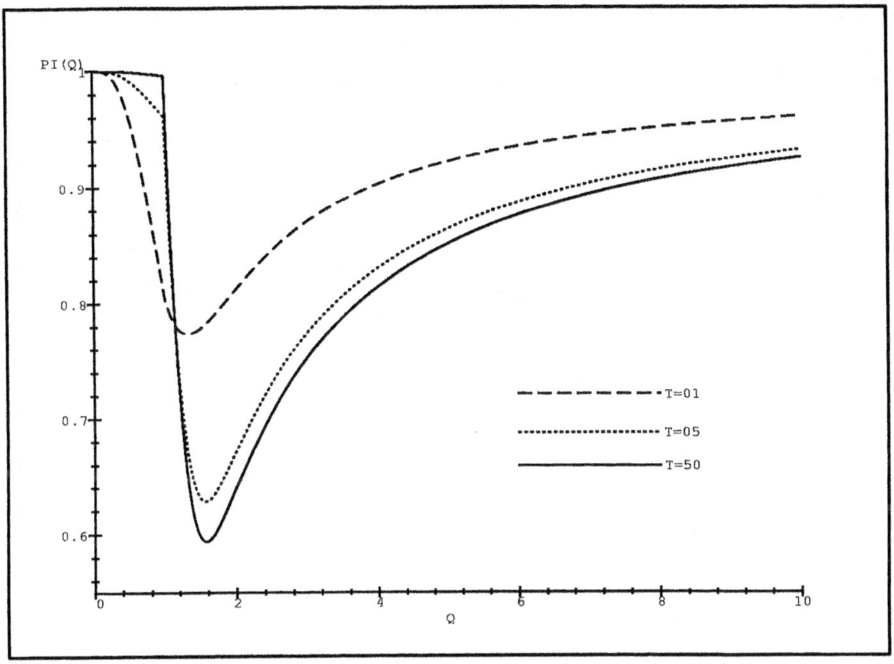

Figure 4.8. Stability function of an (s, nQ) policy for different planning stability horizons

In the region $Q \leq \hat{D}$ for both policies, planning stability decreases with reducing stability horizon (see Figures 4.8 and 4.9). Since the relevance of the single deviation in the planned order releases decreases as the horizon increases (see Table 4.1), the stability performance improves. For large horizons, a stability level of even 100 % is reached.

[26] In the case of an (s, nQ) policy, $T = 50$ is treated as infinite stability horizon. For an (s, S) policy, a closed-form expression for the stability function for $T \to \infty$ can be derived, because the stability quotients can be determined explicitly (see Section 4.2.2). Therefore for the (s, S) policy (4.74) together with (4.11) and (4.36)–(4.38) are used to calculate stability for $T \to \infty$.

The opposite generally applies to sufficiently large lot sizes[27] for $Q > \hat{D}$. In other words, as the horizon is increased, the stability performance of both inventory control rules worsens. This general tendency can be interpreted as follows: The measure of planning stability is given by relating the number of periods with changed setup decisions for two consecutive planning cycles to the total number of periods which can be compared. A change to a planned setup occurs if the actual demand in the first period of planning cycle 0 differs from its forecast. This deviation leads to a shift in the planned order releases in all succeeding periods. For relatively short stability horizons, these changes in later periods will be considered only partially, so that in the long run, stability decreases with rising horizon parameter T.

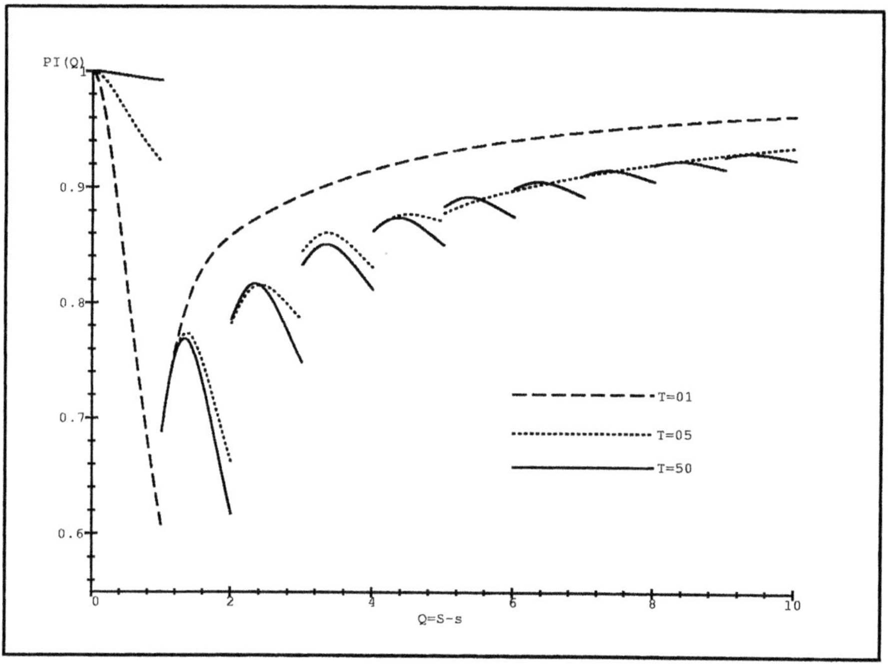

Figure 4.9. Stability function of an (s, S) policy for different planning stability horizons

Nevertheless, for an (s, S) policy for certain values of Q, the increase of the stability horizon may lead to a better stability performance, e.g. in Figure 4.9 for $Q \in (2, 2.4]$ or $Q \in (5, 5.5]$ the stability level for $T \to \infty$ is larger than for $T = 5$. An explanation of this phenomenon is given at the end of this section in connection with the analysis of the impact of the weight parameter. In

[27] For an (s, nQ) policy stability will increase with a reduction of the stability horizon if the lot size is larger than 1.26, whereas in the case of an (s, S) policy the critical minimum reorder quantity has to be larger than 8.

the case of an (s, nQ) policy, the different stability functions have one point of intersection which is attained approximately for $Q = 1.26$ with a stability level of approximately 77 %. Thus for lot sizes which are lower than this point of intersection, the increase of the stability horizon leads to a better stability performance, e.g. for Q close to $\hat{D}$ highest stability is attained for $T \to \infty$. With regard to the worst case performance of stability, for an (s, S) policy in the case of the short-term consideration, minimum stability is reached for $Q = \hat{D}$, whereas for all other considered stability horizons it is attained for $Q = 2\hat{D}$ (see also Table 4.8). In the case of an (s, nQ) policy, minimum stability is attained for $Q = 1.32 \cdot \hat{D}$ if $T = 1$. By increasing the stability horizon, the location of the minimum gets closer to $Q = 1.6 \cdot \hat{D}$ (see also Table 4.7).

Finally, it can also be stated that for both control rules, the influence of the length of the stability horizon on the stability values is reduced with increasing stability horizon, while the increase/reduction of stability for short stability horizons is relatively high. In Figures 4.8 and 4.9, the level of stability for $T = 5$ and $T \to \infty$ are quite similar, in particular for $Q > \hat{D}$ and an (s, nQ) policy, whereas there is also a considerable gap between the levels of stability for $T = 5$ and $T = 1$. Moreover, for the (s, S) rule, the shapes of the stability function look rather different.

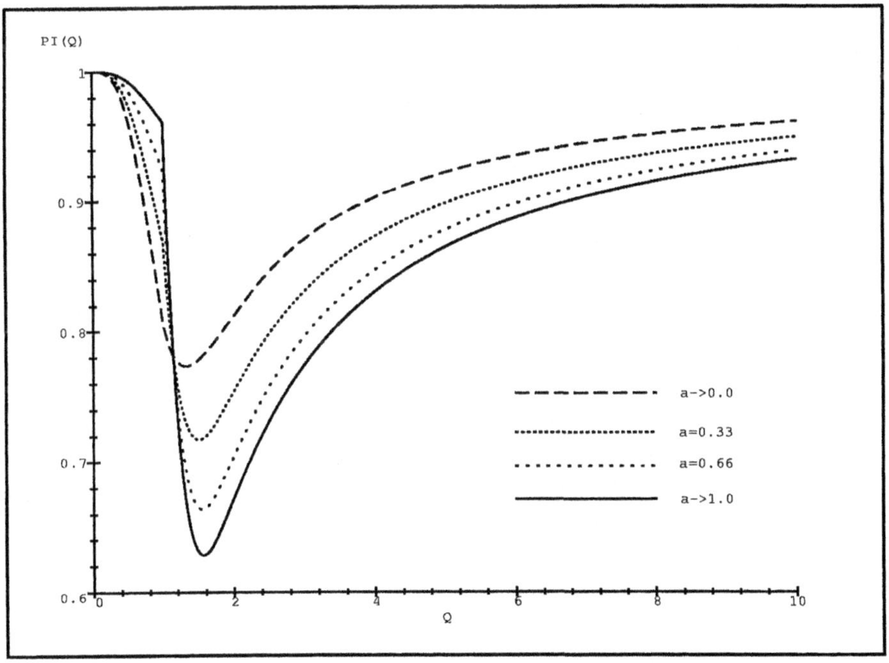

Figure 4.10. Stability function of an (s, nQ) policy with varying a

The shapes of the stability function for $T = 5$ and different values of the weight parameter ($a \to 0$, $a = \frac{1}{3}, \frac{2}{3}$ and $a \to 1$) are visualized in Figures 4.10 and 4.11 (with $c_D^2 = 0.25$). It is evident that for both policies, the case $a \to 0$ corresponds to the short-term consideration with $T = 1$ (see De Kok and Inderfurth [32], and Figures 4.8 and 4.9).

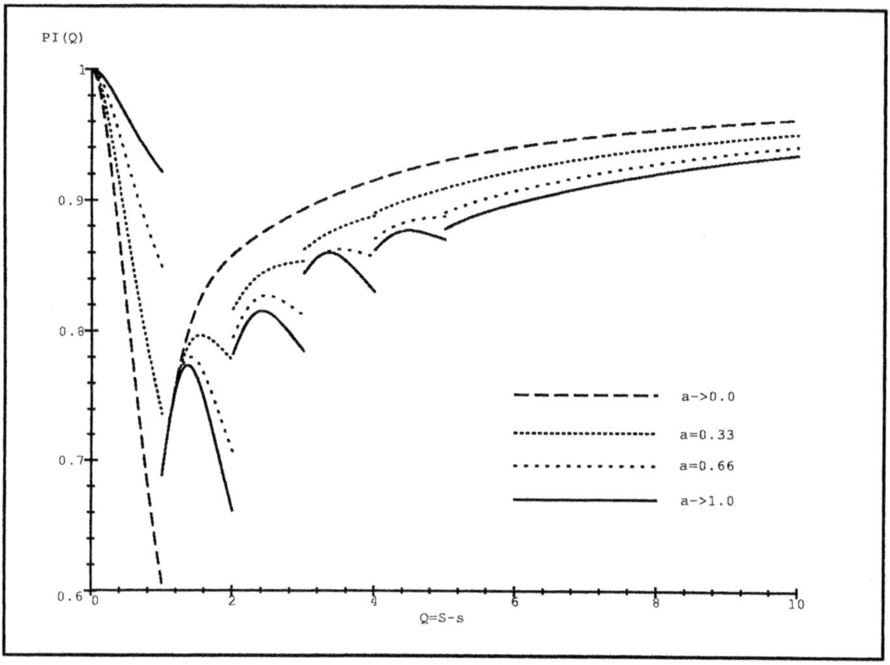

Figure 4.11. Stability function of an (s, S) policy with varying a

Figures 4.10 and 4.11 show almost the same results as for the variation of the stability horizon. For lot sizes which are not larger than the forecasted demand per period for both policies, planning stability decreases as the weight parameter is reduced.

By applying an (s, nQ) policy, it again becomes evident that the stability functions intersect at one point which has the same location as in Figure 4.8, i.e. $Q = 1.26$. For lot sizes which are larger than this critical value, an increase of the weight parameter leads to a reduction in planning stability.

For an (s, S) with $Q > \hat{D}$, stability always decreases with rising a. Thus this latter case is slightly different from an increase in the stability horizon, which may also lead to a better stability performance for some lot sizes. This behaviour of π, which at first glance may seem surprising, can be explained as follows. First, the reduction in planning stability for a given $Q/\hat{D}$-ratio (in the case of $Q > \hat{D}$) with rising weight parameter is clarified. For this reason,

the order sequences in both planning cycles for all values of the minimum lot size and for all possible initial stock levels must be analyzed (see Table 4.2): If we only consider setup changes in the first period of the stability horizon (i.e. $a \to 0$), then there are τ sequences with ***completely*** identical setups and one sequence with ***completely*** different planned order releases ($\tau = 2, .., l$). Since all periods except the first one are (approximately) weighted with zero, τ stability quotients take on values close to 1 and one equals (approximately) 0. As the weight parameter rises, the meaning of plan changes in later periods increases and, vice versa, the value of nearly every stability quotient decreases: For large values of a, which imply that all periods are (almost) equal in weight, identical planned order releases only occur if, in both planning cycles, the first setup takes place in the same period. This means that as the weight parameter increases, the number of stability quotients which are equal to one diminishes, up to a certain value of a (nearby 1) where only a single stability quotient equals one. Simultaneously, the stability quotient which has taken on a value of 0 for $a \to 0$ becomes larger[28]. Since the enhancement of this single stability quotient cannot compensate the reduction of the other ones, planning stability reduces as the weight parameter a increases for given $Q/\hat{D}$-ratios, and maximum stability is attained for the short-term consideration with $a \to 0$ or $T = 1$ (see also Figure 4.9).
It is still necessary to explain why, contrary to the strictly decreasing stability with rising weight parameter, for some values of $Q > \hat{D}$, stability may also increase with rising stability horizon. This is related to the fact that in the case of equally weighted periods, the order sequences are cut off rapidly, and the subsequent periods are not taken into account at all. For periods with different weights this effect is smoothed, and also the planned setup decisions of some weakly weighted periods play a role. Thus in the first (unweighted) case, the values of the stability quotients may change significantly, whereas for the latter, these changes are more moderate. Unfortunately, it is not possible to give a general statement for which parameter settings of $Q/\hat{D}$ with rising T an increase of stability occurs.

As shown in Section 4.3.2, the values of the stability quotients change as long as the $Q/\hat{D}$-ratio parameter l is smaller than the stability horizon. The introduction of a weight parameter cuts off some periods at the end of the regular stability horizon, in particular for small values of a, and leads to a quasi new, shorter stability horizon which is called T^{crit}. Thus in Figure 4.11 for $a = \frac{1}{3}$, the stability function is only discontinuous for $l \leq T^{crit} = 4$. The weights of period 1 up to T^{crit} are positive, whereas the weighting of the following periods is approximately equal to zero. This means that the values of the matching stability quotients change with an increase in the minimum lot size for all $l \leq T^{crit}$. If $l > T^{crit}$, then they are nearly constant, and the stability function has to be continuous.

---

[28] Note that this is true if $l > 2$. For $Q \in (\hat{D}, 2\hat{D}]$, the matching stability quotient is still equal to 0.

Comparing the results with respect to the influence of the stability horizon and weighting of periods for both policies, it is evident that the impact of both parameters is quite similar. In general, with rising T or a, respectively, planning stability increases for $Q \leq \hat{D}$, whereas for larger lot sizes the opposite applies. Nevertheless, it is also true to say that for the short-term consideration (i.e. $T = 1$ or $a \to 0$), the stability performance in the area $Q \cong \hat{D}$ for an (s, nQ) policy is significantly better than for an (s, S) policy (see also De Kok and Inderfurth [32]). For $T > 1$ no one of the considered control rules is superior to another with respect to its performance concerning the length of the stability horizon or the weighting of periods within this horizon.

4.3.4 Minimum Planning Stability

For an (s, nQ) policy, minimum stability is attained for lot sizes which are equal to or slightly larger than the forecasted demand per period, whereas for an (s, S) policy, minimum stability is reached either for $Q = \hat{D}$, $Q \to \hat{D}$ or $Q = 2\hat{D}$ (see also Heisig [49]).
It is intuitively clear that the location of the minimum planning stability depends on both the sequences of order decisions which are reflected by the stability quotients and the underlying demand distribution, which is characterized by its coefficient of demand variation. Tables 4.7 and 4.8 summarize the location of the global minimum for different values of T and c_D^2 for an (s, nQ) policy and an (s, S) control rule, respectively, where $\hat{D} = \bar{D}$ and $a \to 1$. As mentioned above, the behaviour of the stability function depends on the ratio between Q and $\hat{D}$. Consequently, as long as $\hat{D} = \bar{D}$ and for given stability horizon and weight parameter, stability only depends on the TBO. Therefore, in both tables we have depicted minimum stability in dependency on $Q/\hat{D}$. The terms in brackets represent the corresponding levels of minimum stability (in %)[29].
In the case of an (s, nQ) policy for the short-term consideration, minimum stability is reached for $Q = 1$ if demand is (hyper-)exponentially distributed, whereas for $c_D^2 < 1$ minimum stability is attained for lot sizes which are larger than the forecasted demand per period (see also De Kok and Inderfurth [32]). As demand uncertainty decreases, the location of the minimum at first departs more and more from $Q = \hat{D}$, but for $c_D^2 = 0.05$ it approaches $Q = \hat{D}$ once more. As seen in Section 4.3.2, as demand variability increases, the level of stability drops. Obviously, this also applies to the level of minimum stability. For $T > 1$, minimum stability lies around $Q = 1.8 \cdot \hat{D}$ for $c_D^2 \geq 1.0$,

[29] Minimum stability is depicted in dependency on the TBO, i.e. the ratio between the lot size Q and the expected demand per period ($\bar{D} = \hat{D}$). This means, e.g., for $T = 1$ and $c_D^2 = 0.05$ minimum stability is reached for $Q/\hat{D} = 1.261$ with a stability value of 87.3 % in case of an (s, nQ) policy (see Table 4.7), and for $Q/\hat{D} = 1$ with a stability value of 63.2 % in case of an (s, S) policy (see Table 4.8).

$Q = 1.7 \cdot \hat{D}$ for $c_D^2 = 0.5$, $Q = 1.6 \cdot \hat{D}$ for $c_D^2 = 0.25$ and $Q = 1.3 \cdot \hat{D}$ for $c_D^2 = 0.05$. As in the case of $T = 1$ for a given stability horizon, the level of minimum stability is reduced with rising demand uncertainty. Furthermore, the influence of the length of the stability horizon on the location of the minimum is more or less insignificant, e.g. in the case of $c_D^2 = 0.25$ for $T = 5$ minimum stability is reached for TBO= 1.56 and for $T = 50$ it is attained for a critical TBO which is only about 0.02 units larger, i.e. TBO$\cong$ 1.58. Besides, the change in the level of minimum stability is relatively moderate, in particular for low demand variations. If the stability horizon is increased from $T = 2$ to $T = 50$, then for $c_D^2 = 0.05$ minimum stability will be reduced by about 6 %, and for $c_D^2 = 0.25$ it will decrease by approximately 9.5 %.

Table 4.7. Minimum stability in the case of an (s, nQ) policy for different demand variabilities and stability horizons (with $\hat{D} = \bar{D}$ and $a \to 1$)

	c_D^2				
T	0.05	0.25	0.5	1.0	2.0
1	1.261 (87.3)	1.320 (77.4)	1.259 (71.5)	1.000 (63.2)	1.000 (56.9)
2	1.320 (81.4)	1.533 (68.6)	1.625 (62.5)	1.720 (56.1)	1.722 (53.7)
5	1.333 (77.8)	1.562 (62.8)	1.672 (56.4)	1.777 (49.0)	1.789 (46.2)
8	1.333 (76.9)	1.571 (61.4)	1.679 (54.5)	1.786 (47.2)	1.800 (44.3)
12	1.333 (76.4)	1.571 (60.6)	1.680 (53.6)	1.790 (46.2)	1.800 (43.3)
50	1.333 (75.6)	1.572 (59.4)	1.684 (52.2)	1.800 (44.6)	1.813 (41.6)

To summarize, minimum stability decreases for a given stability horizon with increasing demand uncertainty. For given demand variabilities, an increase in the stability horizon from $T = 1$ to $T = 2$ causes a more or less significant change in the location of the minimum stability as well as in its level. The larger c_D^2, the higher this change will be. A further increase of the stability horizon will not have such a large impact on minimum stability.

Most of the results for the (s, nQ) control rule also apply to the dependence of the location of minimum stability on c_D^2 and T in the case of an (s, S) policy. For small demand uncertainties and stability horizons, the global minimum is attained for $Q \cong \hat{D}$[30], and with increasing values of these critical parameters it is more often reached for larger values of the minimum reorder quantity, i.e. $Q = 2\hat{D}$. The level of minimum stability also decreases with rising c_D^2 and T, respectively.

Table 4.8. Minimum stability in the case of an (s, S) policy for different demand variabilities and stability horizons (with $\hat{D} = \bar{D}$ and $a \to 1$)

	c_D^2				
T	0.05	0.25	0.5	1.0	2.0
1	$\frac{Q}{\hat{D}} = 1$ (63.2)	$\frac{Q}{\hat{D}} = 1$ (60.6)	$\frac{Q}{\hat{D}} = 1$ (57.0)	$\frac{Q}{\hat{D}} = 1$ (50.0)	$\frac{Q}{\hat{D}} = 1$ (44.5)
2	$\frac{Q}{\hat{D}} \to 1$ (69.1)	$\frac{Q}{\hat{D}} \to 1$ (68.8)	$\frac{Q}{\hat{D}} = 2$ (66.6)	$\frac{Q}{\hat{D}} = 2$ (58.8)	$\frac{Q}{\hat{D}} = 2$ (56.2)
5	$\frac{Q}{\hat{D}} \to 1$ (69.1)	$\frac{Q}{\hat{D}} = 2$ (66.2)	$\frac{Q}{\hat{D}} = 2$ (58.5)	$\frac{Q}{\hat{D}} = 2$ (48.8)	$\frac{Q}{\hat{D}} = 2$ (45.1)
8	$\frac{Q}{\hat{D}} \to 1$ (69.1)	$\frac{Q}{\hat{D}} = 2$ (64.3)	$\frac{Q}{\hat{D}} = 2$ (56.3)	$\frac{Q}{\hat{D}} = 2$ (46.3)	$\frac{Q}{\hat{D}} = 2$ (42.2)
12	$\frac{Q}{\hat{D}} \to 1$ (69.1)	$\frac{Q}{\hat{D}} = 2$ (63.4)	$\frac{Q}{\hat{D}} = 2$ (55.1)	$\frac{Q}{\hat{D}} = 2$ (44.9)	$\frac{Q}{\hat{D}} = 2$ (40.7)
∞	$\frac{Q}{\hat{D}} \to 1$ (69.1)	$\frac{Q}{\hat{D}} = 2$ (61.2)	$\frac{Q}{\hat{D}} = 2$ (52.9)	$\frac{Q}{\hat{D}} = 2$ (42.2)	$\frac{Q}{\hat{D}} = 2$ (37.7)

In order to explain these results for an (s, S) policy, two effects must be considered. First, an examination of the stability horizon parameter effect which influences the value of the stability quotients. This will be followed by a detailed analysis of the impact of demand uncertainty.

For $Q \leq \hat{D}$, stability increases with an enlargement of the stability horizon parameter, because a setup is planned in nearly every period, no matter what the exact value of the initial stock level and the exact amount of realized demand may be (see Table 4.1). The planning stability of a critical lot size $Q = \hat{D}$ is therefore significantly lower for small stability horizons than for larger ones. Within the region $Q \leq \hat{D}$, stability reaches its minimum for $Q = \hat{D}$, because the larger the lot size, the higher the expected initial stock will be. Therefore, the probability of no setup in the first period of planning cycle 1 is greater.

[30] Note that contrary to the (s, nQ) policy for the short-term consideration with $T = 1$, minimum stability is always reached for $Q = \hat{D}$ (see also De Kok and Inderfurth [32]).

The corresponding order sequences for $\hat{D} < Q \leq 2\hat{D}$ are depicted in Table 4.9. For low initial stock levels, i.e. $Y_0 \leq s + \hat{D}$, there are either completely identical setup decisions or completely different planned order releases in each period of both planning cycles. This means that the stability quotients are either equal to one or equal to zero. The following applies for $Y_0 > s + \hat{D}$: If realized demand is sufficiently large ($D_0 \geq Y_0 - s$), then the planned setups are completely different. If it is moderate, i.e. $Y_0 - s - \hat{D} \leq D_0 < Y_0 - s$, then both sequences of order decisions are identical. If actual demand is very small, i.e. $0 \leq D_0 < Y_0 - s - \hat{D}$, then there is no setup in either planning cycle for the short-term consideration with $T = 1$, but with increasing weight parameter the matching stability quotient converges to zero. Altogether, one can conclude that for $Q \leq \hat{D}$ and $\hat{D} < Q \leq 2\hat{D}$, the length of the stability horizon only influences the value of two stability quotients, namely α_2 and β_3^2 where with rising T the first one rapidly increases and the latter decreases. The other stability quotients are, independent of the length of the stability horizon, either equal to one (α_1, β_1^1 and β_2^2) or equal to zero (β_2^1 and β_1^2).

Table 4.9. Order releases in consecutive planning cycles for (s, S) policy with $Q \in (\hat{D}, 2\hat{D}]$

period	1	2	3	4	5	6	7 ...		
cycle 0	1	0	1	0	1	0	1 ...	$s < Y_0 \leq s + \hat{D}$	$(\tau = 1)$
cycle 1	1	0	1	0	1	0	1 ...	if $D_0 \geq Y_0 - s$	$(\theta = 1)$
	0	1	0	1	0	1	0 ...	if $0 \leq D_0 < Y_0 - s$	$(\theta = 2)$
cycle 0	0	1	0	1	0	1	0 ...	$s + \hat{D} < Y_0 \leq s + Q$	$(\tau = l = 2)$
cycle 1	1	0	1	0	1	0	1 ...	if $D_0 \geq Y_0 - s$	$(\theta = 1)$
	0	1	0	1	0	1	0 ...	if $Y_0 - s - \hat{D} \leq D_0 < Y_0 - s$	$(\theta = 2)$
	0	0	1	0	1	0	1 ...	if $0 \leq D_0 < Y_0 - s - \hat{D}$	$(\theta = 3)$

Additionally, the effect of demand uncertainty influences the location of minimum stability as follows: For low coefficients of demand variation, the probability of small demand ($D_0 < Y_0 - s$) is relatively low, leading to a higher level of planning stability in the region $Q \leq \hat{D}$ because a setup in the first period of cycle 1 is relatively probable. In other words, the stability quotient α_2 is weighted weakly. The same applies to $Q \in (\hat{D}, 2\hat{D}]$ for relatively small initial stock levels where β_1^1 is weighted relatively high. For $s + \hat{D} < Y_0 \leq s + Q$, planning stability is relatively high for moderate demand. For large demand, i.e. $D_0 > Y_0 - s$, stability performance is relatively poor, and for very small demand the corresponding stability quotient β_3^2 depends on the length of the stability horizon as mentioned above.

The following results can be derived from the aforementioned arguments: If the demand density is extremely skewed to the right as for large coefficients of demand variation, then the probability of small demand is relatively high (see also Figure 4.3). For the short-term consideration for $\hat{D} < Q \leq 2\hat{D}$, this leads to a relatively high level of stability[31], whereas for $Q \in [0, \hat{D}]$ the planning stability is relatively low[32]. Therefore minimum stability is reached for critical lot sizes which correspond to the forecasted demand per period. However, this also applies to low demand variabilities like $c_D^2 = 0.25$ or 0.05, because the non-identical setups are still weighted weakly. Note that for large stability horizons, the influence of the demand uncertainty in the region $Q \leq \hat{D}$ is almost negligible, because both stability quotients are (approximately) equal to one. But even an increase from $T = 1$ to $T = 2$ leads to a complete change of the location of minimum stability. Minimum stability is always reached for lot sizes in $(\hat{D}, 2\hat{D}]$. On the one hand, this can be explained by the increase of α_2, and on the other hand, by the reduction of β_3^2. Thus we can conclude that the location of minimum stability is mainly driven by the change in the stability horizon.
Altogether, for the short-term consideration, the stability performance in the region $Q \leq \hat{D}$ is relatively poor, whereas for the opposite region stability is relatively high. Then, minimum planning stability is reached for $Q = \hat{D}$. With increasing T and c_D^2 the stability performance for $Q \in (\hat{D}, 2\hat{D}]$ gets poorer whereas stability for $Q \leq \hat{D}$ increases. Then, minimum stability is either reached for $Q \to \hat{D}$ or for $Q = 2\hat{D}$, depending on the demand uncertainty.

Comparing the level of minimum stability for both inventory control rules, it is clear that minimum stability for the short-term consideration is always greater for the (s, nQ) policy than for the (s, S) control rule. For $T > 1$, there appears to be no clear priority between the policies, e.g. for $c_D^2 = 0.05$ and $c_D^2 = 2.0$ this "worst-case performance" is better in the case of an (s, nQ) policy, whereas for $c_D^2 = 0.25$ and $c_D^2 = 0.5$ the (s, S) policy leads to a higher level of minimum stability.

In order to complete the analysis of minimum stability, the case of a given stability horizon with weighted periods is also considered. As intuitively clear, the influence of the weight parameter on minimum stability is very similar to the impact of the stability horizon (see Tables 4.10 and 4.11, respectively)[33].

[31] Note that the critical stability quotient β_3^2 is equal to one.

[32] Here, in contrast to $Q > \hat{D}$, the critical stability quotient α_2 takes on a value of 0.

[33] It is evident that for $a \to 0$, the results are exactly the same as for $T = 1$, and for $a \to 1$ the outcomes correspond to $T = 5$ (see Tables 4.7 and 4.8). Minimum

With increasing weight parameter, the location of minimum stability changes in the way that the lot sizes get larger (in the case of an (s, nQ) policy) or increase from $Q \cong \hat{D}$ to $Q = 2\hat{D}$ (for an (s, S) policy). Additionally, the level of minimum stability decreases.

Table 4.10. Minimum stability in the case of an (s, nQ) policy for different demand variabilities and weight parameters (with $\hat{D} = \bar{D}$ and $T = 5$)

	demand uncertainty c_D^2				
	0.05	0.25	0.5	1.0	2.0
$a \to 0$	1.261 (87.3)	1.320 (77.4)	1.259 (71.5)	1.000 (63.2)	1.000 (56.9)
$a = \frac{1}{3}$	1.300 (83.4)	1.500 (71.7)	1.583 (66.0)	1.650 (59.9)	1.632 (57.7)
$a = \frac{2}{3}$	1.333 (80.0)	1.545 (66.3)	1.647 (60.0)	1.750 (53.3)	1.750 (50.9)
$a \to 1$	1.333 (77.8)	1.562 (62.8)	1.672 (56.4)	1.777 (49.0)	1.789 (46.2)

For an (s, S) policy, in the case of relatively small weight parameters (like $a = \frac{1}{3}$) for high demand variabilities (as $c_D^2 \geq 0.5$), minimum stability is reached for lot sizes which correspond to the forecasted demand per period, i.e. $Q = \hat{D}$[34]. This is slightly different from the case of short stability horizons where for $c_D^2 \geq 0.5$ even for $T = 2$ minimum stability is attained for $Q = 2\hat{D}$. This effect occurs because low values of a correspond to a high degree to the short-term consideration with $T = 1$, where minimum stability is always reached for $Q = \hat{D}$. Since for low demand uncertainty, the probability of a setup in all periods of planning cycle 0 is comparably high (see Table 4.1), for $c_D^2 \leq 0.25$ even for small weights minimum stability is attained for $Q \in (\hat{D}, 2\hat{D}]$.

For an (s, nQ) policy in Table 4.10 only one case can be found in which the increase of the weight parameter leads to a higher level of minimum stability,

stability is again depicted in dependency on the TBO, i.e. the ratio between the lot size Q and the expected demand per period ($\bar{D} = \hat{D}$). This means, e.g., for $a \to 0$ and $c_D^2 = 0.05$ minimum stability is reached for $Q/\hat{D} = 1.261$ with a stability value of 87.3 % in case of an (s, nQ) policy (see Table 4.10), and for $Q/\hat{D} = 1$ with a stability value of 63.2 % in case of an (s, S) policy (see Table 4.11).

[34] In all other cases, minimum stability in attained for lot sizes $Q \in (\hat{D}, 2\hat{D}]$.

namely if we rise $a \to 0$ to $a = \frac{1}{3}$ for $c_D^2 = 2.0$. In contrast to this, an increase in the stability horizon causes a lower level of minimum stability in any case (see Table 4.7).

Table 4.11. Minimum stability in the case of an (s, S) policy for different demand variabilities and weight parameters (with $\hat{D} = \bar{D}$ and $T = 5$)

	demand uncertainty c_D^2				
	0.05	0.25	0.5	1.0	2.0
$a \to 0$	$\frac{Q}{\hat{D}} = 1$ (63.2)	$\frac{Q}{\hat{D}} = 1$ (60.6)	$\frac{Q}{\hat{D}} = 1$ (57.0)	$\frac{Q}{\hat{D}} = 1$ (50.0)	$\frac{Q}{\hat{D}} = 1$ (44.5)
$a = \frac{1}{3}$	$\frac{Q}{\hat{D}} \to 1$ (69.1)	$\frac{Q}{\hat{D}} \to 1$ (68.9)	$\frac{Q}{\hat{D}} = 1$ (67.7)	$\frac{Q}{\hat{D}} = 1$ (63.2)	$\frac{Q}{\hat{D}} = 1$ (62.2)
$a = \frac{2}{3}$	$\frac{Q}{\hat{D}} \to 1$ (69.1)	$\frac{Q}{\hat{D}} \to 1$ (68.9)	$\frac{Q}{\hat{D}} = 2$ (63.4)	$\frac{Q}{\hat{D}} = 2$ (54.9)	$\frac{Q}{\hat{D}} = 2$ (51.8)
$a \to 1$	$\frac{Q}{\hat{D}} \to 1$ (69.1)	$\frac{Q}{\hat{D}} = 2$ (66.2)	$\frac{Q}{\hat{D}} = 2$ (58.5)	$\frac{Q}{\hat{D}} = 2$ (48.8)	$\frac{Q}{\hat{D}} = 2$ (45.1)

4.3.5 Forecast Accuracy

Here, the influence of forecast errors[35] on planning stability is shown. The demand expectation is therefore fixed, and the value of the forecasted demand per period is varied. Without loss of generality we assume that $Q = 10$, $\bar{D} = 1$ and $T = 5$ with $a \to 1$.

Considering the case $Q \leq \hat{D}$, one finds that for an (s, S) as well as for an (s, nQ) control rule, the stability function does not depend on the value of the forecasted demand per period (see Equations (B.3), (B.11) and (B.43) in Appendix B, and Equations (C.4), (C.6) and (C.7) in Appendix C, respectively). Thus an increase or reduction of the forecasting value does not lead to a change in the stability level, i.e. planning stability with varying forecasts possesses a constant value which depends on c_D^2, $\bar{D}$, Q, T and a as shown in Section 4.3.2 and 4.3.3, respectively, but it is not influenced by $\hat{D}$ as long as $Q \leq \hat{D}$.

In this first scenario, $\hat{D}$ has been varied from 0.1 to 9.9[36]. Note that this

[35] A forecast error occurs if forecasted demand per period $\hat{D}$ deviates from expected demand per period $\bar{D}$.

[36] For $\hat{D} \geq 10$ a constant value of stability is found with $\pi_{s,nQ} \cong \pi_{s,S} \cong 0.82$, because in this case it holds that $Q \leq \hat{D}$.

kind of variation is only relevant from a theoretical point of view, because large forecast errors such as deviations of 100 % or even more between expected value of demand and projected demand should usually not occur[37]. The shape of the stability function for these different values of demand forecasts is visualized in Figures 4.12 and 4.13.

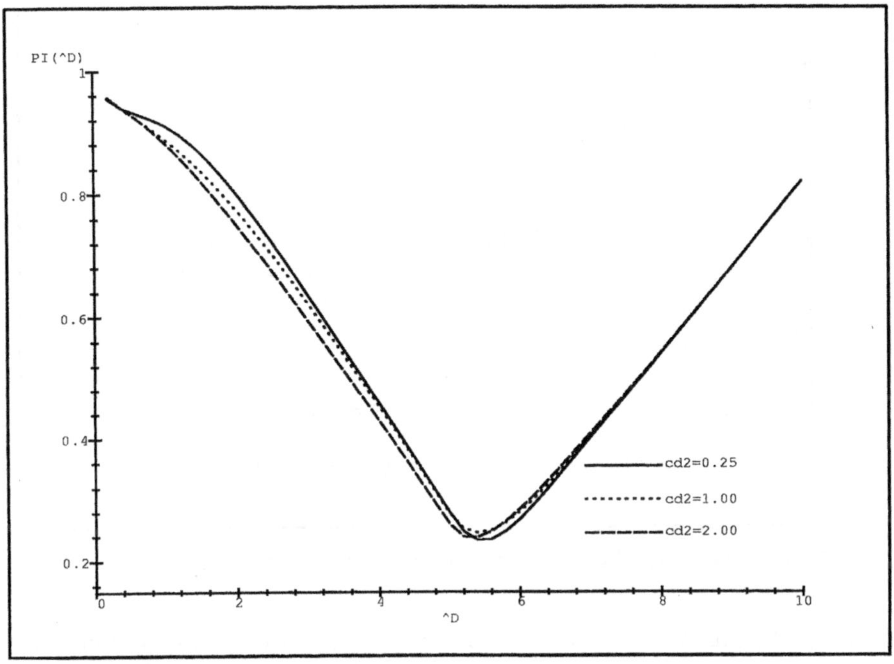

Figure 4.12. Stability function of an (s, nQ) policy with varying $\hat{D}$

In the case of an (s, nQ) policy, it is evident that, for given demand uncertainties with rising forecasted demand per period, at first planning stability decreases, but after reaching a specific value of minimum stability it increases (see Figure 4.12). The different locations of these minima – depending on c_D^2 – are around $\hat{D} = \frac{Q}{2}$. Here, minimum stability is attained for $\hat{D} = 5.5$ ($\pi = 23.33$ % for $c_D^2 = 0.25$), $\hat{D} = 5.4$ ($\pi = 24.62$ % for $c_D^2 = 1.0$) and $\hat{D} = 5.3$ ($\pi = 23.79$ % for $c_D^2 = 2.0$). Moreover, in Figure 4.12, forecasts which are in the neighborhood of or very much larger than the demand expectation lead to a high level of planning stability, i.e. for $\hat{D} \leq 1.8$ and $\hat{D} \geq 9.4$, stability levels which exceed 80 % can be found for all c_D^2-values under consideration. However, the latter case means that forecasted demand deviates from its ex-

[37] A detailed analysis of "realistic" forecasts errors is given at the end of this section.

pected value by more than 900 % which is not very realistic in practice.

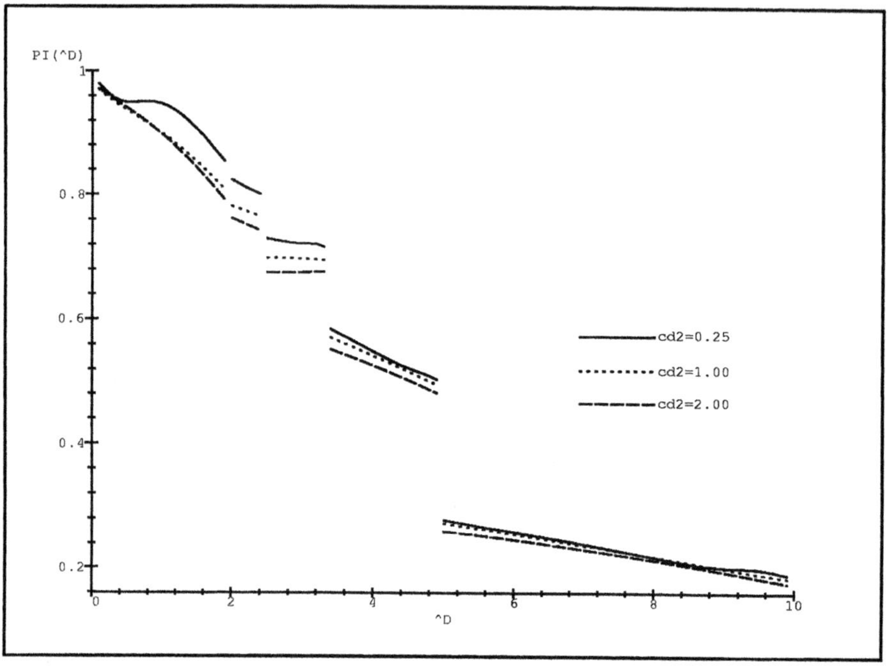

Figure 4.13. Stability function of an (s, S) policy with varying $\hat{D}$

For an (s, S) policy, it is clear that the stability function is discontinuous for lot sizes which correspond to a multiple of the forecasted demand per period. Analogously, in Figure 4.13 the stability function is discontinuous for $\hat{D} = \frac{10}{l}$ with $l \in \mathcal{N}$. Furthermore, minimum stability is attained for values of $\hat{D}$ which are slightly smaller than the minimum reorder quantity Q, i.e $\hat{D} \cong 9.99$ (see also Section 4.3.4). As for an (s, nQ) policy, forecasts which approximately meet the expected demand lead to a high level of planning stability. In the remaining interval, i.e $1.8 < \hat{D} < Q$, the stability performance is relatively poor, especially for values of $\hat{D}$ which belong to the interval $[\frac{Q}{2}, ..., Q)$.

As a first result it can be stated that a good forecasting process, i.e. $\hat{D} = \bar{D}$, leads to a high level of stability for $Q > \hat{D}$. Nevertheless, if the forecasts underestimate the expected demand, i.e. $\hat{D} < \bar{D}$, then the stability performance gets (slightly) better. This fact is related to the influence of the lot size: with decreasing forecasted demand per period and given value of Q, the number of planned setups decreases which leads to a better stability performance.
If the forecasts are only slightly lower than the underlying lot size, then for the (s, nQ) policy, stability is even higher than in the case of accurate forecasts, whereas for an (s, S) policy it reaches its minimum. These results are

also connected with the impact of the lot size: applying an (s, nQ) policy with $\hat{D}$ close to Q means that a setup is planned for release (see Section 3.1) in almost every period in the stability horizon. This means that situations which may create nervousness seldom occur. In most cases, using an (s, S) policy for $\hat{D} < Q \leq 2\hat{D}$ leads to (nearly) completely different planned setups in both planning cycles. The level of stability is therefore comparably low.

To get a better understanding of the influence of "realistic" forecast errors on stability, now only deviations within a range of 50% will be considered. It is again assumed that $T = 5$ with equally weighted periods. Furthermore, this analysis is generally restricted to exponentially distributed demand, i.e. $c_D^2 = 1.0$. We have chosen $\bar{D} = 1$ and varied $\hat{D}$ from 0.5 to 1.5 for different values of Q. The results are shown in Figures 4.14 and 4.15.

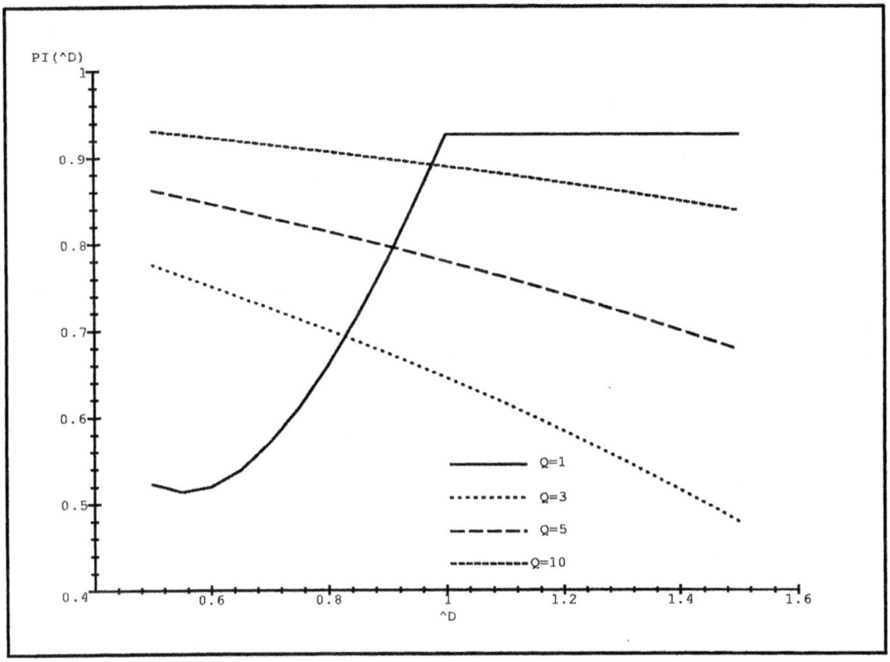

Figure 4.14. Stability function of an (s, nQ) policy with varying $\hat{D}$ and different lot sizes Q

In Figures 4.14 and 4.15 again indicate that accurate forecasts lead to a high level of stability. It can also be seen that for $Q \leq \hat{D}$, the level of stability is constant with increasing projected demand per period.

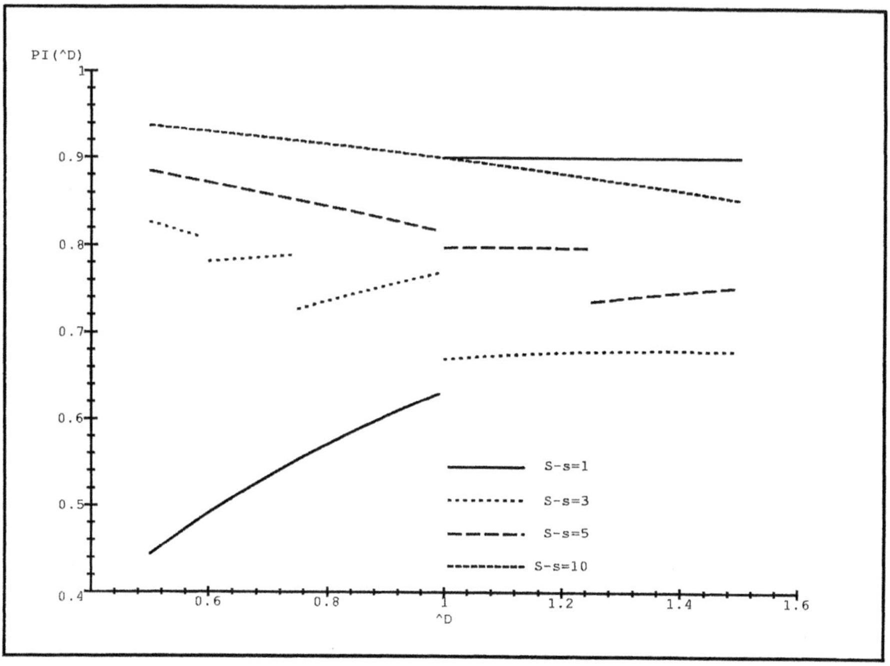

Figure 4.15. Stability function of an (s, S) policy with varying $\hat{D}$ and different minimum reorder quantities $S - s$

For both inventory control rules in the region $\hat{D} < \bar{D}$, stability is even higher than for accurate forecasts in the case of sufficiently large lot sizes, i.e. Q, or $S - s$ must be larger than the expected demand per period $\bar{D}$. For $Q = 1$, stability is (significantly) lower than for accurate forecasts, in particular if the deviation between forecasted and expected value of demand per period increases. Moreover, it is again evident that, in general, an overestimation of expected demand leads to a reduction in stability. Especially for an (s, nQ) control rule, stability (significantly) diminishes if forecasted demand per period is only 50 % higher than expected demand. This applies in particular to relatively small lot sizes, e.g. for $Q = 3$, $\pi = 65\%$ in the case of accurate forecasts, but only a stability level of 47 % for $\hat{D} = 1.5$. In the case of an (s, S) for $\hat{D} > \bar{D}$ stability generally also drops, the higher the deviation between expected and forecasted demand per period. However, the reduction in stability is more moderate than for an (s, nQ) policy. Finally it can be observed that stability increases in most situations with increasing lot size for a given $\hat{D}/\bar{D}$-ratio[38]. Considering an (s, S) policy, it is again apparent that

[38] This is always true if Q is larger than the expected demand per period.

Q-values which are multiples of the forecasted demand per period should be avoided[39]. For instance, in Figure 4.15 for $Q = 3$ local minima are reached for $\hat{D} = 1.00, 0.75, 0.60$.

To conclude, accurate forecasts lead to a good stability performance for both policies. Comparing the value of stability for "realistic" forecast errors in Figures 4.14 and 4.15, the (s, S) policy tends to be a little superior to the (s, nQ) control rule, if the (minimum) lot size Q is larger than the expected demand per period. However, for large lot sizes, such as $Q = 10$ in Figures 4.14 and 4.15, a high level of stability is achieved even if forecast errors of 50 % occur.

4.4 Summary and Managerial Implications

The previous sections present analytical insights into the effects of two basic inventory control rules on long-term setup planning stability. Until now, an analytical examination was only provided by De Kok and Inderfurth [32] for the short-term consideration, which is a special case within this analysis. For the long-term stability, only simulation results have been available (see Jensen [67], [68]).

The main contribution of this work is to give an analytical description of the relationship between setup stability and inventory policies of an (s, S) and (s, nQ) type. This study has shown that some general closed-form formulas can be derived for describing this dependency (see Equations (4.59) – (4.64)). Initial results indicate that the reorder point s does not influence long-term setup stability. Consequently, it is possible to select according to cost and service considerations without affecting stability.

In order to derive more insights, some additional assumptions concerning the distribution of demand have to be made. To keep the analysis tractable, some specific but fairly general types of demand distributions have been selected[40]. For the case of exponentially distributed demand, some of the relationships between lot-sizing parameters and setup stability can even be analytically proven.

Perhaps the most interesting result of this analysis is that no general superiority of one control rule in comparison to the other one has been found[41]. For small lot sizes which are lower than the projected demand per period,

[39] Or, in other words, the quotient $Q/\hat{D}$ should not be an integer.

[40] Simulation studies show that these results also apply to more global situations, see Jensen [68].

[41] The special case of a simple order-up-to-level policy, i.e. $s = S$, obviously shows the best performance with respect to setup stability, but as known from inventory control, this policy may be connected with high costs if setup costs are considerably high.

setup stability of an (s, nQ) policy is greater than the stability of an (s, S) policy. Since in most practical situations the lot size will be larger than the forecasted demand per period, the more interesting region is $Q > \hat{D}$. It turns out that the application of an (s, S) policy for high demand variabilities, (i.e. $c_D^2 \geq 1$) leads to a slightly higher level of setup stability for "moderate" and "large" lot sizes[42]. The stability function of an (s, S) policy for low demand uncertainty possesses local maxima and minima for "low" lot sizes. Setup stability in these maxima is high, and, consequently larger than for an (s, nQ) policy. In contrast, if Q is chosen as a multiple of the projected demand, stability in the case of an (s, S) policy is rather small for sufficiently small minimum lot sizes, and, therefore lower than for an (s, nQ) inventory control rule. For "large" lot sizes, the stability performance of an (s, S) policy is a little better than for an (s, nQ) control rule, and for $Q \to \infty$ the stability levels are (almost) equal.
For the short-term consideration, De Kok and Inderfurth have found similar results (see De Kok and Inderfurth [32], pp.64). For $Q < \hat{D}$ it holds that $\pi_{s,nQ} \geq \pi_{s,S}$, whereas for $Q \cong 2\hat{D}$ and larger Q-values the opposite applies (see also Figures 4.5 and 4.4, p.100). For most practical applications, the latter is valid, thus an (s, S) policy should be preferred. Only under JIT conditions (i.e. $Q < \hat{D}$) is an (s, nQ) inventory control rule advantageous with respect to short-term planning stability.
To sum up, a poor choice of (minimum) lot size leads to a low level of stability for both policies. To protect against a poor setup stability performance, lot sizes in the region twice as large as the forecasted demand should be avoided for both policies. Because of the cyclic patterns of the (s, S) policy for low and moderate Q-values, the sensitivity of setup stability to changes in the lot sizes is higher than for an (s, nQ) inventory control rule. Therefore, in the case of an (s, S) policy, the minimum lot size should not be set as a multiple of the projected demand. This is also valid if the forecasted demand per period deviates from the expected demand per period.

For both policies, the influence of the other critical parameters on setup stability is very similar. It is obvious that for both policies with increasing demand variability, stability significantly diminishes.
An increase in the stability horizon, or in the weighting of periods within this horizon leads to a higher level of stability for low lot sizes (i.e. $Q < \hat{D}$), whereas in most cases, the opposite holds true for larger Q-values. In a multi-stage production system, the length of the stability horizon is, in general, not only a decision variable, but depends also on the cumulative lead time, i.e. it should not be lower than this lead time. Nervousness can be avoided by constructing modified inventory control rules (see Jensen [67]). Therefore, it is important to consider all periods in which plan revisions on a specific production stage may lead to plan changes on upstream stages. Otherwise an

[42] In Figure 4.7 shows $\pi_{s,S} > \pi_{s,nQ}$ for $Q > 2\hat{D}$.

improvement of stability on a downstream stage may lead to nervousness at lower levels. In particular, plan revisions on the MPS level at the end of the planned throughput time lead to short-term adjustments at upstream stages. Finally, the impact of the forecast accuracy[43] on setup stability of both policies is also rather similar[44]. For low lot sizes (i.e. $Q < \hat{D}$) there is no impact of forecast errors on stability. Good forecasts lead to a high level of stability in any case, and for $Q > \bar{D}$, underestimating the expected demand per period (i.e. $\hat{D} < \bar{D}$) even results in an (slightly) better stability performance. The overestimation of expected demand per period, in general, leads to a lower stability level than for accurate forecasts.

It can be concluded that if nervousness plays a role, inventory policies and their control parameters should be determined under consideration of their stability effects. Analogously to service level constraints, which are used instead of costs to ensure a certain level of customer service, the additional factor of nervousness can be incorporated by setting stability constraints. The results in this section give some insights into how lot sizes in a single-stage production system have to be restricted if such constraints are given by the decision makers.
The next section provides some suggestions for further research topics.

4.5 Extensions

The above analysis can be extended in several aspects. One next step is the analysis of quantity-oriented stability as introduced in Section 3.4.2. For the short-term consideration, there are already some analytical results available (see De Kok and Inderfurth [32]). They have found that short-term quantity stability of (s, nQ) policies is always higher than the corresponding stability of (s, S) policies with $Q = S - s$. Simulation studies by Jensen [67],[68] show no superiority of one reorder point policy can be found with respect to long-term quantity stability (see, e.g., Jensen [68], p.173). An analytical examination of long-term quantity stability does not only seem to be interesting, but, unfortunately, also impossible. One main problem is the determination of the maximum order deviations in the denominator of (3.13)[45]. Moreover, the calculation of quantity stability for the short-term consideration is rather difficult, and leads to a large algebraic effort. Therefore, it is assumed that an analytical derivation of closed-form expressions is not feasible for long-term quantity stability, as for setup stability.

43 A forecast error is measured by the deviation of forecasted demand per period $\hat{D}$ from expected demand per period $\bar{D}$.

44 Section 4.5 also describes how stability evolves for more complicated forecasting processes.

45 See also the matching discussion in Section 3.4.2.

Another aspect is the impact of the forecasting procedure. In this analysis, demand is simply projected by using a (quasi-deterministic) constant value, which may deviate from its expectation. In Jensen, the influence of different demand forecasting methods is analyzed (see Jensen [68], pp.186). He considers the method of moving averages, and exponential smoothing. A moving average of order w is defined as the arithmetic average of the most recent w observations. In the case of exponential smoothing, the forecast for the actual period is the weighted average of the last forecasts and the current observations of demand (see, e.g., Nahmias [95], pp.71). The parameter α $(0 < \alpha < 1)$ describes the relative weight of the current observation of demand. Jensen has found that the general shapes of the stability functions for both policies remain almost unchanged by using these demand forecasts instead of a simple constant value. However, in the case of an (s, S) policy with increasing w or α, the cyclical patterns of the stability function are smoothed. Furthermore, for both policies, the level of stability decreases with rising parameter w and α. This result is not surprising, because the nonconstant forecasts generate an additional potential for plan revisions. Finally, Jensen has found that for comparable $w-$ and $\alpha-$values, the method of exponential smoothing is less stable than the moving average procedure. To sum up, it seems that an analytical examination of more complicated forecasting processes with respect to stability aspects might be very useful, e.g., for obtaining greater insight into the impact of the forecast parameters like w or α on stability. However, this analysis is very limited because of the necessary calculation of rather complicated conditional probabilities.

Similar mathematical problems arise when one wishes to incorporate stochastic lead times into an analysis. As mentioned before, the incorporation of deterministic lead times is not crucial, because the planned replenishment decisions only have to be adjusted according to the matching lead time. The integration of stochastic lead times would lead to complicated convolutions of the expected stability. Therefore, an analytical investigation of this aspect is not deemed possible. The same applies if one wishes to focus on non-stationary demand situations. Note that Jensen has analyzed the impact of sporadic demand[46] on stability (see Jensen [68],pp.184). It turns out that, in general, the level of stability decreases with increasing sporadic demand, as long as the fraction of periods with zero demand is lower than 60 %. Thus, it can be assumed that, in general, in the case of non-stationary demand stability decreases.

However, the incorporation of further stochastic impacts in the model leads to additional problems which does not seem to be solved analytically.

Nevertheless, there are still two very interesting open questions which have yet not been answered satisfactory.

First of all, an analytical study of the improvement of stability by introducing

[46] Sporadic demand means that there are a lot of periods, i.e. at least 30-40 %, with zero demand.

a specific stabilization parameter seems to be promising (see Jensen [67], and Jensen [68], pp.200) . This parameter (B) describes a certain limit of tolerance with respect to the amount of available inventory position[47]. Later in this study, a brief description of these modified reorder point policies is given. Planned orders for each period do not only depend on the actual inventory position for this period, but also on the planned lot size calculated in the last planning cycle for this period. If, on the one hand, the actual inventory position falls below the reorder point (i.e. according to the unmodified policy an order has to be scheduled), then this order will be suppressed, if in the previous planning cycle no order has been planned for this period and the undershoot of the reorder point does not exceed B percent of the s-value. Analogously, on the other hand, an order takes place if the actual inventory position is larger than the reorder point, but in the last cycle a setup has been scheduled and the overshoot is in the range of $B \cdot s$. Varying the parameter B Jensen has studied the trade-off between planning stability, costs and the service level achieved[48]. It turns out that for small B-values (i.e. $B \leq 0.2$) stability significantly increases whereas customer service slightly decreases. A further increase of B does not affect stability, but the service level continues to diminish. Costs are hardly influenced, for a modified (s, nQ) they increase a little, and for the modified (s, S) policy they even decrease. As can be also seen in Jensen (see, e.g., Jensen [67]) this stabilization strategy is more effective than the method of freezing a part of each planning cycle. It is more flexible and one can create a stabilization effect in each period, whereas a frozen horizon only "stabilizes" the first periods (which are in this frozen zone) and leads to an "all-or-nothing" stabilization regardless of the actual inventory position. Modeling the dependencies between the lot size parameters, stabilization methods and stability might result in extensions of lot-sizing models which incorporate cost optimization objectives under consideration of a predefined service level as well as stability restrictions[49]. Therefore, the results in this study for the reorder point policies may serve as a basis to incorporate the stability aspect into such models.

Finally, the second interesting question is how stability is affected by production and inventory control in multi-stage systems. There are first simulation experiments for simple systems[50] by Jensen (see, Jensen [68], pp. 219) which indicate that the control rule used at the end-item level has a major influence on the stability performance of the entire system.

If, in a multi-stage system, the end-item level is controlled by a reorder point policy, and a lot-for-lot policy is used on upstream stages, then these results

[47] Note that this strategy is comparable with the use of the Lot size Inflexibility Factor (LIF) in Van Donselaar's FiRST concept (see Section 2.3.3, p.19).

[48] Note that contrary to the unmodified policies, stability now depends also on the size of the reorder point s. For fixed B-values, stability increases with rising s.

[49] See also Kimms [73] for incorporating stability restrictions in decisions making. He presents an iterative method for reducing instability of schedules.

[50] Jensen considers a two-stage serial as well as divergent system.

can directly be applied to such a multi-stage system. Since orders are placed in the same period at all stages, only the size of the order at each level may be altered, but there are no new, previously unplanned orders. Consequently, setup stability at the final product stage represents the planning stability of the entire system[51].

[51] See also Blackburn et al [13], [14], and [15] who suggest the use of the lot-for-lot policy on upstream stages ("lot-for-lot policy after the final product stage") to stabilize lot-sizing (see also Section 3.5).

5. Product Recovery Systems

5.1 Strategic Aspects of Product Recovery Management

This section deals with product recovery management and its relevance for manufacturers of durable products. Product recovery management deals with the management of all used and discarded products, components, and materials for which a producing company is legally, contractually, or otherwise responsible (see, e.g., Thierry [127]). The aim of product recovery management is to regain as much of the economical (and ecological) value of the used or discarded items as is reasonably possible, therefore reducing waste disposal to a minimum.

Literature provides several definitions for the recovery of products. Like Fleischmann et al. [36] and Gungor and Gupta [45][1], for the purpose of this study, the recovery process is categorized into material recovery (recycling) and product recovery (remanufacturing). Recycling recovers the material content of a old product. Remanufacturing preserves the product's identity and returns the product to a desired level of quality. The operations for both recovery options may be disassembly and sorting. In the case of remanufacturing, there is also the assembly of the new products, under certain circumstances, there may also be refurbishing operations necessary.

There are several incentives for companies to take back used products. On the one hand, there are legislative rules, e.g. legislative action encompasses disposal bans for specific product, or recovery quotas. For instance, in Germany, on 7th October 1996, the commercial and industrial waste avoidance and management act (KrW-/AbfG) came into force. It puts the polluter principle into action, and the emphasis is on the product responsibility of the manufacturers and distributors. In addition, the Federal Government has defined several ordinances where the product responsibility for certain products is specified. For instance, recovery goals for sales packaging materials are mandatory between 60 % and 75 % (see packaging ordinance of 1991). The battery ordinance of 1998 obliges customers to return all old device batteries to collecting points or retailers, respectively. The traders have to point out the obligation to return discarded batteries to customers, i.e. consumers must

[1] Gungor and Gupta [45] provide a current overview of the literature in the field of environmentally conscious manufacturing and product recovery.

be supplied with adequate information about this obligation. The electronic scrap ordinance of 1996 sets similar goals for electronic goods, analogously the used car ordinance for all components and materials of cars, e.g., steel, metals, tires,... The European Community has set a law that by the year 2002 no more than 15 % of an automotive product can be disposed of, and in the year 2015 this percentage must be reduced to 5 % (see, e.g., Nasr [96]). In Frosch [39] the development of environmental regulations in the USA is described.

On the other hand, even if legislation is less stringent, environmentally conscious customers increasingly force manufacturers to take back their products after use. By designing and marketing environmentally friendly products, manufacturers may gain advantage in the marketing platform against their competitors (see also Gungor and Gupta [45]). Moreover, the customer pressure is also triggered by increasing product disposal costs. In recent years, these costs have risen significantly as landfill and incineration capacity is being depleted (see, e.g., Thierry [127]). Manufacturers are therefore more and more responsible for the entire life cycle of their products. Considerable efforts are made more recently to re-integrate used items into "traditional" industrial production processes.

In the traditional approach, most products were designed with respect to minimizing materials, assembly and distribution costs, disregarding repair, reuse and disposal costs. These aspects were also not taken into account by most consumers. Minimizing purchasing costs sells products, not optimizing life-cycle performance including maintenance, reuse and disposal issues. As already emphasized, nowadays, both customers and government authorities demand that companies reduce or even avoid waste disposal. Moreover, in addition to enhanced environmental constraints and a "green" image there are also economic drivers for recovering used products (see, e.g., Thierry [127]). On the one hand, a "green" image has also become an important marketing element. By offering "green" products, companies may attract environmentally conscious customers, leading to higher sales. Moreover, producing environmentally friendly products reduces future liabilities, insurance and tax rates, and customers' disposal costs. On the other hand, the reuse of products may lead to savings in material, manufacturing and disposal costs. A first opportunity is to upgrade some parts of the returned old items instead of purchasing all the components to assemble a new product. The product can then be sold as a new one. Furthermore, it may be possible to remanufacture some of the disassembled parts of the returned items and to use these components as spare parts for the original product. Examples from practice include reusable packaging, electronic scrap recycling, or car part remanufacturing. The management of the material flow concerned with the recovery of returned products, which is opposite to the usual supply chain flow, is considered in the recently emerged field of "reverse logistics" (see, e.g., Fleischmann et al. [36]).

5.2 Inventory Management and MRP Concept in Reverse Logistics

One of the issues in the area of reverse logistics is production and inventory management. The major task in this field is to develop appropriate planning and control methods in order to integrate the return flow of used products into the producers' material management. Difficulties arise because of the considerable uncertainties in timing, quantity, and quality of the return flow which is often hard for the producer to influence. One of the consequences of this rising uncertainty is an increase in stock levels in the entire system.
A general framework for an inventory control model incorporating a return flow of used products is depicted in Figure 5.1 (see Fleischmann et al. [36]). Demand for new products is satisfied by a serviceable inventory which is either replenished by manufacturing new products (or outside procurement, respectively), or overhauling old products and bringing them back to "as new" ones. Instead of recovering returned items (which is denoted by remanufacturing from this point, although other processes such as repair or cleaning and testing also apply), some (or even all) of them may also be disposed of. The objective of inventory management is to control the production, remanufacturing and disposal decisions to guarantee a required service level, and to minimize (fixed and variable) costs of the entire recovery system.

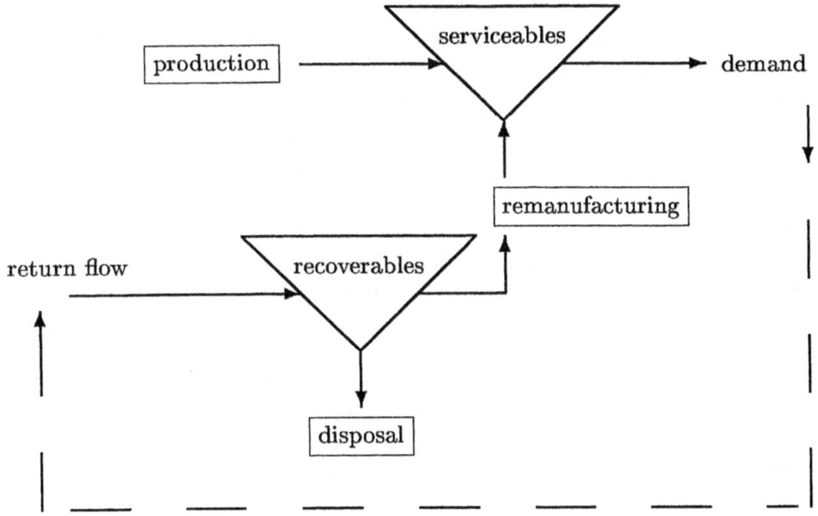

Figure 5.1. Framework inventory management with returns

One approach for dealing with the material coordination problems in such a recovery system is the extension of the mathematical models of inventory control. Inventory control in recovery systems differs from traditional inventory control situations essentially in three aspects (see Fleischmann et al. [36]). First, because of the return flow, the inventory level is not necessarily decreasing, but may also increase. This means a loss of monotonicity of the inventory level which significantly complicates the underlying mathematical models. Second, there are two alternatives for satisfying demand, i.e. "regular production" or "recovery process". This leads to an additional set of decisions. The external orders and the recovery activities have to be coordinated. This situation is equivalent to a two supply mode inventory system where the supply of one mode cannot completely be controlled. Finally, the situation comes down to a two-echelon inventory system due to the distinction between returned products which have yet to undergo a recovery process and serviceables inventory.
A major classification of recovery models in literature can be made by distinguishing between deterministic and stochastic models. In deterministic concepts, the classical EOQ-model is extended (see, e.g., Schrady [110], Mabini et al. [84], and Richter [104]). Since this stdy does not deal with deterministic models, these approaches will not be considered in further detail. The stochastic approaches may be further classified into single versus two level inventory structures (see, e.g., Fleischmann et al. [38]).
Cohen et al. [28] consider a system where recoverable and serviceable inventory coincide, because returns can be reused immediately. It is assumed that a fixed share of the products issued in a given period is returned after a fixed period of time in the market. They show optimality of a periodic review "order upto" policy when only proportional costs play a role. This approach is extended by Kelle and Silver [72] by considering fixed order costs and a stochastic sojourn time in the market. They transform the stochastic model in a deterministic, dynamic lot-sizing problem based on the "net" demand (i.e. demand minus returns) per period, and apply the well-known deterministic lot-sizing procedure[2] to obtain the solution. In a more recent paper, Yuan and Cheung [145] propose a continuous review (s, S) reorder policy. Based on a Markovian approach, the essential operating characteristics of the system are derived, and an algorithm for calculating the optimal control parameters is proposed.

In two-level inventory models, the returned items are, explicitly or implicitly, distinguished from new ones. Then, decisions on new replenishment orders and recovery activities have to be made, and the control parameters must be set accordingly. In periodic review models, the main focus concerns the derivation of the corresponding optimal policy. In an early paper, Simpson [117] considers the trade–off between material savings due to reuse versus ad-

[2] see, e.g., Wagner and Whitin [136]

ditional inventory carrying costs. The optimality of a three parameter policy to control order, repair (or, in other words, remanufacturing), and disposal for the case without fixed costs and lead times is proved. Inderfurth [63] extends this approach by allowing fixed and identical lead times for repair and procurement. He shows that the three parameter policy remains optimal. In a variant of this model, which assumes any returned item to be repaired or disposed of directly, a mixed "order upto - dispose downto" policy is proven to be optimal, provided that the procurement lead time does not exceed the repair lead time by more than one period. Fleischmann and Kuik [37] consider another variant of Simpson's model excluding disposal and prove average cost optimality of an (s, S) policy.

Continuous review models mainly discuss (s, Q)-type-policies, see, e.g., Heyman [51], Muckstadt and Isaac [93], Van der Laan et al. [129, 130], and Fleischmann et al. [38]. Since this study does not consider a continuous review framework setting, these models will not be presented in further detail. A more detailed literature review is given by Fleischmann et al. [36].

Another option for coordinating material flows in recovery systems concerns the extension of the traditional Material Requirements Planning (MRP) concept (a detailed description of the MRP logic is already given in Chapter 2). Extending an MRP system to coordinate recovery options assumes the inclusion of the planning of future return flows within the considered planning horizon. Moreover, planned lead times for the recovery process have to be specified. It is essential to integrate the recovered products at those production stages where they meet the regular forward flow of materials. At these stages, additional computations have to be made, taking into account the return flows and available recovery options, whereas all other production stages can be planned according to the traditional MRP concept. An MRP-framework for a single stage of a recovery system facing product returns can be found in Inderfurth and Jensen [64].

Within the so-called MRRP (Material Requirements and Recovery Planning) approach, some additional steps must be included in the regular MRP scheme. Stocks of returned products have to be considered, and timing and quantity for remanufacturing orders as well as disposal activities for these items have to be determined. In principle, the MRRP calculations follow the MRP rules, but some additional assumptions have to be made. For instance, that net requirements are, as far as possible, fulfilled by remanufacturing returned items before production of new products is considered, or planned future returns are taken into account (proactive planning). Then, the production, remanufacturing and disposal decisions only depend on the respective relevant costs. Disregarding fixed costs as well as capacity constraints, a lot-for-lot ordering policy is economical for both types of serviceables replenishment. If the cost of remanufacturing one unit is larger than the unit production cost plus disposal cost, then all returned items will be disposed of, and the traditional MRP calculations can be used for material coordination. If the opposite applies, then remanufacturing is superior to regular production, and, according to the priority rule mentioned above, all returns are used for satisfying net requirements before production takes place. In the latter case, the storage, or, vice versa, disposal of returned items depends on the relationship between holding costs and the cost benefit of remanufacturing over regular production. Then, a critical runout time for excess returns can be calculated. With these cost considerations, formulas for the computation of all relevant decisions can be given explicitly, analogously to the standard MRP application. Since each of the three decision variables (remanufacturing, production, disposal) only depends on one critical inventory parameter, the complete set of rules can be denoted by a three parameter policy as in stochastic inventory control. Notice that in a case where stockkeeping of returned items is forbidden (e.g. for technical or environmental reasons), the control rule is reduced to a two parameter "order upto - dispose downto" policy. Finally, Inderfurth and Jensen [64] distinguish between proactive and reactive planning. In reactive planning, only those returns are considered which are currently available, i.e. stored in the actual remanufacturing stock. No future expected returns are taken into account. In contrast, proactive MRRP control takes into consideration all expected future returns that (after remanufacturing) can be used to meet future requirements. Remanufacturing and disposal decisions then depend on the possible occurrence of future returns.

To conclude, both the stochastic inventory control approach and the MRRP concept lead to identical or very similar control rules for recovery systems. As in traditional inventory systems, there is a close connection between both approaches. However, the parameter values of the MRRP calculations will usually deviate from the optimal parameters (see Inderfurth and Jensen [64]).

Up to now, the issue of planning stability in recovery systems has only been dealt with by Heisig and Fleischmann [50]. They analyze setup stability for a specific recovery system without stockkeeping of returned items and disposal option which is controlled by a modified, optimal (s, S) policy. These results will be presented in Section 5.4 in detail.

The most basic characteristic distinguishing inventory management in a reuse context from traditional settings is the existence of an exogenous item in-flow. Given this core element of a recovery environment, this study explicitly analyzes how stability is influenced by product recovery by considering a basic recovery model which is introduced in detail in Section 5.3. It is a variant of the system depicted in Figure 5.1, where stockkeeping of returned items is not allowed, i.e. returns either have to be remanufactured or disposed of immediately. Two types of this model are considered, one where disposal of returned products is forbidden, and another one where disposal is allowed. The analysis is closely related to that of a traditional system. Changes in the results due to the integration of a product return flow in a traditional inventory model are shown.

5.3 Basic Recovery Model

This section introduces the product recovery system which will be analyzed with respect to the stability performance of the underlying inventory control rules. To this end, a traditional single item inventory system with an additional in–flow of used items is considered. The interesting recovery system is slightly different from the general framework depicted in Figure 5.1, namely there is no stock point for storing returned items. If returned items are not disposed of, then they undergo a recovery process and can then be used as an alternative to new production to satisfy demand. Figure 5.2 gives a graphical representation of this system.

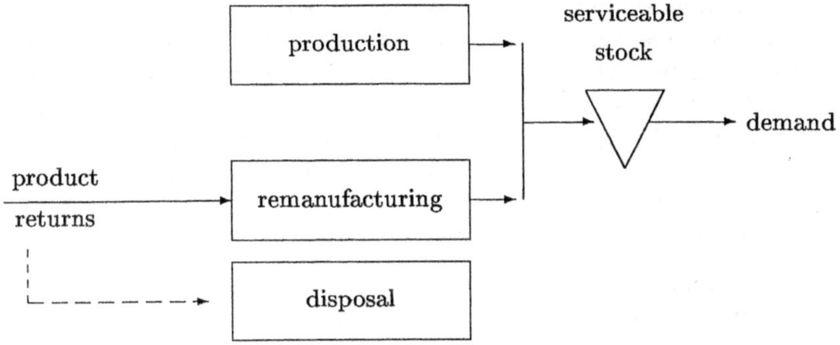

Figure 5.2. Basic recovery system

Two basic scenarios are considered. In the first scenario, all returned products must be remanufactured. In the second scenario, the disposal of returned items is possible. As examples for the system without disposal option, one may think of reusable packages, such as crates and containers, or spare parts dismantled from used equipment, such as in the electronics and automotive industries (see, e.g., Thierry [127]). Furthermore, this recovery system is also relevant if the disposal of returned products is forbidden. This model was introduced by Fleischmann and Kuik [37]. They have shown average cost optimality of a stationary (s, S) policy for production under a fixed plus convex cost structure. If there are no fixed costs, then a simple, modified order-up-to-level (S) inventory control rule is optimal. For the second system with disposal option, the optimal policy is of an (s, S, D)-type (see Van der Laan et al. [130]), and Inderfurth [63] has proved optimality of an "order upto -

dispose downto" (S, D) policy, if no fixed costs are included[3] (see also Section 5.2).
Moreover, as already indicated, these situations are at the core of most other, more complex product recovery systems including, e.g., additional stock points or control options. Typically, the recovery of used products is significantly cheaper than regular production. Therefore, the major challenge in this context concerns the tradeoff between the savings potential and the uncertain availability of the recovery source.
To model the above system, it is assumed that demand and returns are given by independent stochastic processes. As in the traditional system, orders for remanufacturing and production are placed on a periodic review basis. Any unsatisfied demand is backordered. To ease notation, it is assumed that all orders are delivered instantaneously (lead times can be incorporated in the standard way by appropriately redefining the inventory position, under the condition that the remanufacturing lead time does not exceed the manufacturing lead time[4], see, e.g., Fleischmann and Kuik [37], and Inderfurth [63]). In the case of the recovery system without disposal option, remanufacturing is implemented as a push process, i.e. at the beginning of each period all products returned during the previous period are remanufactured. Production orders are the decision variables to control the system. In the case of the system with disposal option, there is an additional decision variable, namely the disposal quantity. For both systems, the following notation is used . Let

$$\begin{aligned} D_t &= \text{demand in period } t; \\ R_t &= \text{returns in period } t; \\ N_t &= D_t - R_t, \text{ net demand in period } t \ , \end{aligned}$$

where $(N_t)_{t \in \mathbb{N}}$ is an i.i.d. sequence of random variables distributed as a random variable N with continuous distribution function Φ, density ϕ, and expected value $\mathbb{E}[N]$. Since the first model does not include a disposal option, one must assume that $\mathbb{E}[N] > 0$, since the inventory level would increase to infinity otherwise. Since, under these circumstances, Fleischmann and Kuik [37] have shown optimality of a stationary (s, S) policy, it is assumed that production orders are placed according to this rule. This means that production orders take place if the inventory position (after remanufacturing) at the beginning of a period is smaller than the reorder point s. Then, stock is increased to the order-upto-level S by production. If inventory is greater than s, no new items are produced. Note that because of the return flow, inventory can also exceed S. If there are no fixed costs for production, then the optimal inventory control rule is a simple order-up-to-level policy. The stability performance of such a type of policy will also be considered, be-

[3] Because of analytical tractability in the case of the recovery system with disposal option, it is only possible to analyze the stability performance of an (S, D) policy, i.e. the system without fixed costs.

[4] If the lead time of remanufacturing is greater than the production lead time, then the optimality of the underlying control rules is not guaranteed.

cause in the case of the recovery system with the disposal option, only the case without fixed costs can be analyzed, i.e. the stability of an (S, D) policy. In order to compare these stability results with the recovery system without disposal option, the S policy for this system must also be examined.

Furthermore, for the recovery system with disposal option it is also assumed that $\mathbb{E}[N] > 0$. The first reason for this assumption is that both systems should be compared with respect to their stability performance. Additionally, the influence of product returns on stability in both systems should be shown and consequently, the same assumptions must be used, in particular the same "structure" of return flow. Moreover, setup stability on the production stage is analyzed. Assuming $\mathbb{E}[N] < 0$ indicates that the demand is mainly satisfied by remanufactured items. The analysis of stability on the remanufacturing stage would then be appropriate. For these reasons, the assumption $\mathbb{E}[N] > 0$ is also maintained in the disposal model. As mentioned before, in the case of excluding fixed costs, the underlying optimal control rule is of an (S, D) type, i.e. a mixed "order upto – dispose downto" policy (see Inderfurth [63]). If inventory position is smaller than S, then it is increased by remanufacturing, and, if necessary, by production. If inventory position exceeds an upper control limit D, then it is decreased by disposal. Between the control limits nothing is produced or disposed of.

Some general stability results are derived for both recovery systems. Starting with the system without disposal option, first the consideration of the (s, S) control rule which is optimal under fixed costs for production. Then, a simple order-up-to-level policy which is optimal if there are no fixed costs. Finally, the consideration of the extension of the latter system without fixed costs where the disposal of returned items is allowed. The stability performance of the optimal (S, D) control rule is analyzed, and these results are compared with the stability of an S policy.

5.4 Recovery System without Disposal Option

This section provides a summary of the results given in Heisig and Fleischmann [50]. Recall that production orders are placed according to an (s, S) policy. A special case of this analysis is the consideration of a simple S policy.
At first, a formal definition of the corresponding mathematical model and notation is given.

5.4.1 Notation and Assumptions

The following notation is used for this analysis:

O_t	=	remanufacturing order size in period t;
Z_t	=	net stock at the beginning of period t after remanufacturing, before production;
Q_t	=	production order size in period t;
Y_t	=	net stock at the beginning of period t after remanufacturing and production.

Then the system dynamics are described by

$$
\begin{aligned}
O_t &= R_{t-1} \\
Z_t &= Y_{t-1} - N_{t-1} \\
Q_t &= \begin{cases} 0 & \text{if } Z_t > s \\ S - Z_t & \text{else} \end{cases} \\
Y_t &= Z_t + Q_t \ .
\end{aligned}
$$

It is worth noting that these relationships are the same as in a traditional (s, S) inventory system apart from the fact that the (net) demand may be negative (see also Chapter 4). In particular, $(Y_t)_{t \in \mathbb{N}}$ forms a discrete time Markov process on $[s, \infty)$. Note that, in contrast with traditional inventory systems, the net inventory is unbounded from above, as a consequence of the stochastic return flow. More specifically, $(Y_t)_{t \in \mathbb{N}}$ is a random walk, which is ergodic due to the condition $\mathbb{E}[N] > 0$ (see Fleischmann and Kuik [37] for a formal proof). Therefore, (Y_t) admits a limiting stationary distribution, which is denoted by F_Y. Furthermore, let Y denote a corresponding random variable.

Planning stability is addressed by analyzing the performance of the above system in a rolling planning horizon setting, such as in a typical MRP environment. An MRP–framework including product recovery is introduced by Inderfurth and Jensen [64] (see also Section 5.2). As in the traditional system, at the beginning of each period a planning cycle of $T + 1$ periods is started, where T is a fixed stability horizon. That is, remanufacturing and production orders are planned for the current plus the next T periods. Orders for the current period are released immediately, whereas planned orders for future periods are only preliminary and may be updated in later periods. $\hat{Q}_t^i$ ($\hat{O}_t^i$) denotes the production (remanufacturing) order size in period t as planned in period i. Analogously, $\hat{Z}_t^i$ ($\hat{Y}_t^i$) denotes the net stock at the beginning of period t before (after) production as planned in period i. Finally, let $\hat{N}$ denote the projected net demand per period and $\hat{D}$ and $\hat{R}$ the projected demand and returns per period, respectively. Since it is assumed that $\mathbb{E}[N] > 0$, it is also supposed that $\hat{N} > 0$. Nevertheless, note that these projections need not necessarily coincide with the corresponding expected values. In particular, setting $\hat{R} = 0$ is a common choice alternative to $\hat{R} = \mathbb{E}[R_t]$. As mentioned in

Section 5.2 these two cases are referred to as reactive and proactive recovery planning, respectively (see, e.g., Inderfurth and Jensen [64]).

To summarize, at the beginning of each period t a sequence of planned production orders $(Q_t, \hat{Q}^t_{t+1}, \hat{Q}^t_{t+2}, \hat{Q}^t_{t+3}, \ldots, \hat{Q}^t_{t+T})$ and remanufacturing orders $(O_t, \hat{O}^t_{t+1}, \hat{O}^t_{t+2}, \hat{O}^t_{t+2}, \ldots, \hat{O}^t_{t+T})$ is generated (see also Figure 5.3 with $t = 0$). The system dynamics are analogous to the above except that demand and returns are replaced by their projected values:

$$
\begin{aligned}
\hat{O}^t_{t+i} &= \hat{R} \\
\hat{Z}^t_{t+i} &= \hat{Y}^t_{t+i-1} - \hat{N} \\
\hat{Q}^t_{t+i} &= \begin{cases} 0 & \text{if } \hat{Z}^t_{t+i} > s \\ S - \hat{Z}^t_{t+i} & \text{else} \end{cases} \\
\hat{Y}^t_{t+i} &= \hat{Z}^t_{t+i} + \hat{Q}^t_{t+i}
\end{aligned}
$$

for $i = 1, ..., T$ (where we define $\hat{Z}^t_t = Z_t$ and analogously for Y_t, Q_t, and O_t). Planning stability then characterizes the variation of $\hat{Q}^i_t$ and $\hat{O}^i_t$ as a function of i, in other words, the difference between subsequent planning updates. In Figure 5.3, the results mentioned above are summarized for two successive planning periods, or planning cycles 0 and 1. Here, Q^t_j $(\hat{Q}^t_j)$ represents the (planned) production decision in period j for planning cycle t, $t = 0, 1$.

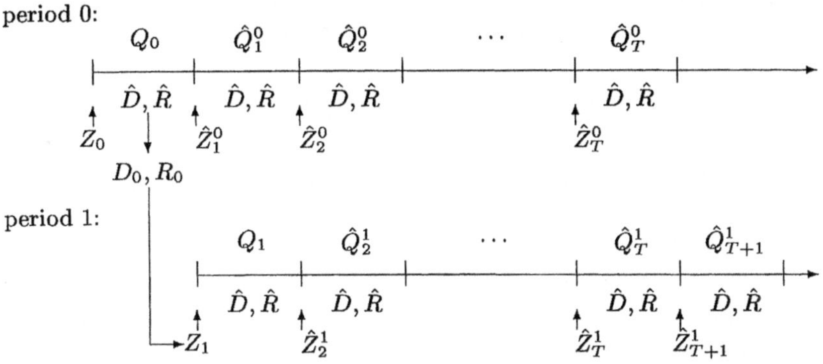

Figure 5.3. Decisions and influences in a product recovery system for two consecutive planning cycles in a rolling horizon framework

The development of the system is exactly the same as in the traditional system, where now the net demand must be considered instead of the demand (see also Figure 3.1): Q_0 will immediately be released while future decisions are only preliminary. After period 0 has passed, a subsequent planning cycle

1 will start. A change of the planned replenishment may only occur if actual net demand $D_0 - R_0$ differs from its forecast $\hat{D} - \hat{R}$. Then, the actual inventory position Z_1 deviates from its planned value $\hat{Z}_1^0$ as calculated in the previous planning cycle. Updating the starting inventory and applying the (s, S) policy generates an adjusted sequence of order releases as depicted in Figure 5.3.

Now, the stability measure for such a situation must be defined. In Chapter 4, a measure was used in which the weighting of periods within the stability horizon is feasible. However, the influence of the weight parameter is very similar to the impact of the length of the stability horizon on stability. Therefore, for the ease of analysis it is assumed that all periods are weighted equally[5]. Moreover, as for traditional inventory systems, only setup stability is considered in order to keep the analysis tractable.
The measure for setup stability is characterized as (see also (3.6))

$$\bar{\pi} = 1 - \frac{1}{T} \sum_{i=1}^{T} |\delta(q_i^0) - \delta(q_i^1)|. \tag{5.1}$$

The measure in (5.1) can be applied to determine the setup stability on both stages in our product recovery system. Stability at production level can be measured using $q_i^t = Q_i^t$ in (5.1), and by setting $q_i^t = R_i^t$, setup stability for the remanufacturing stage is derived[6] (with $t = 0, 1$).
Since initial stock and the replenishment decisions are random variables, stability can again be interpreted as (see also (4.1))

$$\bar{\pi} = \frac{1}{T}\Big[\mathbb{P}\{\delta(\hat{q}_1^0) = \delta(q_1)\} + \mathbb{P}\{\delta(\hat{q}_2^0) = \delta(\hat{q}_2^1)\} + \ldots + \mathbb{P}\{\delta(\hat{q}_T^0) = \delta(\hat{q}_T^1)\}\Big]. \tag{5.2}$$

As for the traditional system, the sequence of these setups must be determined in order to calculate setup stability for production and remanufacturing orders as indicated in (5.2). This will be done in the next section. Moreover, a general expression for $\bar{\pi}$ is derived[7].

[5] Note that the weighting of periods can easily be incorporated in the analysis by applying the same procedure as in Chapter 4.

[6] At the end of Section 5.4.2 there is a brief description of how the setup stability of the remanufacturing stage can be determined.

[7] Section 3.4 introduced the symbol "–" as an indication that all periods within the stability horizon are equal in weight. In the remainder of this study, only this special case will be considered, therefore it will be left out. The same applies to the analysis of the recovery system with disposal option in Section 5.5.

5.4.2 General Results

In order to evaluate the stability measure π introduced in the previous section, the structure of the planned production order sequences $(Q_t, \hat{Q}^t_{t+1}, \ldots, \hat{Q}^t_{t+T})$ (with $t = 0, 1$) are analyzed in more detail.

To calculate π, planned orders must be taken into account $\hat{Q}^j_i$ for $j = 0, 1$ and $i = 1, ..., T$ (see (5.2)). According to the transition rules as discussed in Section 5.4.1 $\hat{Q}^0_i$ for $i \geq 1$ equals 0 whenever the following condition holds

$$\hat{Z}^0_i > s \iff \hat{Y}^0_{i-1} - \hat{N} > s \iff \hat{Z}^0_{i-1} - \hat{N} + \hat{Q}^0_{i-1} > s \ .$$

Thus it is obtained by induction that the smallest $\tau \geq 1$ for which $\hat{Q}^0_\tau > 0$ is valid verifies $(\tau - 1)\hat{N} \leq Y_0 - s < \tau\hat{N}$. Hence the first order after period 0 is planned for period τ where

$$\tau(Y_0) = \lceil \frac{Y_0 - s}{\hat{N}} \rceil \ . \tag{5.3}$$

In the same way, the next order is planned for period $\tau + l$ where

$$l = \lceil \frac{\hat{Y}^0_\tau - s}{\hat{N}} \rceil = \lceil \frac{S - s}{\hat{N}} \rceil \ , \tag{5.4}$$

where $\hat{Y}^0_\tau = S$ follows from the definition of τ and the applied policy . Note that both expressions for l and τ are almost the same as in the traditional system where the demand only has to be replaced by the net demand (see (4.12) and (4.13), respectively). Here, l again characterizes the expected coverage of the minimum order size $S - s$ or, in other words, the expected time between ordering. Subsequently, the same step is repeated until the end of the stability horizon is reached. To summarize, in the planning cycle starting in an arbitrary period 0, production orders after 0 are planned for the periods $\tau + k * l$ for $k \in \mathbb{N}_0$ until the end of the stability horizon. If $\tau > T$ then no order is planned during the entire stability horizon.

Applying this structural result to the planning cycle starting in period 1 yields that the first order after 1 is planned in period $1 + \lceil (Y_1 - s)/\hat{N} \rceil = 1 + \lceil (Y_0 - N_0 - s + Q_1)/\hat{N} \rceil$. In addition, the decision for period 1, i.e. Q_1 has to be taken into account. We have that $Q_1 > 0 \Leftrightarrow Y_0 - N_0 - s \leq 0$. Combining both results yields that the smallest $\theta \geq 1$ for which $\hat{Q}^1_\theta > 0$ is given by[8]

$$\theta(Y_0, N_0) = 1 + \max\{0, \lceil \frac{Y_0 - N_0 - s}{\hat{N}} \rceil\} \ . \tag{5.5}$$

[8] Analogously to cycle 0, this result can also be derived by using equation (4.14) of the traditional system and substituting the demand by the net demand

Thereafter, orders are again planned every l periods until the end of the stability horizon. Hence, in this planning cycle orders are planned for periods $\theta + k * l$ for $k \in \mathbb{N}_0$.

The above considerations show that the planned order sequences generated in each planning cycle have a fairly simple, regular structure. Planning updates in subsequent planning cycles result in a shift of (stochastic) length $\tau - \theta$ of the entire planned order sequence. The same structure is found for traditional (s, S) production systems without product recovery (see Chapter 4). However, the range of possible values for τ and θ are different in both cases. In traditional production systems $\tau \leq l$ and $\theta \leq \tau + 1$. Both relationships do not apply to the product recovery system, since the net demand in a given period may be negative and the net stock may exceed S. Moreover, the probability distributions of τ and θ do, of course, depend on the product returns. This dependence is investigated in more detail in Section 5.4.3.

Furthermore, it is worth noting that for $S - s < \hat{N}$, $l = 1$, i.e. an order is planned for every period after the first setup and the above formulas reduce to the results for a system which is controlled by a simple modified order-up-to-level policy (for details see also Section 5.4.3).

Finally, note that for $S - s >> \hat{N}$ τ and θ may be approximated by

$$\tau(Y) \approx \frac{Y - s}{\hat{N}} \qquad \text{and} \qquad \theta(Y, N) \approx 1 + \frac{Y - N - s}{\hat{N}} .$$

In this case,

$$\mathbb{E}[(\tau(Y) - \theta(Y, N))^2] \approx \mathbb{E}[\frac{(\hat{N} - N)^2}{\hat{N}^2}] = \frac{\text{Var}[N]}{\mathbb{E}[N]^2} . \tag{5.6}$$

Thus the expected squared length of the shift of the order sequence during a planning update is approximately equal to the squared coefficient of variation of the net demand per period. Note that this expression is increasing in both the expected value and the variance of the returns per period. This gives a first indication of the impact of the product returns on the planning updates.

The above results can now be used to evaluate the stability measure π discussed in the previous section. To this end, some additional notation is introduced as follows. Let $V_t := Y_t - s$ for all t. Then $V_t \in [0, \infty)$ for all t. Moreover, recall that Y_t admits a stationary limiting distribution. Hence, the same applies to V_t and the limiting distribution is denoted by F_V. Moreover, let V be a corresponding random variable.

Furthermore, for $\tau, \theta = 1, ...T + 1$ the stability quotient β_θ^τ is defined as the number of periods with identical setup decisions in two subsequent planning cycles with first setups in periods τ and θ divided by the length of the stability horizon T. Note that β_θ^τ equals the planning stability π for fixed values of

τ and θ (see (5.1)). While there is no simple closed form expression for the stability quotients, these values can easily be computed by enumeration. For $\tau > T+1$, $\beta_\theta^\tau = \beta_\theta^{T+1}$ is set and analogously for $\theta > T+1$. Thus, expected setup stability in steady state is given

$$\pi_{s,S}^{rec} = \sum_{\tau=1}^{\infty} \int_{s+(\tau-1)\hat{N}}^{s+\tau\hat{N}} \left[\sum_{\theta=1}^{\infty} \beta_\theta^\tau [\Phi_N(y-s-(\theta-2)\hat{N}) - \Phi_N(y-s-(\theta-1)\hat{N})] \right.$$

$$\left. + \beta_1^\tau [1 - \Phi_N(y-s+\hat{N})] \right] dF_Y(y)$$

$$= \sum_{\tau=1}^{\infty} \int_{(\tau-1)\hat{N}}^{\tau\hat{N}} \left[\sum_{\theta=1}^{\infty} \beta_\theta^\tau [\Phi_N(v-(\theta-2)\hat{N}) - \Phi_N(v-(\theta-1)\hat{N})] \right.$$

$$\left. + \beta_1^\tau [1 - \Phi_N(v+\hat{N})] \right] dF_V(v) \tag{5.7}$$

As is the case for the traditional model, setup stability is defined by weighting the stability quotients with the corresponding net demand probabilities for all possible values of initial stock ($s < Y_0 < \infty$).
Note that $\pi_{s,S}^{rec}$ is independent of the reorder level s just as in traditional production systems. Therefore, s can be chosen according to cost and service considerations without influencing planning stability. In the next section, the value of $\pi_{s,S}^{rec}$ is calculated in an example and its dependence on the system parameters is analyzed.

For the special case of $s = S$

$$\pi_S^{rec} = \sum_{\tau=1}^{\infty} \int_{S+(\tau-1)\hat{N}}^{S+\tau\hat{N}} \left[\sum_{\theta=1}^{\infty} \beta_\theta^\tau [\Phi_N(y-S-(\theta-2)\hat{N}) - \Phi_N(y-S-(\theta-1)\hat{N})] \right.$$

$$\left. + \beta_1^\tau [1 - \Phi_N(y-S+\hat{N})] \right] dF_y(y)$$

Heisig and Fleischmann [50] also analyze the stability of the remanufacturing decisions. This section is concluded by briefly summarizing these results. Since all returned items are remanufactured at the beginning of each period and since R_t is stationary $\hat{O}_{t+i}^t = \hat{R}$ for all t and all $i \geq 1$. Thus, two consecutive planning cycles can only differ with respect to the remanufacturing order in the first period. This is similar to an order-upto-level policy in a traditional production system where an order is placed in each period except for the case of no demand. The specific value of the remanufacturing-oriented planning stability in this model depends on the choice of $\hat{R}$. For

$\hat{R} = 0$ (reactive strategy, compare Section 5.2) the stability measure equals $(\mathbb{P}\{R_t = 0\} + T - 1)/T = (T-1)/T$. In all other cases, maximum stability is obtained $(\mathbb{P}\{R_t > 0\} + T - 1)/T = 1$.

5.4.3 Setup Stability for Exponentially Distributed Demand and Returns

In order to get analytical results, it is assumed that both demand and returns are exponentially distributed. At first glance, this assumption restricts the outcome. However, it is expected that other, more general distributions have a similar impact on stability in recovery systems as they have in traditional systems. Chapter 4 analyzes the impact of different demand distributions including also exponentially distributed demand on stability. It has turned out that as demand uncertainty increases, the stability level decreases, but the general results for all demand distributions are fairly similar. Thus, some general properties of setup stability can be derived despite the limitation of the net demand distribution. Consequently it is realistic to expect that most of the results mentioned below also apply to other distributions of net demand.

For exponentially distributed demand and returns the distribution and density function of net demand N are of the form (see Heisig and Fleischmann [50])

$$\Phi_N(n) = \begin{cases} 1 - \frac{\mu}{\mu+\lambda}\, e^{-\lambda n} & \text{for} \quad n \geq 0 \\ \frac{\lambda}{\mu+\lambda}\, e^{\mu n} & \text{for} \quad n < 0 \end{cases} \tag{5.8}$$

and

$$\phi_N(n) = \begin{cases} \frac{\mu\lambda}{\mu+\lambda}\, e^{-\lambda n} & \text{for} \quad n \geq 0 \\ \frac{\mu\lambda}{\mu+\lambda}\, e^{\mu n} & \text{for} \quad n < 0 \end{cases} \tag{5.9}$$

where $\mathbb{E}[D] = \frac{1}{\lambda}$, and $\mathbb{E}[R] = \frac{1}{\mu}$ are the expected demand and returns, respectively. As mentioned before, it is assumed that $\mu > \lambda$ applies.
Defining again $Q := S - s$ as minimum lot size, the stationary distribution of V is given as (see Appendix D.1.1)

$$F_V(v) = \int_{-\infty}^{v} f_V(x)dx + 1_{v \geq Q}\, p_Q\,,$$

$$\text{with} \qquad f_V(v) = \begin{cases} 0 & \text{for} \quad v < 0 \\ ce^{-(\mu-\lambda)v} & \text{for} \quad v \geq 0 \end{cases}$$

$$\text{and} \quad p_Q = \frac{\mu-\lambda}{\mu(2-e^{-\lambda Q})}$$

$$\text{where} \quad c := p_Q[\lambda + \mu(1-e^{-\lambda Q})].$$

Then, setup stability is given as follows (see Appendix D.1.2).

Case A: For $l \leq T$ we have

$$\pi_{s,S}^{rec} = \frac{c_{\hat{N}}}{\mu+\lambda} + \frac{p_Q}{\mu+\lambda}\left[\beta_1^l \mu e^{-\lambda Q} + \sum_{\theta=2}^{l} \beta_\theta^l \mu c_\lambda e^{-\lambda(Q-(\theta-1)\hat{N})} \right. \tag{5.10}$$
$$+ \beta_{l+1}^l [\mu + \lambda - \mu(1-c_\lambda)e^{-\lambda(Q-l\hat{N})} - \lambda e^{\mu(Q-l\hat{N})}]$$
$$\left. + \sum_{\theta=l+2}^{T+1} \beta_\theta^l \lambda c_\mu e^{\mu(Q-(\theta-1)\hat{N})} + \beta_{T+1}^l \lambda c_T e^{\mu Q}\right]$$

Case B: For $l > T$ we have

$$\pi_{s,S}^{rec} = \frac{c_{\hat{N}}}{\mu+\lambda} + \frac{p_Q}{\mu+\lambda}\left[\beta_1^{T+1} \mu e^{-\lambda Q} + \sum_{\theta=2}^{T+1} \beta_\theta^{T+1} \mu c_\lambda e^{-\lambda(Q-(\theta-1)\hat{N})} \right.$$
$$\left. + \beta_{T+1}^{T+1}(\mu + \lambda - \mu e^{-\lambda(Q-T\hat{N})})\right] \tag{5.11}$$

where

$$c_{\hat{N}} := c\left\{\sum_{\tau=1}^{T}\left[\beta_1^\tau c_\mu e^{-\mu\tau\hat{N}} + \sum_{\theta=2}^{\tau} \beta_\theta^\tau c_\mu c_\lambda e^{-(\mu\tau-\lambda(\theta-1))\hat{N}}\right.\right.$$
$$+ \beta_{\tau+1}^\tau \frac{2}{\mu-\lambda}(\lambda c_\mu(1-c_\lambda) - \mu c_\lambda)e^{-(\mu-\lambda)\tau\hat{N}}$$
$$\left. + \sum_{\theta=\tau+2}^{T+1} \beta_\theta^\tau c_\mu c_\lambda e^{-(\mu(\theta-1)-\lambda\tau)\hat{N}} + \beta_{T+1}^\tau c_T c_\lambda e^{\lambda\tau\hat{N}}\right]$$
$$\left. + \quad \beta_1^{T+1} c_T + \sum_{\theta=2}^{T+1} \beta_\theta^{T+1} c_T c_\lambda e^{\lambda(\theta-1)\hat{N}} + \beta_{T+1}^{T+1} \frac{2\lambda}{\mu-\lambda} e^{-(\mu-\lambda)T\hat{N}}\right\}$$

and $c_\mu := (e^{\mu\hat{N}} - 1)$, $c_\lambda := (1 - e^{-\lambda\hat{N}})$, and $c_T := e^{-\mu T\hat{N}}$.

The distinction between $T \leq l$ and $T > l$ is necessary since F_V has a probability mass in $v = Q$. In the first case, Q is attained for $\tau = l$, whereas in the latter, Q belongs to $\tau = T + 1$. Thus the second term in (5.10) differs from the second one in (5.11).

Note that for the special case of a simple modified S policy, i.e. $s = S$, setup stability is given as[9]

$$\pi_S^{rec} = \frac{p_0}{\mu+\lambda}\left\{ \lambda c_0 + \beta_1^1 \mu + \beta_2^1 \lambda (1 - e^{-\mu \hat{N}}) + \sum_{\theta=3}^{T+1} \beta_\theta^1 \lambda c_\mu e^{-\mu(\theta-1))\hat{N}} + \beta_{T+1}^1 \lambda c_T \right\} \tag{5.12}$$

where

$$\begin{aligned} c_0 := \sum_{\tau=1}^{T} \Bigg[& \beta_1^\tau c_\mu e^{-\mu\tau\hat{N}} + \sum_{\theta=2}^{\tau} \beta_\theta^\tau c_\mu c_\lambda e^{-(\mu\tau-\lambda(\theta-1))\hat{N}} \\ & + \beta_{\tau+1}^\tau \frac{2}{\mu-\lambda}(\lambda c_\mu(1-c_\lambda) - \mu c_\lambda) e^{-(\mu-\lambda)\tau\hat{N}} \\ & + \sum_{\theta=\tau+2}^{T+1} \beta_\theta^\tau c_\mu c_\lambda e^{-(\mu(\theta-1)-\lambda\tau)\hat{N}} + \beta_{T+1}^\tau c_T c_\lambda e^{\lambda\tau\hat{N}} \Bigg] \\ + \; & \beta_1^{T+1} c_T + \sum_{\theta=2}^{T+1} \beta_\theta^{T+1} c_T c_\lambda e^{\lambda(\theta-1)\hat{N}} + \beta_{T+1}^{T+1} \frac{2\lambda}{\mu-\lambda} e^{-(\mu-\lambda)T\hat{N}} \end{aligned}$$

and $p_0 = \dfrac{\mu-\lambda}{\mu}$.

The planning stability in (5.10) and (5.11) only depends on the lot size parameter ($Q = S - s$), the length of the stability horizon (T), and the demand and return expectations ($\bar{D}, \bar{R}$), and forecasts ($\hat{D}, \hat{R}$), respectively.

Note that in the previous analysis, the forecasts may deviate from their expectations. Since the main goal is to provide insights on the influence of product returns on stability, it is now assumed that both coincide. Otherwise there may be some overlapping effects due to the deviation between forecasts and expected values. Hence for the remainder of the study, $\bar{D} = \hat{D}$, $\bar{R} = \hat{R}$, and, consequently $\mathbb{E}[N] = \hat{N}$.

Now the influence of Q, T and $\hat{D}$ as well as $\hat{R}$ on stability will be illustrated. Therefore, different numerical examples will be used. We will see that the relationship between Q and expected net demand ($\hat{D} - \hat{R}$), which is characterized by the parameter l, has a significant influence on $\pi_{s,S}^{rec}$. This is what one might intuitively expect, since the structure of the order sequences essentially depends on the so-called coverage parameter l (see Chapter 4).

Almost the same parameter setting as in Chapter 4 is used, except that (net) demand expectation has been increased, and only exponentially distributed

[9] This result immediately follows from (5.10) by setting $l = 1$.

demand and returns are dealt with. The basic parameter settings are depicted in Table 5.1 where $T = 1$ represents the short-term consideration, and $T = 50$ is set as "infinite" stability horizon.

Table 5.1. Parameter settings for Figure 5.5

$\hat{D}$	$\hat{R}$	T
20	10	1, 5, 50

That means that in Figure 5.5, the rate between returns and demand is equal to 50 %. First, the impact of Q and T on stability is examined, and the results of the traditional model are compared with the recovery model. Therefore, it is assumed that in the traditional model, expected demand is equal to the net demand in the recovery model, i.e 10. Figures 5.4 and 5.5 depict the shape of the stability function for both models.

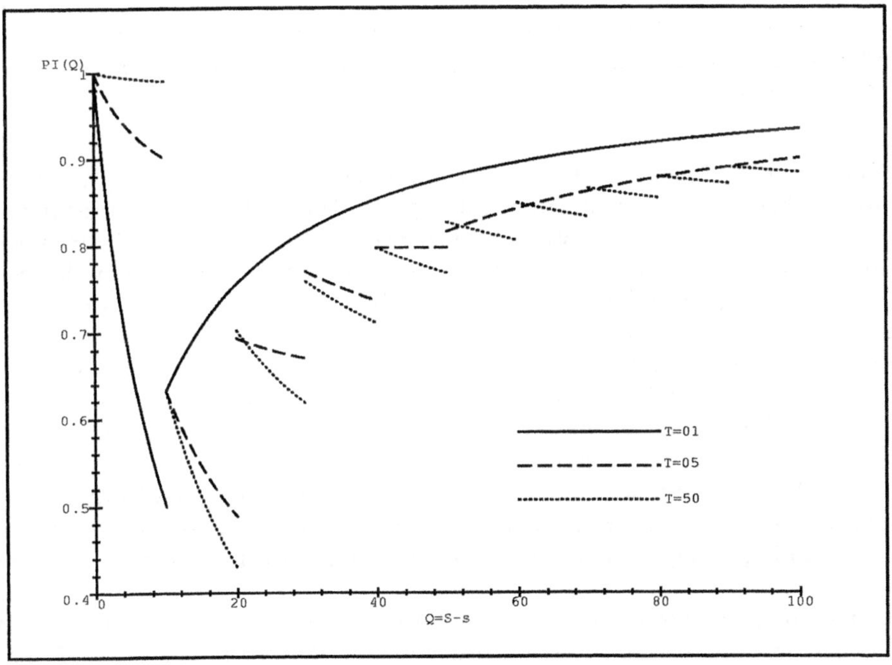

Figure 5.4. Stability function for traditional (s, S) policy (for different stability horizons)

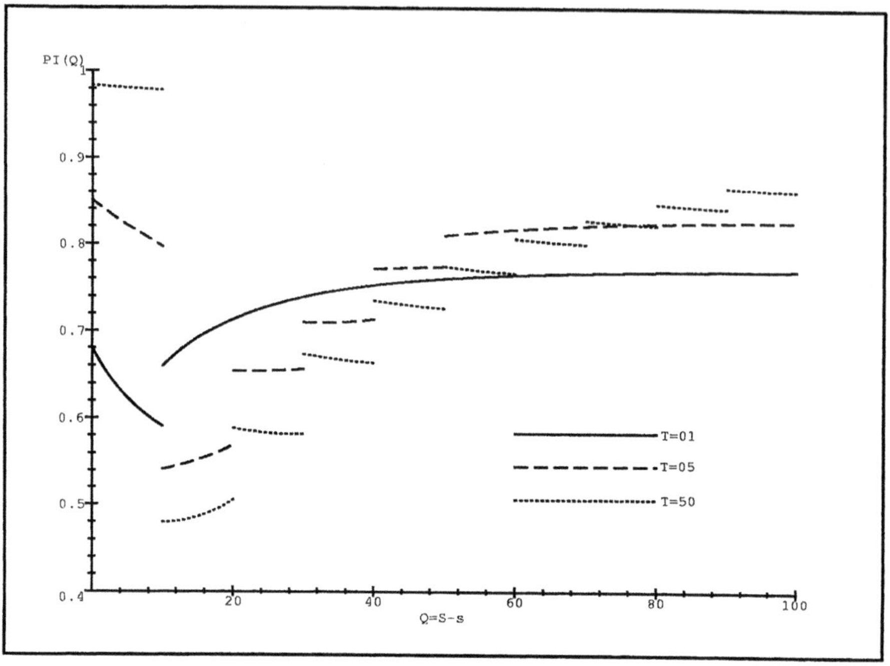

Figure 5.5. Stability function for (s, S) policy in recovery model (for different stability horizons)

Both stability functions are rather similar. With $Q \to \infty$ stability tends to 100 %, because almost no setup takes place. Different from the traditional model, where for $Q \to 0$ stability also reaches 100 %, $\pi^{rec}_{s,S}$ is significantly lower than 1 for small horizons in the recovery model. The shorter the stability horizon, the lower the resulting stability level will be. This different behaviour of the stability function is related to the return flow in the recovery model. In the traditional model for $Q \leq \hat{D}$ a setup occurs in almost every period of the stability horizon. Only if realized demand is very low, there will be no setup in the first period of the second planning cycle (see 4.2.2, Case A). In particular, a setup takes place in each period of the first planning cycle. Because of the unlimited initial stock, in the recovery model there may also be some periods without planned setups in cycle 0 (as well as in cycle 1), thus leading to a general lower level of stability, especially for small stability horizons.

Furthermore, in both models for $l > T$ the shape of the stability function is continuous, whereas for $l \leq T$ it is discontinuous if Q corresponds to multiples of expected (net) demand. For instance, for $T = 5$ the stability functions are continuous for $Q > 50$, and discontinuous in $Q = 10, 20, ..., 50$. Moreover, in the latter case, stability reaches (local) minima in these points of discontinuity. In the traditional model, global minimum stability is reached in $Q = \hat{D}$

for the short-term consideration, and in $Q = 2\hat{D}$ for $T > 1$ (see Section 4.3.2). This can also be observed in Figure 5.4. In Figure 5.5, minimum stability is either reached for $Q = \hat{N}$ ($T = 1$), or for $Q \searrow \hat{N}$ (i.e. Q converges to $\hat{N}$ from above), otherwise. Note that, in general, minimum stability is attained for lot sizes in $(\hat{N}, 2\hat{N})$. It is never reached for lot sizes which are equal to or larger than twice the size of the expected net demand. The reason for this is directly related to the sequence of setups for $\hat{N} < Q \leq 2\hat{N}$. After the first setup is planned to be released, a planned production order can be found in every second period, i.e in cycle 0, setups in periods $\tau + 2n$ (where τ depends on the initial stock), and in cycle 1 setups occur in $\theta + 2n$ (with $n \in \mathbb{N}$). Thus for $\tau = \theta$ identical order decisions can be found in both planning periods. In all other cases, the planned setups deviate significantly, and in the worst case, they may differ in each period. Therefore, the stability level for $l = 2$ is rather low. For larger lot sizes there are no planned order sequences that differ in all periods, since with rising Q, the number of periods with no setups increases in both planning cycles.

Finally, the stability level in the recovery model tends to be lower than in the traditional model in most cases (see Figures 5.4 and 5.5). However, the level of minimum stability in the recovery model is larger than in the traditional one.
Considering the impact of T on $\pi^{rec}_{s,S}$ in Figures 5.4 and 5.5, we find that with rising horizon, stability increases if $Q < \hat{D}$, or $Q < \hat{N}$, respectively. For larger lot sizes there are some cases where stability increases in the traditional model with an enlargement of the stability horizon, but in general it is reduced (see also Section 4.3.2). This general tendency also applies in the recovery model for sufficiently large stability horizons. If we consider the shape of the stability function for $T = 5$ and $T = 50$ in Figure 5.5, then we find that an increase of the stability horizon leads to a lower stability level for most of the lot sizes in the region $Q > \hat{N}$. Nevertheless, for a very large lot size, e.g. $Q > 80$, an increase from $T = 5$ to $T = 50$ leads to a higher stability level. However, in comparing a stability horizon with $T = 8$ to $T = 50$ (see Heisig and Fleischmann [50]), an increase of the stability horizon leads to a lower stability level for all lot sizes $Q > \hat{N}$. Moreover, the shape for the short-term consideration in the traditional model significantly differs from its shape in the recovery system: the stability level in the traditional model is always largest, whereas in the recovery model it is rather small and, in particular, for large values of Q it is lowest.

Now the impact of the expected returns ($\hat{R}$) on stability will be considered. Therefore in Figures 5.6 and 5.7 the following parameter values have been set.

Table 5.2. Parameter settings for Figures 5.6 and 5.7

Q	$\hat{D}$	T
30	20	1, 5, 50

The result is somewhat counterintuitive. For small return rates, planning stability decreases as $\hat{R}$ increases. This is what one might expect since the return flow increases the variability of the net demand per period. However, for large $\hat{R}$ planning stability increases as the return rate increases. For $\hat{R}$ close to $\hat{D}$ stability converges to 1. This effect can be explained by considering the expected stock level (see Figure 5.7). For high return rates, the average stock level increases exponentially in $\hat{R}$, similar to the expected queue length in a single server queue. The high stock level implies that production orders are scheduled very rarely, and hence that the system is very "stable" from a setup perspective. In this way, product returns can increase planning stability, however at the expense of high stock levels. Note that this result applies to arbitrary distributions of demand and returns, because average stock increases in general with increasing return rate, i.e. $\bar{R} \to \bar{D}$.

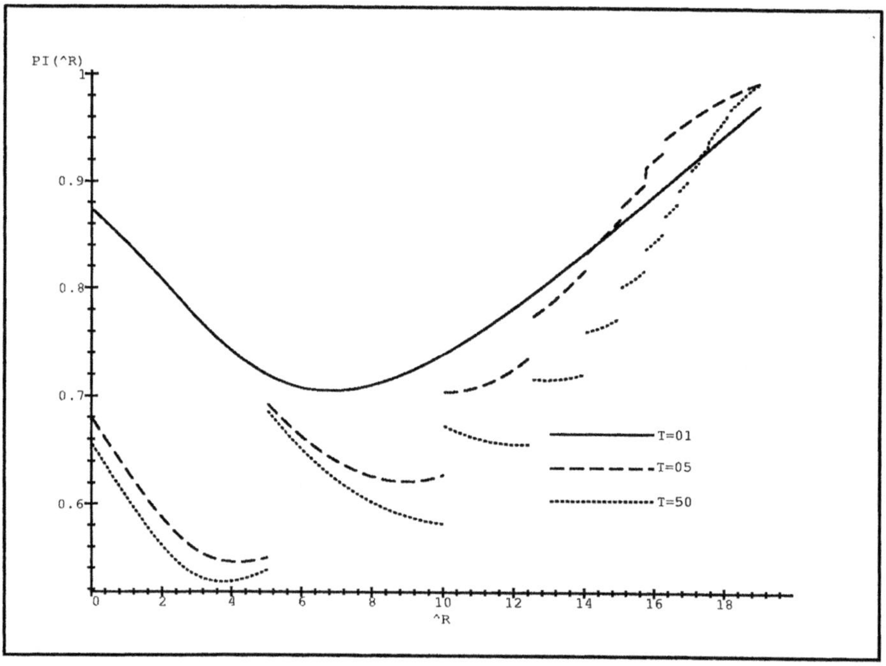

Figure 5.6. Stability function for different return rates $\hat{R}$ for (s, S) policy (for different stability horizons)

Figure 5.6 shows that for the short-term consideration for return/demand-ratios larger than 75 %, the stability level in the recovery model (with $\hat{R} > 0$) is greater than stability in the traditional model (with $\hat{R} = 0$). For smaller return quotas, stability is lower than in the case of no product returns. For larger stability horizons, the same tendency is evident for lower returns quotas. For $T = 5$ and $T = 50$ in the case of $\hat{R}/\hat{D} > 50\%$, stability in the recovery model is greater.
Section 5.4.2 in (5.6) gave an indication of the influence of returns on planning updates. The shift in the order sequence during a planning update is increasing in both the expected value and the variance of the returns per period. Note that (5.6) only considers the difference between τ and θ. Figure 5.6 indicates that stability increases with rising $\hat{R}$ though (5.6) indicates that the expected difference between both planning cycles increases. However, the absolute values of τ and θ also increase as the return rate rises. A long period with non-setup decisions can therefore be found in both planning cycles ultimately leading to a high level of stability for large return rates, even though (5.6) might indicate the opposite.

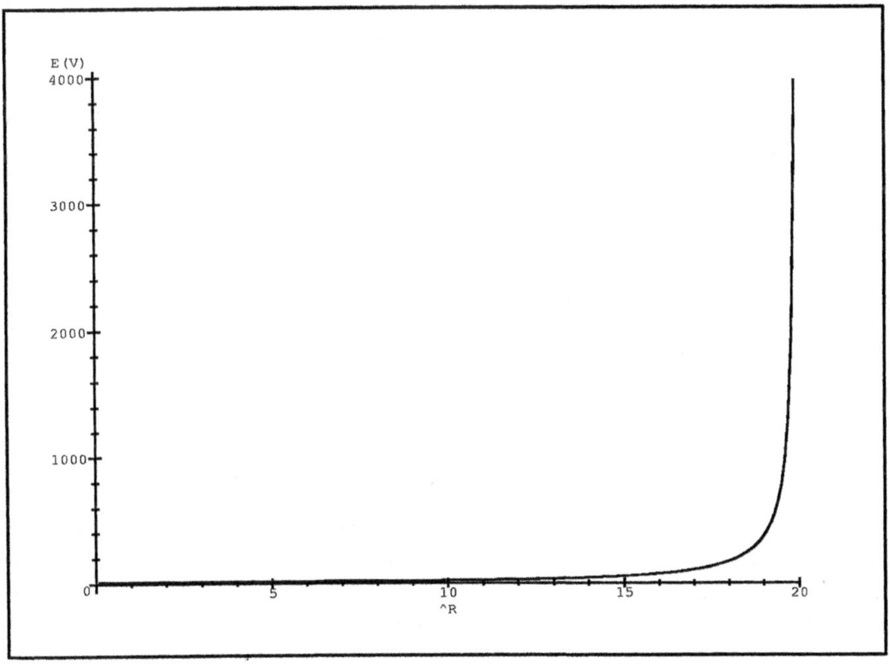

Figure 5.7. Average inventory position $\mathbb{E}[V]$ for (s, S) policy

The adjustment of Q as a function of the return rate has also been examined. To this end, an EOQ-approximation has been used to set the value for

Q depending on the returns[10]. For these adjusted lot sizes, the shape of the stability function as shown in Figure 5.6 only changes insignificantly. This result is not surprising since in the traditional model, an analogous approximation of Q with varying demand rate leads only to a hardly remarkable change of planning stability (see Jensen [68], pp.198).

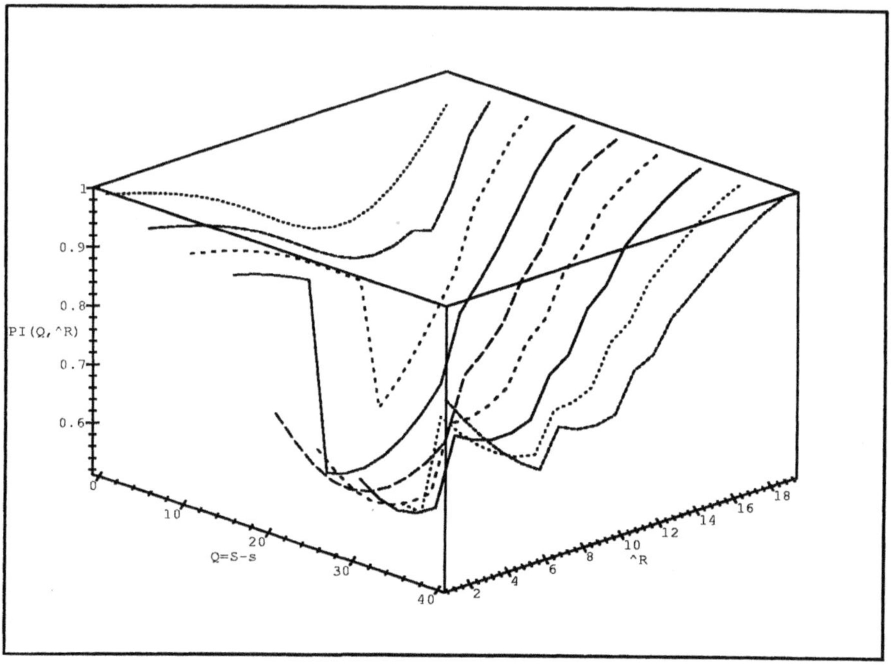

Figure 5.8. Stability function for different lot sizes and return rates ($\hat{D} = 20$ and $T = 5$)

Finally, Q and $\hat{R}$ have been varied simultaneously. In Figure 5.8 depicts the shapes of the stability functions for $T = 5$, $\hat{D} = 20$, $Q = 0, 5, 10, ..., 40$ and $\hat{R} = 0, ..., 19.9$. Here, the case $Q = 0$ corresponds to a simple S policy, and the stability function is continuous. In spite of the points of discontinuity for larger lot sizes, for the sake of clarity, the matching functions in Figure 5.8have been connected. As mentioned above, it can again be observed that, in general, $\pi^{rec}_{s,S}$ decreases for $Q \leq \hat{D} - \hat{R}$, and that it increases otherwise. For small expected returns, stability at first decreases, and then it increases quite fast.

---

[10] $Q = \lfloor [20(\hat{D} - \hat{R})]^{1/2} \rfloor$. This corresponds to a ratio of fixed costs to inventory carrying costs of 10. Moreover, $S = s + Q$.

5.4.4 Recovery System without Fixed Costs for Production

Here, an S policy is proven to be optimal. Then, in the case of exponentially distributed demand and returns, setup stability is given as indicated in (5.12) (see p.144).

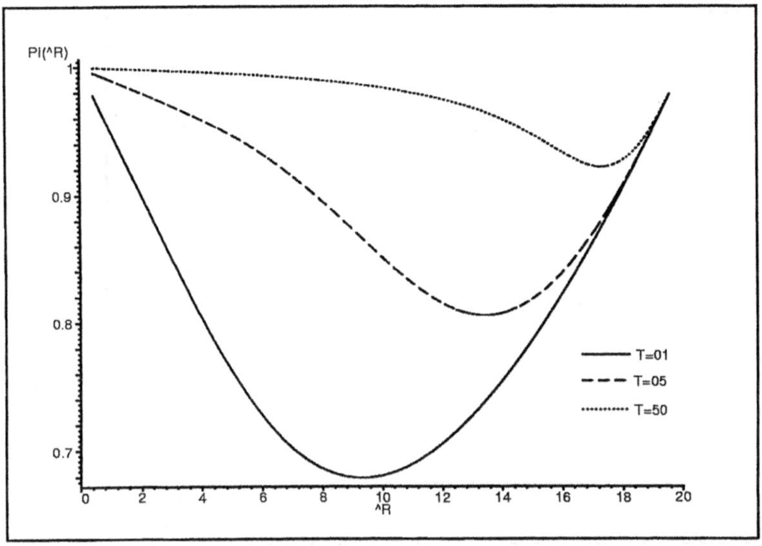

Figure 5.9. Stability function for different return rates $\hat{R}$ for S policy (for different stability horizons)

Since there is no lot-sizing, it is only necessary to consider the impact of expected returns $\hat{R}$ on π_S^{rec}. Therefore, the parameter settings shown in Table 5.3 are used.

Table 5.3. Parameter settings for Figure 5.9

$\hat{D}$	T
20	1, 5, 50

First, it can be noted that the stability function is continuous for all stability horizons, because the coverage parameter l does not change with varying return rate $\hat{R}$. It is always equal to 1. We find that contrary to the (s, S) policy stability[11] tends to 100 % with $\hat{R} \to 0$. This case is equivalent to a traditional

[11] See Figure 5.6.

production system without a remanufacturing option which is controlled by a simple S policy. Thus a production setup is planned for release in each period to raise stock to S. As for the system with fixed costs, stability approaches 100 % for $\hat{R} \rightarrow \hat{D}$. In this case, demand can be satisfied by remanufacturing returned items.

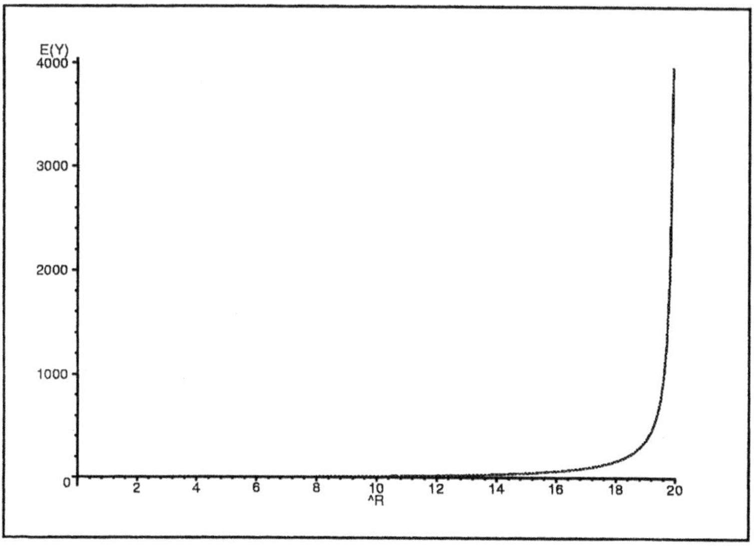

Figure 5.10. Average inventory position $\mathbb{E}[Y]$ for S policy

Moreover, average inventory position evolves like for an (s, S) policy, because again for high return rates average stock increases exponentially in $\hat{R}$ (see Figure 5.10). Thus, production orders occur rarely. Furthermore, with rising stability, horizon stability increases, and the location of minimum stability changes from $\hat{R} \cong \frac{\hat{D}}{2} - 1$ (for $T = 1$) to values of expected returns close to expected demand[12]. Finally, comparing the stability performance of an S policy with that of an (s, S) control rule, findings indicate that the level in the system without fixed costs is larger. This is related to the fact that in the first case, lot-sizing is not possible. Therefore, for "moderate" return rates, production setups occur more frequently than in the system with fixed production costs.

[12] For $T = 100$, findings show that minimum stability is reached for values of $\hat{R}$ which are slightly lower than $\hat{D}$.

5.4.5 Summary

This section provides analytical results on the planning stability of production setups in a basic product recovery system without a disposal option.

As has already been proven, the return flow influences production setup stability considerably. As expected, at first, stability decreases with rising return rate due to the additional uncertainty. However, for large return rates, stability increases again. This fact is related to the increase in the average stock. There is a trade-off between stability and stock level. Hence, the higher level of stability is paid for with a higher stock.

As in traditional inventory models, nervousness is not affected by the reorder point s, but the choice of the minimum lot size $Q = S - s$ and the length of the stability horizon T have a significant impact on stability. The impact of these parameters is very similar to their influence in a traditional system.

Depending on the relationship between $Q/\hat{N}$ and stability horizon T, the stability function either possesses cyclical patterns which lead to a high level of nervousness if the lot size is set to a multiple of the forecasted net demand per period, or it develops continuously. Furthermore, minimum stability is reached for reorder quantities which are equal to the forecasted demand (if $T = 1$), or for lot sizes in the interval $(\hat{N}, 2\hat{N})$ (if $T > 1$). The latter fact is different from the traditional model where minimum long-term stability is always attained for lot sizes which are twice as large as the expected demand. Additionally, a change in the length of the stability horizon leads to a change of the level of planning stability. For small lot sizes, i.e. $Q \leq \hat{N}$, an increase of the stability horizon leads to a higher level of stability. In the other cases, such a general result could not be obtained, but stability tends to decrease with rising stability horizon, except from the short-term consideration where stability for (sufficiently) large lot sizes is rather low in comparison with the traditional model.

For the system without fixed costs, which is controlled by a simple S policy, findings show that stability first decreases with rising return rate, but after reaching a certain level of minimum stability, setup stability increases again. Furthermore, the level of stability is greater than in the recovery system with fixed production costs.

One natural extension of the recovery system introduced in this section is the analysis of a recovery system where used and returned items may also be disposed of. Since in such a recovery system, average stock is limited from above, one may expect a different stability behaviour, compared with our recovery system without disposal. In the next section, the stability performance of a recovery system with a disposal option is analyzed. Because of analytical tractability, we can only consider the case without fixed costs.

5.5 Recovery System with Disposal Option

This section addresses a slightly different recovery system, namely there is an additional option to dispose of returned products. Assuming no fixed costs for production and remanufacturing, the optimal policy for replenishment orders is of an (S, D) type.

5.5.1 Notation and Assumptions

In general, the same assumptions are used as for the recovery system without disposal option, in particular, it is assumed that $\mathbb{E}[N] > 0$ and $\hat{N} > 0$[13]. In addition to the notation in Section 5.4, here an introduction to the following symbols:

M_t	=	disposal quantity in period t;
Z_t	=	net stock at the beginning of t before production, remanufacturing, and disposal[14];
Y_t	=	net stock at the beginning of t after production, remanufacturing, and disposal.

Then the system dynamics are described by

$$M_t = \begin{cases} 0 & \text{if } Z_t \leq D \\ Z_t - D & \text{else} \end{cases}$$

$$Q_t = \begin{cases} 0 & \text{if } Z_t > S \\ S - Z_t & \text{else} \end{cases}$$

$$O_t = R_{t-1} - M_{t-1}$$

$$Z_t = Y_{t-1} - N_{t-1}$$

$$Y_t = Z_t + Q_t - M_t \ .$$

Here, $(Y_t)_{t \in \mathbb{N}}$ forms a discrete time Markov process on $[S, D]$. Note that in contrast with the recovery system without disposal option, the net inventory is bounded from above, as in traditional inventory systems. Therefore, (Y_t) admits a limiting stationary distribution, which is again denoted by F_Y. Moreover, Y denotes the corresponding random variable.

As for the (s, S) policy in Section 5.4, the production setups must be determined for two subsequent planning cycles 0 and 1 (see Figure 5.3). Note that the sequences of production decisions $((Q_t, \hat{Q}^t_{t+1}, \hat{Q}^t_{t+2}, ..., \hat{Q}^t_{t+T})$ with $t = 0, 1)$ are now generated by applying an (S, D) policy. Again it is assumed that all periods are weighted equally, and therefore, the measure of setup stability is used as indicated in (5.1), and (5.2).

[13] Note that for the numerical example in Section 5.5.3, it is again assumed that both values coincide.

[14] Note that Z_t also comprises the returned items of the previous period.

5.5.2 General Results

Since it is assumed that $\hat{N} > 0$, findings show that after the first period t in which a setup takes place, an order is also planned for release in all succeeding periods. The inventory position after replenishment in t is equal to the order-up-to-level S, i.e. $\hat{Y}_t = S$. Thus $\hat{Y}_{t+1} = S - \hat{N}$, which has to be smaller than S due to the aforementioned relationship. Consequently, only the first period with a production setup must be determined.

For this purpose, a parameter K is introduced, which can be determined as follows

$$K = \lfloor \frac{D - S}{\hat{N}} \rfloor. \tag{5.13}$$

Now, the relationship between this range parameter K and the stability horizon parameter T directly influences the structure of the setups in both planning cycles. Therefore, an additional parameter H can be defined as

$$H = \begin{cases} T & \text{for} \quad T \leq K \\ K & \text{for} \quad T > K. \end{cases} \tag{5.14}$$

Cycle 0:

In order to determine the production setups, the region $S \leq Y_0 \leq D$ is divided into several intervals: $S + (\tau - 1)\hat{N} \leq Y_0 < S + \tau\hat{N}$ (for all $\tau = 1, ..., H$) and $S + H\hat{N} \leq Y_0 \leq D$ $(\tau = H + 1)$.

Then, the first setup takes place in period τ. The inventory position of all preceding periods is not smaller than the order-up-to-level, i.e. $\hat{Z}_t^0 = Y_0 - t\hat{N} \geq S$ (for all $t = 1, ...\tau - 1$), but in τ it is lower than S: $\hat{Z}_\tau^0 = Y_0 - \tau\hat{N} < S$, and a setup is planned to be released, i.e. $\hat{Q}_\tau^0 = S - (Y_0 - \tau\hat{N})$ and $\hat{Y}_\tau^0 = S$. Note that if $T \leq K$, i.e. $H = T$, then there are no production setups within the entire stability horizon, because the net demand can be satisfied by the initial inventory position.
To summarize, the period in which the first setup occurs can be calculated as

$$\tau(Y_0) = \lfloor \frac{Y_0 - S}{\hat{N}} \rfloor + 1 \tag{5.15}$$

where $\tau(Y_0)$ can take on values from 1 to $H+1$. It only depends on the initial stock Y_0.

Cycle 1:

The period with a first setup in cycle 1 depends on the realized net demand N_0 and initial stock Y_0. The starting inventory position in the first period of planning cycle 1 is given by $Z_1 = Y_0 - N_0$.
If now the realized net demand is sufficiently large, i.e. $Y_0 - S < N_0 < \infty$,

then the first setup takes place in period 1, i.e. $Q_1 = S - (Y_0 - N_0)$ and $Y_1 = S$, $(\theta = 1)$.
If $N_0 \leq Y_0 - S$, then Y_1 is either given by $Z_1 = Y_0 - N_0$ (if $Y_0 - D \leq N_0 \leq Y_0 - S$) or by the dispose-down-to-level D (if $-\infty < N_0 \leq Y_0 - D$). In both cases, there are no production activities, but in the latter some items are disposed of, i.e. $M_1 = Y_0 - N_0 - D$.

Then, the first setup occurs in period θ for which $Y_0 - S - (\theta - 1)\hat{N} < N_0 \leq Y_0 - S - (\theta - 2)\hat{N}$ $(\theta = 2, ..., H+1)$ and $-\infty < N_0 \leq Y_0 - S - H\hat{N}$ $(\theta = H+2)$ apply. In general, θ is given as

$$\theta(Y_0, N_0) = 1 + max\{0, \lfloor \frac{min(Y_0 - N_0, D) - S}{\hat{N}} \rfloor + 1\} \tag{5.16}$$

for all $\theta = 1, ..., H + 2$.

Table 5.4. Setup decisions in consecutive planning cycles for an (S, D) policy with $T > K$

t	1 ... τ ... K	K+1	K+2 ..		
0	1 ... 1 ... 1	1	1 ...	$S \leq Y_0 < S + \hat{N}$	$(\tau = 1)$
	0 ... 1 ... 1	1	1 ...	$S + (\tau - 1)\hat{N} \leq Y_0 < S + \tau\hat{N}$	$(\tau = 1, ..., K)$
	0 ... 0 ... 0	1	1 ...	$S + K\hat{N} \leq Y_0 \leq D$	$(\tau = K + 1)$
t	1 ... θ ... K	K+1	K+2 ..		
1	1 ... 1 ... 1	1	1 ...	$Y_0 - S < N_0 < \infty$	$(\theta = 1)$
	0 ... 0 ... 1	1	1 ...	$Y_0 - S - (\theta - 1)\hat{N} < N_0 \leq Y_0 - S - (\theta - 2)\hat{N}$	$(\theta = 2, .., K)$
	0 ... 0 ... 0	1	1 ...	$Y_0 - S - K\hat{N} < N_0 \leq Y_0 - S - (K - 1)\hat{N}$	$(\theta = K + 1)$
	0 ... 0 ... 0	0	1 ...	$-\infty < N_0 \leq Y_0 - S - K\hat{N}$	$(\theta = K + 2)$

The sequences of planned setup decisions are summarized in Table 5.4 for $T > K$, and in Table 5.5 for $T \leq K$, respectively. Note that for the latter case, the setups for $\theta = T + 1$ and $\theta = T + 2$ are exactly the same. Both intervals could be summarized to $-\infty < N_0 \leq Y_0 - S - (T - 1)\hat{N}$. But since one closed-form stability function is used for both, $T > K$ and $T \leq K$, we maintain the separation of both intervals.

For $T > K$ (as in Table 5.4), the corresponding stability quotients are given as

$$\beta_\theta^\tau = \begin{cases} \frac{T-(\tau-\theta)}{T} & \text{for} \quad \theta = 1, 2, ..., \tau \\ \frac{T-(\theta-\tau)}{T} & \text{for} \quad \theta = \tau, \tau + 1, ..., K + 2 \end{cases} \qquad \forall \quad \tau = 1, 2, ..., K + 1. \tag{5.17}$$

Table 5.5. Setup decisions in consecutive planning cycles for an (S, D) policy with $T \leq K$

t	$1 \dots \tau \dots T$		
0	$1 \dots 1 \dots 1$	$S \leq Y_0 < S + \hat{N}$	$(\tau = 1)$
	$0 \dots 1 \dots 1$	$S + (\tau - 1)\hat{N} \leq Y_0 < S + \tau\hat{N}$	$(\tau = 1, ..., T)$
	$0 \dots 0 \dots 0$	$S + T\hat{N} \leq Y_0 \leq D$	$(\tau = T + 1)$
t	$1 \dots \theta \dots T$		
1	$1 \dots 1 \dots 1$	$Y_0 - S < N_0 < \infty$	$(\theta = 1)$
	$0 \dots 1 \dots 1$	$Y_0 - S - (\theta - 1)\hat{N} < N_0 \leq Y_0 - S - (\theta - 2)\hat{N}$	$(\theta = 2, ..., T)$
	$0 \dots 0 \dots 0$	$Y_0 - S - T\hat{N} < N_0 \leq Y_0 - S - (T - 1)\hat{N}$	$(\theta = T + 1)$
	$0 \dots 0 \dots 0$	$-\infty < N_0 \leq Y_0 - S - T\hat{N}$	$(\theta = T + 2)$

In the case of $T \leq K$ (see Table 5.5) we get

$$\beta_\theta^\tau = \begin{cases} \frac{T-(\tau-\theta)}{T} & \text{for} \quad \theta = 1, 2, ..., \tau \\ \\ \frac{T-(\theta-\tau)}{T} & \text{for} \quad \theta = \tau, \tau + 1, ..., T + 1 \end{cases} \qquad \forall \ \tau = 1, 2, ..., T + 1, \tag{5.18}$$

$$\text{and} \quad \beta_{T+2}^\tau := \beta_{T+1}^\tau. \tag{5.19}$$

Analogously to the (s, S) policy, with (5.15) and (5.16) expected stability can be written as

$$\pi_{S,D} = \sum_{\tau=1}^{H} \int_{S+(\tau-1)\hat{N}}^{S+\tau\hat{N}} \Big\{ \beta_1^\tau [1 - \Phi_N(y - S)] + \sum_{\theta=2}^{H+1} \beta_\theta^\tau [\Phi_N(y - S - (\theta - 2)\hat{N}) \\ - \Phi_N(y - S - (\theta - 1)\hat{N})] + \beta_{H+2}^\tau \Phi_N(y - S - H\hat{N}) \Big\} dF_Y(y) \tag{5.20}$$

$$+ \int_{S+H\hat{N}}^{D} \Big\{ \beta_1^{H+1} [1 - \Phi_N(y - S)] + \sum_{\theta=2}^{H+1} \beta_\theta^{H+1} [\Phi_N(y - S - (\theta - 2)\hat{N}) \\ - \Phi_N(y - S - (\theta - 1)\hat{N})] + \beta_{H+2}^{H+1} \Phi_N(y - S - H\hat{N}) \Big\} dF_Y(y).$$

In the next section, stability for exponentially distributed demand and returns is calculated, and the influence of the critical parameters on $\pi_{S,D}$ is analyzed.

5.5.3 Setup Stability for Exponentially Distributed Demand and Returns

In the case of exponentially distributed demand and returns, the distribution and density are given by (5.8) and (5.9), respectively. Then, the stationary density of Y is given as (see Appendix D.2.1)

$$F_Y(y) = \int_S^D f_Y(x)dx + \mathbb{1}_{y=S}\, p_S + \mathbb{1}_{y=D}\, p_D\,,$$

$$\text{with} \qquad f_Y(y) = \begin{cases} 0 & \text{for} \quad y < S \\ p_S \lambda e^{(\lambda-\mu)(y-S)} & \text{for} \quad S < y < D \\ 0 & \text{for} \quad y > D \end{cases}$$

$$\text{and} \quad p_S = \tilde{c}_{(S,D)} \mu e^{\lambda S} (e^{-\mu S} - e^{-\lambda(D-S)-\mu D}) \qquad \text{for} \quad y = S$$

$$\text{and} \quad p_D = \tilde{c}_{(S,D)} \lambda e^{-\mu D} (e^{\lambda D} - e^{-\mu(D-S)+\lambda S}) \qquad \text{for} \quad y = D$$

$$\text{where } \tilde{c}_{(S,D)} := \frac{\lambda - \mu}{\lambda^2 e^{-\mu D}(e^{\lambda D} - e^{-\mu(D-S)+\lambda S}) - \mu^2 e^{\lambda S}(e^{-\mu S} - e^{-\lambda(D-S)-\mu D})}.$$

Then, setup stability is given as follows (see Appendix D.2.2).

$$\begin{aligned}
\pi_{S,D} = \frac{p_S}{\lambda+\mu} \Bigg\{ & \beta_1^1 \mu + \beta_2^1 \lambda (1 - e^{-\mu \hat{N}}) + \sum_{\theta=3}^{H+1} \beta_\theta^1 \lambda c_\mu e^{-\mu(\theta-1))\hat{N}} + \beta_{H+2}^1 \lambda c_{H_\mu} \Bigg\} \\
+ \tilde{p} \Bigg\{ & \sum_{\tau=1}^{H} \Bigg[\beta_1^\tau c_\mu e^{-\mu\tau\hat{N}} + \sum_{\theta=2}^{\tau} \beta_\theta^\tau c_\mu c_\lambda e^{-(\mu\tau - \lambda(\theta-1))\hat{N}} \\
& + \beta_{\tau+1}^\tau \frac{2}{\mu-\lambda} (\lambda c_\mu (1 - c_\lambda) - \mu c_\lambda) e^{-(\mu-\lambda)\tau\hat{N}} \\
& + \sum_{\theta=\tau+2}^{H+1} \beta_\theta^\tau c_\mu c_\lambda e^{-(\mu(\theta-1)-\lambda\tau)\hat{N}} + \beta_{H+2}^\tau c_{H_\mu} c_\lambda e^{\lambda\tau\hat{N}} \Bigg] \\
& + \beta_1^{H+1} \tilde{c}_H + \sum_{\theta=2}^{H+1} \beta_\theta^{H+1} \tilde{c}_H c_\lambda e^{\lambda(\theta-1))\hat{N}} \\
& + \beta_{H+2}^{H+1} \Big(\frac{\lambda+\mu}{\mu-\lambda} \hat{c}_H - c_{H_\lambda} \tilde{c}_H \Big) \Bigg\} +
\end{aligned} \qquad (5.21)$$

$$+\frac{p_D}{\lambda+\mu}\Big\{\beta_1^{H+1}\mu c_D+\sum_{\theta=2}^{H+1}\beta_\theta^{H+1}\mu c_D c_\lambda e^{\lambda(\theta-1))\hat{N}}$$
$$+\beta_{H+2}^{H+1}(\lambda+\mu-\mu c_D c_{H_\lambda})\}$$

where

$$\tilde{p}:=\lambda/(\mu+\lambda)p_S,\qquad c_\mu:=(e^{\mu\hat{N}}-1),\qquad c_\lambda:=(1-e^{-\lambda\hat{N}}),$$
$$c_D:=e^{-\lambda(D-S)},\qquad c_{H_\mu}:=e^{-\mu H\hat{N}},\qquad c_{H_\lambda}:=e^{\lambda H\hat{N}},$$
$$\tilde{c}_H:=e^{-\mu H\hat{N}}-e^{-\mu(D-S)},\quad \hat{c}_H:=e^{-(\mu-\lambda)H\hat{N}}-e^{-(\mu-\lambda)(D-S)}.$$

Since $\beta_{T+2}^\tau:=\beta_{T+1}^\tau$ for $T\le K$ (see (5.19)) the result in (5.21) can be simplified to

$$\pi_{S,D}=\frac{p_S}{\lambda+\mu}\Big\{\beta_1^1\mu+\beta_2^1\lambda(1-e^{-\mu\hat{N}})+\sum_{\theta=3}^{T+1}\beta_\theta^1\lambda c_\mu e^{-\mu(\theta-1))\hat{N}}+\beta_{T+1}^1\lambda c_{T_\mu}\Big\}$$
$$+\tilde{p}\Big\{\sum_{\tau=1}^{T}\Big[\beta_1^\tau c_\mu e^{-\mu\tau\hat{N}}+\sum_{\theta=2}^{\tau}\beta_\theta^\tau c_\mu c_\lambda e^{-(\mu\tau-\lambda(\theta-1))\hat{N}}$$
$$+\beta_{\tau+1}^\tau\frac{2}{\mu-\lambda}(\lambda c_\mu(1-c_\lambda)-\mu c_\lambda)e^{-(\mu-\lambda)\tau\hat{N}}$$
$$+\sum_{\theta=\tau+2}^{T+1}\beta_\theta^\tau c_\mu c_\lambda e^{-(\mu(\theta-1)-\lambda\tau)\hat{N}}+\beta_{T+1}^\tau c_{T_\mu}c_\lambda e^{\lambda\tau\hat{N}}\Big]\tag{5.22}$$
$$+\beta_1^{T+1}\tilde{c}_T+\sum_{\theta=2}^{T+1}\beta_\theta^{T+1}\tilde{c}_T c_\lambda e^{\lambda(\theta-1))\hat{N}}$$
$$+\beta_{T+1}^{T+1}(\frac{\lambda+\mu}{\mu-\lambda}\hat{c}_T-c_{T_\lambda}\tilde{c}_T)\Big\}$$
$$+\frac{p_D}{\lambda+\mu}\Big\{\beta_1^{T+1}\mu c_D+\sum_{\theta=2}^{T+1}\beta_\theta^{T+1}\mu c_D c_\lambda e^{\lambda(\theta-1))\hat{N}}$$
$$+\beta_{T+1}^{T+1}(\lambda+\mu-\mu c_D c_{T_\lambda})\}$$

where the stability quotients β_θ^τ are given by (5.18) for all $\theta,\tau=1,...,T+1$.

For $T>K$, one has to use the outcome in (5.21) with $H=K$ and the stability quotients as given by (5.17).

Note that for $D \to \infty$, $p_S = \frac{\mu-\lambda}{\mu}$, $p_D = 0$ and $\tilde{p} = \frac{\lambda}{\mu+\lambda} p_S$. Moreover, $\tilde{c}_T = e^{-\mu T\hat{N}} = c_{T_\mu}$ and $\hat{c}_T = e^{-(\mu-\lambda)T\hat{N}} = c_{T_\mu} c_{T_\lambda}$. Then, exactly the same result is obtained as for the recovery system without disposal and fixed costs, because an infinite value of D implicitly leads to an S policy without disposal option (see (5.12)).

$D \to S$ is a recovery system with disposal option which is controlled by a single parameter S. If, on the one hand, stock is smaller than S, then it is raised to S by remanufacturing returned products, and if necessary, by producing new items. If, on the other hand, stock is larger than S, then the excess is disposed of. In this case, $p_S = \frac{\mu}{\lambda+\mu}$, $p_D = \frac{\lambda}{\lambda+\mu}$, and $\tilde{p} = \frac{\lambda}{\lambda+\mu} p_S$. With these limiting values and $H = 0$, i.e. $K = 0$, in (5.21) findings show that

$$\pi_S^{disposal} = \frac{\beta_1^1 \mu + \beta_2^1 \lambda}{\lambda + \mu}.$$

Since $\beta_1^1 = 1$, and $\beta_2^1 = \frac{T-1}{T}$ (see Table 5.4) ultimately resulting in

$$\pi_S^{disposal} = 1 - \frac{\lambda}{T(\lambda + \mu)}, \tag{5.23}$$

where $\lambda = \frac{1}{\hat{D}}$ and $\mu = \frac{1}{\hat{R}}$.

In general, stability in the recovery system with disposal depends on the policy parameters D and S[15], on the length of the stability horizon (T), and the demand and return expectations, or forecasts, respectively (see (5.21) and (5.22)). As for the recovery system without disposal,it is assumed from this point onwards that demand and return forecasts coincide with their expectations, i.e. $\mathbb{E}[N] = \hat{N}$.

Starting with the impact of $D - S$, and T on setup stability, the same parameters will be used as shown in Table 5.1, i.e. $\hat{D} = 20, \hat{R} = 10$, and $T = 1, 5, 50$. Figure 5.11 depicts the stability function in dependence on $\frac{D-S}{\hat{N}}$ for different stability horizons. Findings show that with increasing $\frac{D-S}{\hat{N}}$, stability at first decreases, and then increases. This can be observed clearly for $T = 1$, where for $0 \leq \frac{D-S}{\hat{N}} < 1$ stability is reduced as the value of $\frac{D-S}{\hat{N}}$ increases, whereas for values larger than 1 it increases. The "jump" in this point can be explained by the calculation of H, i.e. the relationship between T and $K = \lfloor \frac{D-S}{\hat{N}} \rfloor$ (see (5.13) and (5.14), respectively). For $D - S < \hat{N}$, the parameter H equals $K = 0$, and for $D - S \geq \hat{N}$ it is equal to $T = 1$. Therefore, the stability function is discontinuous in $\frac{D-S}{\hat{N}} = 1$. The same applies to $T = 5$, where $H = K$ in the case of $\frac{D-S}{\hat{N}} < 5$, and for larger values $H = 5$ is valid. For $T = 50$, the stability function is discontinuous in $1, 2, 3, ..., 10$. But the

[15] It turns out that the difference between D and S really matters, not the exact amount of D and S. Furthermore, the relation between $D-S$ and $\hat{N}$ significantly influences stability (see also (5.13)).

jumps in these points are relatively small and can hardly be observed in Figure 5.11, because the stability level for large horizons like $T = 50$ is almost equal to 100 %.

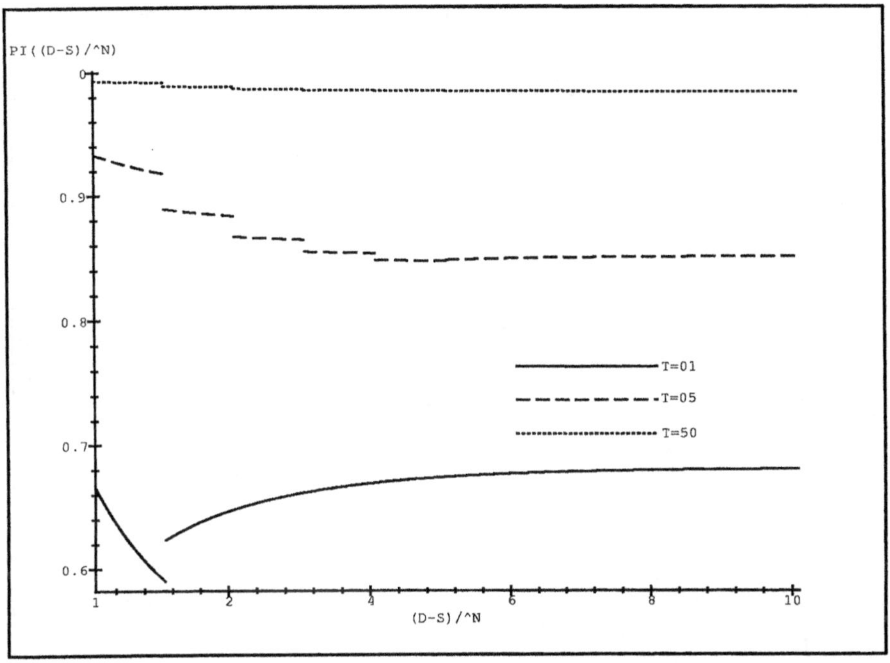

Figure 5.11. Stability function with varying difference between dispose-downto-level D and order-upto-level S (for different stability horizons)

Note that for $D \to S$ stability is given by $\pi_S^{disposal} = 1 - \frac{1}{3T}$ (see (5.23))[16]. For $D \to \infty$ we cannot simplify (5.12) in the same way, because the stability quotients depend in a more complicated way on the length of the stability horizon. But the same level of stability can be observed as in Figure 5.9, and in Figure 5.5 for $Q = 0$, respectively[17].

Finally, Figure 5.11 shows that stability with rising horizon parameter T gets larger. Since for both planning cycles after the first period with a setup, setups also occur in each subsequent period, the setup decisions from the period in which the setup takes place later (i.e. $max\{\tau, \theta\}$) up to period T are identical (see Section 5.5.2). Thus as the stability horizon rises, there are more periods with identical planned setup decisions, and stability increases.

16 Thus we get $\pi_S^{disposal} = 0.66$ for $T = 1$, $\pi_S^{disposal} = 0.93$ for $T = 5$, and $\pi_S^{disposal} = 0.99$ for $T = 50$.

17 $\pi_S^{rec} = 0.68$ for $T = 1$, $\pi_S^{rec} = 0.85$ for $T = 5$, and $\pi_S^{rec} = 0.98$ for $T = 50$.

Figure 5.12 depicts the stability function in dependence on the forecasted returns. Note that in Figure 5.12 the difference between D and S is equal to 30. Exactly the same results can be found for other values of D and S with $D - S = 30$. Therefore it can be concluded that the exact amount of the policy parameters does not influence stability, but the difference between both really matters.

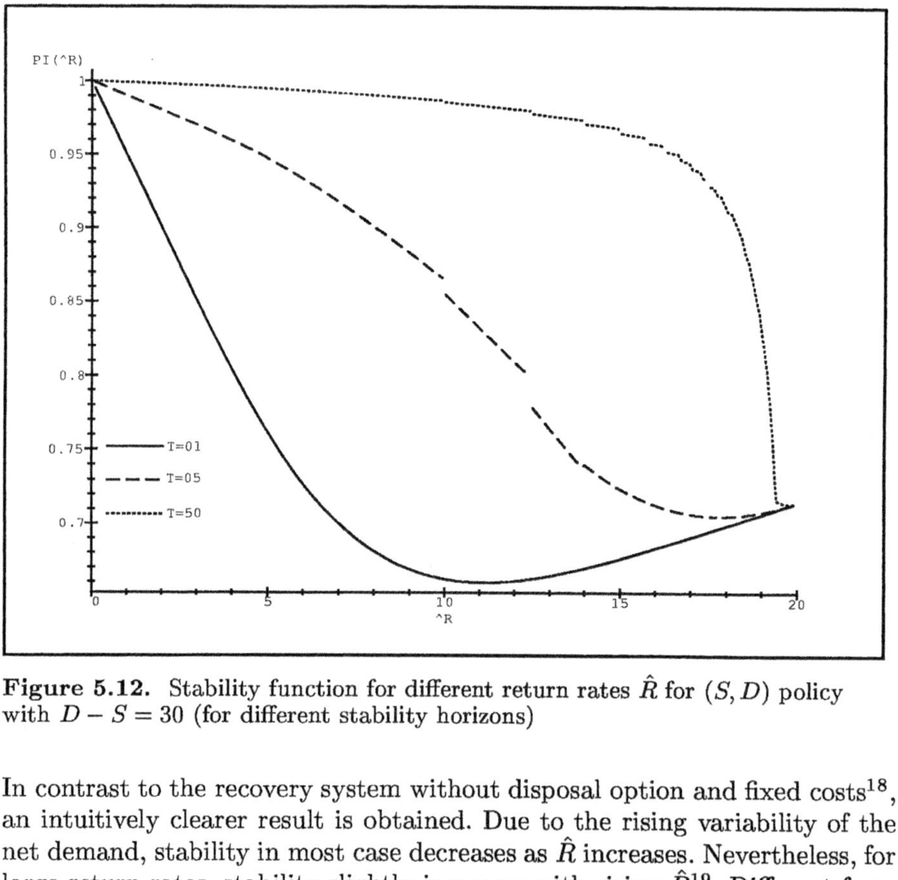

Figure 5.12. Stability function for different return rates $\hat{R}$ for (S, D) policy with $D - S = 30$ (for different stability horizons)

In contrast to the recovery system without disposal option and fixed costs[18], an intuitively clearer result is obtained. Due to the rising variability of the net demand, stability in most case decreases as $\hat{R}$ increases. Nevertheless, for large return rates, stability slightly increases with rising $\hat{R}$[19]. Different from the model in Section 5.4.4, the stability does not converge to 1 (see Figure 5.9). These effects can again be explained by taking a closer look at the expected stock level (see Figure 5.13). With increasing return rate, expected stock also increases, but it does not increase exponentially as in the first recovery system[20] (see Figure 5.7). Moreover, average stock does not reach

[18] See Section 5.4.4.

[19] The larger the stability horizon is, the more moderate the increase of $\pi_{S,D}$ will be.

[20] Note that for $D \to S$, average stock is equal to S. Thus, in this case, it is independent of the return rate. Then, stability decreases with rising return rate

expected demand. Since variability of net demand rises, stability decreases. Nevertheless, depending on the length of the stability horizon, setup stability on the production stage increases from a certain number of $\hat{R}$.

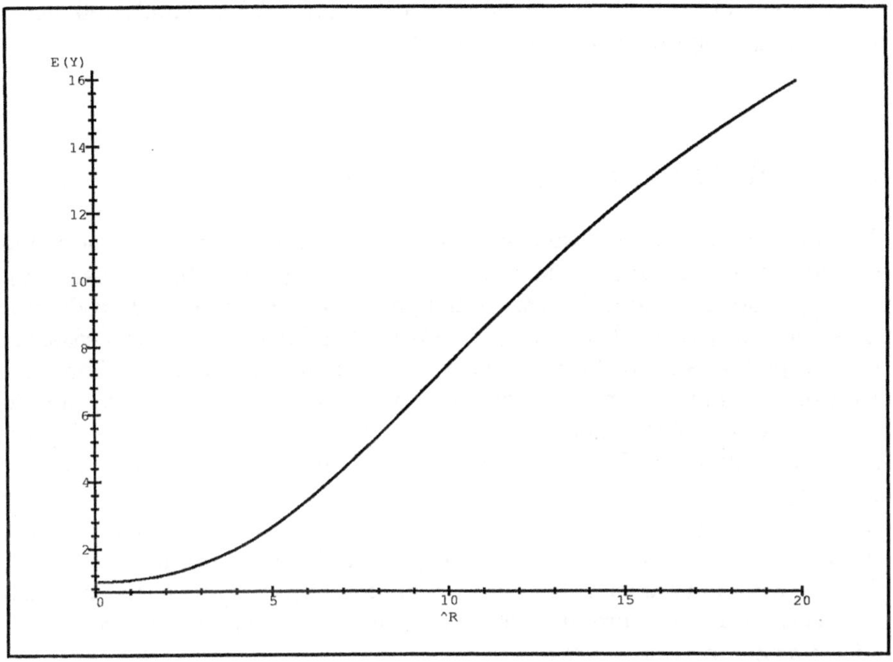

Figure 5.13. Average inventory position $\mathbb{E}[Y]$ for (S, D) policy

5.5.4 Summary

Section 5.5 has shown how stability of production setups depends on the parameters of an (S, D) policy, the length of the stability horizon, and the flow of product returns in a basic recovery system with disposal option.
The return flow leads, in most cases, to a reduction of stability due to the additional uncertainty in net demand. However, as for the S policy in the recovery system without fixed costs and disposal option, for large return rates stability increases due to the fact that expected stock increases[21]; though the increase in stock is comparably low.
It has been found that setup stability is not affected by the value of D and

because of the rising variability of net demand. This can easily be seen in equation (5.23) where with increasing $\hat{R} = \frac{1}{\mu}$ setup stability $\pi_S^{disposal}$ decreases. However, as can also be seen from (5.23), for large stability horizons the level of stability will be rather high.

[21] Note that this is not true for $D \to S$.

S, but the difference $D - S$ really influences stability. For $D = S$, we get the same results as for a "simple" S policy in a recovery system with disposal, and setting $D \to \infty$ comes down to a recovery model without disposal option (see Section 5.4.4). Furthermore, the stability horizon parameter T has a significant impact on $\pi_{S,D}$. It is shown that stability is mainly influenced by the relation between $D - S$, $\hat{N}$ and T.

5.6 Final Remarks and Extensions

The preceding sections have shown how the stability of production setups depends on product returns in two basic recovery systems. In the case of the recovery system without disposal option, only the case with fixed production costs and without fixed production costs is considered. In the first case, the optimal policy is of an (s, S) type, whereas in the latter, the optimal control rule is a simple S policy. For the sake of analytical tractability, for the recovery system with disposal option only the situation without fixed costs has been dealt with. Then, the respective optimal inventory policy is of an (S, D) type. As for traditional inventory systems, the main contribution of this work is to give a first analytical description of the relationship between setup stability, inventory policies, and product returns. Because of the additional variability in net demand, one might have expected that stability decreases with rising product returns. To a certain degree this intuition is not confirmed by this analysis.
If there is no possibility for disposing of returned items, then setup stability at first decreases, but for large return rates it increases again[22]. The higher level of stability is linked to an increase in the average stock. If returned items can be disposed of, then setup stability rises again for relatively large return rates[23], but the increase of stability as well as the increase in the average stock level are comparably moderate.
Thus, if the company can influence the return flow, e.g. by leasing contracts, then it should take into consideration the trade-off between stability and stock level, in particular in the recovery system without disposal.
Additionally, there is evidence that stability is considerably influenced by the length of the stability horizon and the parameters of the underlying control rules. In the case of the recovery system with fixed costs and without disposal option, the influence of s, S, and T is very similar to the impact of these parameters in a traditional inventory system.

For the (S, D) policy, the difference between the order-upto- and dispose-downto-level affects stability. Moreover, findings show that increased T results

[22] Note that this holds for both cases, with and without fixed production costs.
[23] This is valid if D is larger than S, for the special case $D \to S$ stability decreases with rising $\hat{R}$.

in greater stability. The same generally applies to the S policy in the case of the recovery system without disposal. Furthermore, the stability function for both policies looks rather similar. For moderate return ratios like $\hat{R}/\hat{D}$ =50 % even the level of stability is comparable.

For the purpose of analytical tractability, it has been assumed that demand and returns are exponentially distributed. Studies considering the impact of different demand distributions for 'traditional' inventory control systems have shown that stability gets larger, in general, with decreasing demand uncertainty, which is reflected by the coefficient of demand variation (see also Chapter 4, or, e.g., De Kok and Inderfurth [32], Heisig [49], Jensen [68]). Thus it can be expected that for lower variability of demand and returns, the stability level in product recovery systems will also be larger than for exponentially distributed demand and returns. Furthermore, it is expected that the general properties of the stability function remain largely unchanged (see Chapter 4 for an analytical comparison of different demand distributions). However, the examination of other net demand distributions is certainly one aspect for further research.

Besides this topic, the analysis in the previous sections can be extended to several aspects. One may think of similar extensions as proposed for traditional inventory systems like considering quantity-oriented stability, other forecasting processes, stochastic lead times, or improvements of stability by introducing a specific stabilization parameter (see also the discussion of proposals for further research topics in Section 4.5).

Moreover, the investigation of different recovery systems seems desirable. A starting point might be the recovery system introduced in Section 5.2 where the stock keeping of returned products is possible (see Figure 5.1). As mentioned, a three parameter policy is optimal for such a system. The analysis of the stability performance of this policy is then an interesting question. Furthermore, the analysis of stability in multi-stage recovery systems is certainly a topic for further investigations.

6. Conclusions

6.1 Summary of Results

Because of the increasing dynamics and uncertainties in the environment of companies, their planning systems must be able to react to unexpected developments. To cope with uncertainties, the planning system is usually embedded in a framework which permits the incorporation of new information into decision making from one planning period to the next, such as a rolling horizon schedule. The decisions at the top planning level provide input data for subsequent lower planning levels. Therefore, the adjustment of plans for a specific planning level may lead to additional uncertainties at adjoining planning levels. This may lead to a nervous planning system, in particular, since instability at the top level is propagated throughout the entire system. Since material coordination is the central element in the production planning framework, a "stable" material requirements planning system is important to avoid the negative aspects of nervousness, like increasing costs through, e.g., increased overtime, or inventory. For material requirements planning systems, the problems resulting from frequent plan revisions have been discussed extensively in literature. Different strategies have been suggested for reducing nervousness, and the impact of a wide range of parameters of planning concepts and decision rules on instability has been examined. However, a systematic analytical investigation of nervousness for stochastic lot-sizing rules within a rolling horizon schedule has not yet been provided.

The main contribution of this work is to give an analytical description of the relationship between long-term setup stability and basic inventory policies frequently applied in single-stage "traditional" production systems and product recovery systems[1]. Since setup changes cause the main problems in the execution of the planning process, our analysis is restricted to setup stability. Furthermore, long-term stability is dealt with because in multi-level production systems, nervousness at the top level in periods near the end of the stability horizon may lead to plan revisions on lower levels at the beginning of the horizon. In particular, frequent replanning activities on the operational

[1] Notice that for the single-stage system, the (s, S) policy has been proved to be optimal with respect to average cost consideration for a wide range of problems.

level lead to a general loss in planning confidence. For the product recovery system, the examination was restricted to stability at the manufacturing stage, since demand is mainly satisfied by producing new items. Notice that only the case that the expected/forecasted demand is larger than the expected/projected return flow has been dealt with. Some general closed-form formulas are derived for describing the impact of the inventory control rules on stability.

In both traditional production systems and recovery systems, the reorder point s does not influence long-term setup stability. Consequently, it can be chosen according to cost and service considerations without affecting stability.
For both systems, some additional assumptions concerning the distribution of (net) demand have to be made to keep the analysis tractable. For the traditional system, the demand distributions are still of a relatively general type whereas in the case of the recovery system, demand and returns are assumed to be exponentially distributed. However, the development of setup stability for other distributions is expected to be similar to the dependence of setup stability on demand variability in traditional production systems.

For the single-stage system, the most interesting result of this analysis is that no general superiority of one reorder point control rule over another is apparent. However, a simple order-up-to-level policy shows the best performance with respect to setup stability, but this control rule may be connected with high costs.
For low lot sizes, the long-term setup stability of an (s, nQ) policy is greater than stability of an (s, S) policy, i.e. for $Q \leq \hat{D}$ it holds that $\pi_{s,nQ} \geq \pi_{s,S}$. Thus, under JIT conditions, an (s, nQ) inventory control rule is advantageous with respect to stability. Since the lot size will be larger in most other practical situations, the more interesting region is $Q > \hat{D}$. For high demand variabilities, the stability performance of the (s, S) policy is slightly better than for an (s, nQ) rule. For low demand uncertainty, the stability function of an (s, S) policy possesses cyclical patterns for "low" lot sizes. Then, setup stability in the maxima of $\pi_{s,S}$ is high, and, consequently, larger than for an (s, nQ) policy. In contrast, if $S - s$ is chosen as a multiple of the projected demand, stability is rather small, and lower than for an (s, nQ) inventory control rule. For "large" lot sizes, the stability performance of both policies is (almost) equal, and for $Q \to \infty$ setup stability converges to 100 %.
The results for the special case of short-term setup stability are similar (see also De Kok and Inderfurth [32]). For low lot sizes, again an (s, nQ) policy is favorable, whereas for $Q \cong 2\hat{D}$ and larger Q-values the opposite applies. Thus for most practical applications, an (s, S) policy is preferable.
A poor choice of the (minimum) lot size leads in any case to a low level of stability. To protect against a poor setup stability performance, lot sizes in the region twice as large as the forecasted demand should be avoided. Because of

the cyclic patterns of the (s, S) policy for small and moderate Q-values, the sensitivity of setup stability to changes in the lot sizes is higher than for an (s, nQ) inventory control rule. In the case of an (s, S) policy, the minimum lot size should not be set as a multiple of the projected demand.
The influence of the other critical parameters on setup stability is almost identical for both policies. With increasing demand variability, stability significantly diminishes. An increase of the stability horizon, or of the weighting of periods within this horizon, respectively, leads to a higher level of stability for low lot sizes (i.e. $Q < \hat{D}$), whereas for larger Q-values, in general, the opposite applies.

Finally, the impact of the forecast accuracy on the setup stability of both policies is also similar. Good forecasts (in the sense of meeting the expected value of demand) lead in any case to a high level of stability, underestimating the expected demand (i.e. $\hat{D} < \bar{D}$) even results in a (slightly) better stability performance. Otherwise, the overestimation of expected demand leads - for both policies - to a lower stability level than for accurate forecasts.

Regarding the recovery system without disposal option, the results are similar to those for the "traditional" (s, S) policy, i.e. depending on the relation between TBO $(Q/\hat{N})$ and stability horizon T, the stability function either possesses cyclical patterns which may lead to a high level of nervousness (if the lot size is set to a multiple of the forecasted net demand per period), or it develops continuously. Especially, the stability performance for lot sizes equal to or twice the size of the expected net demand is fairly poor. For the (S, D) policy, the difference between the order-upto- and dispose-downto-level really affects stability[2]. Moreover, as the stability horizon increases, nervousness gets lower, whereas for the recovery system without disposal option no clear general tendency can be observed.
Notice that the analysis of these policies also includes the special case of a "simple" S policy with disposal option, which is obtained by setting $s = S$, or $D = S$, respectively.
The main part of this analysis concerns the impact of the return flow on stability in recovery systems with/without disposal option controlled by matching the optimal inventory policy of an (S, D) and (s, S) type, respectively. Since the variability in net demand is increased, one might expect that stability decreases as product returns increase. To a certain degree, this intuition is confuted by this analysis.
If returned items cannot be disposed of, then setup stability indeed decreases for "low"/"moderate" return quotas (up to about 50 %), but for large return rates stability even increases. This higher level of stability is paid for with a high average stock. For the recovery system with disposal option, setup stability rises again for relatively large return rates, but the increase in sta-

[2] Note that $D \to \infty$ comes down to a recovery model without disposal option.

bility as well as the increase in the average stock level are rather moderate in comparison with the recovery model without disposal option.
Thus, if the return flow can be influenced by the company, the trade-off between stability and stock level should also be considered, in particular in the recovery system without disposal.

To sum up, it can be concluded that if nervousness plays a role, inventory policies and their control parameters should be determined under consideration of their stability effects. Analogously to service level constraints, stability constraints should be incorporated. The results in this work give some insights on how inventory control rule parameters in a single-stage production system as well as a recovery system have to be restricted if such constraints are given by the management.

6.2 Further Research

Detailed suggestions for further research have already been provided at the end of Chapter 4 and Chapter 5. Here, a brief summary of these ideas.

An analytical investigation of long-term quantity-oriented stability is certainly desirable, but it does not seem to be possible. Moreover, the examination of other forecasting processes, like exponential smoothing, might also be useful, but the analysis is very limited because of the necessary calculation of rather complicated conditional probabilities. The same applies to considering time-variant demand situations or incorporating stochastic lead times in the analysis. Furthermore, the stability performance of inventory control rules in multi-stage systems has not yet been investigated in a sophisticated analysis. Finally, different recovery systems, like a system where stock keeping of returned products is possible, or multi-stage recovery systems, may be considered.

However, the results in this work may serve as a starting point for the analytical description of the interactions between the control parameters of the inventory policies under consideration and a stabilization parameter as introduced by Jensen [68]. Then, by using the dependencies between the parameters of the inventory control rule, the stabilization parameter and stability, models may be developed which incorporate cost optimization objectives under consideration of a predefined service level as well as stability restrictions. For instance, Kimms [73] shows how stability restrictions can be incorporated in decision making. Using a standard linear mixed-integer problem solver, an iterative method for reducing instability of schedules is presented.

A. Approximation for Renewal Function M(x)

We know that the cdf of X is given by (see Tijms [128])

$$P(X \leq x) = \frac{M(x)}{M(Q)} \qquad 0 \leq x \leq Q \tag{A.1}$$

where $M(x) = \sum_{n=0}^{\infty} \Phi_D^{n*}(x)$.
Note that X has a probability mass in 0,

$$P(X = 0) = \frac{1}{M(Q)}.$$

In general, an exact expression for $M(x)$ is intractable, but for so-called K_2-distributions it has a simple form. A K_2-distribution is defined by the form of its Laplace-Stieltjes transform $\tilde{F}_D(s)$, where $\tilde{F}_D(s) = \int_0^{\infty} e^{-sx} d\Phi_D(x)$. Here, it is given by

$$\tilde{F}_D(s) = \frac{1 + (c_1 - \mathbb{E}(D))s}{1 + c_1 s + c_2 s^2}$$

where c_1, c_2 are constant and $\mathbb{E}(D) = \bar{D}$.
It can be shown that for K_2-distributions $M(x)$ is given by (see De Kok [30])

$$M(x) = 1 + \frac{x}{\bar{D}} + \gamma(1 - e^{-\rho x}), \quad x \geq 0$$

for some constants γ, ρ.
The coefficients γ, ρ are chosen to satisfy the following relation (see, e.g., De Kok [30])

$$\lim_{x \to \infty} [M(x) - (\frac{x}{\bar{D}} + \frac{1 + c_D^2}{2})] = 0$$

where $c_D = \frac{\sigma(D)}{\bar{D}}$ (coefficient of variation).
Thus we obtain

$$\gamma = \frac{c_D^2 - 1}{2}$$

Furthermore, it holds that

$$\lim_{x \to 0} M'(x) = \Phi'(0)$$

which leads to

$$\rho = \frac{2[\Phi'(0) - \mathbb{E}^{-1}(D)]}{c_D^2 - 1}$$

Notice that for exponentially distributed demand, both coefficients are equal to zero, i.e. $\gamma = \rho = 0$.

For mixtures of Erlang distributions defined by a cdf of

$$\Phi_D(x) = 1 - p \sum_{i=0}^{n-1} e^{-\mu_1 x} \frac{(\mu_1 x)^i}{i!} - (1-p) \sum_{i=0}^{r-1} e^{-\mu_2 x} \frac{(\mu_2 x)^i}{i!} \tag{A.2}$$

we get

$$\Phi'_D(0) = \begin{cases} p\mu_1 + (1-p)\mu_2 & n = r = 1 \\ p\mu_1 & n = 1, r \geq 2 \\ (1-p)\mu_2 & n \geq 2, r = 1 \\ 0 & n \geq 2, r \geq 2. \end{cases}$$

A.1 Mixed-Erlang Distribution

From (A.2) we get with $\mu_1 = \mu_2 := \mu$ and thus $n := r - 1$ the cdf of an $E_{k-1,k}$ distribution as (where r in (A.2) is substituted by k)

$$\Phi_D(x) = 1 - p \sum_{i=0}^{k-2} e^{-\mu x} \frac{(\mu x)^i}{i!} - (1-p) \sum_{i=0}^{k-1} e^{-\mu x} \frac{(\mu x)^i}{i!} \tag{A.3}$$

For given demand expectation and coefficient of variation, the parameters k, p and μ can be determined as follows (see Tijms [128], p. 358).

$$\begin{aligned} &\tfrac{1}{k} \leq c_D^2 \leq \tfrac{1}{k-1} \\ &p = \tfrac{1}{1+c_D^2}[kc_D^2 - \sqrt{k(1+c_D^2) - k^2 c_D^2}] \\ &\mu = \tfrac{k-p}{D} \end{aligned} \tag{A.4}$$

A.2 Hyperexponential Distribution

In the case of hyperexponentially distributed demand, we obtain from (A.2) with $n = r = 1$ and $\mu_1 \neq \mu_2$ that (see Tijms [128], pp. 359)

$$\Phi_D(x) = 1 - pe^{-\mu_1 x} - (1-p)e^{-\mu_2 x} \tag{A.5}$$

where (see also Tijms [128], p. 359)

$$\begin{aligned} p &= \tfrac{1}{2}\left(1 + \sqrt{\tfrac{c_D^2 - 1}{c_D^2 + 1}}\right) \\ \mu_1 &= \tfrac{2p}{\bar{D}}, \quad \mu_2 = \tfrac{2(1-p)}{\bar{D}} \end{aligned} \tag{A.6}$$

for given $\bar{D}$ and $c_D^2 > 1$.

B. (s,S) Policy

B.1 General Stability Functions

B.1.1 $Q \leq \hat{D}$

The starting point is (4.59) with

$$\pi^A_{s,S} = \int_0^Q [\alpha_1(1 - \Phi_D(Q-x)) + \alpha_2 \Phi_D(Q-x)] dF_X(x)$$

Rearranging terms and using (A.1) results in (see also Heisig [49])

$$\pi^A_{s,S} = \frac{1}{M(Q)} \left\{ \alpha_1 [\int_0^Q dM(x) - \int_0^Q \Phi_D(Q-x) dM(x)] + \alpha_2 \int_0^Q \Phi_D(Q-x) dM(x) \right\}$$

Since $\int_0^Q 1 dM(x) = M(Q)$ and $\int_0^Q \Phi_D(Q-x) dM(x) = M(Q) - 1$ (see, e.g., De Kok [31], p.153) we obtain

$$\pi^A_{s,S} = \alpha_1 \frac{1}{M(Q)} + \alpha_2 (1 - \frac{1}{M(Q)}) \tag{B.1}$$

B.1.2 $Q > \hat{D}$

Starting from (4.60) with

$$\pi^B_{s,S} = \Bigg\{ \sum_{\tau=1}^{l-1} \int_{Q-\tau\hat{D}}^{Q-(\tau-1)\hat{D}} \{\beta_1^\tau[1-\Phi_D(Q-x)] + \sum_{\theta=2}^{\tau} \beta_\theta^\tau [\Phi_D(Q-x-(\theta-2)\hat{D}) - \Phi_D(Q-x-(\theta-1)\hat{D})] + \beta_{\tau+1}^\tau \Phi_D(Q-x-(\tau-1)\hat{D})\}$$
$$+ \int_0^{Q-(l-1)\hat{D}} \{\beta_1^l[1-\Phi_D(Q-x)] + \sum_{\theta=2}^{l} \beta_\theta^l [\Phi_D(Q-x-(\theta-2)\hat{D}) - \Phi_D(Q-x-(\theta-1)\hat{D})] + \beta_{l+1}^l \Phi_D(Q-x-(l-1)\hat{D})\}\Bigg\} dF_X(x)$$

With (A.1) and rearranging terms we obtain (see also Heisig [49])

$$\pi^B_{s,S} = \Bigg\{ \sum_{\tau=1}^{l-1} \left[\int_{Q-\tau\hat{D}}^{Q-(\tau-1)\hat{D}} \Big(\beta_1^\tau + \sum_{\theta=2}^{\tau+1} (\beta_\theta^\tau - \beta_{\theta-1}^\tau) \Phi_D(Q-x-(\theta-2)\hat{D}) \Big) dM(x) \right]$$
$$+ \int_0^{Q-(l-1)\hat{D}} \Big(\beta_1^l + \sum_{\theta=2}^{l+1} (\beta_\theta^l - \beta_{\theta-1}^l) \Phi_D(Q-x-(\theta-2)\hat{D}) \Big) dM(x) \Bigg\} \frac{1}{M(Q)}$$
$$\forall \quad (l-1)\hat{D} < Q \le l\hat{D} \quad \text{with} \quad l \in \mathcal{N} \setminus \{0,1\} \tag{B.2}$$

B.2 Mixed-Erlang Distributed Demand

B.2.1 $Q \leq \hat{D}$

From (B.1) and (A.2) we obtain that

$$\pi^{A}_{s,S} = \frac{1}{M(Q)}\left\{\alpha_1 + \alpha_2\left[\frac{Q}{\bar{D}} + \gamma(1-e^{-\rho Q})\right]\right\} \tag{B.3}$$

where

$$\frac{1}{M(Q)} = \frac{\bar{D}}{Q + \bar{D}[1+\gamma(1-e^{-\rho Q})]}. \tag{B.4}$$

B.2.2 $Q > \hat{D}$

From (B.2) by substituting $\Phi_D(.)$ from (A.3) and $M(.)$ from (A.2) we find that

$$\pi^{B}_{s,S} = \left\{\sum_{\tau=1}^{l-1}\left[\int_{Q-\tau\hat{D}}^{Q-(\tau-1)\hat{D}} \beta_1^{\tau} d[1+\frac{x}{\bar{D}}+\gamma(1-e^{-\rho x})]\right.\right.$$
$$+\int_{Q-\tau\hat{D}}^{Q-(\tau-1)\hat{D}} \sum_{\theta=2}^{\tau+1}(\beta_\theta^{\tau}-\beta_{\theta-1}^{\tau})[1-p\sum_{i=0}^{k-2}e^{-\mu(Q-x-(\theta-2)\hat{D})}\frac{(\mu(Q-x-(\theta-2)\hat{D}))^i}{i!}$$
$$-(1-p)\sum_{i=0}^{k-1}e^{-\mu(Q-x-(\theta-2)\hat{D})}\frac{(\mu(Q-x-(\theta-2)\hat{D}))^i}{i!}]$$
$$\left. d[1+\frac{x}{\bar{D}}+\gamma(1-e^{-\rho x})]\right] \tag{B.5}$$
$$+\int_{0}^{Q-(l-1)\hat{D}} \beta_1^{l} d[1+\frac{x}{\bar{D}}+\gamma(1-e^{-\rho x})]$$
$$+\int_{0}^{Q-(l-1)\hat{D}} \sum_{\theta=2}^{l+1}(\beta_\theta^{l}-\beta_{\theta-1}^{l})[1-p\sum_{i=0}^{k-2}e^{-\mu(Q-x-(\theta-2)\hat{D})}\frac{(\mu(Q-x-(\theta-2)\hat{D}))^i}{i!}$$
$$-(1-p)\sum_{i=0}^{k-1}e^{-\mu(Q-x-(\theta-2)\hat{D})}\frac{(\mu(Q-x-(\theta-2)\hat{D}))^i}{i!}]$$
$$\left. d[1+\frac{x}{\bar{D}}+\gamma(1-e^{-\rho x})]\right\}\frac{1}{M(Q)}$$

with $\frac{1}{M(Q)}$ as shown in (B.4).

In general, the following applies that (see, e.g., Bronstein and Semendjajew [17], p.71)

$$\int_a^b f(x)dg(x) = \int_a^b f(x)g'(x)dx. \tag{B.6}$$

Thus after some algebraic transformations, we obtain from (B.5) that

$$\pi_{s,S}^B = \Bigg\{ \sum_{\tau=1}^{l-1} \Bigg\{ \frac{1}{\bar{D}} \Bigg[\int_{Q-\tau\hat{D}}^{Q-(\tau-1)\hat{D}} \beta_1^\tau dx$$

$$+ \sum_{\theta=2}^{\tau+1} (\beta_\theta^\tau - \beta_{\theta-1}^\tau) \int_{Q-\tau\hat{D}}^{Q-(\tau-1)\hat{D}} (1 - p \sum_{i=0}^{k-2} e^{-\mu(Q-x-(\theta-2)\hat{D})} \frac{(\mu(Q-x-(\theta-2)\hat{D}))^i}{i!}$$

$$-(1-p) \sum_{i=0}^{k-1} e^{-\mu(Q-x-(\theta-2)\hat{D})} \frac{(\mu(Q-x-(\theta-2)\hat{D}))^i}{i!})dx \Bigg]$$

$$+ \rho\gamma \Bigg[\int_{Q-\tau\hat{D}}^{Q-(\tau-1)\hat{D}} \beta_1^\tau e^{-\rho x} dx$$

$$+ \sum_{\theta=2}^{\tau+1} (\beta_\theta^\tau - \beta_{\theta-1}^\tau) \int_{Q-\tau\hat{D}}^{Q-(\tau-1)\hat{D}} (1 - p \sum_{i=0}^{k-2} e^{-\mu(Q-x-(\theta-2)\hat{D})} \frac{(\mu(Q-x-(\theta-2)\hat{D}))^i}{i!}$$

$$-(1-p) \sum_{i=0}^{k-1} e^{-\mu(Q-x-(\theta-2)\hat{D})} \frac{(\mu(Q-x-(\theta-2)\hat{D}))^i}{i!})e^{-\rho x} \Bigg] dx \Bigg\}$$

$$+ \frac{1}{\bar{D}} \Bigg[\int_0^{Q-(l-1)\hat{D}} \beta_1^l dx$$

$$+ \sum_{\theta=2}^{l+1} (\beta_\theta^l - \beta_{\theta-1}^l) \int_0^{Q-(l-1)\hat{D}} (1 - p \sum_{i=0}^{k-2} e^{-\mu(Q-x-(\theta-2)\hat{D})} \frac{(\mu(Q-x-(\theta-2)\hat{D}))^i}{i!}$$

$$-(1-p) \sum_{i=0}^{k-1} e^{-\mu(Q-x-(\theta-2)\hat{D})} \frac{(\mu(Q-x-(\theta-2)\hat{D}))^i}{i!})dx \Bigg]$$

$$+ \rho\gamma \Bigg[\int_0^{Q-(l-1)\hat{D}} \beta_1^l e^{-\rho x} dx \tag{B.7}$$

$$+\sum_{\theta=2}^{l+1}(\beta_\theta^l-\beta_{\theta-1}^l)\int\limits_0^{Q-(l-1)\hat{D}}(1-p\sum_{i=0}^{k-2}e^{-\mu(Q-x-(\theta-2)\hat{D})}\frac{(\mu(Q-x-(\theta-2)\hat{D}))^i}{i!}$$

$$-(1-p)\sum_{i=0}^{k-1}e^{-\mu(Q-x-(\theta-2)\hat{D})}\frac{(\mu(Q-x-(\theta-2)\hat{D}))^i}{i!})e^{-\rho x}dx\Bigg]$$

$$+\beta_1^l+\sum_{\theta=2}^{l+1}(\beta_\theta^l-\beta_{\theta-1}^l)(1-p\sum_{i=0}^{k-2}e^{-\mu(Q-(\theta-2)\hat{D})}\frac{(\mu(Q-(\theta-2)\hat{D}))^i}{i!}$$

$$-(1-p)\sum_{i=0}^{k-1}e^{-\mu(Q-(\theta-2)\hat{D})}\frac{(\mu(Q-(\theta-2)\hat{D}))^i}{i!})\Bigg\}\frac{1}{M(Q)}$$

with $M(Q)$ as depicted in (B.4).

Some of the integrals in (B.7) are given as follows:

$$\int\limits_{Q-\tau\hat{D}}^{Q-(\tau-1)\hat{D}}dx=\hat{D}$$

$$\int\limits_{Q-\tau\hat{D}}^{Q-(\tau-1)\hat{D}}e^{-\rho x}=\frac{1}{\rho}e^{-\rho(Q-\tau\hat{D})}(1-e^{-\rho\hat{D}})$$

$$\int\limits_0^{Q-(l-1)\hat{D}}dx=Q-(l-1)\hat{D}$$

$$\int\limits_0^{Q-(l-1)\hat{D}}e^{-\rho x}=\frac{1}{\rho}(1-e^{-\rho(Q-(l-1)\hat{D})}).$$

The remaining integrals are of the form

$$-e^{-\mu c}\int\limits_a^b[p\sum_{i=0}^{h-2}\frac{\mu^i(c-x)^i}{i!}+(1-p)\sum_{i=0}^{h-1}\frac{\mu^i(c-x)^i}{i!}]e^{mx}\,dx \tag{B.8}$$

with $c:=Q-(\theta-2)\hat{D}$ and m either equal to μ or $\mu-\rho$.

Applying $\int v(x)u'(x)dx=v(x)u(x)-\int v'(x)u(x)dx$ with $v(x)=e^{mx}$, $u'(x)=\sum\limits_{i=0}^{r-2}\frac{\mu^i(c-x)^i}{i!}$ and $u'(x)=\sum\limits_{i=0}^{r-1}\frac{\mu^i(c-x)^i}{i!}$, respectively, leads to

$$-e^{-\mu c}\left[e^{mx}(\sum_{j=0}^{h-2}\sum_{i=j}^{h-2}\frac{\mu^i(c-x)^{i-j}}{(i-j)!m^{j+1}}+(1-p)\sum_{j=0}^{h-1}\sum_{i=j}^{h-1}\frac{\mu^i(c-x)^{i-j}}{(i-j)!m^{j+1}})\right]_a^b$$

Thus we get for (B.8)

$$-e^{-\mu c}\Big[e^{mb}(p\sum_{j=0}^{h-2}\sum_{i=j}^{h-2}\frac{\mu^i(c-b)^{i-j}}{(i-j)!m^{j+1}}+(1-p)\sum_{j=0}^{h-1}\sum_{i=j}^{h-1}\frac{\mu^i(c-b)^{i-j}}{(i-j)!m^{j+1}}) \tag{B.9}$$

$$-e^{ma}(p\sum_{j=0}^{h-2}\sum_{i=j}^{h-2}\frac{\mu^i(c-a)^{i-j}}{(i-j)!m^{j+1}}+(1-p)\sum_{j=0}^{h-1}\sum_{i=j}^{h-1}\frac{\mu^i(c-a)^{i-j}}{(i-j)!m^{j+1}})\Big]$$

Note that we define $0^0 := 1$.

For the first integral in (B.7) we find with $m = \mu$ that

$$\sum_{\theta=2}^{\tau+1}(\beta_\theta^\tau-\beta_{\theta-1}^\tau)\int_{Q-\tau\hat{D}}^{Q-(\tau-1)\hat{D}}[1-p\sum_{i=0}^{k-2}e^{-\mu(Q-x-(\theta-2)\hat{D})}\frac{(\mu(Q-x-(\theta-2)\hat{D}))^i}{i!}$$

$$-(1-p)\sum_{i=0}^{k-1}e^{-\mu(Q-x-(\theta-2)\hat{D})}\frac{(\mu(Q-x-(\theta-2)\hat{D}))^i}{i!}]\,dx$$

$$=\sum_{\theta=2}^{\tau}(\beta_\theta^\tau-\beta_{\theta-1}^\tau)$$

$$\Big[\hat{D}-e^{-\mu(\tau-\theta+1)\hat{D}}(p\sum_{j=0}^{k-2}\sum_{i=j}^{k-2}\frac{\mu^i((\tau-\theta+1)\hat{D})^{i-j}}{(i-j)!\mu^{j+1}}$$

$$+(1-p)\sum_{j=0}^{k-1}\sum_{i=j}^{k-1}\frac{\mu^i((\tau-\theta+1)\hat{D})^{i-j}}{(i-j)!\mu^{j+1}})$$

$$+e^{-\mu(\tau-\theta+2)\hat{D}}(p\sum_{j=0}^{k-2}\sum_{i=j}^{k-2}\frac{\mu^i((\tau-\theta+2)\hat{D})^{i-j}}{(i-j)!\mu^{j+1}}$$

$$+(1-p)\sum_{j=0}^{k-1}\sum_{i=j}^{k-1}\frac{\mu^i((\tau-\theta+2)\hat{D})^{i-j}}{(i-j)!\mu^{j+1}})\Big]$$

$$+(\beta_{\tau+1}^\tau-\beta_\tau^\tau)\Big[\hat{D}-(p\sum_{j=0}^{k-2}\frac{\mu^j}{\mu^{j+1}}+(1-p)\cdot\sum_{j=0}^{k-1}\frac{\mu^j}{\mu^{j+1}})$$

$$+e^{-\mu\hat{D}}(p\sum_{j=0}^{k-2}\sum_{i=j}^{k-2}\frac{\mu^i\hat{D}^{i-j}}{(i-j)!\mu^{j+1}}+(1-p)\sum_{j=0}^{k-1}\sum_{i=j}^{k-1}\frac{\mu^i\hat{D}^{i-j}}{(i-j)!\mu^{j+1}})\Big]$$

Analogously, we obtain

$$\sum_{\theta=2}^{\tau+1}(\beta_\theta^\tau - \beta_{\theta-1}^\tau) \int\limits_{Q-\tau\hat{D}}^{Q-(\tau-1)\hat{D}} [1-p\sum_{i=0}^{k-2} e^{-\mu(Q-x-(\theta-2)\hat{D})} \frac{(\mu(Q-x-(\theta-2)\hat{D}))^i}{i!}$$

$$-(1-p)\sum_{i=0}^{k-1} e^{-\mu(Q-x-(\theta-2)\hat{D})} \frac{(\mu(Q-x-(\theta-2)\hat{D}))^i}{i!}]e^{-\rho x}\,dx$$

$$= \sum_{\theta=2}^{\tau}(\beta_\theta^\tau - \beta_{\theta-1}^\tau)e^{-\rho(Q-\tau\hat{D})}\left[\frac{1}{\rho}(1-e^{-\rho\hat{D}})\right.$$

$$-e^{-\mu(\tau-\theta+1)\hat{D}}e^{-\rho\hat{D}}(p\sum_{j=0}^{k-2}\sum_{i=j}^{k-2}\frac{\mu^i((\tau-\theta+1)\hat{D})^{i-j}}{(i-j)!(\mu-\rho)^{j+1}}$$

$$+(1-p)\sum_{j=0}^{k-1}\sum_{i=j}^{k-1}\frac{\mu^i((\tau-\theta+1)\hat{D})^{i-j}}{(i-j)!(\mu-\rho)^{j+1}})$$

$$+e^{-\mu(\tau-\theta+2)\hat{D}}(p\sum_{j=0}^{k-2}\sum_{i=j}^{k-2}\frac{\mu^i((\tau-\theta+2)\hat{D})^{i-j}}{(i-j)!(\mu-\rho)^{j+1}}$$

$$\left.+(1-p)\sum_{j=0}^{k-1}\sum_{i=j}^{k-1}\frac{\mu^i((\tau-\theta+2)\hat{D})^{i-j}}{(i-j)!(\mu-\rho)^{j+1}})\right]$$

$$+(\beta_{\tau+1}^\tau - \beta_\tau^\tau)e^{-\rho(Q-\tau\hat{D})}\left[\frac{1}{\rho}(1-e^{-\rho\hat{D}}) - e^{-\rho\hat{D}}(p\sum_{j=0}^{k-2}\frac{\mu^j}{(\mu-\rho)^{j+1}}\right.$$

$$+(1-p)\sum_{j=0}^{k-1}\frac{\mu^j}{(\mu-\rho)^{j+1}})+e^{-\mu\hat{D}}(p\sum_{j=0}^{k-2}\sum_{i=j}^{k-2}\frac{\mu^i\hat{D}^{i-j}}{(i-j)!(\mu-\rho)^{j+1}}$$

$$\left.+(1-p)\sum_{j=0}^{k-1}\sum_{i=j}^{k-1}\frac{\mu^i\hat{D}^{i-j}}{(i-j)!(\mu-\rho)^{j+1}})\right]$$

and

$$\sum_{\theta=2}^{l+1}(\beta_\theta^l-\beta_{\theta-1}^l)\int_0^{Q-(l-1)\hat{D}}[1-p\sum_{i=0}^{k-2}e^{-\mu(Q-x-(\theta-2)\hat{D})}\frac{(\mu(Q-x-(\theta-2)\hat{D}))^i}{i!}$$
$$-(1-p)\sum_{i=0}^{k-1}e^{-\mu(Q-x-(\theta-2)\hat{D})}\frac{(\mu(Q-x-(\theta-2)\hat{D}))^i}{i!}]\,dx$$

$$=\sum_{\theta=2}^{l}(\beta_\theta^l-\beta_{\theta-1}^l)[Q-(l-1)\hat{D}$$
$$-e^{-\mu(l-\theta+1)\hat{D}}(p\sum_{j=0}^{k-2}\sum_{i=j}^{k-2}\frac{\mu^i((l-\theta+1)\hat{D})^{i-j}}{(i-j)!\mu^{j+1}}$$
$$+(1-p)\sum_{j=0}^{k-1}\sum_{i=j}^{k-1}\frac{\mu^i((l-\theta+1)\hat{D})^{i-j}}{(i-j)!\mu^{j+1}})$$
$$+e^{-\mu(Q-(\theta-2)\hat{D})}(p\sum_{j=0}^{k-2}\sum_{i=j}^{k-2}\frac{\mu^i(Q-(\theta-2)\hat{D})^{i-j}}{(i-j)!\mu^{j+1}}$$
$$+(1-p)\sum_{j=0}^{k-1}\sum_{i=j}^{k-1}\frac{\mu^i(Q-(\theta-2)\hat{D})^{i-j}}{(i-j)!\mu^{j+1}})]$$
$$+(\beta_{l+1}^l-\beta_l^l)[Q-(l-1)\hat{D}-(p\sum_{j=0}^{k-2}\frac{\mu^j}{\mu^{j+1}}+(1-p)\sum_{j=0}^{k-1}\frac{\mu^j}{\mu^{j+1}})$$
$$+e^{-\mu(Q-(l-1)\hat{D})}(p\sum_{j=0}^{k-2}\sum_{i=j}^{k-2}\frac{\mu^i(Q-(l-1)\hat{D})^{i-j}}{(i-j)!\mu^{j+1}}$$
$$+(1-p)\sum_{j=0}^{k-1}\sum_{i=j}^{k-1}\frac{\mu^i(Q-(l-1)\hat{D})^{i-j}}{(i-j)!\mu^{j+1}})\Big]$$

Finally we get

$$\sum_{\theta=2}^{\tau+1}(\beta_\theta^l-\beta_{\theta-1}^l)\int_0^{Q-(l-1)\hat{D}}[1-p\sum_{i=0}^{k-2}e^{-\mu(Q-x-(\theta-2)\hat{D})}\frac{(\mu(Q-x-(\theta-2)\hat{D}))^i}{i!}$$
$$-(1-p)\sum_{i=0}^{k-1}e^{-\mu(Q-x-(\theta-2)\hat{D})}\frac{(\mu(Q-x-(\theta-2)\hat{D}))^i}{i!}]e^{-\rho x}\,dx$$

$$=\sum_{\theta=2}^{l}(\beta_\theta^l-\beta_{\theta-1}^l)[\frac{1}{\rho}(1-e^{-\rho(Q-(l-1)\hat{D})})$$

$$-e^{-\mu(l-\theta+1)\hat{D}-\rho(Q-(l-1)\hat{D})}(p\sum_{j=0}^{k-2}\sum_{i=j}^{k-2}\frac{\mu^i((l-\theta+1)\hat{D})^{i-j}}{(i-j)!(\mu-\rho)^{j+1}}$$

$$+(1-p)\sum_{j=0}^{k-1}\sum_{i=j}^{k-1}\frac{\mu^i((l-\theta+1)\hat{D})^{i-j}}{(i-j)!(\mu-\rho)^{j+1}})$$

$$+e^{-\mu(Q-(\theta-2)\hat{D})}(p\sum_{j=0}^{k-2}\sum_{i=j}^{k-2}\frac{\mu^i(Q-(\theta-2)\hat{D})^{i-j}}{(i-j)!(\mu-\rho)^{j+1}}$$

$$+(1-p)\sum_{j=0}^{k-1}\sum_{i=j}^{k-1}\frac{\mu^i(Q-(\theta-2)\hat{D})^{i-j}}{(i-j)!(\mu-\rho)^{j+1}})]$$

$$+(\beta_{l+1}^l-\beta_l^l)[\frac{1}{\rho}(1-e^{-\rho(Q-(l-1)\hat{D})})-e^{-\rho(Q-(l-1)\hat{D})}(p\sum_{j=0}^{k-2}\frac{\mu^j}{(\mu-\rho)^{j+1}}$$

$$+(1-p)\sum_{j=0}^{k-1}\frac{\mu^j}{(\mu-\rho)^{j+1}})$$

$$+e^{-\mu(Q-(l-1)\hat{D})}(p\sum_{j=0}^{k-2}\sum_{i=j}^{k-2}\frac{\mu^i(Q-(l-1)\hat{D})^{i-j}}{(i-j)!(\mu-\rho)^{j+1}}$$

$$+(1-p)\sum_{j=0}^{k-1}\sum_{i=j}^{k-1}\frac{\mu^i(Q-(l-1)\hat{D})^{i-j}}{(i-j)!(\mu-\rho)^{j+1}})]\Bigg]$$

Since $\sum_{j=0}^{a-1}\frac{\mu^j}{\mu^{j+1}}=\frac{a}{\mu}$ and $\sum_{j=0}^{a-1}\frac{\mu^j}{(\mu-\rho)^{j+1}}=\frac{1}{\rho}((\frac{\mu}{\mu-\rho})^a-1)$ we get that

$$p\sum_{j=0}^{k-2}\frac{\mu^j}{\mu^{j+1}}+(1-p)\sum_{j=0}^{k-1}\frac{\mu^j}{\mu^{j+1}}=\frac{k-p}{\mu}$$

$$p\sum_{j=0}^{k-2}\frac{\mu^j}{(\mu-\rho)^{j+1}}+(1-p)\sum_{j=0}^{k-1}\frac{\mu^j}{(\mu-\rho)^{j+1}}=\frac{1}{\rho}[(\frac{\mu}{\mu-\rho})^k(1-\frac{\rho p}{\mu})-1]$$

Using these results we find that planning stability in the case of $c_D^2 \leq 1$ is given by

$$\pi_{s,S}^B=\Bigg\{\sum_{\tau=1}^{l-1}\Bigg\{\frac{1}{\bar{D}}\Bigg[\beta_1^\tau\hat{D}+\sum_{\theta=2}^{\tau}(\beta_\theta^\tau-\beta_{\theta-1}^\tau)[\hat{D}$$

$$-e^{-\mu(\tau-\theta+1)\hat{D}}(p\sum_{j=0}^{k-2}\sum_{i=j}^{k-2}\frac{\mu^i((\tau-\theta+1)\hat{D})^{i-j}}{(i-j)!\mu^{j+1}}$$

$$+(1-p)\sum_{j=0}^{k-1}\sum_{i=j}^{k-1}\frac{\mu^i((\tau-\theta+1)\hat{D})^{i-j}}{(i-j)!\mu^{j+1}})$$

$$+e^{-\mu(\tau-\theta+2)\hat{D}}(p\sum_{j=0}^{k-2}\sum_{i=j}^{k-2}\frac{\mu^i((\tau-\theta+2)\hat{D})^{i-j}}{(i-j)!\mu^{j+1}}$$

$$+(1-p)\sum_{j=0}^{k-1}\sum_{i=j}^{k-1}\frac{\mu^i((\tau-\theta+2)\hat{D})^{i-j}}{(i-j)!\mu^{j+1}})]$$

$$+(\beta_{\tau+1}^{\tau}-\beta_{\tau}^{\tau})[\hat{D}+\frac{p-k}{\mu}+e^{-\mu\hat{D}}(p\sum_{j=0}^{k-2}\sum_{i=j}^{k-2}\frac{\mu^i\hat{D}^{i-j}}{(i-j)!\mu^{j+1}}$$

$$+(1-p)\sum_{j=0}^{k-1}\sum_{i=j}^{k-1}\frac{\mu^i\hat{D}^{i-j}}{(i-j)!\mu^{j+1}})]\Big]$$

$$+\gamma e^{-\rho(Q-\tau\hat{D})}\Big[\beta_1^{\tau}(1-e^{-\rho\hat{D}})+\sum_{\theta=2}^{\tau}(\beta_{\theta}^{\tau}-\beta_{\theta-1}^{\tau})[1-e^{-\rho\hat{D}}$$

$$-\rho e^{-\mu(\tau-\theta+1)\hat{D}}e^{-\rho\hat{D}}(p\sum_{j=0}^{k-2}\sum_{i=j}^{k-2}\frac{\mu^i((\tau-\theta+1)\hat{D})^{i-j}}{(i-j)!(\mu-\rho)^{j+1}}$$

$$+(1-p)\sum_{j=0}^{k-1}\sum_{i=j}^{k-1}\frac{\mu^i((\tau-\theta+1)\hat{D})^{i-j}}{(i-j)!(\mu-\rho)^{j+1}})$$

$$+\rho e^{-\mu(\tau-\theta+2)\hat{D}}(p\sum_{j=0}^{k-2}\sum_{i=j}^{k-2}\frac{\mu^i((\tau-\theta+2)\hat{D})^{i-j}}{(i-j)!(\mu-\rho)^{j+1}}$$

$$+(1-p)\sum_{j=0}^{k-1}\sum_{i=j}^{k-1}\frac{\mu^i((\tau-\theta+2)\hat{D})^{i-j}}{(i-j)!(\mu-\rho)^{j+1}})]$$

$$+(\beta_{\tau+1}^{\tau}-\beta_{\tau}^{\tau})[1-e^{-\rho\hat{D}}-e^{-\rho\hat{D}}((\frac{\mu}{\mu-\rho})^k(1-\frac{\rho p}{\mu})-1)$$

$$+\rho e^{-\mu\hat{D}}(p\sum_{j=0}^{k-2}\sum_{i=j}^{k-2}\frac{\mu^i\hat{D}^{i-j}}{(i-j)!(\mu-\rho)^{j+1}}$$

$$+(1-p)\sum_{j=0}^{k-1}\sum_{i=j}^{k-1}\frac{\mu^i\hat{D}^{i-j}}{(i-j)!(\mu-\rho)^{j+1}})]\Big]\Big\}$$

$$+\frac{1}{\bar{D}}\Big[\beta_1^{l}(Q-(l-1)\hat{D})+\sum_{\theta=2}^{l}(\beta_{\theta}^{l}-\beta_{\theta-1}^{l})[Q-(l-1)\hat{D}$$

$$-e^{-\mu(l-\theta+1)\hat{D}}(p\sum_{j=0}^{k-2}\sum_{i=j}^{k-2}\frac{\mu^i((l-\theta+1)\hat{D})^{i-j}}{(i-j)!\mu^{j+1}}$$

$$+(1-p)\sum_{j=0}^{k-1}\sum_{i=j}^{k-1}\frac{\mu^i((l-\theta+1)\hat{D})^{i-j}}{(i-j)!\mu^{j+1}})$$

$$
\begin{aligned}
&+e^{-\mu(Q-(\theta-2)\hat{D})}(p\sum_{j=0}^{k-2}\sum_{i=j}^{k-2}\frac{\mu^i(Q-(\theta-2)\hat{D})^{i-j}}{(i-j)!\mu^{j+1}} \\
&\qquad +(1-p)\sum_{j=0}^{k-1}\sum_{i=j}^{k-1}\frac{\mu^i(Q-(\theta-2)\hat{D})^{i-j}}{(i-j)!\mu^{j+1}})] \\
&+(\beta_{l+1}^l-\beta_l^l)[Q-(l-1)\hat{D}+\frac{p-k}{\mu} \\
&\qquad +e^{-\mu(Q-(l-1)\hat{D})}(p\sum_{j=0}^{k-2}\sum_{i=j}^{k-2}\frac{\mu^i(Q-(l-1)\hat{D})^{i-j}}{(i-j)!\mu^{j+1}} \\
&\qquad +(1-p)\sum_{j=0}^{k-1}\sum_{i=j}^{k-1}\frac{\mu^i(Q-(l-1)\hat{D})^{i-j}}{(i-j)!\mu^{j+1}})]\Big] \qquad \text{(B.10)} \\
&+\gamma\Big[\beta_1^l(1-e^{-\rho(Q-(l-1)\hat{D})})+\sum_{\theta=2}^{l}(\beta_\theta^l-\beta_{\theta-1}^l)[1-e^{-\rho(Q-(l-1)\hat{D})} \\
&-\rho e^{-\mu(l-\theta+1)\hat{D}-\rho(Q-(l-1)\hat{D})}(p\sum_{j=0}^{k-2}\sum_{i=j}^{k-2}\frac{\mu^i((l-\theta+1)\hat{D})^{i-j}}{(i-j)!(\mu-\rho)^{j+1}} \\
&\qquad +(1-p)\sum_{j=0}^{k-1}\sum_{i=j}^{k-1}\frac{\mu^i((l-\theta+1)\hat{D})^{i-j}}{(i-j)!(\mu-\rho)^{j+1}}) \\
&+\rho e^{-\mu(Q-(\theta-2)\hat{D})}(p\sum_{j=0}^{k-2}\sum_{i=j}^{k-2}\frac{\mu^i(Q-(\theta-2)\hat{D})^{i-j}}{(i-j)!(\mu-\rho)^{j+1}} \\
&\qquad +(1-p)\sum_{j=0}^{k-1}\sum_{i=j}^{k-1}\frac{\mu^i(Q-(\theta-2)\hat{D})^{i-j}}{(i-j)!(\mu-\rho)^{j+1}})] \\
&+(\beta_{l+1}^l-\beta_l^l)[1-e^{-\rho(Q-(l-1)\hat{D})}-e^{-\rho(Q-(l-1)\hat{D})}((\frac{\mu}{\mu-\rho})^k(1-\frac{\rho p}{\mu})-1) \\
&+\rho e^{-\mu(Q-(l-1)\hat{D})}(p\sum_{j=0}^{k-2}\sum_{i=j}^{k-2}\frac{\mu^i(Q-(l-1)\hat{D})^{i-j}}{(i-j)!(\mu-\rho)^{j+1}} \\
&\qquad +(1-p)\sum_{j=0}^{k-1}\sum_{i=j}^{k-1}\frac{\mu^i(Q-(l-1)\hat{D})^{i-j}}{(i-j)!(\mu-\rho)^{j+1}})]\Big] \\
&+\beta_1^l+\sum_{\theta=2}^{l+1}(\beta_\theta^l-\beta_{\theta-1}^l)(1-e^{-\mu(Q-(\theta-2)\hat{D})}(p\sum_{i=0}^{k-2}\frac{(\mu(Q-(\theta-2)\hat{D}))^i}{i!} \\
&\qquad +(1-p)\sum_{i=0}^{k-1}\frac{(\mu(Q-(\theta-2)\hat{D}))^i}{i!}))\Big\}\frac{1}{M(Q)}
\end{aligned}
$$

Now, we can determine the planning stability for $Q \leq \hat{D}$ with (B.3) and for $Q > \hat{D}$ with (B.10) by inserting the corresponding stability quotients and using the relevant coefficients of the distribution function as depicted in Appendix A.1. Note that $\frac{1}{M(Q)}$ is given by (B.4).

B.3 Exponentially Distributed Demand

In the case of exponentially distributed demand, i.e. $c_D^2 = 1$, it holds that $k = 2, p = 1, \mu = \frac{1}{\bar{D}}$ and $\rho = \gamma = 0$ (see Appendix A).

B.3.1 $Q \leq \hat{D}$

Then (B.3) yields

$$\pi_{s,S}^{A} = \alpha_1 \frac{1}{1 + Q/\bar{D}} + \alpha_2 \frac{Q/\bar{D}}{1 + Q/\bar{D}} \tag{B.11}$$

B.3.2 $Q > \hat{D}$

In this case we obtain from (B.10) that

$$\begin{aligned} \pi_{s,S}^{B} = \Bigg\{ \sum_{\tau=1}^{l-1} & \left[\beta_1^{\tau} \frac{\hat{D}}{\bar{D}} + \sum_{\theta=2}^{\tau+1} (\beta_\theta^{\tau} - \beta_{\theta-1}^{\tau}) (\frac{\hat{D}}{\bar{D}} - e^{(\theta-\tau-1)\frac{\hat{D}}{\bar{D}}} + e^{(\theta-\tau-2)\frac{\hat{D}}{\bar{D}}}) \right] \\ & + \beta_1^{l} (\frac{Q - (l-1)\hat{D}}{\bar{D}} + 1) + \sum_{\theta=2}^{l+1} (\beta_\theta^{l} - \beta_{\theta-1}^{l}) \frac{Q - (l-1)\hat{D}}{\bar{D}} \\ & + \sum_{\theta=2}^{l+1} (\beta_\theta^{l} - \beta_{\theta-1}^{l}) (1 - e^{(\theta-l-1)\frac{\hat{D}}{\bar{D}}}) \Bigg\} \frac{1}{1 + Q/\bar{D}} \end{aligned}$$

Factoring out and rearranging terms leads to

$$\begin{aligned} \pi_{s,S}^{B} = \Bigg\{ \sum_{\tau=1}^{l-1} & \Bigg[\beta_1^{\tau} (e^{-(\tau-1)\frac{\hat{D}}{\bar{D}}} - e^{-\tau\frac{\hat{D}}{\bar{D}}}) + \sum_{\theta=2}^{\tau} \beta_\theta^{\tau} (e^{(\theta-\tau)\frac{\hat{D}}{\bar{D}}} - 2e^{(\theta-\tau-1)\frac{\hat{D}}{\bar{D}}} \\ & \qquad + e^{(\theta-\tau-2)\cdot\frac{\hat{D}}{\bar{D}}}) + \beta_{\tau+1}^{\tau} (\frac{\hat{D}}{\bar{D}} - 1 + e^{-\frac{\hat{D}}{\bar{D}}}) \Bigg] \\ & + \beta_1^{l} e^{-(l-1)\frac{\hat{D}}{\bar{D}}} + \sum_{\theta=2}^{l} \beta_\theta^{l} (e^{(\theta-l)\frac{\hat{D}}{\bar{D}}} - e^{(\theta-l-1)\frac{\hat{D}}{\bar{D}}}) \\ & + \beta_{l+1}^{l} \frac{Q - (l-1)\hat{D}}{\bar{D}} \Bigg\} \frac{1}{1 + Q/\bar{D}}. \end{aligned} \tag{B.12}$$

B.3.3 Properties of Stability Function

From this point, only the special case that all periods are weighted equally (i.e. $a \to 1$) and that the forecasted demand corresponds to its expectation are considered in this study (i.e. $\hat{D} = \bar{D}$).

B.3.3.1 Simplification of Stability Function

We get from (B.11)

$$\pi^A_{s,S} = \frac{1}{1+Q/\hat{D}} + \frac{T-1}{T}\frac{Q/\hat{D}}{1+Q/\hat{D}} \tag{B.13}$$

For $Q > \hat{D}$ after some algebraic transformations we get from (B.12)

$$\begin{aligned}\pi^B_{s,S} = \Bigg\{ &\left[\sum_{\tau=2}^{l}(\bar{\beta}^{\tau}_{\tau-1} + \bar{\beta}^{\tau-1}_{\tau}) - \bar{\beta}^{l}_{l} - 2\sum_{\tau=2}^{l-1}\bar{\beta}^{\tau}_{\tau} - \bar{\beta}^{1}_{1}\right] e^{-1} \\ &+ \left[\sum_{\tau=3}^{l}(\bar{\beta}^{\tau}_{\tau-2} - 2\bar{\beta}^{\tau}_{\tau-1}) + \bar{\beta}^{l}_{l-1} - \bar{\beta}^{2}_{1} + \sum_{\tau=2}^{l-1}\bar{\beta}^{\tau}_{\tau}\right] e^{-2} \\ &+ \sum_{j=3}^{l-1}\left[\sum_{\tau=j}^{l-1}\bar{\beta}^{\tau}_{\tau-(j-2)} - 2\sum_{\tau=j+1}^{l-1}\bar{\beta}^{\tau}_{\tau-(j-1)} + \sum_{\tau=j+1}^{l}\bar{\beta}^{\tau}_{\tau-j} - \bar{\beta}^{l}_{l-(j-1)} - \bar{\beta}^{j}_{1}\right] e^{-j} \\ &+ \sum_{\tau=1}^{l}\bar{\beta}^{\tau}_{\tau} - (l-1)\bar{\beta}^{l}_{l+1}\Bigg\}\frac{\hat{D}}{\hat{D}+Q} + \bar{\beta}^{l}_{l+1}\frac{Q}{\hat{D}+Q}\end{aligned} \tag{B.14}$$

This equation can be simplified by using the following result.

Simplification of $\pi^B_{s,S}$

The third term in (B.14) equals zero, i.e.

$$\sum_{j=3}^{l-1}\left[\sum_{\tau=j}^{l-1}\bar{\beta}^{\tau}_{\tau-(j-2)} - 2\sum_{\tau=j+1}^{l-1}\bar{\beta}^{\tau}_{\tau-(j-1)} + \sum_{\tau=j+1}^{l}\bar{\beta}^{\tau}_{\tau-j} - \bar{\beta}^{j}_{1} - \bar{\beta}^{l}_{l-(j-1)}\right] e^{-j} = 0 \;\forall\, l \geq 4.$$

Proof

Due to $e^{-j} > 0$ ($\forall\, j = 3, 4, ..., l-1$) we have to show for all $l \geq 4$ that:

$$\sum_{\tau=j}^{l-1}\bar{\beta}^{\tau}_{\tau-(j-2)} - 2\sum_{\tau=j+1}^{l-1}\bar{\beta}^{\tau}_{\tau-(j-1)} + \sum_{\tau=j+1}^{l}\bar{\beta}^{\tau}_{\tau-j} - \bar{\beta}^{j}_{1} - \bar{\beta}^{l}_{l-(j-1)} = 0 \;\;\forall\, j=3,..,l-1.$$

The result is proved by induction. The strategy for the proof is:

1. Prove that the sum equals zero for $l = 4$
2. Assume that the result is true for $l = n - 1$
3. Show that it holds for $l = n$, $n \in \mathcal{N}$ and $n > 4$.

(1) $l = 4$

We have to show that $\bar{\beta}_2^3 + \bar{\beta}_1^4 - \bar{\beta}_1^3 - \bar{\beta}_2^4 = 0$. The value of the stability quotients depends on the length of the stability horizon. From Table 4.4 (see p.81) we find the following relations. For $\tau = 3$ and $\theta = 1$ we obtain

- from (*ii*) that $\bar{\beta}_1^3 = \frac{T-2L-1}{T}$ for $T = 4L + 1$ and $T = 4L + 2$
- from (*iii*) that $\bar{\beta}_1^3 = \frac{T-2L-2}{T}$ for $T = 4L + 3$
- from (*v*) that $\bar{\beta}_1^3 = \frac{2}{4}$ for $T = 4L$ (with $L > 0$)

Notice that the conditions in (*i*) and (*iv*) are not valid for $\tau = 3$ and $\theta = 1$. Analogously we get for $\tau = 3$ and $\theta = 2$ (where (*iv*) is again not feasible)

- from (*i*) that $\bar{\beta}_2^3 = \frac{T-2L}{T}$ for $T = 4L + 1$
- from (*ii*) that $\bar{\beta}_2^3 = \frac{T-2L-1}{T}$ for $T = 4L + 2$
- from (*iii*) that $\bar{\beta}_2^3 = \frac{T-2L-2}{T}$ for $T = 4L + 3$
- from (*v*) that $\bar{\beta}_2^3 = \frac{2}{4}$ for $T = 4L$ (with $L > 0$)

With the same analysis as above we determine the value of the stability quotients for $\tau = 4$, $\theta = 1$ and $\theta = 2$, respectively.
Thus resulting in:
If $T = 4L + 1$, then $\bar{\beta}_1^4 = \bar{\beta}_1^3 = \frac{T-2L-1}{T}$ and $\bar{\beta}_2^4 = \bar{\beta}_2^3 = \frac{T-2L}{T}$
If $T = 4L + 2$, then $\bar{\beta}_1^4 = \bar{\beta}_1^3 = \bar{\beta}_2^4 = \bar{\beta}_2^3 = \frac{T-2L-1}{T}$
If $T = 4L + 3$, then $\bar{\beta}_1^4 = \bar{\beta}_2^4 = \frac{T-2L-1}{T}$ and $\bar{\beta}_1^3 = \bar{\beta}_2^3 = \frac{T-2L-2}{T}$
If $T = 4L$ (with $L > 0$), then $\bar{\beta}_1^4 = \bar{\beta}_1^3 = \bar{\beta}_2^4 = \bar{\beta}_2^3 = \frac{2}{4}$

From these relations it follows immediately that for each stability horizon T the term in (B.14) equals zero for $l = 4$.
Now that the result has been proved true for $l = 4$, we will prove that it is true for $l = n$, given it is true for $l = n - 1$ (with $n > 4$).

(2) $l = n - 1$

Under the assumption that the result is true for $l = n - 1$ we get

$$\bar{\beta}_{k-1}^{n-1} - \bar{\beta}_k^{n-1} + \ldots + \bar{\beta}_1^{n-(k-1)} - \bar{\beta}_2^{n-(k-1)} + \bar{\beta}_k^{n-2} - \bar{\beta}_{k-1}^{n-2} + \ldots + \bar{\beta}_2^{n-k} - \bar{\beta}_1^{n-k} = 0, \quad (B.15)$$

where $k = 1, 2, \ldots, n - 4$.

(3) $l = n$

For $l = n$ we have to prove for all $k = 1, 2, ..., n-3$ that

$$\bar{\beta}_k^n - \bar{\beta}_{k+1}^n + \bar{\beta}_{k+1}^{n-1} - \bar{\beta}_k^{n-1} + \bar{\beta}_{k-1}^{n-1} - \bar{\beta}_k^{n-1} + ... +$$
$$+\bar{\beta}_1^{n-(k-1)} - \bar{\beta}_2^{n-(k-1)} + \bar{\beta}_k^{n-2} - \bar{\beta}_{k-1}^{n-2} + ... + \bar{\beta}_2^{n-k} - beta_1^{n-k} = 0.$$

With (B.15) the proof reduces to show that

$$\bar{\beta}_k^n - \bar{\beta}_{k+1}^n + \bar{\beta}_{k+1}^{n-1} - \bar{\beta}_k^{n-1} = 0 \quad \forall \quad k = 1, 2, ..., n-3.$$

In order to obtain the value of the stability quotients we have to evaluate the conditions in Table 4.4. We will do this in detail for $\bar{\beta}_k^n$, i.e. $\tau = n$ and $\theta = k$.

From (i) we find that $\bar{\beta}_k^n = \frac{T-2L}{T}$, if $T = Ln+1, ..., Ln+k-1$.

From (ii) follows that $\bar{\beta}_k^n = \frac{T-2L-1}{T}$, if $T = Ln+k, ..., Ln+n-1$.

The conditions in (iii) and (iv) are not feasible for $\tau = n$ and $\theta = k$ with $k \leq n-3$.

Due to (v) we obtain that $\bar{\beta}_k^n = \frac{n-2}{n}$, if $T = Ln$ (with $L > 0$).

Applying the same analysis we get the value of the other relevant stability quotients.
Altogether we obtain:

If $T = Ln+1, ..., Ln+k-1$,

then $\bar{\beta}_k^n = \bar{\beta}_{k+1}^n = \bar{\beta}_{k+1}^{n-1} = \bar{\beta}_k^{n-1} = \frac{T-2L}{T}$

If $T = Ln+k$,

then $\bar{\beta}_{k+1}^n = \bar{\beta}_{k+1}^{n-1} = \frac{T-2L}{T}$ and $\bar{\beta}_k^n = \bar{\beta}_k^{n-1} = \frac{T-2L-1}{T}$

If $T = Ln+k+1, ..., Ln+n-2$,

then $\bar{\beta}_k^n = \bar{\beta}_{k+1}^n = \bar{\beta}_{k+1}^{n-1} = \bar{\beta}_k^{n-1} = \frac{T-2L-1}{T}$

If $T = Ln+n-1$,

then $\bar{\beta}_k^n = \bar{\beta}_{k+1}^n = \frac{T-2L-1}{T}$ and $\bar{\beta}_k^{n-1} = \bar{\beta}_{k+1}^{n-1} = \frac{T-2L-2}{T}$

If $T = Ln$ (with $L > 0$),

then $\bar{\beta}_k^n = \bar{\beta}_{k+1}^n = \bar{\beta}_{k+1}^{n-1} = \bar{\beta}_k^{n-1} = \frac{n-2}{n}$.

With the same arguments as for $l = 4$ the term $\bar{\beta}_k^n - \bar{\beta}_{k+1}^n + \bar{\beta}_{k+1}^{n-1} - \bar{\beta}_k^{n-1}$ equals zero for all T.

q.e.d.

Thus planning stability for $Q > \hat{D}$ can be rewritten as

$$\begin{aligned}\pi^B_{s,S} = \Bigg\{ &\left[\sum_{\tau=2}^{l}(\bar{\beta}^{\tau}_{\tau-1} + \bar{\beta}^{\tau-1}_{\tau}) - \bar{\beta}^{l}_{l} - 2\sum_{\tau=2}^{l-1}\bar{\beta}^{\tau}_{\tau} - \bar{\beta}^{1}_{1}\right] e^{-1} \\ &+ \left[\sum_{\tau=3}^{l}(\bar{\beta}^{\tau}_{\tau-2} - 2\bar{\beta}^{\tau}_{\tau-1}) + \bar{\beta}^{l}_{l-1} - \bar{\beta}^{2}_{1} + \sum_{\tau=2}^{l-1}\bar{\beta}^{\tau}_{\tau}\right] e^{-2} \\ &+ \sum_{\tau=1}^{l}\bar{\beta}^{\tau}_{\tau} - (l-1)\bar{\beta}^{l}_{l+1}\Bigg\}\frac{\hat{D}}{\hat{D}+Q} + \bar{\beta}^{l}_{l+1}\frac{Q}{\hat{D}+Q}.\end{aligned} \tag{B.16}$$

Using the results for the stability quotients in Table 4.4 we can simplify the result in (B.16) as follows. First, we have to determine the relevant stability quotients. It holds that $\bar{\beta}^{\tau}_{\tau} = 1$ for all $\tau = 1, 2, ..., l$. In order to obtain the other expressions we transform and evaluate the conditions in Table 4.4; we will do this in detail for $\bar{\beta}^{\tau}_{\tau-1}$, i.e. $\theta = \tau - 1$. Moreover, it holds that $\bar{\beta}^{\tau}_{\tau-1} = \bar{\beta}^{\tau-1}_{\tau}$. Thus, the outcome for $\bar{\beta}^{\tau-1}_{\tau}$ is not given explicitly. Due to (i), we obtain $\bar{\beta}^{\tau}_{\tau-1} = \frac{T-2L}{T}$ if $T = Ll+1, ..., Ll+\tau-2$. With (ii) it follows that $\bar{\beta}^{\tau}_{\tau-1} = \frac{T-2L-1}{T}$ for $T = Ll+\tau-1$. According to (iii) $\bar{\beta}^{\tau}_{\tau-1} = \frac{T-2L-2}{T}$ for $T = Ll+\tau$. From (iv) we get $\bar{\beta}^{\tau}_{\tau-1} = \frac{T-2L-2}{T}$ for $T = Ll+\tau+1, ..., (L+1)l-1$ and from (v) follows that[1] $\bar{\beta}^{\tau}_{\tau-1} = \frac{T-2L}{T}$ for $T = Ll$ (with $L > 0$).
Thus leading to two different results depending on the stability horizon:

If $T = Ll+1, ..., (L+1)l-1$ (with $L \geq 0$), then we get

$$\bar{\beta}^{\tau}_{\tau-1} = \begin{cases} \frac{T-2L-2}{T} & \text{for} \quad \tau = 2, ..., T-Ll \\ \frac{T-2L-1}{T} & \text{for} \quad \tau = T-Ll+1 \\ \frac{T-2L}{T} & \text{for} \quad \tau = T-Ll+2, ..., l, \end{cases}$$

and

if $T = Ll$ (with $L > 0$), then it holds that

$$\bar{\beta}^{\tau}_{\tau-1} = \frac{T-2L}{T}.$$

With the same analysis as above we obtain the following results for the other stability quotients.

[1] Note that $\frac{l-2}{l} = \frac{T-2L}{T}$ for $T = Ll$. For ease of notation in our further analysis we use the latter expression.

If $T = Ll + 1, ..., (L+1)l - 1$ (with $L \geq 0$), then we obtain

$$\bar{\beta}^{\tau}_{\tau-2} = \begin{cases} \frac{T-2L-2}{T} & \text{for} \quad \tau = 3, ..., T - Ll \\ \frac{T-2L-1}{T} & \text{for} \quad \tau = T - Ll + 1, T - Ll + 2 \\ \frac{T-2L}{T} & \text{for} \quad \tau = T - Ll + 3, ..., l, \end{cases}$$

$$\bar{\beta}^{l}_{l+1} = \frac{T - 2L}{T},$$

and
if $T = Ll$ (with $L > 0$), then it follows that

$$\bar{\beta}^{\tau}_{\tau-2} = \frac{T - 2L}{T} \quad \text{and} \quad \bar{\beta}^{l}_{l+1} = \frac{T - 2L + 1}{T}.$$

Now, the planning stability for both horizon cases can easily be determined.

Case 1: $T = Ll + 1, ..., (L+1)l - 1$

Substituting the relevant stability quotients in (B.16) we obtain

$$\begin{aligned} \pi^{B}_{s,S} = \Bigg\{ 2\Big[\sum_{\tau=2}^{T-Ll} \frac{T - 2L - 2}{T} + \sum_{\tau=T-Ll+1}^{T-Ll+1} \frac{T - 2L - 1}{T} \\ + \sum_{\tau=T-Ll+2}^{l} \frac{T - 2L}{T} - (l-1)\Big] e^{-1} + \Big[\sum_{\tau=3}^{T-Ll} (-\frac{T - 2L - 2}{T}) \\ + \sum_{\tau=T-Ll+1}^{T-Ll+1} (-\frac{T - 2L - 1}{T}) + \sum_{\tau=T-Ll+2}^{T-Ll+2} (-\frac{T - 2L + 1}{T}) \end{aligned}$$

Thus we get

$$\begin{aligned} \pi^{B}_{s,S} = \frac{1}{T} \Bigg\{ \big[2(1 - 2T + 2L)e^{-1} + 2(T - 1 - 2L)e^{-2} + T \\ +2(l-1)L\big] \frac{1}{1 + Q/\hat{D}} + \big[T - 2L\big] \frac{Q/\hat{D}}{1 + Q/\hat{D}} \Bigg\} \end{aligned}$$

Case 2: $T = Ll$ (with $L > 0$)

Using the matching stability quotients as mentioned above we obtain from (B.16) that

$$\begin{aligned} \pi^{B}_{s,S} = \Bigg\{ 2 \left[\sum_{\tau=2}^{l} \frac{T - 2L}{T} - (l-1) \right] e^{-1} + \left[\sum_{\tau=3}^{l} (-\frac{T - 2L}{T}) + l - 2 \right] e^{-2} \\ +l - (l-1) \frac{T - 2L + 1}{T} \Bigg\} \frac{\hat{D}}{\hat{D} + Q} + \frac{T - 2L + 1}{T} \frac{Q}{\hat{D} + Q} \end{aligned}$$

After some simplifications we obtain

$$\pi^B_{s,S} = \frac{1}{T}\Big\{ \big[4(L-T)e^{-1} + 2(T-2L)e^{-2} + T + 1 - l + 2(l-1)L\big]\frac{1}{1+Q/\hat{D}} + \big[T - 2L + 1\big]\frac{1}{1+\hat{D}/Q}\Big\}$$

Substituting L by T/l finally yields to

$$\pi^B_{s,S} = \frac{1}{l}\Big\{ \big[(3-4e^{-1}+2e^{-2})l - 2(1-2e^{-1}+2e^{-2})\big]\frac{1}{1+Q/\hat{D}} + [l-2]\frac{Q/\hat{D}}{1+Q/\hat{D}}\Big\} + \frac{1}{T}\big[1 - \frac{l}{1+Q/\hat{D}}\big]$$

Altogether, for exponentially distributed demand with $a \to 1$ and $\bar{D} = \hat{D}$, stability is given by

$$\pi^A_{s,S} = \frac{1}{1+Q/\hat{D}} + \frac{T-1}{T}\frac{Q/\hat{D}}{1+Q/\hat{D}} \tag{B.17}$$

$$\pi^B_{s,S} = \begin{cases} \frac{1}{T}\Big\{ \big[2(1-2T+2L)e^{-1} + 2(T-2L-1)e^{-2} + T + 2(l-1)L\big]\frac{1}{1+Q/\hat{D}} \\ \quad + \big[T-2L\big]\frac{Q/\hat{D}}{1+Q/\hat{D}}\Big\} \text{ for } T = Ll+1, ..., (L+1)l-1 \ (L \geq 0) \\ \frac{1}{l}\Big\{ \big[(3-4e^{-1}+2e^{-2})l - 2(1-2e^{-1}+2e^{-2})\big]\frac{1}{(1+Q/\hat{D})} \\ \quad + \big[l-2\big]\frac{Q/\hat{D}}{(1+Q/\hat{D})}\Big\} + \frac{1}{T}(1 - \frac{l}{1+Q/\hat{D}}) \text{ for } \quad T = Ll \ (L > 0) \end{cases} \tag{B.18}$$

Since l and L (see (4.12) and (4.17), respectively) are functions of $Q/\hat{D}$ and T, the stability function only depends on the $Q/\hat{D}$-ratio and the length of the stability horizon.

For the special case of an infinite stability horizon we obtain from (B.17) and (B.18), respectively, that

$$\pi^A_{s,S}(T \to \infty) = 1$$

$$\pi^B_{s,S}(T \to \infty) = \frac{(3-4e^{-1}+2e^{-2})l - 2(1-2e^{-1}+2e^{-2})}{l(1+Q/\hat{D})} + \frac{(l-2)Q/\hat{D}}{l(1+Q/\hat{D})}.$$

B.3.3.2 Convexity of Stability Function for $Q < \hat{D}$

In order to prove that $\pi^A_{s,S}$ is a strictly convex function in Q, we analyze the first and second order derivatives of (B.13). It is easy to see that

$$\frac{\partial \pi^A_{s,S}}{\partial Q} = -\frac{1}{T} \frac{\hat{D}}{(\hat{D}+Q)^2} < 0$$

and

$$\frac{\partial^2 \pi^A_{s,S}}{\partial Q^2} = \frac{1}{T} \frac{2\hat{D}}{(\hat{D}+Q)^3} > 0$$

Thus the stability function $\pi^A_{s,S}$ is strictly decreasing and convex.

For $Q = 0$ we get

$$\pi^A_{s,S}(Q = 0) = 1.$$

q.e.d.

B.3.3.3 Discontinuity of Stability Function for $Q = \hat{D}$

For $\pi^A_{s,S}$ with $Q = \hat{D}$ it holds

$$\pi^A_{s,S}(Q = \hat{D}) = 1 - \frac{1}{2T}.$$

For $\pi^B_{s,S}$ we get from (B.16) (with $l = 2$ and $\bar{\beta}^1_1 = \bar{\beta}^2_2 = 1$, $\bar{\beta}^2_1 = \bar{\beta}^1_2 = 0$, and $\bar{\beta}^2_3 = \frac{1}{T}$) that

$$\pi^B_{s,S} = \{[2T(1-e^{-1}) - 1]\hat{D} + Q\} \frac{1}{T} \frac{1}{\hat{D}+Q} \qquad \text{(B.19)}$$

With Q approaching $\hat{D}$ we obtain: $\lim_{Q \to \hat{D}} \pi^B_{s,S} = 1 - e^{-1} \cong 0.63$.

Altogether this results in

$$\pi^A_{s,S}(Q = \hat{D}) \left\{ \begin{matrix} < \\ > \end{matrix} \right\} \lim_{Q \to \hat{D}} \pi^B_{s,S}(Q) \begin{cases} \text{if } T = 1 \\ \text{else.} \end{cases}$$

Thus, the stability function is discontinuous for $Q = \hat{D}$. In the case of the short-term consideration stability for $Q = \hat{D}$ is lower than for lot sizes which are a bit larger than the expected demand per period, for larger stability horizons the opposite applies.

q.e.d.

B.3.3.4 Development of Stability Function for $Q > \hat{D}$

From (B.18), we see that for given demand expectation $\hat{D}$ and stability horizon parameter T the single sections of the stability function are continuous in Q and $Q/\hat{D}$, respectively. With increasing minimum lot size, the $Q/\hat{D}$-ratio-parameter l changes. Thus we have to analyze whether the stability function is continuous with a transition from $Q \in ((l-1)\hat{D}, l\hat{D}]$ to its neighbouring region.

Proof of Continuity for $l > T$

If $l > T$, i.e. $L = 0$, we obtain the following result for $(l-1)\hat{D} < Q \leq l\hat{D}$, i.e. $Q > T\hat{D}$ from the corresponding (first) part of the stability function in (B.18).

$$\pi^B_{s,S} = \{[2(1-2T)e^{-1} + 2(T-1)e^{-2} + T]\hat{D} + TQ\}\frac{1}{T}\frac{1}{\hat{D}+Q}.$$

Thus the stability function depends on Q (as well as on $\hat{D}$ and T), but it is independent of the $Q/\hat{D}$-ratio-parameter l. Therefore it has to be continuous in Q.

q.e.d.

Proof of Concavity for $l > T$

The first and second order derivatives are given by

$$\frac{\partial \pi^B_{s,S}}{\partial Q} = -2\frac{(1-2T)e^{-1} + (T-1)e^{-2}}{T}\frac{\hat{D}}{(\hat{D}+Q)^2}$$

$$\frac{\partial^2 \pi^B_{s,S}}{\partial Q^2} = 4\frac{(1-2T)e^{-1} + (T-1)e^{-2}}{T}\frac{\hat{D}}{(\hat{D}+Q)^3}$$

It is easy to see that $e^{-1} - e^{-2} - (2e^{-1} - e^{-2})T < 0$ for all T.
Thus it follows that $\frac{\partial \pi^B_{s,S}}{\partial Q} > 0$ and $\frac{\partial^2 \pi^B_{s,S}}{\partial Q^2} < 0$, and the stability function has to be strictly concave and increasing.
Notice that the limiting value of $\pi^B_{s,S}$ for Q towards infinity is given by

$$\lim_{Q\to\infty} \pi^B_{s,S}(Q) = \lim_{Q\to\infty} \{\frac{1}{T}\frac{2(1-2T)e^{-1} + 2(T-1)e^{-2} + T}{1 + Q/\hat{D}} + \frac{1}{1+\hat{D}/Q}\} = 1.$$

q.e.d.

Proof of Discontinuity for $l \leq T$

Assumption

The stability function is discontinuous for $l \leq T$, i.e. $L > 0$. In the points of discontinuity it increases by jumps.

Proof

In order to prove this assumption we have to consider two neighbouring regions $Q \in ((h-1)\hat{D}, h\hat{D}]$ and $Q \in (h\hat{D}, (h+1)\hat{D}]$ (for all $h = 2, ..., T$) as shown in Figure B.1.

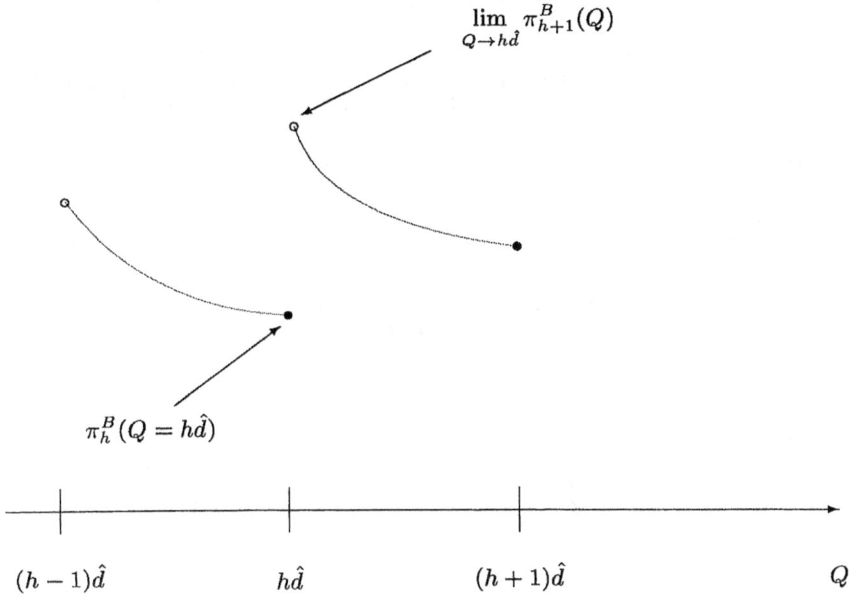

Figure B.1. Planning stability for two neighbouring regions

Notice that the single sections of the stability function in Figure B.1 can also be strictly concave and increasing for specific values of h.

We have to show that

$$\pi_{s,S,(h)}^{B}(Q = h\hat{D}) < \lim_{Q \to h\hat{D}} \pi_{s,S,(h+1)}^{B}(Q) \text{ for all } 1 < h \leq T.$$

The planning stability for the two intervals is given as follows (see (B.18)). For $Q \in ((h-1)\hat{D}, h\hat{D}]$ we get

$$\pi^B_{s,S,(h)}(Q) = \Big\{ [2(1-2T+2L)e^{-1} + 2(T-2L-1)e^{-2} + T + 2(h-1)L]\hat{D} + [T-2L]Q \Big\} \frac{1}{T(\hat{D}+Q)} \qquad \text{(B.20)}$$

$$\text{for } T = Lh+1, ..., (L+1)h-1 \ (L \geq 0)$$

and

$$\pi^B_{s,S,(h)}(Q) = \Big\{ [(3-4e^{-1}+2e^{-2})h - 2(1-2e^{-1}+2e^{-2})]\hat{D} + (h-2)Q \Big\} \frac{1}{h(\hat{D}+Q)} + \frac{1}{T}[1 - \frac{h\hat{D}}{\hat{D}+Q}] \quad \text{for } T = Lh. \qquad \text{(B.21)}$$

Analogously, we obtain for $Q \in (h\hat{D}, (h+1)\hat{D}]$

$$\pi^B_{s,S,(h+1)}(Q) = \Big\{ [2(1-2T+2L)e^{-1} + 2(T-2L-1)e^{-2} + T + 2hL]\hat{D} + [T-2L]Q \Big\} \frac{1}{T(\hat{D}+Q)} \qquad \text{(B.22)}$$

$$\text{for } T = L(h+1)+1, ..., (L+1)(h+1)-1 \ (L \geq 0)$$

and

$$\pi^B_{s,S,(h+1)}(Q) = \Big\{ [(3-4e^{-1}+2e^{-2})(h+1) - 2(1-2e^{-1}+2e^{-2})]\hat{D} + (h-1)Q \Big\} \frac{1}{(h+1)(\hat{D}+Q)} + \frac{1}{T}[1 - \frac{(h+1)\hat{D}}{\hat{D}+Q}] \qquad \text{(B.23)}$$

$$\text{for } T = L(h+1).$$

Note that in the case of (B.20) and (B.22), i.e. $T \neq Lh$ and $T \neq L(h+1)$, it holds that for each h there is exactly one $L \in [\frac{T-1}{h}, ..., \frac{T-(h-1)}{h}]$ or $L \in [\frac{T-1}{h+1}, ..., \frac{T-h}{h+1}]$, respectively.

First, we will analyze for which value of $L \in [\frac{T-1}{h+1}, ..., \frac{T-h}{h+1}]$ the term in (B.22) reaches its *minimum*, if Q approaches $h\hat{D}$ (Result I).
Analogously, we will compute for which $L \in [\frac{T-1}{h}, ..., \frac{T-(h-1)}{h}]$ the term in (B.20) reaches its *maximum*, if Q is equal to $h\hat{D}$ (Result II).

Then, we will describe all possible transitions from the interval h to its successor $h+1$[2]. By using the maximum function values for $\pi^B_{s,S,(h+1)}(Q = h\hat{D})_{L\in[\frac{T-1}{h},\ldots,\frac{T-(h-1)}{h}]}$ and the minimum function values for $\lim_{Q\to h\hat{D}} \pi^B_{s,S,(h+1)}(Q)_{L\in[\frac{T-1}{h+1},\ldots,\frac{T-h}{h+1}]}$ we ensure that our assumption holds, no matter what the exact function value for a given T/h-ratio may be.

Result I

For $\pi^B_{s,S,(h+1)}(Q)$ with $T \neq L(h+1)$ the limiting value of Q approaching $h\hat{D}$ reaches its minimum for $L = \frac{T-h}{h+1}$, i.e.

$$\lim_{Q\to h\hat{D}} \pi^B_{s,S,(h+1)}(Q)_{L=\frac{T-n}{h+1}} < \lim_{Q\to h\hat{D}} \pi^B_{s,S,(h+1)}(Q)_{L=\frac{T-(n-1)}{h+1}} \;\forall\, n = 2,..,h. \tag{B.24}$$

Proof of Result I

In order to prove (B.24), we determine the corresponding planning stability from (B.22). We get

$$\pi^B_{s,S,(h+1)}(Q)_{L=\frac{T-n}{h+1}} = \frac{\{2e^{-1}[h+1-2(Th+n)]+2e^{-2}[Th+2n-(T+h+1)]\}\hat{D}}{(h+1)T(\hat{D}+Q)} + \frac{[(3h+1)T-2hn]\hat{D}+[T(h-1)+2n]Q}{(h+1)T(\hat{D}+Q)}$$

and

$$\begin{aligned}
&\pi^B_{s,S,(h+1)}(Q)_{L=\frac{T-(n-1)}{h+1}} \\
&= \frac{\{2e^{-1}[h+3-2(Th+n)]+2e^{-2}[Th+2n-(T+h+3)]\}\hat{D}}{(h+1)T(\hat{D}+Q)} \\
&+ \frac{[(3h+1)T-2h(n-1)]\hat{D}+[T(h-1)+2(n-1)]Q}{(h+1)T(\hat{D}+Q)}.
\end{aligned}$$

The limiting values are

$$\begin{aligned}
&\lim_{Q\to h\hat{D}} \pi^B_{s,S,(h+1)}(Q)_{L=\frac{T-n}{h+1}} \\
&= \frac{2e^{-1}[h+1-2(Th+n)]+2e^{-2}[Th+2n-(T+h+1)]}{(h+1)^2T} \\
&+ \frac{T(h^2+2h+1)}{(h+1)^2T}
\end{aligned} \tag{B.25}$$

[2] We have to show that the assumption applies for a change from (B.20) to (B.23), (B.20) to (B.22), and (B.21) to (B.22) (see Relations 1 – 3, p.199).

and

$$\lim_{Q \to h\hat{D}} \pi^B_{s,S,(h+1)}(Q)_{L=\frac{T-(n-1)}{h+1}}$$
$$= \frac{2e^{-1}[h+3-2(Th+n)] + 2e^{-2}[Th+2n-(T+h+3)]}{(h+1)^2 T}$$
$$+ \frac{T(h^2+2h+1)}{(h+1)^2 T}. \tag{B.26}$$

Thus the difference between the terms in (B.25) and (B.26) is given by

$$\lim_{Q \to h\hat{D}} \pi^B_{s,S,(h+1)}(Q)_{L=\frac{T-n}{h+1}} - \lim_{Q \to h\hat{D}} \pi^B_{s,S,(h+1)}(Q)_{L=\frac{T-(n-1)}{h+1}} = \frac{4(e^{-2}-e^{-1})}{(h+1)^2 T} < 0.$$

q.e.d

Result II

The right-sided limiting value of $\pi^B_{s,S,(h)}(Q)$ reaches its maximum for $L = \frac{T-(h-1)}{h}$, because

$$\pi^B_{s,S,(h)}(Q = h\hat{D})_{L=\frac{T-(n-1)}{h}} < \pi^B_{s,S,(h)}(Q = h\hat{D})_{L=\frac{T-n}{h}} \; \forall\, n = 2, ..., h-1. \tag{B.27}$$

Proof of Result II

We apply the same analysis as in the proof of (B.24). From (B.20) we obtain with $Q = h\hat{D}$

$$\pi^B_{s,S,(h)}(h\hat{D})_{L=\frac{T-n}{h}} = \frac{2e^{-1}[h-2(T(h-1)+n)] + 2e^{-2}[T(h-2)-h+2n]}{h(h+1)T}$$
$$+ \frac{T(h^2+h-2)+2n}{h(h+1)T} \tag{B.28}$$

and

$$\pi^B_{s,S,(h)}(h\hat{D})_{L=\frac{T-(n-1)}{h}}$$
$$= \frac{2e^{-1}[h-2(T(h-1)+(n-1))] + 2e^{-2}[T(h-2)-h+2(n-1)]}{h(h+1)T}$$
$$+ \frac{T(h^2+h-2)+2(n-1)}{h(h+1)T}.$$

Since $\pi^B_{s,S,(h)}(h\hat{D})_{L=\frac{T-n}{h}} - \pi^B_{s,S,(h)}(h\hat{D})_{L=\frac{T-(n-1)}{h}} = \frac{2[1-2(e^{-1}-e^{-2})]}{h(h+1)T} > 0$ the planning stability increases with rising n.

q.e.d

Using these results it remains to show that with a change from the interval $Q \in ((h-1)\hat{D}, h\hat{D}]$ to the region $Q \in (h\hat{D}, (h+1)\hat{D}]$ the following relations apply:

Relation 1

For a transition from h with $T \neq Lh$ to $h+1$ with $T = L(h+1)$ holds

$$\pi^B_{s,S,(h)}(h\hat{D})_{L=\frac{T-(h-1)}{h}} < \lim_{Q\to h\hat{D}} \pi^B_{s,S,(h+1)}(Q)_{L=\frac{T}{h+1}}.$$

Relation 2

With a change from h with $T \neq Lh$ to $h+1$ with $T \neq L(h+1)$ we find that

$$\pi^B_{s,S,(h)}(h\hat{D})_{L=\frac{T-(h-1)}{h}} < \lim_{Q\to h\hat{D}} \pi^B_{s,S,(h+1)}(Q)_{L=\frac{T-h}{h+1}}.$$

Relation 3

Going over from h with $T = Lh$ to $h+1$ with $T \neq L(h+1)$ results in

$$\pi^B_{s,S,(h+1)}(h\hat{D})_{L=\frac{T}{h}} < \lim_{Q\to h\hat{D}} \pi^B_{s,S,(h+1)}(Q)_{L=\frac{T-h}{h+1}}.$$

The relations mentioned above describe all possible transitions – with respect to the stability horizon – from the interval h to its successor $h+1$. Notice that a change from h with $T = Lh$ to $h+1$ with $T = L(h+1)$ is not possible, because it would follow that $h = 0$, which is a contradiction to $h > 1$.
By using the maximum function values on the left side of relation 1 and 2, respectively, and the minimum on the right side of relation 2 and 3, we ensure that these relations always apply, no matter what the exact function value for a given T/h-ratio may be.

Proof of Relation 1

From (B.28) with $n = h-1$ we obtain

$$\pi^B_{s,S,(h)}(h\hat{D})_{L=\frac{T-(h-1)}{h}} = \frac{2e^{-1}[2(T+1)-h(2T+1)]+2e^{-2}(h-2)(T+1)}{h(h+1)T} + \frac{T(h^2+h-2)+2(h-1)}{h(h+1)T}. \tag{B.29}$$

From (B.23) we get as limiting value

$$\lim_{Q\to h\hat{D}} \pi^B_{s,S,(h+1)}(Q)_{L=\frac{T}{h+1}} = \frac{(3-4e^{-1}+2e^{-2})(h+1)-2(1-2e^{-1}+2e^{-2})+h(h+1)}{(h+1)^2}$$

$$+\frac{1}{T}(1-\frac{h+1}{h+1})$$

$$=\frac{(2e^{-2}-4e^{-1}+2+h)h+1-2e^{-2}}{(h+1)^2}. \tag{B.30}$$

As the difference from (B.29) and (B.30) we obtain

$$\pi^B_{s,S,(h)}(h\hat{D})_{L=\frac{T-(h-1)}{h}} - \lim_{Q\to h\hat{D}} \pi^B_{s,S,(h+1)}(Q)_{L=\frac{T}{h+1}}$$
$$= \frac{[(e^{-1}-e^{-2})(1-h)+(h-T)]h}{h(h+1)^2T}$$
$$- 2\frac{(2e^{-2}-2e^{-1}+1)(T+1)}{h(h+1)^2T}$$
$$\cong \frac{2[0.23(1-h)+(h-T)]h-1.08(T+1)}{h(h+1)^2T}.$$

Since this difference is always lower than zero for $1 < h \leq T$, we have proved relation 1.

q.e.d

Proof of Relation 2

From (B.25) with $n = h$ we obtain

$$\lim_{Q\to h\hat{D}} \pi^B_{s,S,(h+1)}(Q)_{L=\frac{T-h}{h+1}}$$
$$= \frac{2e^{-1}[1-h(2T+1)]+2e^{-2}(T+1)(h-1)+T(h^2+2h+1)}{(h+1)^2T}. \tag{B.31}$$

The difference between (B.29) and (B.31) is given by

$$\pi^B_{s,S,(h)}(h\hat{D})_{L=\frac{T-(h-1)}{h}} - \lim_{Q\to h\hat{D}} \pi^B_{s,S,(h+1)}(Q)_{L=\frac{T-h}{h+1}}$$
$$= 2\frac{h(h-T)-(2e^{-2}-2e^{-1}+1)(T+1)}{h(h+1)^2T}$$
$$\cong \frac{2h(h-T)-1.08(T+1)}{h(h+1)^2T}$$
$$< 0 \quad \forall\, 1 < h \leq T.$$

q.e.d

Proof of Relation 3

Analogously to (B.30) we get from (B.21) with $Q = h\hat{D}$ that

$$\pi^B_{s,S,(h)}(h\hat{D})_{L=\frac{T}{h}} = \frac{[4e^{-1}(1-h)+2e^{-2}(h-2)+(h^2+h-2)]T+h}{h(h+1)T}. \tag{B.32}$$

As difference between (B.32) and (B.31) we get

$$\pi^B_{s,S,(h)}(h\hat{D})_{L=\frac{T}{h}} - \lim_{Q\to h\hat{D}} \pi^B_{s,S,(h+1)}(Q)_{L=\frac{T-h}{h+1}}$$
$$= \frac{[(2(e^{-1}-e^{-2})+1)h-2T]h}{h(h+1)^2T} - \frac{(2(e^{-2}-e^{-1})+1)(2T-h)}{h(h+1)^2T}$$
$$= \frac{(1.47h-2T)h-0.54(2T-h)}{h(h+1)^2T}$$
$$< \quad \forall\, 1 < h \leq T. \qquad \text{q.e.d}$$

Thus we have shown that the planning stability is discontinuous in the critical points $Q = h\hat{D}$ for all $1 < h \leq T$ and increases by jumps with rising Q just a bit from $h\hat{D}$.

q.e.d

Proof of Convexity/Concavity for $l \leq T$

We determine the first and second order derivatives of the sections of the stability function in order to show its convexity/concavity and its monotonicity. According to (B.18) we get

$$\frac{\partial \pi^B_{s,S}}{\partial Q} = \begin{cases} \frac{-2\hat{D}}{T(\hat{D}+Q)^2}\left[(1-2T+2L)e^{-1}+(T-2L-1)e^{-2}+Ll\right] \text{ for } T \neq Ll \\ \frac{-1\hat{D}}{T(\hat{D}+Q)^2}\left[4Te^{-1}\frac{1-l}{l}+2Te^{-2}\frac{l-2}{l}+2T-l\right] \text{ for } T = Ll, \end{cases} \tag{B.33}$$

$$\frac{\partial^2 \pi^B_{s,S}}{\partial Q^2} = \begin{cases} \frac{4\hat{D}}{T(\hat{D}+Q)^3}\left[(1-2T+2L)e^{-1}+(T-2L-1)e^{-2}+Ll\right] \text{ for } T \neq Ll \\ \frac{2\hat{D}}{T(\hat{D}+Q)^3}\left[4Te^{-1}\frac{1-l}{l}+2Te^{-2}\frac{l-2}{l}+2T-l\right] \text{ for } T = Ll. \end{cases}$$

It is obvious that if $\frac{\partial \pi^B_{s,S,(T,l)}(Q)}{\partial Q} > 0$, then $\frac{\partial^2 \pi^B_{s,S,(T,l)}(Q)}{\partial Q^2} < 0$, and vice versa.

Since $\frac{(-1)\hat{D}}{T(\hat{D}+Q)^2} < 0$ and $\frac{\hat{D}}{T(\hat{D}+Q)^3} > 0$ we have to analyze the terms in cornered brackets to determine the sign of the derivatives.

Case 1: $L = 1$, i.e. $l \leq T \leq 2l-1$, or $\lceil \frac{T+1}{2} \rceil \leq l \leq T$, respectively

For $L = 1$ we get for the terms in cornered brackets (see (B.33))

$$(3-2T)e^{-1} + (T-3)e^{-2} + l \text{ if } \quad 2l > T > l \tag{B.34}$$

$$4(1-l)e^{-1} + 2(l-2)e^{-2} + l \quad \text{if} \quad T = l \tag{B.35}$$

1.1. $T = 2l - 1$

For $T = 2l - 1$ we obtain (see (B.34))

$$(5-4l)e^{-1} + (2l-4)e^{-2} + l \begin{cases} > 0 & \text{if} \quad l = 2, ..., 6 \\ < 0 & \text{else.} \end{cases}$$

This results in $\frac{\partial \pi^B_{s,S}(Q)}{\partial Q} \left\{ \begin{matrix} < \\ > \end{matrix} \right\} 0$ and $\frac{\partial^2 \pi^B_{s,S}(Q)}{\partial Q^2} \left\{ \begin{matrix} > \\ < \end{matrix} \right\} 0$ $\begin{cases} \text{if} \quad l = 2, ..., 6 \\ \text{else.} \end{cases}$

Thus $\pi^B_{s,S}(Q)$ is a strictly concave and increasing function for $l > 6$. If $l \leq 6$, then it is strictly decreasing and convex.

1.2. $l < T < 2l - 1$

In order to determine the development of $\pi^B_{s,S}(Q)$ in the interval ($l < T < 2l - 1$) we have to evaluate the following relation (see (B.34))

$$[3(e^{-1} - e^{-2}) - (2e^{-1} - e^{-2})T + l] \left\{ \begin{matrix} \overset{?}{<} \\ \overset{?}{>} \end{matrix} \right\} 0. \qquad \text{(B.36)}$$

This means that we have to determine the critical value for the $Q/\hat{D}$-ratio parameter l in dependence on a given stability horizon, for which the sign of (B.36) changes. Since $l > \frac{T+1}{2}$ (B.36) is always larger than zero for $l < 10$, i.e. the individual segment of the stability function is strictly convex and decreasing.

If $l < (2e^{-1} - e^{-2})T - 3(e^{-1} - e^{-2})$, then (B.36) is lower than zero , i.e. $\frac{\partial \pi^B_{s,S}(Q)}{\partial Q} > 0$ which means that the section of the stability function is strictly concave and increasing.

Analogously it is larger than zero for $l > (2e^{-1} - e^{-2})T - 3(e^{-1} - e^{-2})$, i.e. $\pi^B_{s,S}(Q)$ is strictly convex and decreasing.

Altogether we obtain

$$\frac{\partial \pi^B_{s,S}(Q)}{\partial Q} \left\{ \begin{matrix} < \\ > \end{matrix} \right\} 0, \; \frac{\partial^2 \pi^B_{s,S}(Q)}{\partial Q^2} \left\{ \begin{matrix} > \\ < \end{matrix} \right\} 0 \text{ if } \begin{cases} \lceil (2e^{-1} - e^{-2})T - 3(e^{-1} - e^{-2}) \rceil \leq l < T \\ \frac{T+1}{2} < l \leq \lfloor (2e^{-1} - e^{-2})T - 3(e^{-1} - e^{-2}) \rfloor . \end{cases}$$

1.3. $T = l$

For $T = l$ it holds that (see (B.35))

$$4(1-l)e^{-1} + 2(l-2)e^{-2} + l \begin{cases} > 0 & \text{if} \quad l = 2, 3, 4 \\ < 0 & \text{else.} \end{cases}$$

Thus $\frac{\partial \pi^B_{s,S}(Q)}{\partial Q} \left\{ \begin{matrix} < \\ \\ > \end{matrix} \right\} 0$ and $\frac{\partial^2 \pi^B_{s,S}(Q)}{\partial Q^2} \left\{ \begin{matrix} > \\ \\ < \end{matrix} \right\} 0$ $\begin{cases} \text{if} \quad l = 2,3,4 \\ \\ \text{else.} \end{cases}$

We observe that $\pi^B_{s,S}(Q)$ is strictly increasing and concave for $l > 4$; otherwise it is strictly decreasing and convex.

Case 2: $L > 1$, i.e. $T \geq 2l$, or $l < \frac{T+1}{2}$, respectively

For $L > 1$ we assume that the segments of the stability function are strictly convex, i.e. $\frac{\partial \pi^B_{s,S}(Q)}{\partial Q} < 0$ and $\frac{\partial^2 \pi^B_{s,S}(Q)}{\partial Q^2} > 0$.

Thus we have to show that (see (B.33))

$$4Te^{-1}\frac{1-l}{l} + 2Te^{-2}\frac{l-2}{l} + 2T - l > 0 \text{ if } \quad T = Ll \tag{B.37}$$

$$(1 - 2T + 2L)e^{-1} + (T - 2L - 1)e^{-2} + Ll > 0 \text{ if } \quad T \neq Ll. \tag{B.38}$$

Substituting T with Ll in (B.37) leads to

$$4(e^{-1} - e^{-2})L + 2(1 - 2e^{-1} + e^{-2})Ll - l > 0.$$

Since $2(1-2e^{-1}+e^{-2})Ll > l$ and $4(e^{-1}-e^{-2})L > 0$, for $L > 1$, this condition is always valid.
For (B.38) we obtain after some transformations

$$T < \frac{e^{-1} - e^{-2}}{2e^{-1} - e^{-2}} + \frac{2(e^{-1} - e^{-2})L}{2e^{-1} - e^{-2}} + \frac{Ll}{2e^{-1} - e^{-2}}.$$

Since $T = (L+1)l - 1 < \frac{Ll}{2e^{-1}-e^{-2}}$, and $\frac{(e^{-1}-e^{-2})(2L+1)}{2e^{-1}-e^{-2}} > 0$, it is obvious that (B.38) is always true for $L > 1$.

Thus $\frac{\partial \pi^B_{s,S}(Q)}{\partial Q} < 0$, and the section of the stability function is a strictly convex and decreasing function in Q for $l < \frac{T+1}{2}$.

B.3.3.5 Minimum Stability for long-term Setup Stability

It holds that

- $\pi^A_{s,S}$ is strictly convex and decreasing (see Section B.3.3)
- $\pi^A_{s,S}(Q = \hat{D}) > \lim_{Q \to \hat{D}} \pi^B_{s,S}(Q)$ for $T > 1$ (see Section B.3.3)
- $\pi^B_{s,S}$ increases by jumps in the points of discontinuity (see Section B.3.3), i.e. $\pi^B_{s,S,(h)}(Q = h\hat{D}) < \lim_{Q \to h\hat{D}} \pi^B_{s,S,(h+1)}(Q)$ for all $1 < h \leq T$

- $\pi^B_{s,S}$ is continuous, strictly concave and increasing for $h > T$ (see Section B.3.3).

In order to prove that planning stability reaches its minimum for $Q = 2\hat{D}$ in the case of $T > 1$ it remains to show that

$$\pi^B_{s,S,(h)}(Q = h\hat{D}) < \pi^B_{s,S,(h+1)}(Q = (h+1)\hat{D}) \text{ for all } 1 < h \leq T.$$

This is depicted in Figure B.2.

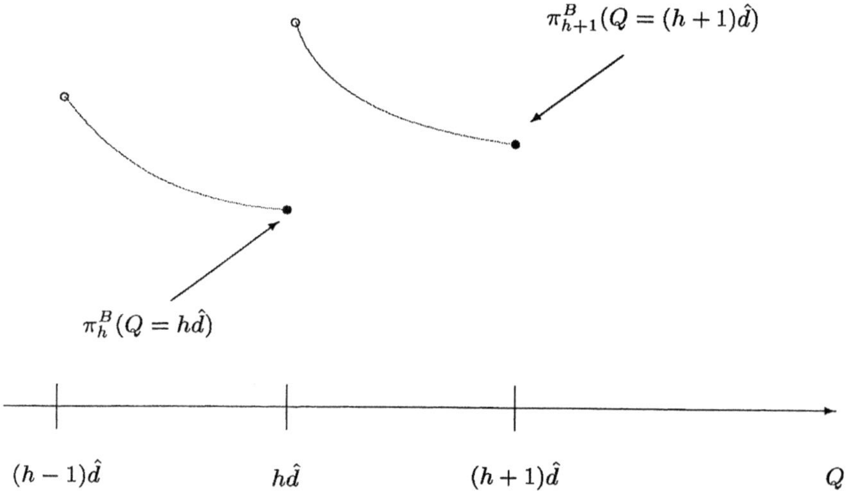

Figure B.2. Minimum planning stability for two neighbouring regions

Analogously to the proof of the discontinuity of $\pi^B_{s,S}$ for $l \leq T$ (see Section B.3.3) we have to show that the following relations are valid:

Relation 1

For a transition from h with $T \neq Lh$ to $h+1$ with $T = L(h+1)$ it holds

$$\pi^B_{s,S,(h)}(h\hat{D})_{L=\frac{T-(h-1)}{h}} < \pi^B_{s,S,(h+1)}((h+1)\hat{D})_{L=\frac{T}{h+1}}.$$

Relation 2

With a change from h with $T \neq Lh$ to $h+1$ with $T \neq L(h+1)$ we find that

$$\pi^B_{s,S,(h))}(h\hat{D})_{L=\frac{T-(h-1)}{h}} < \pi^B_{s,S,(h+1)}((h+1)\hat{D})_{L=\frac{T-1}{h+1}}.$$

Relation 3

Going over from h with $T = Lh$ to $h+1$ with $T \neq L(h+1)$ results in

$$\pi^B_{s,S,(h)}(h\hat{D})_{L=\frac{T}{h}} < \pi^B_{s,S,(h+1)}((h+1)\hat{D})_{L=\frac{T-1}{h+1}}.$$

From Result II (see p.198) it follows that $\pi^B_{s,S,(h)}(h\hat{D})$ achieves its *maximum* for $L = \frac{T-(h-1)}{h}$ if $T \neq Lh$ and $\pi^B_{s,S,(h+1)}((h+1)\hat{D})$ achieves its *minimum* for $L = \frac{T-1}{h+1}$ if $T \neq L(h+1)$, respectively. By using the maximum function values in the point $Q = h\hat{D}$ and the minimum values in $Q = (h+1)\hat{D}$, we ensure that the relations mentioned above always hold, no matter what the exact function value for a given T/h-ratio may be.

Proof of Relation 1

From (B.29) we know that

$$\pi^B_{s,S,(h)}(h\hat{D})_{L=\frac{T-(h-1)}{h}} = \frac{2e^{-1}[2(T+1)-h(2T+1)]+2e^{-2}(h-2)(T+1)+}{h(h+1)T} + \frac{T(h^2+h-2)+2(h-1)}{h(h+1)T}. \tag{B.39}$$

From (B.23) we get

$$\pi^B_{s,S,(h+1)}((h+1)\hat{D})_{L=\frac{T}{h+1}} = \frac{-4hTe^{-1}+2(h-2)Te^{-2}+h^2T+h(3T+1)+1}{(h+1)(h+2)T}. \tag{B.40}$$

As difference from (B.39) and (B.40) we obtain

$$\pi^B_{s,S,(h)}(h\hat{D})_{L=\frac{T-(h-1)}{h}} - \pi^B_{s,S,(h+1)}((h+1)\hat{D})_{L=\frac{T}{h+1}} \cong \frac{(0.54h-1.20T+1)h-2.14(T+1)}{h(h+1)(h+2)T}$$

which is always lower than zero for $1 < h \leq T$. Thus we have proved relation 1.

q.e.d

Proof of Relation 2

From (B.22) we obtain

$$\pi^B_{s,S,(h+1)}((h+1)\hat{D})_{L=\frac{T-1}{h+1}} = \frac{2[h(1-2T)-1]e^{-1}+2(T-1)(h-1)e^{-2}}{(h+1)(h+2)T} + \frac{hT(h+3)+2}{(h+1)(h+2)T}. \tag{B.41}$$

The difference between (B.39) and (B.41) is given by

$$\begin{aligned}\pi^B_{s,S,(h)}(h\hat{D})_{L=\frac{T-(h-1)}{h}} - \pi^B_{s,S,(h+1)}((h+1)\hat{D})_{L=\frac{T-1}{h+1}} &\cong \frac{(0.81h-1.20T-0.27)h}{h(h+1)(h+2)T} \\ &- \frac{2[0.70(T+1)+0.37]}{h(h+1)(h+2)T} \\ &< 0 \text{ for all } 1<h\leq T.\end{aligned}$$

q.e.d

Proof of Relation 3

From (B.32) we get

$$\pi^B_{s,S,(h)}(h\hat{D})_{L=\frac{T}{h}} = \frac{[4e^{-1}(1-h)+2e^{-2}(h-2)+(h^2+h-2)]T+h}{h(h+1)T} \tag{B.42}$$

The difference between (B.42) and (B.41) is given by

$$\begin{aligned}\pi^B_{s,S,(h)}(h\hat{D})_{L=\frac{T}{h}} - \pi^B_{s,S,(h+1)}((h+1)\hat{D})_{L=\frac{T-1}{h+1}} &\cong \frac{(0.54h-1.20T+0.47)h-2.14(T+1)}{h(h+1)(h+2)T} \\ &< 0 \text{ for all } 1<h\leq T.\end{aligned}$$

q.e.d

Thus we have shown that planning stability in a critical point $Q = h\hat{D}$ is always lower than stability in $Q = (h+1)\hat{D}$ for all $1 < h \leq T$. With the properties mentioned on page 203 the planning stability reaches its minimum for $Q = 2\hat{D}$ if $T > 1$.

q.e.d

The concrete value of minimum stability in dependence of T can easily be determined from (B.19)[3]. For $Q = 2\hat{D}$ in (B.19) we get

$$\pi^B_{s,S}(2\hat{D},T) = \frac{2}{3}(1-e^{-1}) + \frac{1}{3T} \quad \forall T.$$

[3] Note that it can also be obtained from (B.18) where with $l = 2$ both cases, i.e. $T = 2L+1$ and $T = 2L$, lead to the same result.

B.4 Hyperexponentially Distributed Demand

B.4.1 $Q \leq \hat{D}$

As for mixtures of Erlang demand distributions stability can be calculated as follows (see (B.3)).

$$\pi^A_{s,S} = \frac{1}{M(Q)}\left\{\alpha_1 + \alpha_2\left[\frac{Q}{\bar{D}} + \gamma(1-e^{-\rho Q})\right]\right\} \tag{B.43}$$

with $\frac{1}{M(Q)}$ as shown in (B.4).

B.4.2 $Q > \hat{D}$

From (B.2) by substituting $\Phi_D(.)$ from (A.5) and $M(.)$ from (A.2) we find that

$$\begin{aligned}
\pi^B_{s,S} = \Bigg\{ \sum_{\tau=1}^{l-1} \Bigg[& \int\limits_{Q-\tau\hat{D}}^{Q-(\tau-1)\hat{D}} \beta_1^\tau d[1 + \frac{x}{\bar{D}} + \gamma(1-e^{-\rho x})] \\
& + \int\limits_{Q-\tau\hat{D}}^{Q-(\tau-1)\hat{D}} \sum_{\theta=2}^{\tau+1} (\beta_\theta^\tau - \beta_{\theta-1}^\tau)[1 - pe^{-\mu_1(Q-x-(\theta-2)\hat{D})} \\
& -(1-p)e^{-\mu_2(Q-x-(\theta-2)\hat{D})}]\, d\,[1 + \frac{x}{\bar{D}} + \gamma(1-e^{-\rho x})]\Bigg] \\
& + \int\limits_{0}^{Q-(l-1)\hat{D}} \beta_1^l d[1 + \frac{x}{\bar{D}} + \gamma(1-e^{-\rho x})] \\
& + \int\limits_{0}^{Q-(l-1)\hat{D}} \sum_{\theta=2}^{l+1} (\beta_\theta^l - \beta_{\theta-1}^l)[1 - pe^{-\mu_1(Q-x-(\theta-2)\hat{D})} \\
& -(1-p)e^{-\mu_2(Q-x-(\theta-2)\hat{D})}]\, d\,[1 + \frac{x}{\bar{D}} + \gamma(1-e^{-\rho x})]\Bigg\} \frac{1}{M(Q)}
\end{aligned}$$

with $\frac{1}{M(Q)}$ given by (B.4).

Using (B.6) we obtain after some algebraic transformations

$$\pi^B_{s,S} = \Bigg\{ \sum_{\tau=1}^{l-1} \Bigg\{ \frac{1}{\bar{D}} \Bigg[\int\limits_{Q-\tau\hat{D}}^{Q-(\tau-1)\hat{D}} \beta_1^\tau dx$$

$$+ \int\limits_{Q-\tau\hat{D}}^{Q-(\tau-1)\hat{D}} \sum_{\theta=2}^{\tau+1} (\beta_\theta^\tau - \beta_{\theta-1}^\tau)(1 - pe^{-\mu_1(Q-x-(\theta-2)\hat{D})}$$

$$-(1-p)e^{-\mu_2(Q-x-(\theta-2)\hat{D})})dx \Bigg]$$

$$+\rho\gamma \Bigg[\int\limits_{Q-\tau\hat{D}}^{Q-(\tau-1)\hat{D}} \beta_1^\tau e^{-\rho x} dx$$

$$+ \int\limits_{Q-\tau\hat{D}}^{Q-(\tau-1)\hat{D}} \sum_{\theta=2}^{\tau+1} (\beta_\theta^\tau - \beta_{\theta-1}^\tau)(1 - pe^{-\mu_1(Q-x-(\theta-2)\hat{D})}$$

$$-(1-p)e^{-\mu_2(Q-x-(\theta-2)\hat{D})})e^{-\rho x} dx \Bigg] \Bigg\}$$

$$+\frac{1}{\bar{D}} \Bigg[\int\limits_0^{Q-(l-1)\hat{D}} \beta_1^l dx$$

$$+ \int\limits_0^{Q-(l-1)\hat{D}} \sum_{\theta=2}^{l+1} (\beta_\theta^l - \beta_{\theta-1}^l)(1 - pe^{-\mu_1(Q-x-(\theta-2)\hat{D})}$$

$$-(1-p)e^{-\mu_2(Q-x-(\theta-2)\hat{D})})dx \Bigg] \tag{B.44}$$

$$+\rho\gamma \Bigg[\int\limits_0^{Q-(l-1)\hat{D}} \beta_1^l e^{-\rho x} dx$$

$$+ \int\limits_0^{Q-(l-1)\hat{D}} \sum_{\theta=2}^{l+1} (\beta_\theta^l - \beta_{\theta-1}^l)(1 - pe^{-\mu_1(Q-x-(\theta-2)\hat{D})}$$

$$-(1-p)e^{-\mu_2(Q-x-(\theta-2)\hat{D})})e^{-\rho x} dx \Bigg]$$

$$+\beta_1^l + \sum_{\theta=2}^{l+1}(\beta_\theta^l - \beta_{\theta-1}^l)(1 - pe^{-\mu_1(Q-(\theta-2)\hat{D})}$$

$$-(1-p)e^{-\mu_2(Q-(\theta-2)\hat{D})})\Bigg\}\frac{1}{M(Q)}$$

Some of the integrals in (B.44) are exactly the same as for Erlangian distributed demand. The others are given by

$$\int_{Q-\tau\hat{D}}^{Q-(\tau-1)\hat{D}} e^{-\mu_i(Q-x-(\theta-2)\hat{D})} = \frac{1}{\mu_i}e^{-\mu_i(\tau-\theta+1)\hat{D}}(1-e^{-\mu_i\hat{D}})$$

$$\int_{Q-\tau\hat{D}}^{Q-(\tau-1)\hat{D}} e^{-\rho x}e^{-\mu_i(Q-x-(\theta-2)\hat{D})} = \frac{1}{\mu_i-\rho}e^{-\rho(Q-\tau\hat{D})}(e^{-\rho\hat{D}}-e^{-\mu_i\hat{D}})e^{-\mu_i(\tau-\theta+1)\hat{D}}$$

$$\int_{0}^{Q-(l-1)\hat{D}} e^{-\mu_i(Q-x-(\theta-2)\hat{D})} = \frac{1}{\mu_i}e^{\mu_i(\theta-2)\hat{D}}(e^{-\mu_i(l-1)\hat{D}}-e^{-\mu_i Q})$$

$$\int_{0}^{Q-(l-1)\hat{D}} e^{-\rho x}e^{-\mu_i(Q-x-(\theta-2)\hat{D})} = \frac{1}{\mu_i-\rho}e^{\mu_i(\theta-2)\hat{D}}(e^{-(\mu_i-\rho)(l-1)\hat{D}}e^{-\rho Q}-e^{-\mu_i Q})$$

for $i = 1, 2$.

Using these results we get

$$\pi_{s,S}^B = \Bigg\{\sum_{\tau=1}^{l-1}\Bigg\{\frac{1}{\bar{D}}\Bigg[\beta_1^\tau\hat{D} + \sum_{\theta=2}^{\tau+1}(\beta_\theta^\tau - \beta_{\theta-1}^\tau)[\hat{D} + \frac{p}{\mu_1}e^{-\mu_1(\tau-\theta+1)\hat{D}}(e^{-\mu_1\hat{D}}-1)$$

$$+\frac{1-p}{\mu_2}e^{-\mu_2(\tau-\theta+1)\hat{D}}(e^{-\mu_2\hat{D}}-1)]\Bigg]$$

$$+\gamma e^{-\rho(Q-\tau\hat{D})}\Bigg[\beta_1^\tau(1-e^{-\rho\hat{D}}) + \sum_{\theta=2}^{\tau+1}(\beta_\theta^\tau - \beta_{\theta-1}^\tau)[1 - e^{-\rho\hat{D}}$$

$$+\frac{p\rho}{\mu_1-\rho}e^{-\mu_1(\tau-\theta+1)\hat{D}}(e^{-\mu_1\hat{D}} - e^{-\rho\hat{D}})$$

$$+\frac{(1-p)\rho}{\mu_2-\rho}e^{-\mu_2(\tau-\theta+1)\hat{D}}(e^{-\mu_2\hat{D}} - e^{-\rho\hat{D}})]\Bigg]\Bigg\}$$

$$+\frac{1}{\bar{D}}\Bigg[\beta_1^l(Q-(l-1)\hat{D}) + \sum_{\theta=2}^{l+1}(\beta_\theta^l - \beta_{\theta-1}^l)[Q-(l-1)\hat{D}$$

$$
\begin{aligned}
&+\frac{p}{\mu_1}e^{\mu_1(\theta-2)\hat{D}}(e^{-\mu_1 Q}-e^{-\mu_1(l-1)\hat{D}}) \\
&+\frac{1-p}{\mu_2}e^{\mu_2(\theta-2)\hat{D}}(e^{-\mu_2 Q}-e^{-\mu_2(l-1)\hat{D}})]\Bigg] \\
+\gamma\Bigg[&\beta_1^l(1-e^{-\rho(Q-(l-1)\hat{D})})+\sum_{\theta=2}^{l+1}(\beta_\theta^l-\beta_{\theta-1}^l)[1-e^{-\rho(Q-(l-1)\hat{D})} \\
&+\frac{p\rho}{\mu_1-\rho}e^{\mu_1(\theta-2)\hat{D}}(e^{-\mu_1 Q}-e^{-(\mu_1-\rho)(l-1)\hat{D}}e^{-\rho Q}) \\
&+\frac{(1-p)\rho}{\mu_2-\rho}e^{\mu_2(\theta-2)\hat{D}}(e^{-\mu_2 Q}-e^{-(\mu_2-\rho)(l-1)\hat{D}}e^{-\rho Q}]\Bigg] \\
+\beta_1^l&+\sum_{\theta=2}^{l+1}(\beta_\theta^l-\beta_{\theta-1}^l)(1-pe^{-\mu_1(Q-(\theta-2)\hat{D})} \\
&\qquad -(1-p)e^{-\mu_2(Q-(\theta-2)\hat{D})})\Bigg\}\frac{1}{M(Q)}.
\end{aligned}
\tag{B.45}
$$

As for Mixed-Erlang distributed demand we can compute planning stability for $Q \leq \hat{D}$ with (B.43) and for $Q > \hat{D}$ with (B.10) by inserting the corresponding stability quotients and using the relevant coefficients of the distribution function as depicted in Appendix A.2. Again $\frac{1}{M(Q)}$ is given by (B.4).

B.5 Short-term Planning Stability

For $Q \leq \hat{D}$ we get for $T = 1$, i.e. $\alpha_1 = 1$ and $\alpha_2 = 0$, from (B.1) that

$$\pi_{s,S}^A = \frac{1}{M(Q)}.$$

From (4.65) with $F_X(x) = \frac{M(X)}{M(Q)}$ we get for $Q > \hat{D}$ that

$$\pi_{s,S}^B = \left\{M(Q)-M(Q-\hat{D})+2\int_0^{Q-\hat{D}}\Phi_D(Q-x)dM(x)-(M(Q)-1)\right\}\frac{1}{M(Q)}.$$

Thus we obtain

$$\pi_{s,S}^B = \left\{1-M(Q-\hat{D})+2\int_0^{Q-\hat{D}}\Phi_D(Q-x)dM(x)\right\}\frac{1}{M(Q)}.$$

By inserting the corresponding distributions for Erlangian distributed demand and hyperexponentially distributed demand, respectively, we can obtain some closed-form expressions for the stability functions. These stability functions can also be achieved by setting $T = 1$ and using the aforementioned values for the stability functions in (B.3), (B.10), (B.43), and (B.45). We will not give these results explicitly, because they can easily be determined from the matching stability functions in Appendices B.2 and B.4, respectively.

For the special case of exponentially distributed demand we obtain for $Q \leq \hat{D}$ from (B.11) that

$$\pi^A_{s,S} = \frac{1}{1 + Q/\bar{D}}.$$

For $Q > \hat{D}$ we get from (B.12)

$$\pi^B_{s,S} = \frac{1}{Q + \bar{D}}(Q - \hat{D} + 2\bar{D}(1 - e^{-\frac{\hat{D}}{\bar{D}}})).$$

With $\bar{D} = \hat{D}$ these results are exactly the same as in Inderfurth [61].

C. (s,nQ) Policy

C.1 General Stability Functions

C.1.1 $Q \leq \hat{D}$

The starting point is (4.61) with

$$\pi^A_{s,nQ} = \int_0^Q \{\alpha_1[1 - \Phi_D(Q-x)] + \alpha_2 \Phi_D(Q-x)\} dF_X(x).$$

In the case of an (s, nQ) policy it holds that (see, e.g., Hadley and Whitin [47], pp.245)

$$P(X \leq x) = \frac{x}{Q} \quad \forall \quad 0 \leq x \leq Q. \tag{C.1}$$

Rearranging terms results in

$$\pi^A_{s,nQ} = \frac{1}{Q}\{\alpha_1 Q - \alpha_1 \int_0^Q \Phi_D(Q-x)dx + \alpha_2 \int_0^Q \Phi_D(Q-x)dx\}.$$

Thus we finally get

$$\pi^A_{s,nQ} = \alpha_1 - \frac{\alpha_1 - \alpha_2}{Q} \int_0^Q \Phi_D(x)dx. \tag{C.2}$$

C.1.2 $Q > \hat{D}$

Here, starting from (4.62) with

$$\pi^B_{s,nQ} = \sum_{\omega=1}^{\zeta} \int_{Q-\frac{\omega}{\eta}\hat{D}}^{Q-\frac{\omega-1}{\eta}\hat{D}} \Big\{ \sum_{n_1=1}^{\infty} \Big[\sum_{\kappa=1}^{\zeta} \beta^{\omega}_{1,\kappa} (\Phi_D(Q - x + \frac{n_1\zeta - (\kappa-1)}{\eta}\hat{D})$$

$$-\Phi_D(Q - x + \frac{n_1\zeta - \kappa}{\eta}\hat{D}))\Big] +$$

$$+\sum_{\kappa=1}^{\omega-1}\beta_{2,\kappa}^{\omega}\big(\Phi_D(Q-x-\frac{\kappa-1}{\eta}\hat{D})-\Phi_D(Q-x-\frac{\kappa}{\eta}\hat{D})\big)+$$
$$+\beta_{2,\omega}^{\omega}\Phi_D(Q-x-\frac{\omega-1}{\eta}\hat{D})\Big\}dF_X(x).$$

With (C.1) we obtain

$$\pi_{s,nQ}^{B}=\frac{1}{Q}\Big\{\sum_{\omega=1}^{\zeta}\int_{\frac{\omega-1}{\eta}\hat{D}}^{\frac{\omega}{\eta}\hat{D}}\Big[\sum_{n_1=1}^{\infty}\Big(\sum_{\kappa=1}^{\zeta}\beta_{1,\kappa}^{\omega}\big(\Phi_D(x+\frac{n_1\zeta-(\kappa-1)}{\eta}\hat{D})$$
$$-\Phi_D(x+\frac{n_1\zeta-\kappa}{\eta}\hat{D})\big)\Big) \tag{C.3}$$
$$+\sum_{\kappa=1}^{\omega-1}\beta_{2,\kappa}^{\omega}\big(\Phi_D(x-\frac{\kappa-1}{\eta}\hat{D})-\Phi_D(x-\frac{\kappa}{\eta}\hat{D})\big)$$
$$+\beta_{2,\omega}^{\omega}\Phi_D(x-\frac{\omega-1}{\eta}\hat{D})\Big]dx\Big\}.$$

C.2 Mixed-Erlang Distributed Demand

C.2.1 $Q \leq \hat{D}$

(C.2) together with (A.3) leads to

$$\pi_{s,nQ}^{A}=\alpha_2+\frac{\alpha_1-\alpha_2}{Q}[p\int_0^Q\sum_{i=0}^{k-2}e^{-\mu x}\frac{(\mu x)^i}{i!}dx+(1-p)\int_0^Q\sum_{i=0}^{k-1}e^{-\mu x}\frac{(\mu x)^i}{i!}dx].$$

Since, in general, (see also (B.9))

$$\int_0^b\sum_{i=0}^{h-1}e^{-mx}\frac{(mx)^i}{i!}dx=-\frac{1}{m}\Big[e^{-mb}\sum_{j=0}^{h-1}\sum_{i=j}^{h-1}\frac{(mb)^{i-j}}{(i-j)!}-h\Big]$$

it follows that

$$\pi_{s,nQ}^{A}=\alpha_2+\frac{\alpha_2-\alpha_1}{Q}\Big[\frac{p}{\mu}(e^{-\mu Q}\sum_{j=0}^{k-2}\sum_{i=j}^{k-2}\frac{(\mu Q)^{i-j}}{(i-j)!}-(k-1)) \tag{C.4}$$
$$+\frac{(1-p)}{\mu}(e^{-\mu Q}\sum_{j=0}^{k-1}\sum_{i=j}^{k-1}\frac{(\mu Q)^{i-j}}{(i-j)!}-k)\Big].$$

C.2.2 $Q > \hat{D}$

From (C.3) together with (A.3) we get

$$\pi^B_{s,nQ} = \frac{1}{Q} \sum_{\omega=1}^{\zeta} \int_{\frac{\omega-1}{\eta}\hat{D}}^{\frac{\omega}{\eta}\hat{D}} \Bigg\{ \sum_{n_1=1}^{\infty} \Bigg[\sum_{\kappa=1}^{\zeta} \beta^{\omega}_{1,\kappa} \Bigg(1 - p \sum_{i=0}^{k-2} e^{-\mu(x+\frac{n_1\zeta-(\kappa-1)}{\eta}\hat{D})} \cdot \frac{(\mu(x+\frac{n_1\zeta-(\kappa-1)}{\eta}\hat{D}))^i}{i!}$$

$$-(1-p)\sum_{i=0}^{k-1} e^{-\mu(x+\frac{n_1\zeta-(\kappa-1)}{\eta}\hat{D})} \frac{(\mu(x+\frac{n_1\zeta-(\kappa-1)}{\eta}\hat{D}))^i}{i!}$$

$$-1 + p\sum_{i=0}^{k-2} e^{-\mu(x+\frac{n_1\zeta-\kappa}{\eta}\hat{D})} \frac{(\mu(x+\frac{n_1\zeta-\kappa}{\eta}\hat{D}))^i}{i!}$$

$$+(1-p)\sum_{i=0}^{k-1} e^{-\mu(x+\frac{n_1\zeta-\kappa}{\eta}\hat{D})} \frac{(\mu(x+\frac{n_1\zeta-\kappa}{\eta}\hat{D}))^i}{i!} \Bigg) \Bigg]$$

$$+ \sum_{\kappa=1}^{\omega-1} \beta^{\omega}_{2,\kappa} \Bigg[1 - p\sum_{i=0}^{k-2} e^{-\mu(x-\frac{\kappa-1}{\eta}\hat{D})} \frac{(\mu(x-\frac{\kappa-1}{\eta}\hat{D}))^i}{i!}$$

$$-(1-p)\sum_{i=0}^{k-1} e^{-\mu(x-\frac{\kappa-1}{\eta}\hat{D})} \frac{(\mu(x-\frac{\kappa-1}{\eta}\hat{D}))^i}{i!}$$

$$-1 + p\sum_{i=0}^{k-2} e^{-\mu(x-\frac{\kappa}{\eta}\hat{D})} \frac{(\mu(x-\frac{\kappa}{\eta}\hat{D}))^i}{i!}$$

$$+(1-p)\sum_{i=0}^{k-1} e^{-\mu(x-\frac{\kappa}{\eta}\hat{D})} \frac{(\mu(x-\frac{\kappa}{\eta}\hat{D}))^i}{i!} \Bigg]$$

$$+\beta^{\omega}_{2,\omega} \Bigg[1 - p\sum_{i=0}^{k-2} e^{-\mu(x-\frac{\omega-1}{\eta}\hat{D})} \frac{(\mu(x-\frac{\omega-1}{\eta}\hat{D}))^i}{i!}$$

$$-(1-p)\sum_{i=0}^{k-1} e^{-\mu(x-\frac{\omega-1}{\eta}\hat{D})} \frac{(\mu(x-\frac{\omega-1}{\eta}\hat{D}))^i}{i!} \Bigg] \Bigg\} dx.$$

This can be rewritten as

$$\pi^B_{s,nQ} = \frac{1}{Q} \sum_{\omega=1}^{\zeta} \Bigg\{ \sum_{n_1=1}^{\infty} \Bigg[\sum_{\kappa=1}^{\zeta} \beta^{\omega}_{1,\kappa} \Bigg(p e^{-\mu\frac{n_1\zeta-\kappa}{\eta}\hat{D}} \int_{\frac{\omega-1}{\eta}\hat{D}}^{\frac{\omega}{\eta}\hat{D}} [\sum_{i=0}^{k-2} \frac{(\mu(x+\frac{n_1\zeta-\kappa}{\eta}\hat{D}))^i}{i!}$$

$$-e^{-\mu\frac{1}{\eta}\hat{D}} \sum_{i=0}^{k-2} \frac{(\mu(x+\frac{n_1\zeta-(\kappa-1)}{\eta}\hat{D}))^i}{i!}]e^{-\mu x}dx$$

$$+(1-p)e^{-\mu\frac{n_1\zeta-\kappa}{\eta}\hat{D}} \int\limits_{\frac{\omega-1}{\eta}\hat{D}}^{\frac{\omega}{\eta}\hat{D}} [\sum_{i=0}^{k-1} \frac{(\mu(x+\frac{n_1\zeta-\kappa}{\eta}\hat{D}))^i}{i!}$$

$$-e^{-\mu\frac{1}{\eta}\hat{D}} \sum_{i=0}^{k-1} \frac{(\mu(x+\frac{n_1\zeta-(\kappa-1)}{\eta}\hat{D}))^i}{i!}]e^{-\mu x}dx\Big)$$

$$+\sum_{\kappa=1}^{\omega-1} \beta_{2,\kappa}^{\omega}\Big(pe^{\mu\frac{\kappa}{\eta}\hat{D}} \int\limits_{\frac{\omega-1}{\eta}\hat{D}}^{\frac{\omega}{\eta}\hat{D}} [\sum_{i=0}^{k-2} \frac{(\mu(x-\frac{\kappa}{\eta}\hat{D}))^i}{i!}$$

$$-e^{-\mu\frac{1}{\eta}\hat{D}} \sum_{i=0}^{k-2} \frac{(\mu(x-\frac{\kappa-1}{\eta}\hat{D}))^i}{i!}]e^{-\mu x}dx$$

$$+(1-p)e^{\mu\frac{\kappa}{\eta}\hat{D}} \int\limits_{\frac{\omega-1}{\eta}\hat{D}}^{\frac{\omega}{\eta}\hat{D}} [\sum_{i=0}^{k-1} \frac{(\mu(x-\frac{\kappa}{\eta}\hat{D}))^i}{i!}$$

$$-e^{-\mu\frac{1}{\eta}\hat{D}} \sum_{i=0}^{k-1} \frac{(\mu(x-\frac{\kappa-1}{\eta}\hat{D}))^i}{i!}]e^{-\mu x}dx\Big)$$

$$+\beta_{2,\omega}^{\omega} \int\limits_{\frac{\omega-1}{\eta}\hat{D}}^{\frac{\omega}{\eta}\hat{D}} \Big[1-pe^{\mu\frac{\omega-1}{\eta}\hat{D}} \sum_{i=0}^{k-2} \frac{(\mu(x-\frac{\omega-1}{\eta}\hat{D}))^i}{i!}e^{-\mu x}$$

$$-(1-p)e^{\mu\frac{\omega-1}{\eta}\hat{D}} \sum_{i=0}^{k-1} \frac{(\mu(x-\frac{\omega-1}{\eta}\hat{D}))^i}{i!}e^{-\mu x}\Big]dx\Big\}$$

It holds $\int\limits_{\frac{\omega-1}{\eta}\hat{D}}^{\frac{\omega}{\eta}\hat{D}} 1dx = \frac{\hat{D}}{\eta}$.

The remaining integrals can be solved by using the following general relation.

$$\int_a^b \sum_{i=0}^{h-1} \frac{(m(x+c))^i}{i!}e^{-mx} = -\frac{1}{m}\Big[\sum_{j=0}^{h-1}\sum_{i=j}^{h-1} \frac{m^i(x+c)^{i-j}}{(i-j)!}e^{-mx}\Big]_a^b$$

$$= \frac{1}{m}\Big[\sum_{j=0}^{h-1}\sum_{i=j}^{h-1} \frac{m^i(a+c)^{i-j}}{(i-j)!}e^{-ma} - \sum_{j=0}^{h-1}\sum_{i=j}^{h-1} \frac{m^i(b+c)^{i-j}}{(i-j)!}e^{-mb}\Big]$$

Thus we get

$$\pi^B_{s,nQ} = \sum_{\omega=1}^{\zeta}\Bigg\{\sum_{n_1=1}^{\infty}\Bigg[\sum_{\kappa=1}^{\zeta}\beta^{\omega}_{1,\kappa}\Bigg(p\frac{e^{-\mu\frac{n_1\zeta-\kappa}{\eta}\hat{D}}}{\mu}[\sum_{j=0}^{k-2}\sum_{i=j}^{k-2}\frac{(\mu\frac{\omega-1+n_1\zeta-\kappa}{\eta}\hat{D})^{i-j}}{(i-j)!}e^{-\mu\frac{\omega-1}{\eta}\hat{D}}$$

$$-\sum_{j=0}^{k-2}\sum_{i=j}^{k-2}\frac{(\mu\frac{\omega+n_1\zeta-\kappa}{\eta}\hat{D})^{i-j}}{(i-j)!}e^{-\mu\frac{\omega}{\eta}\hat{D}}$$

$$-e^{-\mu\frac{1}{\eta}\hat{D}}(\sum_{j=0}^{k-2}\sum_{i=j}^{k-2}\frac{(\mu\frac{\omega+n_1\zeta-\kappa}{\eta}\hat{D})^{i-j}}{(i-j)!}e^{-\mu\frac{\omega-1}{\eta}\hat{D}}$$

$$-\sum_{j=0}^{k-2}\sum_{i=j}^{k-2}\frac{(\mu\frac{\omega+n_1\zeta-\kappa+1}{\eta}\hat{D})^{i-j}}{(i-j)!}e^{-\mu\frac{\omega}{\eta}\hat{D}})]$$

$$+(1-p)\frac{e^{-\mu\frac{n_1\zeta-\kappa}{\eta}\hat{D}}}{\mu}[\sum_{j=0}^{k-1}\sum_{i=j}^{k-1}\frac{(\mu\frac{\omega-1+n_1\zeta-\kappa}{\eta}\hat{D})^{i-j}}{(i-j)!}e^{-\mu\frac{\omega-1}{\eta}\hat{D}}$$

$$-\sum_{j=0}^{k-1}\sum_{i=j}^{k-1}\frac{(\mu\frac{\omega+n_1\zeta-\kappa}{\eta}\hat{D})^{i-j}}{(i-j)!}e^{-\mu\frac{\omega}{\eta}\hat{D}}$$

$$-e^{-\mu\frac{1}{\eta}\hat{D}}(\sum_{j=0}^{k-1}\sum_{i=j}^{k-1}\frac{(\mu\frac{\omega+n_1\zeta-\kappa}{\eta}\hat{D})^{i-j}}{(i-j)!}e^{-\mu\frac{\omega-1}{\eta}\hat{D}}$$

$$-\sum_{j=0}^{k-1}\sum_{i=j}^{k-1}\frac{(\mu\frac{\omega+n_1\zeta-\kappa+1}{\eta}\hat{D})^{i-j}}{(i-j)!}e^{-\mu\frac{\omega}{\eta}\hat{D}})]\Bigg)\Bigg]$$

$$+\sum_{\kappa=1}^{\omega-1}\beta^{\omega}_{2,\kappa}\Bigg(p\frac{e^{\mu\frac{\kappa}{\eta}\hat{D}}}{\mu}[\sum_{j=0}^{k-2}\sum_{i=j}^{k-2}\frac{(\mu\frac{\omega-1-\kappa}{\eta}\hat{D})^{i-j}}{(i-j)!}e^{-\mu\frac{\omega-1}{\eta}\hat{D}}$$

$$-\sum_{j=0}^{k-2}\sum_{i=j}^{k-2}\frac{(\mu\frac{\omega-\kappa}{\eta}\hat{D})^{i-j}}{(i-j)!}e^{-\mu\frac{\omega}{\eta}\hat{D}}$$

$$-e^{-\mu\frac{1}{\eta}\hat{D}}(\sum_{j=0}^{k-2}\sum_{i=j}^{k-2}\frac{(\mu\frac{\omega-\kappa}{\eta}\hat{D})^{i-j}}{(i-j)!}e^{-\mu\frac{\omega-1}{\eta}\hat{D}}$$

$$-\sum_{j=0}^{k-2}\sum_{i=j}^{k-2}\frac{(\mu\frac{\omega-\kappa+1}{\eta}\hat{D})^{i-j}}{(i-j)!}e^{-\mu\frac{\omega}{\eta}\hat{D}})]$$

$$+(1-p)\frac{e^{\mu\frac{\kappa}{\eta}\hat{D}}}{\mu}[\sum_{j=0}^{k-1}\sum_{i=j}^{k-1}\frac{(\mu\frac{\omega-1-\kappa}{\eta}\hat{D})^{i-j}}{(i-j)!}e^{-\mu\frac{\omega-1}{\eta}\hat{D}}$$

$$-\sum_{j=0}^{k-1}\sum_{i=j}^{k-1}\frac{(\mu\frac{\omega-\kappa}{\eta}\hat{D})^{i-j}}{(i-j)!}e^{-\mu\frac{\omega}{\eta}\hat{D}}$$

$$-e^{-\mu\frac{1}{\eta}\hat{D}}(\sum_{j=0}^{k-1}\sum_{i=j}^{k-1}\frac{(\mu\frac{\omega-\kappa}{\eta}\hat{D})^{i-j}}{(i-j)!}e^{-\mu\frac{\omega-1}{\eta}\hat{D}}$$

$$-\sum_{j=0}^{k-1}\sum_{i=j}^{k-1}\frac{(\mu\frac{\omega-\kappa+1}{\eta}\hat{D})^{i-j}}{(i-j)!}e^{-\mu\frac{\omega}{\eta}\hat{D}})]\Bigg)$$

$$+\ \beta_{2,\omega}^{\omega}\left(\frac{1}{\eta}\hat{D}-p\frac{e^{\mu\frac{\omega-1}{\eta}\hat{D}}}{\mu}[\sum_{j=0}^{k-2}\sum_{i=j}^{k-2}\frac{(\mu\frac{\omega-1-\omega+1}{\eta}\hat{D})^{i-j}}{(i-j)!}e^{-\mu\frac{\omega-1}{\eta}\hat{D}}\right.$$

$$-\sum_{j=0}^{k-2}\sum_{i=j}^{k-2}\frac{(\mu\frac{\omega-\omega+1}{\eta}\hat{D})^{i-j}}{(i-j)!}e^{-\mu\frac{\omega}{\eta}\hat{D}}]$$

$$-(1-p)\frac{e^{\mu\frac{\omega-1}{\eta}\hat{D}}}{\mu}[\sum_{j=0}^{k-1}\sum_{i=j}^{k-1}\frac{(\mu\frac{\omega-1-\omega+1}{\eta}\hat{D})^{i-j}}{(i-j)!}e^{-\mu\frac{\omega-1}{\eta}\hat{D}}$$

$$\left.-\sum_{j=0}^{k-1}\sum_{i=j}^{k-1}\frac{(\mu\frac{\omega-\omega+1}{\eta}\hat{D})^{i-j}}{(i-j)!}e^{-\mu\frac{\omega}{\eta}\hat{D}}]\right)\Bigg\}\frac{1}{Q}$$

After some transformations we finally obtain

$$\pi_{s,nQ}^{B}=\sum_{\omega=1}^{\zeta}\Bigg\{\sum_{n_1=1}^{\infty}\Bigg[\sum_{\kappa=1}^{\zeta}\beta_{1,\kappa}^{\omega}\Bigg(\frac{p}{\mu}e^{-\frac{\mu(\omega+n_1\zeta-\kappa)\hat{D}}{\eta}}[\sum_{j=0}^{k-2}\sum_{i=j+1}^{k-2}(\frac{(\frac{\mu(\omega-1+n_1\zeta-\kappa)\hat{D}}{\eta})^{i-j}}{(i-j)!}e^{\frac{\mu\hat{D}}{\eta}}$$

$$-2\frac{(\frac{\mu(\omega+n_1\zeta-\kappa)\hat{D}}{\eta})^{i-j}}{(i-j)!}$$

$$+\frac{(\frac{\mu(\omega+n_1\zeta-\kappa+1)\hat{D}}{\eta})^{i-j}}{(i-j)!}e^{-\frac{\mu\hat{D}}{\eta}})$$

$$+(k-1)(e^{\frac{\mu\hat{D}}{\eta}}-2+e^{\frac{-\mu\hat{D}}{\eta}})]$$

$$+\frac{1-p}{\mu}e^{-\frac{\mu(\omega+n_1\zeta-\kappa)\hat{D}}{\eta}}[\sum_{j=0}^{k-1}\sum_{i=j+1}^{k-1}(\frac{(\frac{\mu(\omega-1+n_1\zeta-\kappa)\hat{D}}{\eta})^{i-j}}{(i-j)!}e^{\frac{\mu\hat{D}}{\eta}}$$

$$-2\frac{(\frac{\mu(\omega+n_1\zeta-\kappa)\hat{D}}{\eta})^{i-j}}{(i-j)!}$$

$$+\frac{(\frac{\mu(\omega+n_1\zeta-\kappa+1)\hat{D}}{\eta})^{i-j}}{(i-j)!}e^{-\frac{\mu\hat{D}}{\eta}})$$

$$+k(e^{\frac{\mu\hat{D}}{\eta}} - 2 + e^{\frac{-\mu\hat{D}}{\eta}})]\Big)\Big] \quad (C.5)$$

$$+\sum_{\kappa=1}^{\omega-1}\beta_{2,\kappa}^{\omega}\Big(\frac{p}{\mu}e^{\frac{\mu(\kappa-\omega)\hat{D}}{\eta}}[\sum_{j=0}^{k-2}\sum_{i=j+1}^{k-2}(\frac{(\frac{\mu(\omega-1-\kappa)\hat{D}}{\eta})^{i-j}}{(i-j)!}e^{\frac{\mu\hat{D}}{\eta}} - 2\frac{(\frac{\mu(\omega-\kappa)\hat{D}}{\eta})^{i-j}}{(i-j)!}$$
$$+\frac{(\frac{\mu(\omega-\kappa+1)\hat{D}}{\eta})^{i-j}}{(i-j)!}e^{-\frac{\mu\hat{D}}{\eta}}) + (k-1)(e^{\frac{\mu\hat{D}}{\eta}} - 2 + e^{\frac{-\mu\hat{D}}{\eta}})]$$
$$+\frac{1-p}{\mu}e^{\frac{\mu(\kappa-\omega)\hat{D}}{\eta}}[\sum_{j=0}^{k-1}\sum_{i=j+1}^{k-1}(\frac{(\frac{\mu(\omega-1-\kappa)\hat{D}}{\eta})^{i-j}}{(i-j)!}e^{\frac{\mu\hat{D}}{\eta}} - 2\frac{(\frac{\mu(\omega-\kappa)\hat{D}}{\eta})^{i-j}}{(i-j)!}$$
$$+\frac{(\frac{\mu(\omega-\kappa+1)\hat{D}}{\eta})^{i-j}}{(i-j)!}e^{-\frac{\mu\hat{D}}{\eta}}) + k(e^{\frac{\mu\hat{D}}{\eta}} - 2 + e^{\frac{-\mu\hat{D}}{\eta}})]\Big)$$

$$+\beta_{2,\omega}^{\omega}\Big(\frac{\hat{D}}{\eta}+\frac{p}{\mu}\sum_{j=0}^{k-2}\sum_{i=j+1}^{k-2}\frac{(\frac{\mu\hat{D}}{\eta})^{i-j}}{(i-j)!}e^{-\frac{\mu\hat{D}}{\eta}} + \frac{(1-p)}{\mu}\sum_{j=0}^{k-1}\sum_{i=j+1}^{k-1}\frac{(\frac{\mu\hat{D}}{\eta})^{i-j}}{(i-j)!}e^{-\frac{\mu\hat{D}}{\eta}}$$
$$-\frac{p(k-1)}{\mu}(1-e^{-\frac{\mu\hat{D}}{\eta}}) - \frac{(1-p)k}{\mu}(1-e^{-\frac{\mu\hat{D}}{\eta}})\Big)\Big\}\frac{1}{Q}.$$

Now, we can determine the planning stability for given values of $\bar{D}$ and $c_D^2 \leq 1$ for $Q \leq \hat{D}$ with (C.4) and for $Q > \hat{D}$ with (C.5) by inserting the corresponding stability quotients and by using the relevant coefficients of the demand distribution as depicted in Appendix A.1.

C.3 Exponentially Distributed Demand

In the case of exponentially distributed demand it holds that $k = 2$, $p = 1$ and $\mu = \frac{1}{\bar{D}}$.

C.3.1 $Q \leq \hat{D}$

From (C.4) we find that

$$\pi_{s,nQ}^{A} = \alpha_2 + \frac{\alpha_2 - \alpha_1}{Q/\bar{D}}\Big[e^{-\frac{Q}{\bar{D}}} - 1\Big]. \quad (C.6)$$

C.3.2 $Q > \hat{D}$

From (C.5) we obtain

$$\pi^B_{s,nQ} = \sum_{\omega=1}^{\zeta} \Bigg\{ \sum_{n_1=1}^{\infty} \Bigg[\sum_{\kappa=1}^{\zeta} \beta^{\omega}_{1,\kappa} \bar{D} e^{-\frac{(\omega+n_1\zeta-\kappa)\hat{D}}{\bar{D}\eta}} (e^{\frac{\hat{D}}{\bar{D}\eta}} - 2 + e^{\frac{-\hat{D}}{\bar{D}\eta}}) \Bigg]$$
$$+ \sum_{\kappa=1}^{\omega-1} \beta^{\omega}_{2,\kappa} \bar{D} e^{\frac{(\kappa-\omega)\hat{D}}{\bar{D}\eta}} (e^{\frac{\hat{D}}{\bar{D}\eta}} - 2 + e^{\frac{-\hat{D}}{\bar{D}\eta}}) + \beta^{\omega}_{2,\omega} \left(\frac{\hat{D}}{\eta} - \bar{D}(1 - e^{-\frac{\hat{D}}{\bar{D}\eta}}) \right) \Bigg\} \frac{1}{Q}.$$

Thus we get

$$\pi^B_{s,nQ} = \sum_{\omega=1}^{\zeta} \Bigg\{ \sum_{\kappa=1}^{\zeta} \beta^{\omega}_{1,\kappa} \frac{e^{-\frac{(\omega+\zeta-\kappa)\hat{D}}{\bar{D}\eta}}}{1 - e^{-\frac{\zeta\hat{D}}{\bar{D}\eta}}} (e^{\frac{\hat{D}}{\bar{D}\eta}} - 2 + e^{\frac{-\hat{D}}{\bar{D}\eta}})$$
$$+ \sum_{\kappa=1}^{\omega-1} \beta^{\omega}_{2,\kappa} e^{\frac{(\kappa-\omega)\hat{D}}{\bar{D}\eta}} (e^{\frac{\hat{D}}{\bar{D}\eta}} - 2 + e^{\frac{-\hat{D}}{\bar{D}\eta}}) + \beta^{\omega}_{2,\omega} \left(\frac{\hat{D}}{\bar{D}\eta} - (1 - e^{-\frac{\hat{D}}{\bar{D}\eta}}) \right) \Bigg\} \frac{\bar{D}}{Q}$$

for all $\zeta > \eta$ with $Q = \frac{\zeta}{\eta}\hat{D}$.

C.4 Hyperexponentially Distributed Demand

C.4.1 $Q \leq \hat{D}$

(C.2) together with (A.5) leads to

$$\pi^A_{s,nQ} = \alpha_2 + \frac{\alpha_1 - \alpha_2}{Q} [p \int_0^Q e^{-\mu_1 x} dx + (1-p) \int_0^Q e^{-\mu_2 x} dx].$$

Thus it follows that

$$\pi^A_{s,nQ} = \alpha_2 + \frac{\alpha_2 - \alpha_1}{Q} \left[\frac{p}{\mu_1} (e^{-\mu_1 Q} - 1) + \frac{(1-p)}{\mu_2} (e^{-\mu_2 Q} - 1) \right]. \quad \text{(C.7)}$$

C.4.2 $Q > \hat{D}$

From (C.3) together with (A.5) we get

$$\pi^B_{s,nQ} = \frac{1}{Q} \sum_{\omega=1}^{\zeta} \int_{\frac{\omega-1}{\eta}\hat{D}}^{\frac{\omega}{\eta}\hat{D}} \Bigg\{ \sum_{n_1=1}^{\infty} \Bigg[\sum_{\kappa=1}^{\zeta} \beta^{\omega}_{1,\kappa} \Big(1 - p e^{-\mu_1 (x + \frac{n_1\zeta-(\kappa-1)}{\eta}\hat{D})}$$
$$- (1-p) e^{-\mu_2 (x + \frac{n_1\zeta-(\kappa-1)}{\eta}\hat{D})}$$

$$-1+pe^{-\mu_1(x+\frac{n_1\zeta-\kappa}{\eta}\hat{D})}$$
$$+(1-p)e^{-\mu_2(x+\frac{n_1\zeta-\kappa)}{\eta}\hat{D})}\Big)\Big]$$
$$+\sum_{\kappa=1}^{\omega-1}\beta_{2,\kappa}^{\omega}\Big[1-pe^{-\mu_1(x-\frac{\kappa-1}{\eta}\hat{D})}-(1-p)e^{-\mu_2(x-\frac{\kappa-1}{\eta}\hat{D})}$$
$$-1+pe^{-\mu_1(x-\frac{\kappa}{\eta}\hat{D})}+(1-p)e^{-\mu_2(x-\frac{\kappa}{\eta}\hat{D})}\Big]$$
$$+\beta_{2,\omega}^{\omega}\Big[1-pe^{-\mu_1(x-\frac{\omega-1}{\eta}\hat{D})}-(1-p)e^{-\mu_2(x-\frac{\omega-1}{\eta}\hat{D})}\Big]\Big\}dx.$$

This can be rewritten as

$$\pi_{s,nQ}^{B}=\frac{1}{Q}\sum_{\omega=1}^{\zeta}\Big\{\sum_{n_1=1}^{\infty}\Big[\sum_{\kappa=1}^{\zeta}\beta_{1,\kappa}^{\omega}\Big(pe^{-\mu_1\frac{n_1\zeta-\kappa}{\eta}\hat{D}}[1-e^{-\mu_1\frac{1}{\eta}\hat{D}}]\int_{\frac{\omega-1}{\eta}\hat{D}}^{\frac{\omega}{\eta}\hat{D}}e^{-\mu_1 x}dx$$
$$+(1-p)e^{-\mu_2\frac{n_1\zeta-\kappa}{\eta}\hat{D}}[1-e^{-\mu_2\frac{1}{\eta}\hat{D}}]\int_{\frac{\omega-1}{\eta}\hat{D}}^{\frac{\omega}{\eta}\hat{D}}e^{-\mu_2 x}dx\Big)$$
$$+\sum_{\kappa=1}^{\omega-1}\beta_{2,\kappa}^{\omega}\Big(pe^{\mu_1\frac{\kappa}{\eta}\hat{D}}[1-e^{-\mu_1\frac{1}{\eta}\hat{D}}]\int_{\frac{\omega-1}{\eta}\hat{D}}^{\frac{\omega}{\eta}\hat{D}}e^{-\mu_1 x}dx$$
$$+(1-p)e^{\mu_2\frac{\kappa}{\eta}\hat{D}}[1-e^{-\mu_2\frac{1}{\eta}\hat{D}}]\int_{\frac{\omega-1}{\eta}\hat{D}}^{\frac{\omega}{\eta}\hat{D}}e^{-\mu_2 x}dx\Big)$$
$$+\beta_{2,\omega}^{\omega}\int_{\frac{\omega-1}{\eta}\hat{D}}^{\frac{\omega}{\eta}\hat{D}}\Big[1-pe^{\mu_1\frac{\omega-1}{\eta}\hat{D}}e^{-\mu_1 x}-(1-p)e^{\mu_2\frac{\omega-1}{\eta}\hat{D}}e^{-\mu_2 x}\Big]dx\Big\}.$$

It holds that $\int_{\frac{\omega-1}{\eta}\hat{D}}^{\frac{\omega}{\eta}\hat{D}}1dx=\frac{\hat{D}}{\eta}$ and $\int_{\frac{\omega-1}{\eta}\hat{D}}^{\frac{\omega}{\eta}\hat{D}}e^{-\mu_i x}dx=\frac{1}{\mu_i}(e^{-\mu_i(\omega-1)\hat{D}}-e^{-\mu_i\omega\hat{D}})$ for $i=1,2$.

Thus we finally get

$$\pi_{s,nQ}^{B}=\sum_{\omega=1}^{\zeta}\Big\{\sum_{n_1=1}^{\infty}\Big[\sum_{\kappa=1}^{\zeta}\beta_{1,\kappa}^{\omega}\Big(\frac{p}{\mu_1}e^{-\frac{\mu_1(\omega+n_1\zeta-\kappa)\hat{D}}{\eta}}(e^{\frac{\mu_1\hat{D}}{\eta}}-2+e^{\frac{-\mu_1\hat{D}}{\eta}})$$

$$+\frac{1-p}{\mu_2}e^{-\frac{\mu_2(\omega+n_1\zeta-\kappa)\hat{D}}{\eta}}(e^{\frac{\mu_2\hat{D}}{\eta}}-2+e^{\frac{-\mu_2\hat{D}}{\eta}})\Big)\Big] \quad \text{(C.8)}$$

$$+\sum_{\kappa=1}^{\omega-1}\beta_{2,\kappa}^{\omega}\Big(\frac{p}{\mu_1}e^{\frac{\mu_1(\kappa-\omega)\hat{D}}{\eta}}(e^{\frac{\mu_1\hat{D}}{\eta}}-2+e^{\frac{-\mu_1\hat{D}}{\eta}})$$

$$+\frac{1-p}{\mu_2}e^{\frac{\mu(\kappa-\omega)\hat{D}}{\eta}}(e^{\frac{\mu_2\hat{D}}{\eta}}-2+e^{\frac{-\mu_2\hat{D}}{\eta}})\Big)$$

$$+\beta_{2,\omega}^{\omega}\Big(\frac{\hat{D}}{\eta}-\frac{p}{\mu_1}(1-e^{-\frac{\mu_1\hat{D}}{\eta}})-\frac{1-p}{\mu_2}(1-e^{-\frac{\mu_2\hat{D}}{\eta}})\Big)\Big\}\frac{1}{Q}.$$

Now, stability can be determined for $Q \leq \hat{D}$ with (C.7) and for $Q > \hat{D}$ with (C.8) by inserting the corresponding stability quotients and by using the relevant coefficients of the demand distribution as depicted in Appendix A.2.

C.5 Short-Term Planning Stability

For $Q \leq \hat{D}$ we obtain (see De Kok and Inderfurth [32])

$$\pi_{s,nQ}^{A} = 1 - \frac{1}{Q}\int_{0}^{Q}\Phi_D(x)dx. \quad \text{(C.9)}$$

This result can also be derived from (C.2) with $\alpha_1 = 1$ and $\alpha_2 = 0$.

For $Q > \hat{D}$ stability in (4.66) can be written as

$$\pi_{s,nQ}^{B} = \frac{1}{Q}\{\int_{0}^{\hat{D}}[1-\Phi_D(x)]dx + \int_{\hat{D}}^{Q}\Phi_D(x)dx\},$$

and we get (see De Kok and Inderfurth [32])

$$\pi_{s,nQ}^{B} = \frac{1}{Q}\{\hat{D} - \int_{0}^{Q}\Phi_D(x)dx + 2\int_{\hat{D}}^{Q}\Phi_D(x)dx\}. \quad \text{(C.10)}$$

For Mixed-Erlang distributed demand we get from (C.9) together with (A.3) for $Q \leq \hat{D}$

$$\pi^A_{s,nQ} = \frac{1}{Q}\Bigg[\frac{p}{\mu}(k-1-\sum_{j=0}^{k-2}\sum_{i=j}^{k-2}\frac{(\mu Q)^{i-j}}{(i-j)!}e^{-\mu Q}) + \frac{(1-p)}{\mu}(k-\sum_{j=0}^{k-1}\sum_{i=j}^{k-1}\frac{(\mu Q)^{i-j}}{(i-j)!}e^{-\mu Q})\Bigg].$$

For $Q > \hat{D}$ we obtain from (C.10) together with (A.3) that

$$\begin{aligned}\pi^B_{s,nQ} = \frac{1}{Q}\Bigg\{&\hat{D} - Q + \frac{p}{\mu}(k-1-\sum_{j=0}^{k-2}\sum_{i=j}^{k-2}\frac{(\mu Q)^{i-j}}{(i-j)!}e^{-\mu Q}) \\ &+\frac{(1-p)}{\mu}(k-\sum_{j=0}^{k-1}\sum_{i=j}^{k-1}\frac{(\mu Q)^{i-j}}{(i-j)!}e^{-\mu Q}) \\ &+2\Bigg[Q-\hat{D}-\frac{p}{\mu}(\sum_{j=0}^{k-2}\sum_{i=j}^{k-2}\frac{(\mu \hat{D})^{i-j}}{(i-j)!}e^{-\mu\hat{D}} - \sum_{j=0}^{k-2}\sum_{i=j}^{k-2}\frac{(\mu Q)^{i-j}}{(i-j)!}e^{-\mu Q}) \\ &-\frac{1-p}{\mu}(\sum_{j=0}^{k-1}\sum_{i=j}^{k-1}\frac{(\mu \hat{D})^{i-j}}{(i-j)!}e^{-\mu\hat{D}} - \sum_{j=0}^{k-1}\sum_{i=j}^{k-1}\frac{(\mu Q)^{i-j}}{(i-j)!}e^{-\mu Q})\Bigg]\Bigg\}.\end{aligned}$$

Finally this leads to

$$\begin{aligned}\pi^B_{s,nQ} = \frac{1}{Q}\Bigg\{&Q - \hat{D} + \frac{p}{\mu}(k-1+\sum_{j=0}^{k-2}\sum_{i=j}^{k-2}\frac{(\mu Q)^{i-j}}{(i-j)!}e^{-\mu Q}) \\ &+\frac{(1-p)}{\mu}(k+\sum_{j=0}^{k-1}\sum_{i=j}^{k-1}\frac{(\mu Q)^{i-j}}{(i-j)!}e^{-\mu Q}) \\ &-2(\frac{p}{\mu}\sum_{j=0}^{k-2}\sum_{i=j}^{k-2}\frac{(\mu \hat{D})^{i-j}}{(i-j)!}e^{-\mu\hat{D}} + \frac{(1-p)}{\mu}\sum_{j=0}^{k-1}\sum_{i=j}^{k-1}\frac{(\mu \hat{D})^{i-j}}{(i-j)!}e^{-\mu\hat{D}})\Bigg\}.\end{aligned}$$

In the case of exponentially distributed demand we get from (C.9) for $Q \leq \hat{D}$ that

$$\pi^A_{s,nQ} = \frac{1}{Q/\bar{D}}\Big[1 - e^{-\frac{Q}{\bar{D}}}\Big].$$

Analogously we find from (C.10)

$$\pi^B_{s,nQ} = 1 - \frac{\hat{D}}{Q} + \frac{1}{Q/\bar{D}}\Big\{1 + e^{-\frac{Q}{\bar{D}}} - 2e^{-\frac{\hat{D}}{\bar{D}}}\Big\}.$$

With $\bar{D} = \hat{D}$ we get the same outcome as given in Inderfurth [61].

For hyperexponentially distributed demand we obtain for $Q \leq \hat{D}$ from (C.9) together with (A.5)

$$\pi^A_{s,nQ} = \frac{1}{Q}\left[\frac{p}{\mu_1}(1 - e^{-\mu_1 Q}) + \frac{(1-p)}{\mu}(1 - e^{-\mu_2 Q})\right].$$

For $Q > \hat{D}$ we find from (C.10) together with (A.5) that

$$\pi^B_{s,nQ} = \frac{1}{Q}\left\{\hat{D} - Q + \frac{p}{\mu_1}(1 - e^{-\mu_1 Q}) + \frac{(1-p)}{\mu_2}(1 - e^{-\mu_2 Q})\right.$$
$$\left. +2\left[Q - \hat{D} - \frac{p}{\mu_1}(e^{-\mu_1 \hat{D}} - e^{-\mu_1 Q}) - \frac{1-p}{\mu_2}(e^{-\mu_2 \hat{D}} - e^{-\mu_2 Q})\right]\right\}.$$

This yields to

$$\pi^B_{s,nQ} = \frac{1}{Q}\left\{Q - \hat{D} + \frac{p}{\mu_1}(1 + e^{-\mu_1 Q}) + \frac{(1-p)}{\mu_2}(1 + e^{-\mu_2 Q})\right.$$
$$\left. -2(\frac{p}{\mu_1}e^{-\mu_1 \hat{D}} + \frac{(1-p)}{\mu_2}e^{-\mu_2 \hat{D}})\right\}.$$

C.6 Proof of Algorithm I

The algorithm is proved by induction. The strategy of the proof is:

1. Prove that algorithm I is true for $\omega = 1$
   1.1 Prove that it holds for $t = 1$
   1.2 Assume that the algorithm is valid for $t = \Theta - 1$
   1.3 Show that it is true for $t = \Theta$.
2. Assume that the algorithm holds for $\omega = \varpi - 1$.
3. Show that it is valid for $\omega = \varpi$
   3.1 Prove that it holds for $t = 1$
   3.2 Assume that the algorithm is valid for $t = \Theta - 1$
   3.3 Show that it is true for $t = \Theta$.

1. $\omega = 1$ (i.e. $s < Y_0 \leq s + \frac{1}{\eta}\hat{D}$)

It holds that $c_0 = 0$.

1.1 $t = 1$

From (4.6) we get $\hat{Z}^0_1 = Y_0 - \hat{D}$ which we also obtain by using (4.42). Since $Y_0 \leq s + \frac{1}{\eta}\hat{D}$ it is evident that $\hat{Z}^0_1 \leq s$ and a setup must be released. By applying (4.43) we also find that $\hat{Q}^0_1 = \frac{\varsigma}{\eta}\hat{D} > 0$, because

$c_0 = 0 < \eta$. With (4.5) we get $\hat{Y}_1^0 = Y_0 + \frac{\zeta-\eta}{\eta}\hat{D}$. From (4.45) we find that $c_1 = (\zeta - \eta) \bmod \zeta$. Since $\zeta > \eta$ it is evident that $c_1 = \zeta - \eta$ which leads to the same stock level after replenishment as applying (4.5).

1.2 $t = \Theta - 1$

Under the assumption that the algorithm is true for $t = \Theta - 1$ we get $\hat{Z}^0_{\Theta-1} = Y_0 + \frac{c_{\Theta-2}-\eta}{\eta}\hat{D}$ (see 4.42) where $c_{\Theta-2} = ((\Theta - 2)(\zeta - \eta)) \bmod \eta$. If now $c_{\Theta-2} < \eta$, then we obtain from (4.43) that $\hat{Q}^0_{\Theta-1} = \frac{\zeta}{\eta}\hat{D}$, otherwise no setup is scheduled. With (4.44) we get $\hat{Y}^0_{\Theta-1} = Y_0 + \frac{c_{\Theta-1}}{\eta}\hat{D}$ with $c_{\Theta-1} = ((\Theta - 1)(\zeta - \eta)) \bmod \zeta$.

1.3 $t = \Theta$

The starting planned inventory position in period Θ is given by $\hat{Z}^0_\Theta = \hat{Y}^0_{\Theta-1} - \hat{D} = Y_0 + \frac{c_{\Theta-1}-\eta}{\eta}\hat{D}$ with $c_{\Theta-1}$ as mentioned above.
If $c_{\Theta-1} < \eta$, then $\hat{Q}^0_\Theta = \frac{\zeta}{\eta}\hat{D}$, because the initial stock level Y_0 is assumed to be smaller than or equal to $s + \frac{1}{\eta}\hat{D}$. Thus in the case of $c_{\Theta-1} < \eta$ we find that $\hat{Z}^0_\Theta \leq s$.
If on the other hand $c_{\Theta-1} \geq \eta$, then the starting inventory position in period Θ will exceed the reorder point, because $Y_0 > s$. Then, no order is planned to be released, i.e. $\hat{Q}^0_\Theta = 0$.
The stock level after replenishment is given by $\hat{Y}^0_\Theta = \hat{Z}^0_\Theta + \hat{Q}^0_\Theta = Y_0 + \frac{c_{\Theta-1}-\eta}{\eta}\hat{D} + \hat{Q}^0_\Theta$.

Case 1: $\hat{Q}^0_\Theta = \frac{\zeta}{\eta}\hat{D}$

Thus we get $\hat{Y}^0_\Theta = Y_0 + \frac{c_{\Theta-1}-\eta+\zeta}{\eta}\hat{D}$.

In order to prove (4.44) we have to show that $c_\Theta = c_{\Theta-1} - \eta + \zeta$. Since $c_{\Theta-1} - \eta < 0$ it also holds that $c_{\Theta-1} - \eta + \zeta < \zeta$. Thus it is evident that $c_\Theta = (c_{\Theta-1} - \eta + \zeta) \bmod \zeta = c_{\Theta-1} - \eta + \zeta$.
Case 2: $\hat{Q}^0_\Theta = 0$

Thus we get $\hat{Y}^0_\Theta = Y_0 + \frac{c_{\Theta-1}-\eta}{\eta}\hat{D}$.

Here, we have to show that $c_\Theta = c_{\Theta-1} - \eta$. Since $c_{\Theta-1} - \eta \geq 0$ it also holds that $c_{\Theta-1} - \eta + \zeta \geq \zeta$. Now, we find that $c_\Theta = (c_{\Theta-1} - \eta + \zeta) \bmod \zeta = c_{\Theta-1} - \eta$. Thus we have proved (4.44).

2. $\omega = \varpi - 1$ (i.e. $s + \frac{\varpi-2}{\eta}\hat{D} < Y_0 \leq s + \frac{\varpi-1}{\eta}\hat{D}$)

We assume that algorithm I is true for $\omega = \varpi - 1$.

3. $\omega = \varpi$ (i.e. $s + \frac{\varpi-1}{\eta}\hat{D} < Y_0 \leq s + \frac{\varpi}{\eta}\hat{D}$)

It holds that $c_0 = \varpi - 1$.

3.1 $t = 1$

From (4.6) we find that $\hat{Z}_1^0 = Y_0 - \hat{D}$ which we also obtain by using (4.42).
If $\varpi - 1 < \eta$, then $\hat{Z}_1^0 \leq s$, because the forecasted demand $\hat{D}$ exceeds the initial stock level Y_0 for which holds that $Y_0 \leq s + \frac{\varpi}{\eta}\hat{D}$. Thus in the case of $\varpi - 1 < \eta$ we find that $\hat{Q}_1^0 > 0$.
If $\varpi - 1 \geq \eta$, then $\hat{Q}_1^0 = 0$, because the forecasted demand can be satisfied by the initial stock level without reaching the reorder point: $Y_0 > s + \frac{\varpi-1}{\eta}\hat{D}$, i.e. $\hat{Z}_1^0 > s$.

The same results can be deduced immediately from (4.43).

The stock level after replenishment is given by $\hat{Y}_1^0 = \hat{Z}_1^0 + \hat{Q}_1^0$.

Case 1: $\hat{Q}_1^0 = \frac{\zeta}{\eta}\hat{D}$

Thus we get $\hat{Y}_1^0 = Y_0 + \frac{\zeta-\eta}{\eta}\hat{D}$.

In order to prove (4.44)[1] we have to show that $c_1 = \varpi - 1 - \eta + \zeta$. Since $\varpi - 1 - \eta < 0$ it holds that $\varpi - 1 - \eta + \zeta < \zeta$. Thus it is evident that $c_1 = (\varpi - 1 - \eta + \zeta) \bmod \zeta = \varpi - 1 - \eta + \zeta$.

Case 2: $\hat{Q}_1^0 = 0$

Thus we get $\hat{Y}_1^0 = Y_0 - \hat{D}$.

Here, we have to show that $c_1 = \varpi - 1 - \eta$ which is straightforward. Since $\varpi - 1 - \eta \geq 0$ it holds that $\varpi - 1 - \eta + \zeta \geq \zeta$. Thus it is evident that $c_1 = (\varpi - 1 - \eta + \zeta) \bmod \zeta = \varpi - 1 - \eta$.

3.2 $t = \Theta - 1$

Under the assumption that algorithm I is true for $t = \Theta - 1$ we get $\hat{Z}_{\Theta-1}^0 = Y_0 + \frac{c_{\Theta-2} - \eta - (\varpi-1)}{\eta}\hat{D}$ (see 4.42) where $c_{\Theta-2} = (\varpi - 1 + (\Theta - 2)(\zeta - \eta)) \bmod \eta$.
If now $c_{\Theta-2} < \eta$, then we obtain from (4.43) that $\hat{Q}_{\Theta-1}^0 = \frac{\zeta}{\eta}\hat{D}$, otherwise

[1] From (4.44) we find that $\hat{Y}_1^0 = Y_0 + \frac{c_1 - (\varpi-1)}{\eta}\hat{D}$.

no setup is scheduled. With (4.44) we get $\hat{Y}^0_{\Theta-1} = Y_0 + \frac{c_{\Theta-1}-(\varpi-1)}{\eta}\hat{D}$ with $c_{\Theta-1} = (\varpi - 1 + (\Theta-1)(\zeta-\eta)) \bmod \zeta$.

3.3 $t = \Theta$

The starting planned inventory position is given by $\hat{Z}^0_\Theta = \hat{Y}^0_{\Theta-1} - \hat{D} = Y_0 + \frac{c_{\Theta-1}-(\varpi-1)-\eta}{\eta}\hat{D}$ with $c_{\Theta-1}$ as mentioned in 3.2.

If $c_{\Theta-1} < \eta$, then $\hat{Q}^0_\Theta = \frac{\zeta}{\eta}\hat{D}$. By rearranging the terms of the starting stock level in period Θ we get $\hat{Z}^0_\Theta = Y_0 - \frac{\varpi}{\eta}\hat{D} + \frac{c_{\Theta-1}-\eta+1}{\eta}\hat{D}$. Since $Y_0 - \frac{\varpi}{\eta}\hat{D} \leq s$ and $\frac{c_{\Theta-1}-\eta+1}{\eta}\hat{D} \leq 0$ in the case of $c_{\Theta-1} < \eta$ it is evident that $\hat{Z}^0_\Theta \leq s$ which leads to a planned setup in period Θ.

If $c_{\Theta-1} \geq \eta$, then $\hat{Z}^0_\Theta > s$, because $Y_0 - \frac{\varpi-1}{\eta}\hat{D} > s$ and $\frac{c_{\Theta-1}-\eta}{\eta}\hat{D} \geq 0$. Thus no setup is scheduled, i.e. $\hat{Q}^0_\Theta = 0$.

The stock after replenishment is given by $\hat{Y}^0_\Theta = \hat{Z}^0_\Theta + \hat{Q}^0_\Theta = Y_0 + \frac{c_{\Theta-1}-(\varpi-1)-\eta}{\eta}\hat{D} + \hat{Q}^0_\Theta$.

Case 1: $\hat{Q}^0_\Theta = \frac{\zeta}{\eta}\hat{D}$

Thus we get $\hat{Y}^0_\Theta = Y_0 + \frac{c_{\Theta-1}-(\varpi-1)-\eta+\zeta}{\eta}\hat{D}$.

Since $c_\Theta = c_{\Theta-1} - \eta + \zeta$ (see 1.3, Case 1) we have proved (4.44). From (4.44) we find that $\hat{Y}^0_\Theta = Y_0 + \frac{c_\Theta-(\varpi-1)}{\eta}\hat{D}$.

Case 2: $\hat{Q}^0_\Theta = 0$

Thus we get $\hat{Y}^0_\Theta = Y_0 + \frac{c_{\Theta-1}-(\varpi-1)-\eta}{\eta}\hat{D}$.

Since $c_\Theta = c_{\Theta-1} - \eta$ (see 1.3, Case 2) we have shown that (4.44) is true, because it holds that $\hat{Y}^0_\Theta = Y_0 + \frac{c_\Theta-(\varpi-1)}{\eta}\hat{D}$.

Thus the proof of algorithm I is completed.

q.e.d.

Notes on Algorithm I

1. It holds that

$$c_t = (c_{t-1} + \zeta - \eta) \bmod \zeta = (c_0 + t(\zeta-\eta)) \bmod \zeta. \tag{C.11}$$

Proof (by induction):

1. $t = 1$: $c_1 = (c_0 + \zeta - \eta) \bmod \zeta$.

2. Assume that (C.11) is true for $t = \Theta - 1$.

3. $t = \Theta$: $c_\Theta = (c_{\Theta-1} + \zeta - \eta) \bmod \zeta$.
   With $c_{\Theta-1} = (c_0 + (\Theta-1)(\zeta-\eta)) \bmod \zeta$ we get:

$$c_\Theta = [(c_0 + (\Theta-1)(\zeta-\eta)) \bmod \zeta + \zeta - \eta] \bmod \zeta \tag{C.12}$$

   Lemma:

   For $x, y, z \geq 0$ it holds that $(x+y) \bmod z = (x \bmod z + y) \bmod z$. This is straightforward: $(x+y) \bmod z = (x \bmod z + y \bmod z) \bmod z = (x \bmod z + y) \bmod z$.

   With $x = c_0 + (\Theta-1)(\zeta-\eta) \geq 0$ ($c_0 \geq 0, \zeta > \eta$), $y = \zeta - \eta > 0$ and $z = \zeta$ as in (C.12) it is easy to see that $c_\Theta = (c_0 + (\Theta-1)(\zeta-\eta) + \zeta - \eta) \bmod \zeta$. This finally results in

$$c_\Theta = (c_0 + \Theta(\zeta-\eta)) \bmod \zeta.$$

q.e.d.

2. We find for all $\omega = 1, 2, ..., \zeta$ that the setup decisions from period 1 to ζ will be repeated in periods $\zeta+1...2\zeta$, $2\zeta+1...3\zeta$, and so on (as far as the stability horizon is not exceeded). This implies that

$$\hat{Z}_1^0 = \hat{Z}_{i\zeta+1}^0 = Y_0 - \hat{D} \qquad \forall \qquad i \in \mathcal{N} \tag{C.13}$$

   Proof:

   From (4.42) we obtain $\hat{Z}_1^0 = Y_0 - \hat{D}$. Additionally we find $\hat{Z}_{i\zeta+1}^0 = Y_0 + \frac{c_{i\zeta} - c_0}{\eta}\hat{D} - \hat{D}$. Here, $c_{i\zeta}$ is given by $(c_0 + i\zeta(\zeta-\eta)) \bmod \zeta$. Applying the aforementioned Lemma we find $c_{i\zeta} = (c_0 \bmod \zeta + i\zeta(\zeta-\eta) \bmod \zeta) \bmod \zeta$. Since $i\zeta(\zeta-\eta) \bmod \zeta = 0$ it is easy to see that $c_{i\zeta} = c_0 \bmod \zeta = c_0$, because $c_0 = \omega - 1 < \zeta$. Thus we have shown that $\hat{Z}_{i\zeta+1}^0 = Y_0 - \hat{D}$.

q.e.d.

3. Moreover, the setup decisions from period 1 up to $T+1$ for a given value of $\omega = \varpi$ (with $\varpi = 1, ..., \eta$) will be repeated in periods Θ up to $T+1$ for a certain value of $\omega = (\Theta-1)\eta + \varpi$ whereas from 1 up to $\Theta - 1$ no setups are planned to be released.

   Proof:

   For $s + \frac{(\Theta-1)\eta+(\varpi-1)}{\eta} < Y_0 \leq s + \frac{(\Theta-1)\eta+\varpi}{\eta}$ the starting inventory position at the beginning of period Θ is given by $\hat{Z}_\Theta^0 = Y_0 - \Theta\hat{D}$, because the initial stock level Y_0 is large enough to satisfy the cumulative forecasted demand from period 1 to $\Theta - 1$. Thus no orders take place in these periods.

   Transformation: $\chi_0 := Y_0 - (\Theta-1)\hat{D}$.

Thus we get $\hat{Z}_{\Theta}^{0} = \chi_0 - \hat{D}$ with $s + \frac{\varpi - 1}{\eta} < \chi_0 \leq s + \frac{\varpi}{\eta}$. Since Y_0 (or χ_0, respectively) has no further influence on the application of algorithm I, the planned setups from period 1 to $T+1$ for $\omega = \varpi$ must be identical to the planned setup decisions from period Θ to $T+1$ for $\omega = (\Theta-1)\eta+\varpi$.

q.e.d.

D. Product Recovery Systems

D.1 (s,S) Policy

D.1.1 Stationary Density of (s, S) Policy

Here, an explicit expression for the stationary distribution of the net stock level for the case of exponentially distributed demand and returns is determined (see also Heisig and Fleischmann [50]). Recall that D_t and R_t are exponentially distributed for each t with parameters λ and μ, respectively. Notice that the assumption $\mathbb{E}(D) > \mathbb{E}(R)$ implies that $\mu > \lambda$. Furthermore, recall that $V_t = Y_t - s$ where Y_t denotes the net stock at the beginning of period t after remanufacturing and production as defined in Section 5.4.1. As discussed in Section 5.4.1, the existence and uniqueness of a stationary distribution F_V of the process (V_t) on $[0, \infty)$ follow from the fact that (V_t) is an ergodic random walk (see Fleischmann and Kuik [37]). Hence, it suffices to determine the explicit form of F_V. This is done so by considering the stationarity equation of the process (V_t). As before, let $\Phi_N(n) = \mathbb{P}\{N \leq n\}$ denote the distribution of the net demand in an arbitrary period and $\phi_N(n)$ the corresponding density function. Assuming exponential distributions for D_t and R_t yields

$$\phi_N(n) = \begin{cases} \frac{\mu\lambda}{\mu+\lambda}\, e^{-\lambda n} & \text{for } n \geq 0 \\ \frac{\mu\lambda}{\mu+\lambda}\, e^{\mu n} & \text{for } n < 0 \end{cases} \quad \text{and } \Phi_N(n) = \begin{cases} 1 - \frac{\mu}{\mu+\lambda}\, e^{-\lambda n} & \text{for } n \geq 0 \\ \frac{\lambda}{\mu+\lambda}\, e^{\mu n} & \text{for } n < 0\ . \end{cases} \tag{D.1}$$

Furthermore, for $x \geq 0$ and $v \in \mathbb{R}$ let

$$q(x, v) = \mathbb{P}\{V_{t+1} \leq v \mid V_t = x\}\ .$$

Inserting the transition probabilities of V_t yields

$$q(x, v) = \int_0^v \phi_N(x - j)dj + \mathbb{1}_{v \geq Q}(1 - \Phi_N(x))\ ,$$

where $\mathbb{1}_{v \geq Q}$ denotes the indicator function of the condition $v \geq Q$. Stationarity of F_V with respect to (V_t) implies

$$F_V(v) = \int_0^\infty q(x, v) F_V(dx)\ \ \forall\ \ v \in \mathbb{R}\ . \tag{D.2}$$

Suppose that F_V can be written in the form

$$F_V(v) = \int_0^v f_V(x)dx + 1\!\!1_{v \geq Q}\, p_Q \,,$$

where the first term denotes an absolutely continuous part and the second term denotes a probability mass at $v = Q$. Then (D.2) is equivalent with

$$\int_0^v f_V(x)dx + 1\!\!1_{v \geq Q}\, p_Q = \int_0^\infty \Big(\int_0^v \phi_N(j-x)dx + 1\!\!1_{v \geq Q}(1-\phi_N(j))\Big) f_V(j)dj$$
$$+\, p_Q\Big(\int_0^v \phi_N(Q-x)dx + 1\!\!1_{v \geq Q}(1-\Phi_N(Q))\Big) \;\forall\, v \in I\!\!R.$$

Letting $v \to Q$ yields

$$p_Q = \int_0^\infty (1-\Phi_N(j))f_V(j)dj + p_Q(1-\Phi_N(Q)) \tag{D.3}$$

and therefore

$$\int_0^v f_V(x)dx = \int_0^v \Big(\int_0^\infty \phi_N(j-x)f_V(j)dj + p_Q\phi_N(Q-x)\Big)dx \;\;\forall\;\; v \in I\!\!R,$$

and further

$$f_V(x) = \int_0^\infty \phi_N(j-x)f_V(j)dj + p_Q\phi_N(Q-x) \;\;\forall\;\; x \in I\!\!R\,. \tag{D.4}$$

Solving (D.3) for p_Q and inserting into (D.4) yields the following integral equation

$$f_V(x) = \int_0^\infty \Big(\phi_N(j-x) + \frac{\phi_N(Q-x)}{\Phi_N(Q)}(1-\Phi_N(j))\Big)\, f_V(j)\,dj \quad \forall\;\; x \in I\!\!R\,. \tag{D.5}$$

We can rewrite this condition further by using (D.1). To this end we must distinguish two cases, namely $x \leq Q$ and $x > Q$. Let us first assume that $x \leq Q$. Then (D.5) yields

$$\begin{aligned} f_V(x) = \frac{\mu\lambda}{\mu+\lambda}\Big[& e^{-\mu x}\int_0^x e^{\mu j} f_V(j)dj \\ + \;& e^{\lambda x}\int_x^\infty e^{-\lambda j} f_V(j)dj \\ + \;& e^{\lambda x}\int_0^\infty e^{-\lambda Q}\frac{\mu e^{-\lambda j}}{\lambda+\mu(1-e^{-\lambda Q})} f_V(j)dj \Big] \quad \forall\;\; x \leq Q. \end{aligned}$$

Repeatedly differentiating this equation leads to the following differential equation for f_V

$$f_V'''(x) = (\lambda-\mu)f_V''(x) \qquad \forall\;\; x \leq Q. \tag{D.6}$$

Moreover, we find that inserting (D.1) into (D.5) for $x > Q$ leads to the same differential equation. Hence (D.6) must hold for all $x \geq 0$. Clearly, the general solution of (D.6) has the form

$$f_V(x) = a + b\,x + c\,e^{(\lambda-\mu)\,x}$$

with some constants a, b and c. Since $\lim_{x\to\infty} f_V(x)$ must equal zero we get that $a = b = 0$. Moreover, replacing then $f_V(x) = c\,e^{(\lambda-\mu)\,x}$ in (D.3) leads to

$$p_Q = \frac{c}{\lambda + \mu(1 - e^{-\lambda Q})}$$

Using the fact that $\int_0^\infty f_V(x)dx + p_Q$ must equal one yields the value of the constant c. It is given by

$$c = \frac{(\mu - \lambda)(\lambda + \mu(1 - e^{-\lambda Q}))}{\mu(2 - e^{-\lambda Q})}.$$

Thus we finally get

$$F_V(v) = \int_{-\infty}^{v} f_V(x)dx + 1_{v \geq Q}\, p_Q \ ,$$

$$\text{with} \quad p_Q = \frac{\mu - \lambda}{\mu(2 - e^{-\lambda Q})}$$

$$\text{and} \quad f_V(v) = \begin{cases} 0 & \text{for} \quad v < 0 \\ ce^{-(\mu-\lambda)v} & \text{for} \quad v \geq 0 \end{cases}$$

$$\text{where} \quad c = p_Q[\lambda + \mu(1 - e^{-\lambda Q})] \ .$$

D.1.2 Exponentially Distributed Demand and Returns

The starting point is (5.7) with

$$\pi_{s,S}^{rec} = \sum_{\tau=1}^{\infty} \int_{(\tau-1)\hat{N}}^{\tau\hat{N}} \Bigg[\sum_{\theta=1}^{\infty} \beta_\theta^\tau [\Phi_N(v - (\theta-2)\hat{N}) - \Phi_N(v - (\theta-1)\hat{N})]$$

$$+ \beta_1^\tau [1 - \Phi_N(v + \hat{N})] \Bigg] dF_V(v).$$

Using the fact that $\beta_\theta^{T+k} = \beta_\theta^{T+1}$ for all $k \geq 1$ and all θ (and analogous for $\theta \geq T+1$) and taking into account the form of the stationary distribution of V derived in Appendix D.1.1 we can rewrite $\pi_{s,S}^{rec}$ as follows.

$$\pi_{s,S}^{rec} = \sum_{\tau=1}^{T} \int\limits_{(\tau-1)\hat{N}}^{\tau\hat{N}} \Bigg[\beta_1^{\tau}[1-\Phi_N(v)] + \sum_{\theta=2}^{T+1} \beta_\theta^{\tau}[\Phi_N(v-(\theta-2)\hat{N}) - \Phi_N(v-(\theta-1)\hat{N})]$$

$$+ \beta_{T+1}^{\tau}\Phi_N(v - T\hat{N})\Bigg] f_V(v)dv$$

$$+ \int\limits_{T\hat{N}}^{\infty} \Bigg[\beta_1^{T+1}[1-\Phi_N(v)] + \sum_{\theta=2}^{T+1} \beta_\theta^{T+1}[\Phi_N(v-(\theta-2)\hat{N}) - \Phi_N(v-(\theta-1)\hat{N})]$$

$$+ \beta_{T+1}^{T+1}\Phi_N(v - T\hat{N})\Bigg] f_V(v)dv$$

$$+ p_Q \Bigg[\beta_1^{l}[1-\Phi_N(Q)] + \sum_{\theta=2}^{T+1} \beta_\theta^{l}[\Phi_N(Q-(\theta-2)\hat{N}) - \Phi_N(Q-(\theta-1)\hat{N})]$$

$$+ \beta_{T+1}^{l}\Phi_N(Q - T\hat{N})\Bigg]$$

where $\Phi_N(.)$ is the cdf of net demand (see (5.8)) and $f_V(v)$ is the density distribution of v (with $v = y - s$) as derived in Appendix D.1.1.

Since

$$\Phi_N(b) - \Phi_N(a) = \int\limits_{a}^{b} \phi_N(n)dn \tag{D.7}$$

we can rewrite $\pi_{s,S}^{rec}$ further as follows.

$$\pi_{s,S}^{rec} = \sum_{\tau=1}^{T} \int\limits_{(\tau-1)\hat{N}}^{\tau\hat{N}} \Bigg[\beta_1^{\tau} \int\limits_{v}^{\infty} \phi_N(n)\, dn + \sum_{\theta=2}^{T+1} \beta_\theta^{\tau} \int\limits_{v-(\theta-1)\hat{N}}^{v-(\theta-2)\hat{N}} \phi_N(n)\, dn$$

$$+ \beta_{T+1}^{\tau} \int\limits_{-\infty}^{v-T\hat{N}} \phi_N(n)\, dn\Bigg] f_V(v)dv$$

$$+ \int\limits_{T\hat{N}}^{\infty} \Bigg[\beta_1^{T+1} \int\limits_{v}^{\infty} \phi_N(n)\, dn + \sum_{\theta=2}^{T+1} \beta_\theta^{T+1} \int\limits_{v-(\theta-1)\hat{N}}^{v-(\theta-2)\hat{N}} \phi_N(n)\, dn$$

$$+ \beta_{T+1}^{T+1} \int\limits_{-\infty}^{v-T\hat{N}} \phi_N(n)\, dn\Bigg] f_V(v)dv$$

$$+ p_Q \left[\beta_1^l \int_Q^\infty \phi_N(n)\, dn + \sum_{\theta=2}^{T+1} \beta_\theta^l \int_{Q-(\theta-1)\hat{N}}^{Q-(\theta-2)\hat{N}} \phi_N(n)\, dn + \beta_{T+1}^l \int_{-\infty}^{Q-T\hat{N}} \phi_N(n)\, dn \right]$$

where $\phi_N(n)$ is given by (5.9).

Hence, for $a < b$ we have

$$\int_a^b \phi_N(n) dn = \begin{cases} \frac{\mu}{\mu+\lambda} \left(e^{-\lambda a} - e^{-\lambda b}\right) & \text{for } 0 \le a < b \\ 1 - \frac{\mu}{\mu+\lambda} e^{-\lambda b} - \frac{\lambda}{\mu+\lambda} e^{\mu a} & \text{for } a < 0 \le b \\ \frac{\lambda}{\mu+\lambda} \left(e^{\mu b} - e^{\mu a}\right) & \text{for } a < b < 0. \end{cases}$$

Inserting the expressions for the distribution of N (see (5.9)) and V (see Appendix D.1.1) we can evaluate the integrals as follows.

$$\int_v^\infty \phi_N(n) dn = \frac{\mu}{\mu+\lambda} e^{-\lambda v}$$

$$\int_{v-(\theta-1)\hat{N}}^{v-(\theta-2)\hat{N}} \phi_N(n) dn = \begin{cases} \frac{\mu}{\mu+\lambda} e^{-\lambda(v-(\theta-1)\hat{N})} \left(1 - e^{-\lambda \hat{N}}\right) & \text{for } \theta \le v+1 \\ 1 - \frac{\mu}{\mu+\lambda} e^{-\lambda(v-(\theta-2)\hat{N})} \\ - \frac{\lambda}{\mu+\lambda} e^{\mu(v-(\theta-1)\hat{N})} & \text{for } v+1 < \theta \le v+2 \\ \frac{\lambda}{\mu+\lambda} e^{\mu(v-(\theta-1)\hat{N})} \left(e^{\mu \hat{N}} - 1\right) & \text{for } v+2 < \theta \end{cases}$$

$$\int_{-\infty}^{v-T\hat{N}} \phi_N(n) dn = \frac{\lambda}{\mu+\lambda} e^{\mu(v-T\hat{N})}$$

Further, setting $\tilde{c} := c/(\mu+\lambda)$, we get

$$\int_{(\tau-1)\hat{N}}^{\tau\hat{N}} \int_v^\infty \phi_N(n) f_V(v) dn dv = \tilde{c}\, e^{-\mu\tau\hat{N}} \left(e^{\mu\hat{N}} - 1\right)$$

$$\int_{(\tau-1)\hat N}^{\tau\hat N}\int_{v-(\theta-1)\hat N}^{v-(\theta-2)\hat N}\phi_N(n)f_V(v)dndv=\begin{cases}\tilde c\,(1-e^{-\lambda\hat N})(e^{\mu\hat N}-1)e^{\lambda(\theta-1)\hat N}e^{-\mu\tau\hat N} \\ \qquad\qquad\qquad\qquad \text{for } \theta\le\tau \\ \frac{2\tilde c}{\mu-\lambda}\,e^{-(\mu-\lambda)\tau\hat N}(\lambda e^{(\mu-\lambda)\hat N} \\ +(\mu-\lambda)e^{-\lambda\hat N}-\mu) \qquad \text{for } \theta=\tau+1 \\ \tilde c\,(1-e^{-\lambda\hat N})(e^{\mu\hat N}-1)e^{\lambda\tau\hat N}e^{-\mu(\theta-1)\hat N} \\ \qquad\qquad\qquad\qquad \text{for } \theta\ge\tau+2\end{cases}$$

$$\int_{(\tau-1)\hat N}^{\tau\hat N}\int_{-\infty}^{v-T\hat N}\phi_N(n)f_V(v)dndv=\tilde c\,e^{-\mu T\hat N}(1-e^{-\lambda\hat N})e^{\lambda\tau\hat N}$$

$$\int_{T\hat N}^{\infty}\int_{v}^{\infty}\phi_N(n)f_V(v)dndv=\tilde c\,e^{-\mu T\hat N}$$

$$\int_{T\hat N}^{\infty}\int_{v-(\theta-1)\hat N}^{v-(\theta-2)\hat N}\phi_N(n)f_V(v)dndv=\tilde c\,(1-e^{-\lambda\hat N})e^{-\mu T\hat N}e^{\lambda(\theta-1)\hat N}$$

$$\int_{T\hat N}^{\infty}\int_{-\infty}^{v-T\hat N}\phi_N(n)f_V(v)dndv=\frac{2\tilde c\,\lambda}{\mu-\lambda}\,e^{-(\mu-\lambda)T\hat N}.$$

We can now put all these results together. For ease of notation we set $c_\mu := (e^{\mu\hat N}-1)$, $c_\lambda := (1-e^{-\lambda\hat N})$, and $c_T := e^{-\mu T\hat N}$. We need to distinguish two cases concerning the relation of l and T. (Note that the distinction only affects the last term.)

Case A: For $l\le T$ we have

$$\pi^{rec}_{s,S}=\tilde c\left\{\sum_{\tau=1}^{T}\left[\beta_1^\tau c_\mu e^{-\mu\tau\hat N}+\sum_{\theta=2}^{\tau}\beta_\theta^\tau c_\mu c_\lambda e^{-(\mu\tau-\lambda(\theta-1))\hat N}\right.\right.$$
$$+\frac{2\beta_{\tau+1}^\tau}{\mu-\lambda}(\lambda c_\mu(1-c_\lambda)-\mu c_\lambda)e^{-(\mu-\lambda)\tau\hat N}$$
$$\left.+\sum_{\theta=\tau+2}^{T+1}\beta_\theta^\tau c_\mu c_\lambda e^{-(\mu(\theta-1)-\lambda\tau)\hat N}+\beta_{T+1}^\tau c_T c_\lambda e^{\lambda\tau\hat N}\right]$$

$$+ \quad \beta_1^{T+1} c_T + \sum_{\theta=2}^{T+1} \beta_\theta^{T+1} c_T c_\lambda e^{\lambda(\theta-1)\hat{N}} + \beta_{T+1}^{T+1} \frac{2\lambda}{\mu - \lambda} e^{-(\mu-\lambda)T\hat{N}} \Bigg\}$$

$$+ \quad \frac{p_Q}{\mu+\lambda} \Bigg[\beta_1^l \mu e^{-\lambda Q} + \sum_{\theta=2}^{l} \beta_\theta^l \mu c_\lambda e^{-\lambda(Q-(\theta-1)\hat{N})}$$

$$+ \beta_{l+1}^l (\mu + \lambda - \mu(1-c_\lambda) e^{-\lambda(Q-l\hat{N})}$$

$$- \lambda e^{\mu(Q-l\hat{N})}) + \sum_{\theta=l+2}^{T+1} \beta_\theta^l \lambda c_\mu e^{\mu(Q-(\theta-1)\hat{N})} + \beta_{T+1}^l \lambda c_T e^{\mu Q} \Bigg].$$

Case B: For $l > T$ we have

$$\pi_{s,S}^{rec} = \tilde{c} \Bigg\{ \sum_{\tau=1}^{T} \Bigg[\beta_1^\tau c_\mu e^{-\mu\tau\hat{N}} + \sum_{\theta=2}^{\tau} \beta_\theta^\tau c_\mu c_\lambda e^{-(\mu\tau - \lambda(\theta-1))\hat{N}}$$

$$+ \frac{2\beta_{\tau+1}^\tau}{\mu - \lambda} (\lambda c_\mu (1 - c_\lambda) - \mu c_\lambda) e^{-(\mu-\lambda)\tau\hat{N}}$$

$$+ \sum_{\theta=\tau+2}^{T+1} \beta_\theta^\tau c_\mu c_\lambda e^{-(\mu(\theta-1) - \lambda\tau)\hat{N}} + \beta_{T+1}^\tau c_T c_\lambda e^{\lambda\tau\hat{N}} \Bigg]$$

$$+ \quad \beta_1^{T+1} c_T + \sum_{\theta=2}^{T+1} \beta_\theta^{T+1} c_T c_\lambda e^{\lambda(\theta-1)\hat{N}} + \beta_{T+1}^{T+1} \frac{2\lambda}{\mu-\lambda} e^{-(\mu-\lambda)T\hat{N}} \Bigg\}$$

$$+ \frac{p_Q}{\mu+\lambda} \Bigg[\beta_1^l \mu e^{-\lambda Q} + \sum_{\theta=2}^{T+1} \beta_\theta^l \mu c_\lambda e^{-\lambda(Q-(\theta-1)\hat{N})}$$

$$+ \beta_{T+1}^l (\mu + \lambda - \mu e^{-\lambda(Q-T\hat{N})}) \Bigg].$$

D.2 (S,D) Policy

D.2.1 Stationary Density of (S, D) Policy

The derivation of the stationary density for an (S, D) policy is very similar to the determination of the stationary density for an (s, S) policy. D_t and R_t denote exponentially distributed demand and returns for each t with parameters λ and μ, respectively, where $\mu > \lambda$ always holds. The net demand N_t for period t is given by $D_t - R_t$, its distribution is denoted by $\Phi_N(n)$ (see (5.8)) and its density is given by $\phi_N(n)$ (see (5.9)). Finally, recall that Y_t denotes the net stock at the beginning of period t after production, remanufacturing and disposal as defined in Section 5.5.1.
For $x \geq 0$ and $y \in \mathbb{R}$ let

$$q(x, y) = \mathbb{P}\{Y_{t+1} \leq y \mid Y_t = x\} \ .$$

Inserting the transition probabilities of Y_t yields

$$q(x, y) = \int_S^D \phi_N(x - j)dj + \mathbb{1}_{y=S}(1 - \Phi_N(x - S)) + \mathbb{1}_{y=D}\Phi_N(x - D) \ ,$$

where $\mathbb{1}_{y=S}$ denotes the indicator function of the condition $y = S$, and analogously $\mathbb{1}_{y=D}$ for $y = D$. Stationarity of F_Y with respect to (Y_t) implies

$$F_Y(y) = \int_S^D q(x, y)F_Y(dx) \ \ \forall \ y \in \mathbb{R} \ . \tag{D.8}$$

Suppose that F_Y can be written in the form

$$F_Y(y) = \int_S^D f_Y(x)dx + \mathbb{1}_{y=S}\, p_S + \mathbb{1}_{y=D}\, p_D \ ,$$

where the first term denotes an absolutely continuous part and the second and third term denotes a probability mass at $y = S$ and $y = D$, respectively.

Then (D.8) is equivalent to

$$\int_S^D f_Y(x)dx + 1\!\!1_{y=S}\, p_S + 1\!\!1_{y=D}\, p_D$$

$$= \int_S^D \Big(\int_S^D \phi(j-x)dx + 1\!\!1_{y=S}(1-\Phi_N(j-S)) + 1\!\!1_{y=D}\Phi_N(j-D)\Big) f_Y(j)dj$$

$$+\ p_S\Big(\int_S^D \phi(S-x)dx + 1\!\!1_{y=S}(1-\Phi_N(0)) + 1\!\!1_{y=D}\Phi_N(S-D)\Big)$$

$$+\ p_D\Big(\int_S^D \phi(D-x)dx + 1\!\!1_{y=S}(1-\Phi_N(D-S)) + 1\!\!1_{y=D}\Phi_N(0)\Big)\ \ \forall y \in \mathbb{R}.$$

Letting $y \to S$ yields

$$p_S = \int_S^D (1-\Phi_N(j-S))f_Y(j)dj + p_S(1-\Phi_N(0)) + p_D(1-\Phi_N(D-S)), \quad \text{(D.9)}$$

and $y \to D$ leads to

$$p_D = \int_S^D \Phi_N(j-D))f_Y(j)dj + p_S\Phi_N(S-D) + p_D\Phi_N(0), \quad \text{(D.10)}$$

and therefore

$$\int_S^D f_Y(x)dx = \int_S^D \Big(\int_S^D \phi_N(j-x)f_Y(j)dj + p_S\phi_N(S-x) + p_D\phi_N(D-x)\Big)dx\ \forall\ y \in \mathbb{R},$$

and further

$$f_Y(x) = \int_S^D \phi_N(j-x)f_Y(j)dj + p_S\phi_N(S-x) + p_D\phi_N(D-x)\ \ \forall\ \ x \in \mathbb{R}\,. \quad \text{(D.11)}$$

For exponentially distributed demands and returns $\Phi_N(n)$ and $\phi(n)$ are given by (5.8) and (5.9).
Thus we get from (D.9)–(D.11) that

$$p_S = \frac{\mu}{\mu+\lambda}\Big\{\int_S^D e^{-\lambda(j-S)} f_Y(j)dj + p_S + e^{-\lambda(D-S)}p_D\Big\}, \quad \text{(D.12)}$$

$$f_Y(x) = \frac{\lambda\mu}{\lambda+\mu}\Bigg\{ \int_x^D e^{-\lambda(j-x)} f_Y(j)dj + \int_S^x e^{\mu(j-x)} f_Y(j)dj$$

$$+e^{\mu(S-x)}p_S + e^{-\lambda(D-x)}p_D \Bigg\}, \tag{D.13}$$

$$p_D = \frac{\lambda}{\mu+\lambda}\Bigg\{ \int_S^D e^{\mu(j-D)} f_Y(j)dj + e^{\mu(S-D)}p_S + p_D \Bigg\}. \tag{D.14}$$

From (D.12) and (D.14) we find that

$$p_S = \frac{1}{1-e^{-(\mu+\lambda)(D-S)}}[e^{-\lambda(D-S)} \int_S^D e^{-\mu(D-j)} f(j)dj + \frac{\mu}{\lambda} \int_S^D e^{-\lambda(j-S)} f(j)dj], \tag{D.15}$$

$$p_D = \frac{1}{1-e^{-(\mu+\lambda)(D-S)}}[e^{-\mu(D-S)} \int_S^D e^{-\lambda(j-S)} f(j)dj + \frac{\lambda}{\mu} \int_S^D e^{-\mu(D-j)} f(j)dj]. \tag{D.16}$$

For (D.13) with (D.15) and (D.16) we find as for the (s, S) policy (see Appendix D.1.1)

$$f_Y'''(x) = (\lambda - \mu) f_Y''(x)$$

which implies with the same arguments as in the case of the (s, S) policy that

$$f_Y(x) = \frac{ce^{(\lambda-\mu)x}}{(\lambda-\mu)^2} \tag{D.17}$$

where c is a constant.
Replacing f_Y in (D.15) and (D.16), respectively, yields to

$$p_S = \frac{ce^{\lambda S}}{(1-e^{-(\mu+\lambda)(D-S)})\lambda(\lambda-\mu)^2}[e^{-\mu S} - e^{-\lambda(D-S)-\mu D}] \tag{D.18}$$

$$p_D = \frac{ce^{-\mu D}}{(1-e^{-(\mu+\lambda)(D-S)})\mu(\lambda-\mu)^2}[e^{\lambda D} - e^{-\mu(D-S)+\lambda S}]. \tag{D.19}$$

Using $p_S + \int_S^D f_Y(y)dy + p_D = 1$ the value of the constant c can easily be determined. It is given by

$$c = \frac{\mu\lambda(\lambda-\mu)^3(1-e^{-(\lambda+\mu)(D-S)})}{\lambda^2 e^{-\mu D}(e^{\lambda D} - e^{-\mu(D-S)+\lambda S}) - \mu^2 e^{\lambda S}(e^{-\mu S} - e^{-\lambda(D-S)-\mu D})}. \tag{D.20}$$

With (D.20) in (D.17) – (D.19) we finally get

$$F_Y(y) = \int_S^D f_Y(x)dx + \mathbb{1}_{y=S}\, p_S + \mathbb{1}_{y=D}\, p_D \ ,$$

$$\text{with} \qquad f_Y(y) = \begin{cases} 0 & \text{for } y<S \\ p_S \lambda e^{(\lambda-\mu)(y-S)} & \text{for } S<y<D \\ 0 & \text{for } y>D \end{cases}$$

$$\text{and} \quad p_S = \tilde{c}_{(S,D)}\mu e^{\lambda S}(e^{-\mu S} - e^{-\lambda(D-S)-\mu D}) \qquad \text{for } y=S$$

$$\text{and} \quad p_D = \tilde{c}_{(S,D)}\lambda e^{-\mu D}(e^{\lambda D} - e^{-\mu(D-S)+\lambda S}) \qquad \text{for } y=D$$

where

$$\tilde{c}_{(S,D)} := \frac{\lambda - \mu}{\lambda^2 e^{-\mu D}(e^{\lambda D} - e^{-\mu(D-S)+\lambda S}) - \mu^2 e^{\lambda S}(e^{-\mu S} - e^{-\lambda(D-S)-\mu D})} .$$

D.2.2 Exponentially Distributed Demand and Returns

The starting point is (5.20). Using the stationary density of Y as depicted in Appendix D.2.1 we get

$$\pi_{S,D} = \sum_{\tau=1}^{H} \int_{(\tau-1)\hat{N}}^{\tau\hat{N}} \{\beta_1^\tau[1-\Phi_N(y-S)] + \sum_{\theta=2}^{H+1} \beta_\theta^\tau[\Phi_N(y-S-(\theta-2)\hat{N})$$

$$-\Phi_N(y-S-(\theta-1)\hat{N})] + \beta_{H+2}^\tau \Phi_N(y-S-H\hat{N})\} f_Y(y)dy$$

$$+ \int_{H\hat{N}}^{D-S} \{\beta_1^{H+1}[1-\Phi_N(y-S)] + \sum_{\theta=2}^{H+1} \beta_\theta^{H+1}[\Phi_N(y-S-(\theta-2)\hat{N})$$

$$-\Phi_N(y-S-(\theta-1)\hat{N})] + \beta_{H+2}^{H+1}\Phi_N(y-S-H\hat{N})\} f_Y(y)dy$$

$$+p_S\left[\beta_1^1[1-\Phi_N(0)] + \sum_{\theta=2}^{H+1} \beta_\theta^1[\Phi_N(-(\theta-2)\hat{N}) - \Phi_N(-(\theta-1)\hat{N})\right.$$

$$\left. +\beta_{H+2}^1 \Phi(-H\hat{N})\right]$$

$$+p_D \left[\beta_1^{H+1}[1 - \Phi_n(D-S)] + \sum_{\theta=2}^{H+1} \beta_\theta^{H+1}[\Phi_N(D-S-(\theta-2)\hat{N}) \right.$$
$$\left. -\Phi_N(D-S-(\theta-1)\hat{N})] + \beta_{H+2}^{H+1}\Phi_N(D-S-H\hat{N}) \right]$$

Let $U := Y - S$ and F_U denote the matching distribution. It is given by (see Appendix D.2.1)

$$F_U(u) = \int_0^{D-S} f_U(x)dx + 1\!\!1_{u=0}\, p_S + 1\!\!1_{u=D-S}\, p_D \,,$$

$$\text{with} \qquad f_U(u) = \begin{cases} 0 & \text{for } u<0 \\ p_S \lambda e^{(\lambda-\mu)u} & \text{for } 0<u<D-S \\ 0 & \text{for } u>D-S \end{cases}$$

$$\text{and} \quad p_S = \tilde{c}_{(S,D)} \mu e^{\lambda S}(e^{-\mu S} - e^{-\lambda(D-S)-\mu D}) \qquad \text{for } u=0$$

$$\text{and} \quad p_D = \tilde{c}_{(S,D)} \lambda e^{-\mu D}(e^{\lambda D} - e^{-\mu(D-S)+\lambda S}) \qquad \text{for } u=D-S$$

where

$$\tilde{c}_{(S,D)} := \frac{\lambda - \mu}{\lambda^2 e^{-\mu D}(e^{\lambda D} - e^{-\mu(D-S)+\lambda S}) - \mu^2 e^{\lambda S}(e^{-\mu S} - e^{-\lambda(D-S)-\mu D})}$$

Then by using (D.7) $\pi_{S,D}$ can be written as

$$\pi_{S,D} = \sum_{\tau=1}^{H} \int_{(\tau-1)\hat{N}}^{\tau\hat{N}} \left[\beta_1^\tau \int_u^\infty \phi_N(n)\, dn + \sum_{\theta=2}^{H+1} \beta_\theta^\tau \int_{u-(\theta-1)\hat{N}}^{u-(\theta-2)\hat{N}} \phi_N(n)\, dn \right.$$
$$\left. + \beta_{H+2}^\tau \int_{-\infty}^{u-H\hat{N}} \phi_N(n)\, dn \right] f_U(u)du$$
$$+ \int_{H\hat{N}}^{D-S} \left[\beta_1^{H+1} \int_u^\infty \phi_N(n)\, dn + \sum_{\theta=2}^{H+1} \beta_\theta^{H+1} \int_{u-(\theta-1)\hat{N}}^{u-(\theta-2)\hat{N}} \phi_N(n)\, dn \right.$$
$$\left. + \beta_{H+2}^{H+1} \int_{-\infty}^{u-H\hat{N}} \phi_N(n)\, dn \right] f_U(u)du \qquad \text{(D.21)}$$

$$+p_S\left[\beta_1^1\int_0^{\infty}\phi_N(n)\,dn+\sum_{\theta=2}^{H+1}\beta_\theta^1\int_{-(\theta-1)\hat{N}}^{-(\theta-2)\hat{N}}\phi_N(n)\,dn\right.$$

$$\left.+\,\beta_{H+2}^1\int_{-\infty}^{-H\hat{N}}\phi_N(n)\,dn\right]$$

$$+p_D\left[\beta_1^{H+1}\int_{D-S}^{\infty}\phi_N(n)\,dn+\sum_{\theta=2}^{H+1}\beta_\theta^{H+1}\int_{D-S-(\theta-1)\hat{N}}^{D-S-(\theta-2)\hat{N}}\phi_N(n)\,dn\right.$$

$$\left.+\,\beta_{H+2}^{H+1}\int_{-\infty}^{D-S-H\hat{N}}\phi_N(n)\,dn\right]$$

where $\phi_N(n)$ is given by (5.9).

Analogously to the (s,S) policy we find that

$$\int_u^{\infty}\phi_N(n)dn=\frac{\mu}{\mu+\lambda}\,e^{-\lambda u}$$

$$\int_{u-(\theta-1)\hat{N}}^{u-(\theta-2)\hat{N}}\phi_N(n)dn=\begin{cases}\frac{\mu}{\mu+\lambda}\,e^{-\lambda(u-(\theta-1)\hat{N})}(1-e^{-\lambda\hat{N}}) & \text{for } \theta\le u+1\\ 1-\frac{\mu}{\mu+\lambda}\,e^{-\lambda(u-(\theta-2)\hat{N})} & \\ -\frac{\lambda}{\mu+\lambda}e^{\mu(u-(\theta-1)\hat{N})} & \text{for } u+1<\theta\le u+2\\ \frac{\lambda}{\mu+\lambda}\,e^{\mu(u-(\theta-1)\hat{N})}(e^{\mu\hat{N}}-1) & \text{for } u+2<\theta\end{cases}$$

$$\int_{-\infty}^{u-H\hat{N}}\phi_N(n)dn=\begin{cases}1-\frac{\mu}{\mu+\lambda}\,e^{-\lambda(u-H\hat{N})} & \text{for } u=H+1\\ \frac{\lambda}{\mu+\lambda}\,e^{\mu(u-H\hat{N})} & \text{for } u\le H\end{cases}$$

Inserting the densities of N and U, and using the aforementioned results we get for the integrals in (D.21)

$$\int_{(\tau-1)\hat{N}}^{\tau\hat{N}}\int_u^{\infty}\phi_N(n)f_U(u)dndu=\tilde{p}e^{-\mu\tau\hat{N}}(e^{\mu\hat{N}}-1)$$

$$\int_{(\tau-1)\hat{N}}^{\tau\hat{N}} \int_{u-(\theta-1)\hat{N}}^{u-(\theta-2)\hat{N}} \phi_N(n) f_U(u) dn du = \begin{cases} \tilde{p}(1-e^{-\lambda\hat{N}})(e^{\mu\hat{N}}-1)e^{\lambda(\theta-1)\hat{N}}e^{-\mu\tau\hat{N}} & \text{for } \theta \le \tau \\ \frac{2\tilde{p}}{\mu-\lambda} e^{-(\mu-\lambda)\tau\hat{N}}(\lambda e^{(\mu-\lambda)\hat{N}} \\ +(\mu-\lambda)e^{-\lambda\hat{N}}-\mu) & \text{for } \theta=\tau+1 \\ \tilde{p}(1-e^{-\lambda\hat{N}})(e^{\mu\hat{N}}-1)e^{\lambda\tau\hat{N}}e^{-\mu(\theta-1)\hat{N}} & \text{for } \theta \ge \tau+2 \end{cases}$$

$$\int_{(\tau-1)\hat{N}}^{\tau\hat{N}} \int_{-\infty}^{u-H\hat{N}} \phi_N(n) f_U(u) dn du = \tilde{p} e^{-\mu H\hat{N}}(1-e^{-\lambda\hat{N}})e^{\lambda\tau\hat{N}}$$

$$\int_{H\hat{N}}^{D-S} \int_{u}^{\infty} \phi_N(n) f_U(u) dn du = \tilde{p}(e^{-\mu H\hat{N}} - e^{-\mu(D-S)})$$

$$\int_{H\hat{N}}^{D-S} \int_{u-(\theta-1)\hat{N}}^{u-(\theta-2)\hat{N}} \phi_N(n) f_U(u) dn du = \tilde{p}(1-e^{-\lambda\hat{N}})e^{\lambda(\theta-1)\hat{N}}(e^{-\mu H\hat{N}} - e^{-\mu(D-S)})$$

$$\int_{H\hat{N}}^{D-S} \int_{-\infty}^{u-H\hat{N}} \phi_N(n) f_U(u) dn du = \tilde{p}\,[\frac{\lambda+\mu}{\mu-\lambda}(e^{-(\mu-\lambda)H\hat{N}} - e^{-(\mu-\lambda)(D-S)}) + e^{\lambda H\hat{N}}(e^{-\mu(D-S)} - e^{-\mu H\hat{N}})]$$

where $\tilde{p} := \lambda/(\mu+\lambda)p_S$.

For ease of notation we set $c_\mu := (e^{\mu\hat{N}}-1)$, $c_\lambda := (1-e^{-\lambda\hat{N}})$, $c_D := e^{-\lambda(D-S)}$, and $c_{H_\mu} := e^{-\mu H\hat{N}}$, $c_{H_\lambda} := e^{\lambda H\hat{N}}$. Further we define $\tilde{c}_H := e^{-\mu H\hat{N}} - e^{-\mu(D-S)}$ as well as $\hat{c}_H := e^{-(\mu-\lambda)H\hat{N}} - e^{-(\mu-\lambda)(D-S)}$.

Then, we finally obtain

$$\pi_{S,D} = \frac{p_S}{\lambda+\mu}\left\{ \beta_1^1\mu + \beta_2^1\lambda(1-e^{-\mu\hat{N}}) + \sum_{\theta=3}^{H+1} \beta_\theta^1 \lambda c_\mu e^{-\mu(\theta-1))\hat{N}} + \beta_{H+2}^1 \lambda c_{H_\mu} \right\}$$

$$+\tilde{p}\left\{\sum_{\tau=1}^{H} \left[\beta_1^\tau c_\mu e^{-\mu\tau\hat{N}} + \sum_{\theta=2}^{\tau} \beta_\theta^\tau c_\mu c_\lambda e^{-(\mu\tau-\lambda(\theta-1))\hat{N}} \right.\right.$$

$$+ \frac{2\beta_{\tau+1}^\tau}{\mu-\lambda}(\lambda c_\mu(1-c_\lambda) - \mu c_\lambda)e^{-(\mu-\lambda)\tau\hat{N}}$$

$$+\sum_{\theta=\tau+2}^{H+1} \beta_\theta^\tau c_\mu c_\lambda e^{-(\mu(\theta-1)-\lambda\tau)\hat{N}} + \beta_{H+2}^\tau c_{H_\mu} c_\lambda e^{\lambda\tau\hat{N}}\Bigg]$$

$$+\beta_1^{H+1}\tilde{c}_H + \sum_{\theta=2}^{H+1} \beta_\theta^{H+1}\tilde{c}_H c_\lambda e^{\lambda(\theta-1))\hat{N}}$$

$$+\beta_{H+2}^{H+1}(\frac{\lambda+\mu}{\mu-\lambda}\hat{c}_H - c_{H_\lambda}\tilde{c}_H)\Bigg\}$$

$$+\frac{p_D}{\lambda+\mu}\Bigg\{\beta_1^{H+1}\mu c_D + \sum_{\theta=2}^{H+1} \beta_\theta^{H+1}\mu c_D c_\lambda e^{\lambda(\theta-1))\hat{N}}$$

$$+\beta_{H+2}^{H+1}(\lambda+\mu-\mu c_D c_{H_\lambda})\Bigg\}.$$

List of Abbreviations

Abbreviation	Meaning
BOM	Bill of Material
cd2	squared coefficient of demand variation
cdf	cumulative distribution function
ECR	Efficient Consumer Response
e.g.	for example
ERP	Enterprise Resource Planning
EOQ	Economic Order Quantity
FiRST	Flexible intergral Requirements planning STrategy
FOQ	Fixed Order Quantity
gcd	greatest common divisor
i.e.	id est
JIT	Just-in-Time
KrW-/AbfG	Commercial and Industrial Waste Avoidance Management Act (Kreislaufwirtschafts- und Abfallgesetz)
LIF	Lot-size Inflexibility Factor
LRP	Line Requirements Planning
max	maximum operator
min	minimum operator
mod	mode operator
MPS	Master Production Schedule
MRP	Material Requirements Planning
no.	number
p.	page
PI	setup stability
POQ	Period Order Quantity
pp.	pages
q.e.d.	quod erat demonstrandum
SIC	Stochastic Inventory Control
TBO	Time Between Orders

List of Symbols

Nervousness and stability measures

Symbol	Meaning
ν_S	setup oriented nervousness measure
ν_Q	quantity oriented nervousness measure
π_S	setup stability
$\bar{\pi}_S$	setup stability with equally weighted periods
π_{IS}	short-term setup stability
π_Q	quantity stability
$\bar{\pi}_Q$	quantity stability with equally weighted periods
π_{IQ}	short-term quantity stability
$\pi_{s,S}$, $\pi_{s,nQ}$	setup stability for (s, S) policy, and (s, nQ) policy, respectively
$\pi^A_{s,S}$, $\pi^A_{s,nQ}$	setup stability for $Q \leq \hat{D}$ ((s, S) and (s, nQ) policy)
$\pi^B_{s,S}$, $\pi^B_{s,nQ}$	setup stability for $Q > \hat{D}$ ((s, S) and (s, nQ) policy)
$\pi^{rec}_{s,S}$	setup stability for (s, S) policy in recovery system without disposal option, with fixed production costs
$\pi_{S,D}$	setup stability for (S, D) policy in recovery system with disposal option, without fixed production costs
π^{rec}_S	setup stability for S policy in recovery system without disposal option, without fixed production costs
$\pi^{disposal}_S$	setup stability for S policy in recovery system with disposal option, without fixed production costs

Variables and parameters within planning framework

Symbol	Meaning
a	weight parameter for periods
$\bar{D}$, $\hat{D}$	expected, forecasted demand per period
D_t, $\hat{D}^j_t$	stochastic demand in period t, demand in t as projected in cycle j
D_{max}	maximum reasonable demand per period
M	total number of orders over all planning cycles

M_t	disposal quantity in period t
N	number of planning cycles
$\bar{N}$, $\hat{N}$	expected, forecasted net demand per period
N_t, $\hat{N}_t^j$	stochastic net demand in period t, net demand in t as projected in cycle j
O_t ($\hat{O}_t^j$)	remanufacturing order size in period t (as planned in cycle j)
P	length of planning horizon
q_t ($\hat{q}_t^j$)	replenishment order in period t (as planned in cycle j)
$\hat{Q}_t$ ($\hat{Q}_t^j$)	production order size in period t (as planned in cycle j)
$\bar{R}$, $\hat{R}$	expected, forecasted returns per period
R_t, $\hat{R}_t^j$	stochastic returns in period t, returns in t as projected in cycle j
T	stability horizon parameter
V_t	stochastic difference between net stock at the beginning of t after replenishment and reorder point s
X_t	stochastic difference between maximum and actual stock at the beginning of t
Y_t	stochastic stock level after replenishment at the beginning of t
$\hat{Y}_t^j$	stock level after replenishment at the beginning of t as planned in cycle j
Z_t	stochastic stock level before replenishment at the beginning of t
$\hat{Z}_t^j$	stock level before replenishment at the beginning of t as planned in cycle j
ΔP	length of frozen zone
Δq_{max}	maximum quantity that can be changed between two successive planning cycles
Λ	lead time, or throughput time, respectively

Variables and parameters of decision rules

Symbol	Meaning
B	stabilization parameter
D	dispose-down-to-level
H	parameter for (S, D) policy, $H = \begin{cases} T & \text{if } T \leq K \\ K & \text{else} \end{cases}$
K	range parameter in the case of (S, D) policy

L	number of order sequences for (s,S) policy
l	coverage parameter for (s,S) policy
n_t $(\hat{n}_t^j)$	multiplier for lot size Q in the case of an (s,nQ) policy in period t (as projected in cycle j)
Q	(minimum) lot size
R	number of time periods between ordering for (R,S) policy
s	reorder point
S	order-up-to-level
ζ	numerator of lot size Q in the case of (s,nQ) policy
η	denominator of lot size Q in the case of (s,nQ) policy

Stability quotients

Symbol	Meaning
α_θ	stability quotient for $Q \leq \hat{D}$ (for (s,S) and (s,nQ) policy)
β_θ^τ	stability quotient for $Q > \hat{D}$ (for (s,S) policy)
$\beta_{\vartheta,\kappa}^\omega$	stability quotient for $Q > \hat{D}$ (for (s,nQ) policy)
$\bar{\alpha}_\theta$, $\bar{\beta}_\theta^\tau$, $\bar{\beta}_{\vartheta,\kappa}^\omega$	stability quotients with equally weighted periods
τ	period with first setup in cycle 0 for (s,S) policy
θ	period with first setup in cycle 1 for (s,S) policy
ω	inventory case parameter for $Q > \hat{D}$ in the case of (s,nQ) policy
ϑ, κ	demand case parameters for $Q > \hat{D}$ in the case of (s,nQ) policy

Indices, Sets, and Functions

Symbol	Meaning
p, k, μ	parameter of Erlangian $E_{k-1,k}$ distribution
p, μ_1, μ_2	parameter of hyperexponential H_2 distribution
γ, ρ	parameter of renewal function
t	period index
c_D	coefficient of demand variation
σ_D	standard deviation of demand
$\phi_D(.)$, $\phi_R(.)$, $\phi_N(.)$	density function of demand, returns, and net demand, respectively
$\Phi_D(.)$, $\Phi_R(.)$, $\Phi_N(.)$	cdf of demand, returns and net demand, respectively
$\mathbb{E}(W)$	expected value of a stochastic variable W
E_k	Erlang-k distribution

$f_V(.)$, $f_X(.)$, $f_Y(.)$	density function of V, X, and Y, respectively
$F_V(.)$, $F_X(.)$, $F_Y(.)$	cdf of V, X, and Y, respectively
$M(.)$	renewal function
p_Q	probability mass at $v = Q$
$\mathbb{P}\{W\}$	probability of W
$\mathbb{N}$	set of natural numbers
$\mathbb{R}$	set of rational numbers
$\lceil x \rceil$	next integer equal to or larger than x
$\|\lceil x \rceil\|$	next integer larger than x
$\lfloor x \rfloor$	next integer equal to or smaller than x
δ	Kronecker-symbol: $\delta(x) = \begin{cases} 1 & \text{if} \quad x > 0 \\ 0 & \text{else} \end{cases}$
$[x]^+$	indicator function: $[x]^+ = \begin{cases} x & \text{if} \quad x > 0 \\ 0 & \text{else} \end{cases}$
$1\!\!1_{x=y}$	indicator function: $1\!\!1_{x=y} = \begin{cases} 1 & \text{if} \quad x = y \\ 0 & \text{else} \end{cases}$

List of Figures

List of Tables

References

1. Alscher, J., and H. Schneider (1982) *Zur Interdependenz von Fehlmengenkosten und Servicegrad.* Kostenrechnungs-Praxis 6, 257-271
2. Arthur Andersen Report (1987) *Cars and Competition: Management Challenges.* Chicago, IL: Arthur Andersen & Co.
3. Axsäter, S., Ch. Schneeweiß and E.A. Silver (eds.) *Multi-stage production planning and inventory control.* Berlin, 1986
4. Anderson, E.J., and A.G. Lagodimos (1989) *Service levels in single-stage MRP systems with demand uncertainty.* Engineering Costs and Production Economics 17, 125-133
5. Baker, K.R. (1977) *An experimental study of the effectiveness of rolling schedules in production planning.* Decision Sciences 8, 19-27
6. Baker, K.R., and D.W. Peterson (1979) *An analytic framework for evaluating rolling schedules.* Management Science 25, 341-351
7. Baker, K.R. *Requirements planning.* In: [42] Graves, S.C., A.H.G. Rinnooy Kan, and P.H. Zipkin (eds.) *Handbook in Operations Research and Management Science (Volume 4): Logistics of production and inventory.* Amsterdam, 1993, 571-627
8. Bartezzaghi, E., and R. Verganti (1995) *Managing demand uncertainty through order overplanning.* International Journal of Production Economics 40, 107-120
9. Bean, J., R. Smith, and C. Yano (1987) *Forecast horizons for the discounted dynamic lot size model allowing speculative motive.* Naval Research Logistics 34, 761-774
10. Blackburn, J.D., and R.A. Millen (1980) *Heuristic lot-sizing performance in a rolling-schedule environment.* Decision Sciences 11, 691-701
11. Blackburn, J.D., and R.A. Millen (1982a) *The impact of a rolling schedule in a multi-level MRP system.* Journal of Operations Management 2(2), 125-135
12. Blackburn, J.D., and R.A. Millen (1982b) *Improved heuristics for multi-stage requirements planning systems.* Management Science 28(1), 44-56
13. Blackburn, J.D., D.H. Kropp, and R.A. Millen (1985) *MRP system nervousness: causes and cures.* Engineering Costs and Production Economics 9, 141-146
14. Blackburn, J.D., D.H. Kropp, and R.A. Millen (1986) *A comparison of strategies to dampen nervousness in MRP systems.* Management Science 32, 413-429
15. Blackburn, J.D., D.H. Kropp, and R.A. Millen (1987) *Alternative approaches to schedule instability: a comparative analysis.* International Journal of Production Research 25, 1739-1749
16. Blackburn, J.D., and H. Kunreuther (1974) *Planning horizons for the dynamic lot size model with backlogging.* Management Science 21, 251-255
17. Bronstein, I.N., and K.A. Semendjajew (1990) *Ergänzende Kapitel zum Taschenbuch der Mathematik.* 6. Aufl., Teubner, Leipzig
18. Buzacott, J.A., and J.G. Shanthikumar (1994) *Safety stock versus safety time in MRP controlled production systems.* Management Science 40(12), 1678-1689

19. Campbell, G.M. (1992) *Master production scheduling under rolling planning horizons with fixed order intervals.* Decisions Sciences 23, 312-331
20. Campbell, K.L. (1971) *Scheduling is not the problem.* Production and Inventory Management 12(3), 53-60
21. Carlson, R.C., S.L. Beckman, and D.H. Kropp (1982) *The effectiveness of extending the horizon in rolling production scheduling.* Decision Sciences 13, 129-146
22. Carlson, R.C., J.V. Jucker, and D.H. Kropp (1979) *Less Nervous MRP Systems: A Dynamic Economic Lot-Sizing Approach.* Management Science 25, 754-761
23. Carlson, R.C., and D.H. Yano (1986) *Safety stocks in MRP Systems with emergency setups for components.* Management Science 32, 403-412
24. Chapman, S.N. (1990) *Schedule stability and the implementation of Just-In-Time.* Production and Inventory Management Journal 31(3), 66-70
25. Chu, C.-H., and J.C. Hayya (1988) *Buffering decisions under MRP environment: A review.* Omega 16, 325-331
26. Chung, C.-H. and L.J. Krajewski *Replanning frequencies for Master Production Schedules.* Decision Sciences 17, 263-273
27. Clark, A.J., and H. Scarf (1960) *Optimal policies for a multi-echelon inventory problem.* Management Science 6, 475-490
28. Cohen, M.A., S. Nahmias, and W.P. Pierskalla (1980) *A dynamic inventory system with recycling.* Naval Research Logistics Quarterly 27(2): 289-296
29. Daniels, R.L., and P. Kouvelis (1995) *Robust scheduling to hedge against processing time uncertainty in single-stage production.* Management Science 41(2), 363-376
30. De Kok, A.G. (1985) *Computational results for a dam problem with variable release rate and service level constraints.* Communications in Statistics-Stochastic Models 1, 291-315
31. De Kok, A.G., *Production-inventory control models: approximations and algorithms.* CWI, Amsterdam, 1987
32. De Kok, A.G., and K. Inderfurth (1997) *Nervousness in inventory management: comparison of basic control rules.* European Journal of Operations Research 103, 55-82
33. De Leeuw, A.C.J, and H.W. Volberda (1996) *On the concept of flexibility: A dual control perspective.* Omega 24, 121-139
34. Federgruen, A., and M. Tzur (1994) *Minimal forecast horizons and a new planning procedure for the general dynamic lot sizing model: nervousness revisited.* Operations Research 42(3), 456-468
35. Federgruen, A., and M. Tzur (1995) *Fast solution and detection of minimal forecast horizons in dynamic programs with a single indicator of the future: applications to dynamic lot-sizing models.* Management Science 41, 874-893
36. Fleischmann, M., J.M. Bloemhof-Ruwaard, R. Dekker, E. van der Laan, J.A.E.E. van Nunen, and L.N. van Wassenhove (1997) *Quantitative models for reverse logistics: A review.* European Journal of Operations Research 103, 1-17
37. Fleischmann, M., and R. Kuik (1998) *On optimal Inventory Control with Stochastic Item Returns.* Management Report No. 21, Erasmus University Rotterdam
38. Fleischmann, M., R. Kuik, and R. Dekker (1999) *Controlling inventories with stochastic item returns: A basic model.* To appear in European Journal of Operational Research
39. Frosch, R.A. (1995) *Industrial ecology: adapting technology for a sustainable world.* Environment 37(10), 16-37
40. Forrester, J.W. *Industrial Dynamics.* MIT Press, Cambridge, MA, 1961

41. Grasso, E.T., and B.W. Taylor (1984) *A simulation-based experimental investigation of supply/timing uncertainty in MRP systems.* International Journal of Production Research 22(3), 485-497
42. Graves, S.C., A.H.G. Rinnooy Kan, and P.H. Zipkin (eds.) *Handbook in Operations Research and Management Science (Volume 4): Logistics of production and inventory.* Elsevier, Amsterdam, 1993
43. Grubbström, R.W. et al. (eds.) *Production Economics: Issues and challenges for the 90th.* Elsevier, Amsterdam, 1991
44. Grubbström, R.W., and O. Tang *Modelling rescheduling activities in a multi-period production-inventory system.* Tenth International Working Seminar on Production Economics, Pre-Prints Vol. 2, Igls, 1998, 67-84
45. Gungor, A., and S.M. Gupta (2000) *Issues in environmentally conscious manufacturing and product recovery: a survey.* To appear in Computers and Industrial Engineering
46. Gupta, S.K. and J. Rosenhaed (1968) *Robustness in sequential investment decisions.* Management Science 15, B18-B29
47. Hadley, G., and T.M. Whitin, *Analysis of inventory systems.* Prentice-Hall, New Jersey, 1963
48. Hanssmann, F. *Einführung in die Systemforschung.* München und Wien, 1987
49. Heisig, G. (1998) *Planning stability under (s,S) Inventory Control Rules.* OR Spektrum 20, 215-228
50. Heisig, G., and M. Fleischmann (2001) *Planning stability in a product recovery system.* OR Spektrum 23, 25-50
51. Heyman, D.P. (1977) *Optimal disposal policies for a single-item inventory system with returns.* Naval Research Logistics Quaterly 24, 385-405
52. Hillier, F.S., and G.J. Lieberman. *Introduction to Operations Research.* Fifth edition, McGraw-Hill, 1990
53. Ho, C. (1989) *Evaluating the impact of operating environments on MRP system nervousness.* International Journal of Production Research 27(7), 1115-1135
54. Ho, C. (1992) *An examination of dampening procedures considering rescheduling costs.* Omega 20(2), 257-269
55. Ho, C., and P.L. Carter (1996) *An investigation of alternative dampening procedures to cope with MRP system nervousness.* International Journal of Production Research 34(1), 137-156
56. Ho, C., and T.C. Ireland (1993) *A diagnostic analysis of the impact of forecast errors on production planning via MRP system nervousness.* Production Planning & Control 4(4), 311-322
57. Ho, C., and T.C. Ireland (1998) *Correlating MRP system nervousness with forecast errors.* International Journal of Production Research 36(8), 2285-2299
58. Ho, C., W.-K. Law, and R. Rampal (1995) *Uncertainty-dampening methods for reducing MRP system nervousness.* International Journal of Production Research 33(2), 483-496
59. Ho, C., R. Narasimhan, S.A. Melnyk, and P.L.Carter (1992) *Research framework for investigating the effectiveness of dampening procedures to cope with MRP system nervousness.* International Journal of Operations & Production Management 12(6), 30-43
60. Inderfurth, K. *Safety stock optimization in multi-stage inventory systems.* In: [43] Grubbström, R.W. et al. (eds.) *Production Economics: Issues and challenges for the 90th.* Amsterdam, 1991
61. Inderfurth, K. (1994) *Nervousness in inventory control: analytical results.* OR Spektrum 16, 113-123
62. Inderfurth, K., and T. Jensen (1997) *Planungsnervosität im Rahmen der Produktionsplanung und -steuerung.* ZfB 8, 817-843

63. Inderfurth, K. (1997) *Simple optimal replenishment and disposal policies for a product recovery system with leadtimes.* OR Spektrum 19:111-122
64. Inderfurth, K., and T. Jensen *Analysis of MRP Policies with Recovery Options.* In: [81] Leopold-Wildburger, U., G. Feichtinger, and K.-P. Kistner (eds.) *Modelling and Decisions in Economics.* Physica, Heidelberg, 189-228
65. Inderfurth,K., and S. Minner (1998) *Safety stocks in multi-stage inventory systems under different service measures.* European Journal of Operational Research 106, 57-73
66. Inman, R.R., and D.J.A. Gonsalvez (1997) *The Causes of Schedule Instability in an Automative Supply Chain.* Production and Inventory Management 38, 2nd Quarter, 26-31
67. Jensen, T. (1993) *Measuring and improving planning stability of reorder-point lot-sizing policies.* International Journal of Production Economics 30-31, 167-178
68. Jensen, T., *Planungsstabilität in der Material-Logistik.* PhD thesis, Physica, Heidelberg, 1996
69. Kadipasaoglu, S.N. (1995) *The effect of freezing the master production schedule on cost in multilevel MRP systems.* Production and Inventory Management 36, Third Quarter, 30-36
70. Kadipasaoglu, S.N., and S.V. Sridharan (1995) *Alternative approaches for reducing instability in multistage manufacturing under demand uncertainty.* Journal of Operations Management 13, 193-211
71. Kadipasaoglu, S.N., and S.V. Sridharan (1997) *Measurement of instability in multi-level MRP systems.* International Journal of Production Research 35, 713-737
72. Kelle, P., and E.A. Silver (1989) *Purchasing policy of new containers considering the random returns of previously issued containers.* IIE Transactions 21(4), 349-354
73. Kimms, A. (1998) *Stability measures for rolling schedules with applications to capacity expansion planning, master production scheduling, and lot sizing.* Omega 26(3), 355-366
74. Kouvelis, P.; A.A. Kurawarwala; and G.J. Gutierrez (1992) *Algorithms for robust single and multiple period layout planning for manufacturing systems.* European Journal of Operational Research 63, 287-303
75. Kropp, D.H., R.C. Carlson, and J.V. Jucker (1983) *Heuristic lot-sizing approaches for dealing with MRP system nervousness.* Decision Sciences 14, 156-169
76. Kropp, D.H., and R.C. Carlson (1984) *A Lot-Sizing Algorithm for Reducing Nervousness in MRP Systems.* Management Science 30, 240-244
77. Kühn, M. *Flexibilität in logistischen Systemen.* Heidelberg 1989
78. Lagodimos, A.G., and E.J. Anderson (1993) *Optimal positioning of safety stocks in MRP.* International Journal of Production Research 31, 1797-1813
79. Lasserre, J.B. and C. Mercè (1990) *Robust Hierarcical Production Planning under Uncertainty.* Annals of Operations Research 26, 73-87
80. Lee, H.L., and S. Nahmias *Single-Product, Single-Location Models.* In: [42] Graves, S.C., A.H.G. Rinnooy Kan, and P.H. Zipkin (eds.) *Handbook in Operations Research and Management Science (Volume 4): Logistics of production and inventory.* Amsterdam, 1993, 3-55
81. Leopold-Wildburger, U., G. Feichtinger, and K.-P. Kistner (eds.) *Modelling and Decisions in Economics.* Physica, Heidelberg
82. Lin, N.-P., and L. Krajewski (1992) *A model for master production scheduling in uncertain environments.* Decision Sciences 23, 839-861

83. Lundin, R.A., and T.E. Morton (1975) *Planning horizons for the dynamic lot size model: Zabel vs. protective procedures and computational results.* Operations Research 23, 711-734
84. Mabini M.C., L.M. Pintelon, and L.F. Gelders (1992) *EOQ type formulations for controlling repairable inventories.* International Journal of Production Economics 28, 21-33
85. Magee, J.E., *Production Planning and Inventory Control.* McGraw-Hill, New York, 1958
86. Mather, H. (1977) *Reschedule the reschedules you just rescheduled–way of life for MRP?* Production and Inventory Management 18, First Quarter, 60-79
87. Meier-Barthold, D., *Flexibilität in der Material-Logistik.* Gabler, Wiesbaden, 1999
88. Miller, J.G. *Hedging the Master Schedule.* In: [107] Ritzman, L.P. et al. (eds.) *Disaggregation problems in manufacturing and service organisation.* Boston, 1979, 237-256
89. Milwaukee Chapter Inc. (1977) *MRP symposium.* Production and Inventory Management 18, Second Quarter, 29-39
90. Minifie, J.R., and R.A. Davis (1986) *Survey of MRP nervousness issues.* Production and Inventory Management 27, Third Quarter, 111-120
91. Minifie, J.R., and R.A. Davis (1990) *Interaction effects on MRP nervousness.* International Journal of Production Research 28, 173-183
92. Minner, S., *Strategic safety stocks in supply chains.* PhD thesis, Otto-von-Guericke-Universität Magdeburg, 1999
93. Muckstadt, J.A., and H.M. Isaac (1981) *An analysis of single item inventory systems with returns.* Naval Research Logistics Quarterly, 28, 237-254
94. Murthy, D.N.P., and L. Ma (1991) *MRP with uncertainty: A review and some extensions.* International Journal of Production Economics 25, 51-64
95. Nahmias, S., *Production and Operations Analysis.* 3rd edition, McGraw-Hill, Irwin, 1997
96. Nasr, N. (1997) *Environmentally conscious manufacturing.* Careers and the Engineer, Spring 1997, 26-27
97. Orlicky, J.A., *Material requirements planning.* McGraw Hill, 1975
98. Orlicky, J.A. (1976) *Rescheduling with tomorrow's MRP system.* Production and Inventory Management 17, Second Quarter, 38-48
99. Penlesky, R.J., W.L. Berry, and U. Wemmerlöv (1989) *Open order due data maintenance in MRP systems.* Management Science 35(5), 571-584
100. Penlesky, R.J., U. Wemmerlöv, and W.L. Berry (1991) *Filtering heuristics for reschuling in open orders MRP systems.* International Journal of Production Research 29, 2279-2296
101. Portioli, A. (1998) *Investigation on the relative performances of overplanning and safety stocks.* Tenth International Working Seminar on Production Economics, Pre-Prints Vol. 2, Igls, 1998, 279-293
102. Pyke, D.F., and M.A. Cohen (1990) *Push and pull in manufacturing and distribution systems.* Journal of Operations Management 9(1), 24-43
103. Richter, K. (1987) *Stability of the constant cost dynamic lot size model.* European Journal of Operational Research 31, 61-65
104. Richter, K. (1996) *The extended EOQ repair and waste disposal model.* International Journal of Production Economics 45, 443-448
105. Richter and Vörös (1989) *On the stability region for mulit-level inventory problems.* European Journal of Operational Research 411, 169-173
106. Richter and Vörös (1990) *Stability of a two-stage production and inventory model.* Engineering Costs and Production Economics 20, 65-71

107. Ritzman, L.P. et al (eds.), *Disaggregation problems in manufacturing and service organisation.* Boston, 1979
108. Rosenblatt, M.J., and H.L. Lee (1987) *A robustness approach to facilities design.* International Journal of Production Research 25, 479-486
109. Rosenhead, J.; M. Elton; and S.K. Gupta (1972) *Robustness and optimality as criteria for strategic decisions.* Operations Research Quarterly 23, 413-431
110. Schrady, D.A. (1967) *A deterministic inventory model for repairable items.* Naval Research Logistics Quarterly 14, 391-398
111. Schmitt, T.G. (1984) *Resolving uncertainty in manufacturing systems.* Journal of Operations Management 4(4), 331-345
112. Schneeweiß , Ch., *Some modelling theoretic remarks on multi-stage production planning.* In: [3] Axsäter, S., Ch. Schneeweiß and E.A. Silver (eds.) *Multi-stage production planning and inventory control.* Berlin, 1986, 1-8
113. Schneeweiß , Ch., *Planung (Band 2) - Konzepte der Prozeß - und Modellgestaltung.* Berlin, 1992
114. Schneider, H., and J.L. Ringuest (1990) *Power approximation for computing (s, S) policies using service level.* Management Science 39, 822-834
115. Sherbrooke, C.C. *Optimal inventory modeling of systems, mulit-echelon techniques.* John Wiley & Sons, New York, 1992
116. Silver E.A., D.F. Pyke, and R. Peterson, *Inventory Management and Production Planning and Scheduling.* 3rd edition, John Wiley & Sons, New York, 1998
117. Simpson, V.P. (1978) *Optimum solution structure for a repairable inventory problem.* Operations Reseaarch 26(2), 270-281
118. Spencer, M.S., and J.F. Cox (1994) *Sales and manufacturing coordination in repetitive manufacturing: Characteristics and Problems.* International Journal of Production Econimics 37, 73-81
119. Sridharan, S.V., W.L. Berry, and V. Udayabhanu (1987) *Freezing the master production schedule under rolling planning horizons.* Management Science 33, 1137-1149
120. Sridharan, S.V., W.L. Berry, and V. Udayabhanu (1988) *Measuring master production schedule stability under rolling planning horizons.* Decision Sciences 19, 147-166
121. Sridharan, S.V., and W.L. Berry (1990) *Master production scheduling make-to-stock products: a framework analysis.* International Journal of Production Research 28, 541-558
122. Sridharan, S.V., and R.L. LaForge (1989) *The impact of safety stock on schedule instability, cost and service.* Journal of Operations Management 8(4), 327-347
123. Sridharan, S.V., and R.L. LaForge (1990) *An analysis of alternative policies to achieve schedule stability.* Journal of Manufacturing and Operations Management 3, 53-73
124. Steele, D.C. (1975) *The nervous MRP system: How to do battle.* Production and Inventory Management 16, Second Quarter, 1-18
125. Stockinger, S. and R. Dutter (1987) *Robust Time Series Analysis: A survey* Kybernetika 23, 1-90
126. Tempelmeier, H., *Material-Logistik.* 4th edition, Springer, Berlin, 1999
127. Thierry, M., *An analysis of the impact of product recovery management on manufacturing companies.* PhD thesis, Erasmus University Rotterdam, Rotterdam, 1997
128. Tijms, H.C., *Stochastic models: an algorithmic approach.* Wiley, New York, 1994

129. Van der Laan, E.A., and M. Salomon (1997) *Production planning and inventory control with remanufacturing and disposal.* European Journal of Operational Research 102, 264-278
130. Van der Laan, E.A., M. Salomon, R. Dekker, and L.N. van Wassenhove (1999) *Inventory control in hybrid systems with remanufacturing.* Management Science 45(5), 733-747
131. Van Donselaar, K., *Material coordination under uncertainty.* PhD thesis, Eindhoven, 1989
132. Van Donselaar, K. (1992) *The use of MRP and LRP in a stochastic environment.* Production Planning & Control 3(3), 239-246
133. Van Donselaar, K., Van den Nieuwenhof, J., and J. Visschers (2000) *The impact of material coordination concepts on planning stability in supply chains.* Submitted to International Journal of Production Economics
134. Venkataraman R. (1996) *Frequency of replanning in a rolling horizon master production schedule for a process industry environment: A case study.* Production and Operations Management 5(3), 255-265
135. Vollmann, T.E., W.L. Berry, and D.C. Whybark, *Manufacturing planning and control systems.* 4th edition, Irwin, Homewood, Ill., 1997
136. Wagner, H.M., and T.M. Whitin (1958) *Dynamic version of the economic lot size model.* Management Science 5, 89-96
137. Weinmann, A. *Uncertain models and robust control.* Wien u. New York, 1991
138. Wemmerlöv, U. (1979) *Design factors in MRP systems: A limited survey.* Production and Inventory Management 20, Fourth Quarter, 15-35
139. Wemmerlöv, U., and D.C. Whybark (1984) *Lot-sizing under uncertainty in a rolling schedule environment.* International Journal of Production Research 22(3), 467-484
140. Wemmerlöv, U. (1986) *A time-phased order-point system in environments with and without demand uncertainty: a comparative analysis of non-monetary performance variables.* International Journal of Production Research 24(2), 343-358
141. Whybark, D.C., and J.G. Williams (1976) *Material requirements planning under uncertainty.* Decision Sciences 7, 595-606
142. Wijngaard, J., and J.C. Wortmann (1985) *MRP and Inventories.* European Journal of Operational Research 20, 281-293
143. Wild, B. *Die Flexibilität von Betriebsvereinbarungen zur Arbeitszeit.* Physica, Heidelberg, 1995
144. Yano, C.A., and R.C. Carlson (1987) *Interaction between frequency of rescheduling and the role of safety stock in material requirements planning systems.* International Journal of Production Research 25, 221-232
145. Yuan X.-M., and K.L. Cheung (1998) *Modeling returns of merchandise in an inventory system.* OR Spektrum 20(3), 147-154
146. Zäpfel, G. (1996) *Auftragsgetriebene Produktion zur Bewältigung der Nachfrageungewißheit.* Zeitschrift für Betriebswirtschaft 66, 861-877
147. Zahn, E., and U. Schmid, *Produktionswirtschaft I: Grundlagen und operatives Produktionsmanagement.* Lucius & und Lucius Verlag, Stuttgart, 1996
148. Zhao, X., J.C. Goodale J.C., and T.S. Lee (1995) *Lot-sizing rules and freezing the master production schedule in material requirements planning systems under demand uncertainty.* International Journal of Production Research 33(8), 2241-2276
149. Zhao, X., and K. Lam (1997) *Lot-sizing rules and freezing the master production schedule in material requirements planning systems.* International Journal of Production Economics 53, 281-305

150. Zhao, X., and T.S. Lee (1993) *Freezing the master production schedule for material requirements planning systems under demand uncertainty.* Journal of Operations Management 11, 185-205
151. Zhao, X., and T.S. Lee (1996) *Freezing the master production schedule in multilevel material requirements planning systems under deterministic demand.* Production Planning & Control 7(2), 144-161

Printing: Strauss GmbH, Mörlenbach
Binding: Schäffer, Grünstadt

Lecture Notes in Economics and Mathematical Systems

For information about Vols. 1–320
please contact your bookseller or Springer-Verlag

Vol. 325: P. Ferri, E. Greenberg, The Labor Market and Business Cycle Theories. X, 183 pages. 1989.

Vol. 326: Ch. Sauer, Alternative Theories of Output, Unemployment, and Inflation in Germany: 1960–1985. XIII, 206 pages. 1989.

Vol. 327: M. Tawada, Production Structure and International Trade. V, 132 pages. 1989.

Vol. 328: W. Güth, B. Kalkofen, Unique Solutions for Strategic Games. VII, 200 pages. 1989.

Vol. 329: G. Tillmann, Equity, Incentives, and Taxation. VI, 132 pages. 1989.

Vol. 330: P.M. Kort, Optimal Dynamic Investment Policies of a Value Maximizing Firm. VII, 185 pages. 1989.

Vol. 331: A. Lewandowski, A.P. Wierzbicki (Eds.), Aspiration Based Decision Support Systems. X, 400 pages. 1989.

Vol. 332: T.R. Gulledge, Jr., L.A. Litteral (Eds.), Cost Analysis Applications of Economics and Operations Research. Proceedings. VII, 422 pages. 1989.

Vol. 333: N. Dellaert, Production to Order. VII, 158 pages. 1989.

Vol. 334: H.-W. Lorenz, Nonlinear Dynamical Economics and Chaotic Motion. XI, 248 pages. 1989.

Vol. 335: A.G. Lockett, G. Islei (Eds.), Improving Decision Making in Organisations. Proceedings. IX, 606 pages. 1989.

Vol. 336: T. Puu, Nonlinear Economic Dynamics. VII, 119 pages. 1989.

Vol. 337: A. Lewandowski, I. Stanchev (Eds.), Methodology and Software for Interactive Decision Support. VIII, 309 pages. 1989.

Vol. 338: J.K. Ho, R.P. Sundarraj, DECOMP: An Implementation of Dantzig-Wolfe Decomposition for Linear Programming. VI, 206 pages.

Vol. 339: J. Terceiro Lomba, Estimation of Dynamic Econometric Models with Errors in Variables. VIII, 116 pages. 1990.

Vol. 340: T. Vasko, R. Ayres, L. Fontvieille (Eds.), Life Cycles and Long Waves. XIV, 293 pages. 1990.

Vol. 341: G.R. Uhlich, Descriptive Theories of Bargaining. IX, 165 pages. 1990.

Vol. 342: K. Okuguchi, F. Szidarovszky, The Theory of Oligopoly with Multi-Product Firms. V, 167 pages. 1990.

Vol. 343: C. Chiarella, The Elements of a Nonlinear Theory of Economic Dynamics. IX, 149 pages. 1990.

Vol. 344: K. Neumann, Stochastic Project Networks. XI, 237 pages. 1990.

Vol. 345: A. Cambini, E. Castagnoli, L. Martein, P Mazzoleni, S. Schaible (Eds.), Generalized Convexity and Fractional Programming with Economic Applications. Proceedings, 1988. VII, 361 pages. 1990.

Vol. 346: R. von Randow (Ed.), Integer Programming and Related Areas. A Classified Bibliography 1984–1987. XIII, 514 pages. 1990.

Vol. 347: D. Ríos Insua, Sensitivity Analysis in Multi-objective Decision Making. XI, 193 pages. 1990.

Vol. 348: H. Störmer, Binary Functions and their Applications. VIII, 151 pages. 1990.

Vol. 349: G.A. Pfann, Dynamic Modelling of Stochastic Demand for Manufacturing Employment. VI, 158 pages. 1990.

Vol. 350: W.-B. Zhang, Economic Dynamics. X, 232 pages. 1990.

Vol. 351: A. Lewandowski, V. Volkovich (Eds.), Multiobjective Problems of Mathematical Programming. Proceedings, 1988. VII, 315 pages. 1991.

Vol. 352: O. van Hilten, Optimal Firm Behaviour in the Context of Technological Progress and a Business Cycle. XII, 229 pages. 1991.

Vol. 353: G. Ricci (Ed.), Decision Processes in Economics. Proceedings, 1989. III, 209 pages 1991.

Vol. 354: M. Ivaldi, A Structural Analysis of Expectation Formation. XII, 230 pages. 1991.

Vol. 355: M. Salomon. Deterministic Lotsizing Models for Production Planning. VII, 158 pages. 1991.

Vol. 356: P. Korhonen, A. Lewandowski, J . Wallenius (Eds.), Multiple Criteria Decision Support. Proceedings, 1989. XII, 393 pages. 1991.

Vol. 357: P. Zörnig, Degeneracy Graphs and Simplex Cycling. XV, 194 pages. 1991.

Vol. 358: P. Knottnerus, Linear Models with Correlated Disturbances. VIII, 196 pages. 1991.

Vol. 359: E. de Jong, Exchange Rate Determination and Optimal Economic Policy Under Various Exchange Rate Regimes. VII, 270 pages. 1991.

Vol. 360: P. Stalder, Regime Translations, Spillovers and Buffer Stocks. VI, 193 pages . 1991.

Vol. 361: C. F. Daganzo, Logistics Systems Analysis. X, 321 pages. 1991.

Vol. 362: F. Gehrels, Essays in Macroeconomics of an Open Economy. VII, 183 pages. 1991.

Vol. 363: C. Puppe, Distorted Probabilities and Choice under Risk. VIII, 100 pages . 1991

Vol. 364: B. Horvath, Are Policy Variables Exogenous? XII, 162 pages. 1991.

Vol. 365: G. A. Heuer, U. Leopold-Wildburger. Balanced Silverman Games on General Discrete Sets. V, 140 pages. 1991.

Vol. 366: J. Gruber (Ed.), Econometric Decision Models. Proceedings, 1989. VIII, 636 pages. 1991.

Vol. 367: M. Grauer, D. B. Pressmar (Eds.), Parallel Computing and Mathematical Optimization. Proceedings. V, 208 pages. 1991.

Vol. 368: M. Fedrizzi, J. Kacprzyk, M. Roubens (Eds.), Interactive Fuzzy Optimization. VII, 216 pages. 1991.

Vol. 369: R. Koblo, The Visible Hand. VIII, 131 pages.1991.

Vol. 370: M. J. Beckmann, M. N. Gopalan, R. Subramanian (Eds.), Stochastic Processes and their Applications. Proceedings, 1990. XLI, 292 pages. 1991.

Vol. 371: A. Schmutzler, Flexibility and Adjustment to Information in Sequential Decision Problems. VIII, 198 pages. 1991.

Vol. 372: J. Esteban, The Social Viability of Money. X, 202 pages. 1991.

Vol. 373: A. Billot, Economic Theory of Fuzzy Equilibria. XIII, 164 pages. 1992.

Vol. 374: G. Pflug, U. Dieter (Eds.), Simulation and Optimization. Proceedings, 1990. X, 162 pages. 1992.

Vol. 375: S.-J. Chen, Ch.-L. Hwang, Fuzzy Multiple Attribute Decision Making. XII, 536 pages. 1992.

Vol. 376: K.-H. Jöckel, G. Rothe, W. Sendler (Eds.), Bootstrapping and Related Techniques. Proceedings, 1990. VIII, 247 pages. 1992.

Vol. 377: A. Villar, Operator Theorems with Applications to Distributive Problems and Equilibrium Models. XVI, 160 pages. 1992.

Vol. 378: W. Krabs, J. Zowe (Eds.), Modern Methods of Optimization. Proceedings, 1990. VIII, 348 pages. 1992.

Vol. 379: K. Marti (Ed.), Stochastic Optimization. Proceedings, 1990. VII, 182 pages. 1992.

Vol. 380: J. Odelstad, Invariance and Structural Dependence. XII, 245 pages. 1992.

Vol. 381: C. Giannini, Topics in Structural VAR Econometrics. XI, 131 pages. 1992.

Vol. 382: W. Oettli, D. Pallaschke (Eds.), Advances in Optimization. Proceedings, 1991. X, 527 pages. 1992.

Vol. 383: J. Vartiainen, Capital Accumulation in a Corporatist Economy. VII, 177 pages. 1992.

Vol. 384: A. Martina, Lectures on the Economic Theory of Taxation. XII, 313 pages. 1992.

Vol. 385: J. Gardeazabal, M. Regúlez, The Monetary Model of Exchange Rates and Cointegration. X, 194 pages. 1992.

Vol. 386: M. Desrochers, J.-M. Rousseau (Eds.), Computer-Aided Transit Scheduling. Proceedings, 1990. XIII, 432 pages. 1992.

Vol. 387: W. Gaertner, M. Klemisch-Ahlert, Social Choice and Bargaining Perspectives on Distributive Justice. VIII, 131 pages. 1992.

Vol. 388: D. Bartmann, M. J. Beckmann, Inventory Control. XV, 252 pages. 1992.

Vol. 389: B. Dutta, D. Mookherjee, T. Parthasarathy, T. Raghavan, D. Ray, S. Tijs (Eds.), Game Theory and Economic Applications. Proceedings, 1990. IX, 454 pages. 1992.

Vol. 390: G. Sorger, Minimum Impatience Theorem for Recursive Economic Models. X, 162 pages. 1992.

Vol. 391: C. Keser, Experimental Duopoly Markets with Demand Inertia. X, 150 pages. 1992.

Vol. 392: K. Frauendorfer, Stochastic Two-Stage Programming. VIII, 228 pages. 1992.

Vol. 393: B. Lucke, Price Stabilization on World Agricultural Markets. XI, 274 pages. 1992.

Vol. 394: Y.-J. Lai, C.-L. Hwang, Fuzzy Mathematical Programming. XIII, 301 pages. 1992.

Vol. 395: G. Haag, U. Mueller, K. G. Troitzsch (Eds.), Economic Evolution and Demographic Change. XVI, 409 pages. 1992.

Vol. 396: R. V. V. Vidal (Ed.), Applied Simulated Annealing. VIII, 358 pages. 1992.

Vol. 397: J. Wessels, A. P. Wierzbicki (Eds.), User-Oriented Methodology and Techniques of Decision Analysis and Support. Proceedings, 1991. XII, 295 pages. 1993.

Vol. 398: J.-P. Urbain, Exogeneity in Error Correction Models. XI, 189 pages. 1993.

Vol. 399: F. Gori, L. Geronazzo, M. Galeotti (Eds.), Nonlinear Dynamics in Economics and Social Sciences. Proceedings, 1991. VIII, 367 pages. 1993.

Vol. 400: H. Tanizaki, Nonlinear Filters. XII, 203 pages. 1993.

Vol. 401: K. Mosler, M. Scarsini, Stochastic Orders and Applications. V, 379 pages. 1993.

Vol. 402: A. van den Elzen, Adjustment Processes for Exchange Economies and Noncooperative Games. VII, 146 pages. 1993.

Vol. 403: G. Brennscheidt, Predictive Behavior. VI, 227 pages. 1993.

Vol. 404: Y.-J. Lai, Ch.-L. Hwang, Fuzzy Multiple Objective Decision Making. XIV, 475 pages. 1994.

Vol. 405: S. Komlósi, T. Rapcsák, S. Schaible (Eds.), Generalized Convexity. Proceedings, 1992. VIII, 404 pages. 1994.

Vol. 406: N. M. Hung, N. V. Quyen, Dynamic Timing Decisions Under Uncertainty. X, 194 pages. 1994.

Vol. 407: M. Ooms, Empirical Vector Autoregressive Modeling. XIII, 380 pages. 1994.

Vol. 408: K. Haase, Lotsizing and Scheduling for Production Planning. VIII, 118 pages. 1994.

Vol. 409: A. Sprecher, Resource-Constrained Project Scheduling. XII, 142 pages. 1994.

Vol. 410: R. Winkelmann, Count Data Models. XI, 213 pages. 1994.

Vol. 411: S. Dauzère-Péres, J.-B. Lasserre, An Integrated Approach in Production Planning and Scheduling. XVI, 137 pages. 1994.

Vol. 412: B. Kuon, Two-Person Bargaining Experiments with Incomplete Information. IX, 293 pages. 1994.

Vol. 413: R. Fiorito (Ed.), Inventory, Business Cycles and Monetary Transmission. VI, 287 pages. 1994.

Vol. 414: Y. Crama, A. Oerlemans, F. Spieksma, Production Planning in Automated Manufacturing. X, 210 pages. 1994.

Vol. 415: P. C. Nicola, Imperfect General Equilibrium. XI, 167 pages. 1994.

Vol. 416: H. S. J. Cesar, Control and Game Models of the Greenhouse Effect. XI, 225 pages. 1994.

Vol. 417: B. Ran, D. E. Boyce, Dynamic Urban Transportation Network Models. XV, 391 pages. 1994.

Vol. 418: P. Bogetoft, Non-Cooperative Planning Theory. XI, 309 pages. 1994.

Vol. 419: T. Maruyama, W. Takahashi (Eds.), Nonlinear and Convex Analysis in Economic Theory. VIII, 306 pages. 1995.

Vol. 420: M. Peeters, Time-To-Build. Interrelated Investment and Labour Demand Modelling. With Applications to Six OECD Countries. IX, 204 pages. 1995.

Vol. 421: C. Dang, Triangulations and Simplicial Methods. IX, 196 pages. 1995.

Vol. 422: D. S. Bridges, G. B. Mehta, Representations of Preference Orderings. X, 165 pages. 1995.

Vol. 423: K. Marti, P. Kall (Eds.), Stochastic Programming. Numerical Techniques and Engineering Applications. VIII, 351 pages. 1995.

Vol. 424: G. A. Heuer, U. Leopold-Wildburger, Silverman's Game. X, 283 pages. 1995.

Vol. 425: J. Kohlas, P.-A. Monney, A Mathematical Theory of Hints. XIII, 419 pages, 1995.

Vol. 426: B. Finkenstädt, Nonlinear Dynamics in Economics. IX, 156 pages. 1995.

Vol. 427: F. W. van Tongeren, Microsimulation Modelling of the Corporate Firm. XVII, 275 pages. 1995.

Vol. 428: A. A. Powell, Ch. W. Murphy, Inside a Modern Macroeconometric Model. XVIII, 424 pages. 1995.

Vol. 429: R. Durier, C. Michelot, Recent Developments in Optimization. VIII, 356 pages. 1995.

Vol. 430: J. R. Daduna, I. Branco, J. M. Pinto Paixão (Eds.), Computer-Aided Transit Scheduling. XIV, 374 pages. 1995.

Vol. 431: A. Aulin, Causal and Stochastic Elements in Business Cycles. XI, 116 pages. 1996.

Vol. 432: M. Tamiz (Ed.), Multi-Objective Programming and Goal Programming. VI, 359 pages. 1996.

Vol. 433: J. Menon, Exchange Rates and Prices. XIV, 313 pages. 1996.

Vol. 434: M. W. J. Blok, Dynamic Models of the Firm. VII, 193 pages. 1996.

Vol. 435: L. Chen, Interest Rate Dynamics, Derivatives Pricing, and Risk Management. XII, 149 pages. 1996.

Vol. 436: M. Klemisch-Ahlert, Bargaining in Economic and Ethical Environments. IX, 155 pages. 1996.

Vol. 437: C. Jordan, Batching and Scheduling. IX, 178 pages. 1996.

Vol. 438: A. Villar, General Equilibrium with Increasing Returns. XIII, 164 pages. 1996.

Vol. 439: M. Zenner, Learning to Become Rational. VII, 201 pages. 1996.

Vol. 440: W. Ryll, Litigation and Settlement in a Game with Incomplete Information. VIII, 174 pages. 1996.

Vol. 441: H. Dawid, Adaptive Learning by Genetic Algorithms. IX, 166 pages.1996.

Vol. 442: L. Corchón, Theories of Imperfectly Competitive Markets. XIII, 163 pages. 1996.

Vol. 443: G. Lang, On Overlapping Generations Models with Productive Capital. X, 98 pages. 1996.

Vol. 444: S. Jørgensen, G. Zaccour (Eds.), Dynamic Competitive Analysis in Marketing. X, 285 pages. 1996.

Vol. 445: A. H. Christer, S. Osaki, L. C. Thomas (Eds.), Stochastic Modelling in Innovative Manufactoring. X, 361 pages. 1997.

Vol. 446: G. Dhaene, Encompassing. X, 160 pages. 1997.

Vol. 447: A. Artale, Rings in Auctions. X, 172 pages. 1997.

Vol. 448: G. Fandel, T. Gal (Eds.), Multiple Criteria Decision Making. XII, 678 pages. 1997.

Vol. 449: F. Fang, M. Sanglier (Eds.), Complexity and Self-Organization in Social and Economic Systems. IX, 317 pages, 1997.

Vol. 450: P. M. Pardalos, D. W. Hearn, W. W. Hager, (Eds.), Network Optimization. VIII, 485 pages, 1997.

Vol. 451: M. Salge, Rational Bubbles. Theoretical Basis, Economic Relevance, and Empirical Evidence with a Special Emphasis on the German Stock Market.IX, 265 pages. 1997.

Vol. 452: P. Gritzmann, R. Horst, E. Sachs, R. Tichatschke (Eds.), Recent Advances in Optimization. VIII, 379 pages. 1997.

Vol. 453: A. S. Tangian, J. Gruber (Eds.), Constructing Scalar-Valued Objective Functions. VIII, 298 pages. 1997.

Vol. 454: H.-M. Krolzig, Markov-Switching Vector Autoregressions. XIV, 358 pages. 1997.

Vol. 455: R. Caballero, F. Ruiz, R. E. Steuer (Eds.), Advances in Multiple Objective and Goal Programming. VIII, 391 pages. 1997.

Vol. 456: R. Conte, R. Hegselmann, P. Terna (Eds.), Simulating Social Phenomena. VIII, 536 pages. 1997.

Vol. 457: C. Hsu, Volume and the Nonlinear Dynamics of Stock Returns. VIII, 133 pages. 1998.

Vol. 458: K. Marti, P. Kall (Eds.), Stochastic Programming Methods and Technical Applications. X, 437 pages. 1998.

Vol. 459: H. K. Ryu, D. J. Slottje, Measuring Trends in U.S. Income Inequality. XI, 195 pages. 1998.

Vol. 460: B. Fleischmann, J. A. E. E. van Nunen, M. G. Speranza, P. Stähly, Advances in Distribution Logistic. XI, 535 pages. 1998.

Vol. 461: U. Schmidt, Axiomatic Utility Theory under Risk. XV, 201 pages. 1998.

Vol. 462: L. von Auer, Dynamic Preferences, Choice Mechanisms, and Welfare. XII, 226 pages. 1998.

Vol. 463: G. Abraham-Frois (Ed.), Non-Linear Dynamics and Endogenous Cycles. VI, 204 pages. 1998.

Vol. 464: A. Aulin, The Impact of Science on Economic Growth and its Cycles. IX, 204 pages. 1998.

Vol. 465: T. J. Stewart, R. C. van den Honert (Eds.), Trends in Multicriteria Decision Making. X, 448 pages. 1998.

Vol. 466: A. Sadrieh, The Alternating Double Auction Market. VII, 350 pages. 1998.

Vol. 467: H. Hennig-Schmidt, Bargaining in a Video Experiment. Determinants of Boundedly Rational Behavior. XII, 221 pages. 1999.

Vol. 468: A. Ziegler, A Game Theory Analysis of Options. XIV, 145 pages. 1999.

Vol. 469: M. P. Vogel, Environmental Kuznets Curves. XIII, 197 pages. 1999.

Vol. 470: M. Ammann, Pricing Derivative Credit Risk. XII, 228 pages. 1999.

Vol. 471: N. H. M. Wilson (Ed.), Computer-Aided Transit Scheduling. XI, 444 pages. 1999.

Vol. 472: J.-R. Tyran, Money Illusion and Strategic Complementarity as Causes of Monetary Non-Neutrality. X, 228 pages. 1999.

Vol. 473: S. Helber, Performance Analysis of Flow Lines with Non-Linear Flow of Material. IX, 280 pages. 1999.

Vol. 474: U. Schwalbe, The Core of Economies with Asymmetric Information. IX, 141 pages. 1999.

Vol. 475: L. Kaas, Dynamic Macroeconomics with Imperfect Competition. XI, 155 pages. 1999.

Vol. 476: R. Demel, Fiscal Policy, Public Debt and the Term Structure of Interest Rates. X, 279 pages. 1999.

Vol. 477: M. Théra, R. Tichatschke (Eds.), Ill-posed Variational Problems and Regularization Techniques. VIII, 274 pages. 1999.

Vol. 478: S. Hartmann, Project Scheduling under Limited Resources. XII, 221 pages. 1999.

Vol. 479: L. v. Thadden, Money, Inflation, and Capital Formation. IX, 192 pages. 1999.

Vol. 480: M. Grazia Speranza, P. Stähly (Eds.), New Trends in Distribution Logistics. X, 336 pages. 1999.

Vol. 481: V. H. Nguyen, J. J. Strodiot, P. Tossings (Eds.). Optimation. IX, 498 pages. 2000.

Vol. 482: W. B. Zhang, A Theory of International Trade. XI, 192 pages. 2000.

Vol. 483: M. Königstein, Equity, Efficiency and Evolutionary Stability in Bargaining Games with Joint Production. XII, 197 pages. 2000.

Vol. 484: D. D. Gatti, M. Gallegati, A. Kirman, Interaction and Market Structure. VI, 298 pages. 2000.

Vol. 485: A. Garnaev, Search Games and Other Applications of Game Theory. VIII, 145 pages. 2000.

Vol. 486: M. Neugart, Nonlinear Labor Market Dynamics. X, 175 pages. 2000.

Vol. 487: Y. Y. Haimes, R. E. Steuer (Eds.), Research and Practice in Multiple Criteria Decision Making. XVII, 553 pages. 2000.

Vol. 488: B. Schmolck, Ommitted Variable Tests and Dynamic Specification. X, 144 pages. 2000.

Vol. 489: T. Steger, Transitional Dynamics and Economic Growth in Developing Countries. VIII, 151 pages. 2000.

Vol. 490: S. Minner, Strategic Safety Stocks in Supply Chains. XI, 214 pages. 2000.

Vol. 491: M. Ehrgott, Multicriteria Optimization. VIII, 242 pages. 2000.

Vol. 492: T. Phan Huy, Constraint Propagation in Flexible Manufacturing. IX, 258 pages. 2000.

Vol. 493: J. Zhu, Modular Pricing of Options. X, 170 pages. 2000.

Vol. 494: D. Franzen, Design of Master Agreements for OTC Derivatives. VIII, 175 pages. 2001.

Vol. 495: I Konnov, Combined Relaxation Methods for Variational Inequalities. XI, 181 pages. 2001.

Vol. 496: P. Weiß, Unemployment in Open Economies. XII, 226 pages. 2001.

Vol. 497: J. Inkmann, Conditional Moment Estimation of Nonlinear Equation Systems. VIII, 214 pages. 2001.

Vol. 498: M. Reutter, A Macroeconomic Model of West German Unemployment. X, 125 pages. 2001.

Vol. 499: A. Casajus, Focal Points in Framed Games. XI, 131 pages. 2001.

Vol. 500: F. Nardini, Technical Progress and Economic Growth. XVII, 191 pages. 2001.

Vol. 501: M. Fleischmann, Quantitative Models for Reverse Logistics. XI, 181 pages. 2001.

Vol. 502: N. Hadjisavvas, J. E. Martínez-Legaz, J.-P. Penot (Eds.), Generalized Convexity and Generalized Monotonicity. IX, 410 pages. 2001.

Vol. 503: A. Kirman, J.-B. Zimmermann (Eds.), Economics with Heterogenous Interacting Agents. VII, 343 pages. 2001.

Vol. 504: P.-Y. Moix (Ed.),The Measurement of Market Risk. XI, 272 pages. 2001.

Vol. 505: S. Voß, J. R. Daduna (Eds.), Computer-Aided Scheduling of Public Transport. XI, 466 pages. 2001.

Vol. 506: B. P. Kellerhals, Financial Pricing Models in Continuous Time and Kalman Filtering. XIV, 247 pages. 2001.

Vol. 507: M. Koksalan, S. Zionts, Multiple Criteria Decision Making in the New Millenium. XII, 481 pages. 2001.

Vol. 508: K. Neumann, C. Schwindt, J. Zimmermann, Project Scheduling with Time Windows and Scarce Resources. XI, 335 pages. 2002.

Vol. 509: D. Hornung, Investment, R&D, and Long-Run Growth. XVI, 194 pages. 2002.

Vol. 510: A. S. Tangian, Constructing and Applying Objective Functions. XII, 582 pages. 2002.

Vol. 511: M. Külpmann, Stock Market Overreaction and Fundamental Valuation. IX, 198 pages. 2002.

Vol. 512: W.-B. Zhang, An Economic Theory of Cities.XI, 220 pages. 2002.

Vol. 513: K. Marti, Stochastic Optimization Techniques. VIII, 364 pages. 2002.

Vol. 514: S. Wang, Y. Xia, Portfolio and Asset Pricing. XII, 200 pages. 2002.

Vol. 515: G. Heisig, Planning Stability in Material Requirements Planning System. XII, 264 pages. 2002.